John F. Kennedy

A BIBLIOGRAPHY

Photograph of John F. Kennedy courtesy of the John F. Kennedy Library #AR7595B.

John F. Kennedy
A BIBLIOGRAPHY

Compiled by
JAMES N. GIGLIO

Bibliographies of the Presidents of the United States,
Number 34

GREENWOOD PRESS
Westport, Connecticut • London

Library of Congress Cataloging-in-Publication Data

Giglio, James N.
    John F. Kennedy : a bibliography / compiled by James N. Giglio.
       p.   cm.—(Bibliographies of the presidents of the United
States, ISSN 1061–6500 ; no. 34)
    Includes index.
    ISBN 0–313–28192–0 (alk. paper)
    1. Kennedy, John F. (John Fitzgerald), 1917–1963—Bibliography.
I. Title. II. Series.
Z8462.8.G54 1995
[E842]
016.973922—dc20   95–15450

British Library Cataloguing in Publication Data is available.

Library of Congress Catalog Card Number: 95–15450
ISBN: 0–313–28192–0
ISSN: 1061–6500

First published in 1995

Greenwood Press, 88 Post Road West, Westport, CT 06881
An imprint of Greenwood Publishing Group, Inc.

Printed in the United States of America

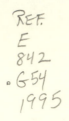

The paper used in this book complies with the
Permanent Paper Standard issued by the National
Information Standards Organization (Z39.48–1984).

10 9 8 7 6 5 4 3 2 1

To Donald R. McCoy, mentor and friend

Contents

Foreword

Nothing in the American constitutional order continues to excite so much scholarly interest, debate, and controversy as the role of the presidency. This remains the case in spite of the complaint, so common in the historical profession a generation ago, about the tyranny of "the presidential synthesis" in the writing of American history.

This complaint had its point. It is true enough that the deep currents in social, economic, and intellectual history, in demography, family structure, and collective mentalities, flow on without regard to presidential administrations. To deal with these underlying trends, the "new history" began, in the 1950s and 1960s, to reach out beyond traditional history to anthropology, sociology, psychology, and statistics. For a season social-science history pushed politics and personalities off the historical stage.

But in time social-science history displayed its limitations. It did not turn out to be, as its apostles had promised, a philosopher's--or historian's--stone. "Most of the great problems of history," wrote Lawrence Stone, himself a distinguished practitioner of the new history, " remains as insoluble as ever, if not more so." In particular, the new history had no interest in public policy--the decisions a nation makes through the political process--and proved impotent to explain it. Yet one can reasonably argue that, at least in a democracy, public policy reveals the true meaning of the past, the moods, preoccupations, values, and dreams of a nation, more clearly and trenchantly than almost anything else.

The tide of historical interest is now turning again--from deep currents to events, from underlying trends to decisions. While the history of public policy requires an accounting of the total culture from which national decisions emerge, such history must center in the end on the decisions themselves and on the people who make (and resist) them. Historians today are returning to the insights of classical history--to the recognition that the state, political authority, military power, elections, statutes, wars, the ideas, ambitions, delusions, and wills of individuals make a difference to history.

This is far from a reversion to "great man" theories. But it is a valuable corrective to the assumption, nourished by social-science history, that public policy is merely a passive reflection of underlying historical forces. For the ultimate fascination of history lies precisely in the interplay between the individual and his environment. "It is true," wrote Tocqueville, "that around every man a fatal circle is traced beyond which he cannot pass; but within the wide verge of that circle he is powerful and free; as it is with man, so with communities."

The *Bibliographies of the Presidents* series therefore needs no apology. Public policy is a powerful key to an understanding of the past; and in the United States the presidency is the battleground where issues of public policy are fought and resolved. The history of American presidents is far from the total history of America. But American history without the presidents would leave the essential part of the story untold.

Recent years have seen a great expansion in the resources available for students of the presidency. The National Historical Publications Commission has done superb work in stimulating and sponsoring editions, both letterpress and microform, of hitherto inaccessible materials. "Documents," as President Kennedy said in 1963, "are the primary sources of history; they are the means by which later generations draw close to historical events and enter into the thoughts, fears and hopes of the past." He saluted the NHPC program as "this great effort to enable the American people to repossess its historical heritage."

At the same time, there has been a rich outpouring of scholarly monographs on presidents, their associates, their problems, and their times. And the social-science challenge to narrative history has had its impact on presidential scholarship. The interdisciplinary approach has raised new questions, developed new methods and uncovered new sources. It has notably extended the historian's methodological arsenal.

This profuse presidential literature has heretofore lacked a guide. The *Bibliographies of the Presidents* series thus fills a great lacuna in American scholarship. It provides comprehensive annotated bibliographies, president by president, covering manuscripts and archives, biographies and monographs, articles and dissertations, government documents and oral histories, libraries, museums, and iconographic resources. The editors are all scholars who have mastered their presidents. The series places the study of American presidents on a solid bibliographical foundation.

In so doing, it will demonstrate the wide sweep of approaches to our presidents, from analysis to anecdotage, from hagiography to vilification. It will illustrate the rise and fall of presidential reputations--fluctuations that often throw as much light on historians as on presidents. It will provide evidence for and against Bryce's famous proposition "Why Great Men Are Not Chosen Presidents." It will remind us that superior men have somehow made it to the White House but also that, as the Supreme Court said in *ex parte Milligan*, the republic has "no right to expect that it will always have wise and humane rulers, sincerely attached to the principles of the Constitution. Wicked men, ambitious of power, with hatred of liberty and contempt of law, may fill the place once occupied by Washington and Lincoln."

Above all, it will show how, and to what degree, the American presidency has been the focus of the concerns, apprehensions and aspirations of the people and the times. The history of the presidency is a history of nobility and of pettiness, of courage and of cunning, of forthrightness and of trickery, of quarrel and of consensus. The turmoil perennially swirling around the White House illuminates the heart of American democracy. The literature reflects the turmoil, and the *Bibliographies of the Presidents* supply at last the light that will enable scholars and citizens to find their way through the literature.

Arthur Schlesinger, Jr.

Editor's Preface

Individuals who rise to the highest elected office offered by the American people hold a special fascination. Their backgrounds, their philosophies over time, the way they "rise" are matters of enduring observation, commentary, and analysis. The Greenwood Bibliographies of the Presidents of the United States, splendidly begun by the late Carol Fitzgerald in 1988, provides to both the specialist and generalist a comprehensive guide to every aspect of those unique individuals.

Each volume records the mundane and the critical--from early education, to contemporary news and political analysis, family reminiscences, scholarly analysis and revision, partisan attacks, official papers, personal manuscripts, visual records, and, for administrations of our day, the film and video record.

The Greenwood series offers the possibility of complete access to every instant of the Chief Executive's career or preparation. Taken together, the volumes provide chronological, precise, and detailed accounts of how each President has risen, administered, and withdrawn--and how scholars, pundits, and the American people have weighed that progress.

Mary Ellen McElligott

Introduction

President John Fitzgerald Kennedy, the first Catholic president of the United States, served a scant 1,033 days, less than any other elected president in the twentieth century with the exception of Warren G. Harding. Kennedy would be the first to admit that he had departed with many promises unfulfilled. Even so, he remains paradoxically our most popular chief executive. In part this is due to his Hollywood appearance, his perceived idealism and vision, and his captivating style that had inspired young people to dedicate themselves to national service and to public life. Indeed, he helped make politics once again a respectable endeavor. Most of us who lived during the Kennedy years experienced a renewed sense of optimism and idealism as a result of his presidency. Revealingly, he never fell below a 59 percent approval rating in the Gallup Polls. Our remembrance of him and his rhetoric and of that time has been enhanced by the circumstances of his death, which left his youthful image forever frozen in our national memory. His brutal assassination also left in the wake an elegant wife, two attractive children, and realizable dreams and promises that soon soured as our social fabric unraveled in the face of the Vietnam escalation, the student protest movement, and the urban riots of the late 1960s; Watergate and other transgressions followed in the 1970s and 1980s. No wonder many Americans have come to feel that Kennedy's departure had somehow contributed to all of this and that had he lived he would have fulfilled our democratic ideals.

Most recent scholars have been much more measured in their assessments. They have successfully challenged both the early appraisals of the Camelot school of scholarship dominated mainly by former Kennedy associates such as Theodore Sorensen and Arthur Schlesinger, Jr., that emphasized Kennedy's greatness and the reactive revisionists of the 1970s, including Henry Fairlie and Bruce Miroff, that portrayed Kennedy as a strident cold warrior and ineffectual on domestic affairs. What remains today is an above average president who is remembered in foreign policy for his inspiring initiatives--for example, the Peace Corps, which exposed young Americans to the Third World; the Alliance for Progress, even though promising more than it could ever deliver to Latin America; and the Nuclear Test Ban Treaty of 1963, which contributed to an emerging détente with the Soviet Union.

Kennedy also strengthened the country militarily, enabling it to withstand Khrushchev's menacing moves in Berlin in 1961. He at the same time helped to abate the crisis in Laos by agreeing to support a coalition government headed by a neutralist. Even though scholars today rightly recognize that Kennedy contributed to an unnecessary missile crisis in Cuba, his response to Soviet nuclear weaponry there was measured, prudent, and courageous. By the fall of 1962, he seemed a much more effective leader than during the Bay of Pigs debacle of 1961, unquestionably his greatest foreign policy failure. Still, Vietnam remained his most serious challenge at the time of his death. His emphasis on counterinsurgency had increased American military advisers to 16,000 and his support of the overthrow of the Diem regime in South Vietnam had committed the United States even more to that war. Where all of this would have led is a matter of conjecture. One thing seems certain: Kennedy would not have unilaterally withdrawn American forces by 1965.

On the domestic front, due to his narrow election victory, a recalcitrant Congress, and his own weaknesses as a legislative leader, Kennedy failed to accomplish most of his major objectives such as medicare, federal aid to education, and civil rights. Nevertheless, probably no president up to his time had embraced the black cause to the same extent by the summer of 1963, and he had done much to pave the way for the Civil Rights Act of 1964. He also addressed some of the problems of housing, juvenile delinquency, mental retardation, agricultural overproduction, and organized crime. His economic policies, culminating with the tax cut of 1964, ended economic stagnation and reduced unemployment and the balance of payments deficit, making the early 1960s a good time to live for most Americans.

Recent scholars have also appraised Kennedy's personal life, often in a negative way. They have alluded to his enormous ego and occasional pettiness, his obsession with image, and above all his womanizing. His relationship with Judith Campbell Exner exposed him to the mob, and his dalliances with Marilyn Monroe also threatened to imperil his presidency as did women casually smuggled into the White House without FBI background checks. But Kennedy loved to live on the edge despite physical debilitations that included a severe chronic back problem and Addison's disease, a malfunction of the adrenal glands, which required a daily ingestion of steroids. Scholars have also recently confirmed that Kennedy indeed relied on potentially dangerous amphetamines to overcome the stress, exhaustion, and back pain that constantly plagued him.

Yet one still leaves Kennedy with admiration for having overcome serious medical problems not only through medication but through remarkable will and fortitude. He managed to retain his buoyant personality, his vigor, and his genuine love of people. Therein, perhaps, lies his real profile in courage.

Despite having published a book on the Kennedy presidency, I have found this undertaking extremely challenging because of the enormous amount of primary and secondary sources on Kennedy--more than one would expect of a president who served less than three years. I had been aware of the voluminous publications on the Cuban missile crisis and the Kennedy assassination, but I was surprised that so much was written on Kennedy and Catholicism during the election of 1960 or on such foreign policy topics as U.S.-Canadian relations during the Kennedy administration. The innumerable number of doctoral dissertations, especially in the foreign policy area, also surprised me. Most of them were done by political scientists and students of international relations. Obviously space constraints dictated that I could not include everything. Nevertheless, I have made a determined effort to incorporate all of the primary sources--the manuscripts, oral histories, and published documents--that directly relate to Kennedy or to his presidency. The same thing is true of the published scholarly works. I was more selective regarding contemporary journalistic publications, including articles in news magazines and other magazines or journals. Much depended on how much scholarly work existed on a topic. The thoughtfulness of the contemporary piece represented another consideration. Thus, I was more apt to select an essay from the *New Republic* rather than one from *Newsweek*. I did not include book reviews unless Kennedy himself wrote them or unless a review essay went well beyond the books under consideration. Neither did I include Kennedy's published speeches, which can be found in various compilations.

Since this is an annotated bibliography, some comment is necessary regarding the annotations. For the most part, they are intended merely to describe the cited work. If the study is significant, the annotation instead might be evaluative. In a few cases it was impossible to secure information on some works that obviously touched on Kennedy. Consequently, I included them without annotation. In any event, I have purused the vast majority of the published scholarly work. In the case of most dissertations, I have depended on *Dissertation Abstracts International.* On some works I have also relied on other published bibliographies or on the annotations provided by *America: History and Life.*

After spending nearly three years on this study, I would be remiss in not providing some observations about work that still needs to be done on the Kennedy presidency. I was amazed that no scholarly study exists on Native Americans during the Kennedy period; except for the steel crisis, labor matters have also been ignored, as have environmental issues and housing policy. In general there is a greater need to study the domestic side of the Kennedy presidency. Despite the extensive publications on foreign affairs, I am unaware of any book-length study or scholarly article on Kennedy and Japan. Little has been done on North Africa and on Eastern Europe or on Mexico and Korea. Other country studies are also needed. Moreover, there is no work that I know that provides a systematic analysis of Kennedy's voting record while in Congress. Many biographies still need to be written, including one on Secretary of Interior Stewart Udall, Labor Secretary Arthur Goldberg, and Kennedy adviser Theodore Sorensen.

Lastly, and most importantly, I wish to express my indebtedness to the many people who assisted me. At the top of the list are my wife Fran Jendrisak Giglio, who wrote the chronology, helped with the contemporary articles, and remained supportive in so many other ways, and Willa Garrett of the Duane Meyer Library, Southwest Missouri State University, who knows as much about Kennedy as anyone I know and who assisted in the contemporary articles and other bibliographic-related matters. The following Southwest Missouri State University graduate students also provided assistance on the contemporary articles: Lane Beardall, Jean Griffith, Brian Butler, and Cathy Marcum. I am indebted to the interlibrary loan department of the Meyer library, especially Francie Rottman, who bore my countless requests with efficiency and grace. Assistance also came from Byron Stewart, Lynn Cline, and Charlotte Dugan of the Meyer library. Thanks to colleagues Dominic Capeci, who aided me more than he knows, and Matthew Mancini, who, as department head, provided crucial support. My indebtedness is significant to Kenneth Johnston of Computer Services for his unlimited computer skills. Colleague Bob Miller also assisted me in the computer area at a crucial time. A special thanks to to history department secretary Margie von der Heide, who helped me in the printing of the manuscript, and to SMSU colleagues Wayne Bartee and Beat Kernen for translating German and Russian texts, respectively. I also appreciate the summer fellowship from Southwest Missouri State University, which enabled me to complete this study.

I also desire to thank several other individuals and libraries. Ronald E. Whealan and Meagan Desnoyers of the John Fitzgerald Kennedy Library were most invaluable in sending me material. Whealan, who advised me throughout the project, and Professor James T. Crown of New York University read the manuscript in its entirety. Thanks too to Marie Nitschke of Robert W. Woodruff Library, of the Emory Library, who sent me RLIN database information on the Columbia Oral History Project; Ronald J. Grele, Mary Marshall Clark, and Pamela Simon of the Columbia Oral History Project; Allen Fisher and Linda Hanson of the Lyndon Baines Johnson Library; and Raymond H. Geselbracht of the Harry S. Truman Library. I also profited from the excellent Dwight David Eisenhower bibliography compiled by Professor R. Alton Lee of the University of South Dakota, published by Scholarly Resources, Inc.

Chronology

1917

May 29. John Fitzgerald Kennedy born in Brookline, Massachusetts, a suburb of Boston, the second child of Joseph P. and Rose Kennedy.

1921

Entered kindergarten at Edward Devotion School in Brookline.

1927

Moved with family to Bronxville, New York.

1931

Entered the Choate School, a boarding school in Wallingford, Connecticut.

1935

October. Because of illness withdrew without attending classes from the London School of Economics.

December. Withdrew from Princeton University because of illness.

1940

June. Graduated cum laude from Harvard University with a bachelor of science degree in political science.

August. Wilfred Funk, Inc. published Kennedy's *Why England Slept*, an adaptation of his senior thesis, "Appeasement at Munich."

1941

Appointed an ensign in the U.S. Naval Reserve and reported for active duty in the Office of Naval Operations in Washington, D.C.

1943

August 2. Kennedy's PT-109 was rammed and destroyed by a Japanese destroyer in the Solomon Islands.

August 7. Rescued from a South Pacific island, weak and injured.

October 1. Promoted to lieutenant.

1944

June 12. Received the Navy and Marine Corps medal.

June 23. Had unsuccessful back surgery at New England Baptist Hospital, Boston.

August 12. Death of Joseph P., Jr., Kennedy's older brother, in an airplane explosion in Europe.

1945

July. Worked as a Hearst news correspondent in London and reported on the U. N. founding conference in San Francisco for the Hearst chain.

1946

June 18. Won the Democratic nomination for Congress from Massachusetts' Eleventh Congressional District.

November 5. Elected to the U.S. House of Representatives.

1948

May 13. Death of Kennedy's sister, Kathleen "Kick" Kennedy, in an airplane crash in France.

November 2. Reelected to a second term in the House of Representatives.

1950

November 7. Reelected to a third term in the House of Representatives.

1952

November 4. Elected to the U.S. Senate.

1953

September 12. Married Jacqueline Lee Bouvier in Newport, Rhode Island.

1954

October 21. Underwent major spinal surgery in New York.   Because of complications related to Addison's disease, Kennedy nearly died and had to undergo surgery again in 1955.

1956

January. Harper and Row published Kennedy's *Profiles in Courage,* which benefited from the research and writing of Jules Davids and Theodore Sorensen. *Profiles* won the Pulitzer Prize for biography in 1957.

August 16. Nominated Adlai Stevenson at the Democratic National Convention in Chicago.

August 17. Narrowly lost the vice presidential nomination to Estes Kefauver but emerged as a national figure.

1957

January. Appointed to the Senate Foreign Relations Committee.

November 27. Birth of Caroline Bouvier Kennedy.

1958

November 5. Reelected to the U.S. Senate.

1960

January 2. Announced candidacy for the U.S. presidency.

April 5. Won the Wisconsin primary.

May 10. Won the West Virginia primary.

July 13. Won the presidential nomination on the first ballot at the Democratic National Convention in Los Angeles.

July 15. Gave his acceptance speech before the convention in which he talked about a New Frontier.

September 26. The first of four nationally televised presidential debates contributed to Kennedy's surpassing Richard Nixon in the preference polls.

November 8. Elected president with a plurality of less than 120,000 votes but with a 303 to 219 electoral tally.

November 25. Birth of John Fitzgerald Kennedy, Jr., in Washington, D. C.

December 16. Appointed his brother, Robert, U. S. Attorney General.

1961

January 20. Inaugurated as president of the United States.

January 25. Held first presidential news conference, the first president to hold a "live" televised news conference.

January 30. Delivered his first State of the Union message to Congress.

January 31. By a close vote administration forces managed to enlarge the House of Representatives Rules Committee.

March 1. Signed an executive order establishing the Peace Corps.

March 7. Signed an executive order establishing the President's Committee on Equal Employment Opportunity.

March 13. Announced a plan for an Alliance for Progress.

March 28. Delivered special message to Congress requesting appropriations for the largest peacetime military buildup in history.

April 17. The Bay of Pigs invasion.

April 20. Spoke to the American Society of Newspaper Editors in Washington regarding the Bay of Pigs debacle.

May 5. Alan Shepard, America's first astronaut, made a fifteen-minute suborbital flight.

May 5. Signed the minimum wage bill.

May 16. Traveled to Canada on his first state visit for two days of talks with Prime

Minister John Diefenbaker.

May 31. Arrived with Mrs. Kennedy in Paris for talks with French and NATO officials.

June 3. Arrived in Vienna for two days of meetings with Soviet Premier Nikita Khrushchev.

June 30. Signed the Housing Act of 1961.

July 25. Somberly addressed the American people on television concerning the Berlin crisis in which he asked Americans to endure sacrifices.

August 8. Signed the Agricultural Act of 1961.

August 13. The Berlin Wall was erected.

August 30. The Soviet Union resumed nuclear testing.

September 5. The U.S. resumed underground nuclear testing.

September 22. Signed the Peace Corps Act.

September 25. Delivered a moving speech before the General Assembly of the United Nations on the death of Secretary General Dag Hammarskjold.

October. The Taylor-Rostow mission to South Vietnam led to the recommendation to escalate American involvement there.

December 14. Established the Commission on the Status of Women.

December 19. Father Joseph P. Kennedy suffered a stroke in Palm Beach, Florida.

1962

January 5. Named *Time* magazine "Man of the Year."

January 18. Submitted to Congress a balanced budget for fiscal 1963.

February 3. Ordered a trade embargo of Cuba.

February 14. "A Tour of the White House with Mrs. John F. Kennedy" is broadcast over the CBS and NBC networks.

February 20. John Glenn orbited the earth.

March 15. Signed the Manpower Development and Training Act.

April 11. Attacked the steel industry for price increases.

May 1. Signed the Educational Television Act.

June 29. Began a three-day diplomatic visit to Mexico with Mrs. Kennedy.

July 23. Through the efforts mainly of Kennedy negotiator Averell Harriman, nineteen nations signed the Geneva Protocol, agreeing to respect Laos' territorial integrity and sovereignty.

August 13. Signed the Work Hours Standards Act.

August 31. Signed the Communications Satellite Act.

September 7. Asked Congress for the authority to call 150,000 reserves to active duty in response to Soviet activity in Cuba.

September 30. Delivered a national address concerning the violence over the enrollment of James Meredith at the University of Mississippi.

October 10. Signed the Drug Reform Bill.

October 15. Reconnaissance flights showed evidence of Soviet missiles in Cuba.

October 22. Addressed the nation concerning the military buildup in Cuba and announced the quarantine of offensive military equipment headed for Cuba.

October 23. The U.N. Security Council held an emergency meeting on the Cuban missile crisis.

October 23. The Organization of American States voted to support the blockade of Cuba.

October 28. Khrushchev indicated that the offensive missiles in Cuba would be removed in return for the United States ending the blockade and promising never to invade Cuba. Kennedy secretly and informally had also pledged to remove Jupiter missiles from Turkey.

November 20. Signed Executive Order #11063 ending discrimination in public housing.

December 18. Began four days of meetings with Prime Minister Harold Macmillan in Nassau, The Bahamas, on the matter of nuclear defense.

December 21. Negotiated an agreement with Fidel Castro for the release of Bay of Pigs prisoners.

1963

May 12. Made a national address concerning the racial disturbance in Birmingham.

May 28. Congress approved the Equal Pay Act, which guaranteed equal pay to women.

June 10. Discussed the importance of a nuclear test ban agreement in perhaps his most significant foreign policy address, delivered at American University.

June 11. Signed a proclamation ordering the governor of Alabama to curtail the blocking of black students from entering the University of Alabama.

June 11. Delivered a national address in which he movingly called civil rights a moral issue.

June 23. Arrived in Bonn, West Germany, for four days of talks.

June 26. Spoke before the Berlin Wall in one of his most stirring speeches.

June 26. Arrived in Ireland for four days.

July 2. Met with Pope Paul VI at the Vatican.

July 26. Delivered a national address, announcing the nuclear test ban agreement with the Soviet Union.

August 7. The birth of Patrick Bouvier Kennedy, five weeks premature.

August 9. Patrick Kennedy died.

August 28. Mass civil rights demonstration in Washington where Dr. Martin Luther King, Jr., delivered his "I have a dream" speech.

August 30. The communications "hot line" was established, linking Washington and Moscow.

September 10. National Guard troops in Alabama were federalized to enforce the desegregation of the University of Alabama.

September 24. Began a five-day cross-country trip to encourage the conservation of natural resources.

September 25. The tax cut bill passed the House of Representatives. The Senate would approve it in early 1964.

October 7. Signed the Nuclear Test Ban Treaty.

October 9. Announced the sale of surplus wheat to the Soviet Union.

October 29. Kennedy's civil rights bill passed the House Judiciary Committee with bipartisan support.

November 1. Military coup in South Vietnam. The following day President Ngo Dinh Diem and his brother-in-law were assassinated.

November 21. Left with Mrs. Kennedy for a political trip to Texas.

November 22. Assassinated at 12:30 p.m. while traveling in a motorcade through the streets of Dallas. Lyndon Johnson took the oath of office as president.

November 23. Lee Harvey Oswald was charged with the death of President Kennedy.

November 24. Oswald was shot and killed by Jack Ruby.

November 24. Kennedy's body lay in state in the Capitol Rotunda.

November 25. The nation observed a national day of mourning as Kennedy was laid to rest in Arlington National Cemetery and the eternal flame was lit.

November 29. President Johnson appointed members to a commission to investigate Kennnedy's death.

1964

September 24. The Warren Commission presented its report on the Kennedy assassination to President Johnson.

1994

May 19. Jacqueline Kennedy Onassis died in New York City of cancer.

1

Manuscript and Archival Sources

A. MANUSCRIPT SOURCES FOR JOHN F. KENNEDY IN THE JOHN FITZGERALD KENNEDY LIBRARY

The John Fitzgerald Kennedy Papers in the John Fitzgerald Kennedy Library remains the best single source on Kennedy's life and career. The collection, containing 4,145 linear feet of papers, 49 rolls of microfilm, 127 audiotapes, and 73 dictabelts, provides data on his writings, materials relating to his service in the Navy, U.S. Congress, U.S. Senate, and the White House. In addition there are correspondence with family members, childhood letters, a diary, academic records and notebooks, financial papers, medical records, manuscripts of his books, *Why England Slept* and *Profiles in Courage*, presidential doodles, scrapbooks, campaign files, transition files, and many items from the presidential administration and post-assassination period. About 12 percent of the papers is still closed to researchers. A guide to the collection and related holdings, *Historical Materials in the John Fitzgerald Kennedy Library*, can be obtained from the John Fitzgerald Kennedy Library, Columbia Point, Boston, MA 02125.

A breakdown of the collection follows:

1. John F. Kennedy Personal Papers, 1917-1963. This is an artificial and fragmentary collection created by the library staff for the convenience of research use.

2. John F. Kennedy Pre-presidential Papers. Includes papers on Kennedy's congressional and senatorial career, the 1960 campaign, and the presidential transition.

3. President's Office Files. A subfile of the presidential papers, it contains general correspondence, special correspondence, speech files, legislative files, staff memorandums, departments and agencies material, personal secretary's files, and presidential recordings.

4. National Security Files. Another subfile of the presidential papers, it constitutes the working files of McGeorge Bundy, special assistant to the president for national Security Affairs. This represents the primary foreign policy file of the Kennedy White House.

5. White House Central Files. Set up as a reference service for the president and his staff and to document White House activities, it consists of four major subdivisions: White House Central Subject File (papers sent from various offices in the White House), White House Central Name File (an index to the Subject File by personal or organizational name), Chronological File (copies of JFK's outgoing correspondence), and Security Classified File (national security classified material withdrawn from the Subject File by the White House staff). Oversized materials are kept separately, including reports, printed materials, and attachments to correspondence.

6. White House Staff Files. Files of Lawrence F. O'Brien, Kenneth P. O'Donnell, Walter Rostow, Pierre Salinger, and twenty-seven other staffers.

7. Bureau of the Budget Bill Reports. Memorandums to the president from the assistant director of the Bureau of the Budget for legislative reference, recommendations from agency heads to the bureau, and committee reports.

8. White House Social Files. Incorporates the papers and records of Mrs. John F. Kennedy and the White House Social Office under the direction of Letitia Baldrige and Pamela Turnure. This largely unprocessed collection is open upon request.

9. Miscellaneous Presidential Files. This consists of congratulations, greetings, get-well messages, president's appointment books, public opinion mail, White House telephone memorandums and toll tickets, and White House operating expenses.

10. Papers of the Post-Assassination Period. Mostly condolence books, correspondence, dedications, resolutions, scrapbooks regarding the death of John Kennedy.

B. MANUSCRIPT AND ARCHIVAL SOURCES FOR JOHN F. KENNEDY IN OTHER REPOSITORIES

11. John F. Kennedy Assassination Records Collection. National Archives. A mammoth collection that includes materials from the Warren Commission, the House Select Committee on Assassinations, the Central Intelligence Agency, and the Federal Bureau of Investigation.

12. John F. Kennedy FBI file in the Freedom of Information Act Reading Room, Federal Bureau of Investigation Headquarters, Washington. Also available on microfilm from Scholarly Resources, Inc., Wilmington, De., 1994.

C. PUBLISHED JOHN F. KENNEDY PAPERS

13. Adler, Bill, ed. *The Complete Kennedy Wit*. New York: Citadel Press, 1967. Expansion of Adler's *The Kennedy Wit* (1964) and *More Kennedy Wit* (1965).

14. Bagnall, Joseph A., ed. *President Kennedy's Grand and Global Alliance: World Order for the New Century*. Lanham, NY: University Press of America, 1992. Through Kennedy's own words, this is an attempt to acquaint a new generation with a major dimension of the Kennedy legacy--his strategy for survival in the thermonuclear age.

15. Barbarash, Ernest E., comp. *John F. Kennedy on Israel, Zionism, and Jewish Issues*. New York: Herzl Press, 1965. Published for the Zionist Organization of America. A brief compilation from speeches and writings on Kennedy's support of Israel.

16. Chase, Harold W. and Allen H. Lerman, eds. *Kennedy and the Press*. New York: Thomas Crowell, 1965. Contains the texts of President Kennedy's sixty-four news conferences and eight special interviews.

17. *Freedom of Communications, Part I: The Speeches, Remarks, Press Conferences, and Statements of Senator John F. Kennedy, August 1 through November 7, 1960*. Washington.: Government Printing Office, 1961. An essential source for covering the 1960 campaign.

18. Gardner, Gerald C., ed. *The Quotable Mr. Kennedy*. New York: Abelard-Schuman, 1962. Brief compilation of quotations without references.

19. _____, ed. *The Shining Moments: The Words and Moods of John F. Kennedy*. Montreal: Pocket Books, 1964. Forty-six photographs along with quotations.

20. Goldman, Alex J. *The Quotable Kennedy*. New York: Citadel Press, 1965. Kennedy's "brilliant" sayings, passages, and comments are extracted from his writings and speeches.

21. Herndon, Booton, comp. *The Humor of JFK*. New York: Fawcett Publications, 1964. Brief, pithy quips and humorous remarks from Kennedy from childhood to the presidency.

22. Israel, Fred L. *The State of the Union Messages of the Presidents, 1790-1966*. 3 vols. New York: Chelsea House, 1966. 3:3122-54. Includes an introduction by Arthur Schlesinger, Jr.

23. *John Fitzgerald Kennedy: A Compilation of Statements and Speeches Made* *during His Service in the United States Senate and House of Representatives.* Washington: Government Printing Office, 1964. An indispensable source in any study of Kennedy's congressional years.

24. Kennedy, John F. *The Burden and the Glory.* Edited by Allan Nevins. New York: Harper and Row, 1964. Covers President Kennedy's public statements and speeches in 1962 and 1963.

25. _____. *The Strategy of Peace.* Edited by Allan Nevins. New York: Harper and Row, 1960. A compilation of speeches and statements on Kennedy's foreign policy position on the eve of the 1960 campaign.

26. _____. Edited by John W. Gardner. *To Turn the Tide.* New York: Harper and Row, 1962. Covers JFK's public statements from his election through 1961.

27. *The Kennedy Press Conferences.* New York: E. M. Coleman Enterprises, 1978.

28. Meyersohn, Maxwell, comp. *Memorable Quotations of John F. Kennedy.* New York: Crowell, 1965. The most complete compilation of Kennedy quotations.

29. Moss, William, comp. *Public Statements on Vietnam, 1961-1963.* Boston: John F. Kennedy Library, 1973.

30. O'Hara, William T., ed. *John F. Kennedy on Education.* New York: Teachers College Press, Columbia University, 1966. Based on JFK's writings and speeches from 1951 through 1963.

31. *Public Papers of the Presidents of the United States, John F. Kennedy, Containing the Public Messages, Speeches, and Statements of the President, 1961-1963.* 3 vols. Washington: Government Printing Office, 1962-1964. Essential supplement to the manuscript materials on the Kennedy presidency at the Kennedy Library.

32. Schneider, Nicholas, comp. *Religious Views of President John F. Kennedy in His Own Words.* St. Louis: Herder, 1965. Nearly all of the references come from the *Public Papers of the Presidents of the United States, John F. Kennedy.*

33. Schneider, Nicholas, and Nathalie S. Rockhill, comps. *John F. Kennedy Talks to Young People.* New York: Hawthorn Books, 1968. Designed to inspire young people with the messages of the late president.

34. Settel, T. S., ed. *The Faith of JFK.* New York: E. P. Dutton, 1965. A eulogistic introduction by Richard Cardinal Cushing, along with President Kennedy's biblical or other inspirational quotations mostly extracted from speeches.

35. _____, ed. *The Wisdom of JFK*. New York: E. P. Dutton, 1965. Short excerpts from his presidential speeches.

36. Sorensen, Theodore, comp. *Let the Word Go Forth: The Speeches, Statements, and Writings of John F. Kennedy, 1947-1963*. New York: Delacorte Press, 1988. Familiar and not so familiar speeches, statements, and remarks compiled by Kennedy's special counsel and chief speechwriter.

37. Wszelaki, Jan, ed. *John F. Kennedy and Poland: Selection of Documents, 1948-63*. New York: Polish Institute of Arts and Sciences in America, 1964. Contains Kennedy's press conference and speech statements and selected correspondence on Poland from 1948 through November 1963.

D. UNPUBLISHED PERSONAL AND ADMINISTRATIVE PAPERS OF PRESIDENTIAL ASSOCIATES IN THE KENNEDY LIBRARY

38. Alfsen, Fritz. Fragmentary collection of trade consultant, Department of Commerce.

39. Amory, Robert. Served as deputy director of the Central Intelligence Agency.

40. Ball, George W. As Undersecretary of State, Ball played a key role in foreign policy matters.

41. Batt, William L. Labor Department official.

42. Bayley, Edwin R. A small collection of an administration public information figure.

43. Beaty, Oren. A small collection of an assistant to the Secretary of the Interior.

44. Beer, Samuel H. The papers of the national chairman of the Americans for Democratic Action (1959-62).

45. Behrman, Jack N. Served as Assistant Secretary of Commerce for International Affairs (1961-62).

46. Belk, Samuel E. Belk was on the National Security Council staff (1959-65).

47. Bell, David E. Kennedy's director of the Bureau of the Budget (1961-62) and administrator, Agency for International Development (1963-66).

48. Bennett, James V. Director of the Bureau of Prisons, Department of Justice.

49. Bernhard, Berl I. Bernhard was on the Commission on Civil Rights (1958-63).

50. Billings, K. LeMoyne. A very small collection of Kennedy's close friend since prep school.

51. Birkhead, Kenneth M. Assistant to the Secretary of Agriculture for Congressional Liaison (1961-63).

52. Black, David. Black served in the Interior Department (1961-63) and on the Federal Power Commission (1963-66).

53. Boggs, Elizabeth M. Member of the President's Panel on Mental Retardation.

54. Boutin, Bernard L. The Deputy Administrator and Administrator, General Services Administration (1961-64).

55. Bradshaw, James S. Press adviser to the Secretary General, Organization of American States (1961-62).

56. Broder, David S. An important journalist and author. Permission required.

57. Bruno, Gerald J. A political advance man for President Kennedy.

58. Bundy, McGeorge. The papers of JFK's National Security adviser which relate to the John F. Kennedy Library and the John F. Kennedy School of Government, Harvard University, and transcriptions of presidential recordings on the Cuban missile crisis.

59. Burke, James A. Papers of a congressional representative from the 86th through the 95th Congress.

60. Bush, Gerald W. Director of training for the Far East, Peace Corps (1962-64).

61. Byrne, John E. Press secretary to the governor of Maine, who worked in the 1960 presidential campaign and on Kennedy's November 1963 trip to Texas.

62. Cabot, John Moors. Kennedy's ambassador to Poland (1962-63).

63. Carver, John A. JFK's Assistant Secretary of the Interior for Public Lands Management (1961-63).

64. Chase, Gordon. Served on the National Security Council staff (1962-63).

65. Chayes, Abram. Legal adviser, Department of State (1961-63).

66. Christie, Alexander K. Labor figure, legislative consultant.

67. Cleveland, (James) Harlan. Assistant Secretary of State for International Organization Affairs (1961-63).

68. Clifford, Clark. Select papers of one who served as an adviser and family lawyer handling matters relating to *Profiles in Courage*.

69. Coleman, Barbara J. A journalist who served as White House press aide (1961-62).

70. Corson, John. Management consultant for the Kennedy administration.

71. Crockett, William J. Served as Assistant Secretary of State for Administration (1961-63) and Deputy Undersecretary of State for Administration (1963).

72. Daane, (James) Dewey. The Deputy United States Treasurer for Monetary Affairs (1961-63) and governor of Federal Reserve System (1963).

73. Daly, Charles U. Staff Assistant to the President for Congressional Liaison (1962-63).

74. Democratic National Committee. Records, 1952-63. Includes the 1956 and 1960 conventions and presidential campaigns.

75. Dillon, C. Douglas. Secretary of the Treasury.

76. Dixon, Paul Randall. Chairman and commissioner of the Federal Trade Commission (1961-63).

77. Dunfey, William L. Kennedy campaign coordinator in New England and New York (1960).

78. Dungan, Ralph A. Special Assistant to the President (1961-63).

79. Dunlop, John T. Member, Presidential Railroad Commission (1960-62).

80. Estabrook, Robert H. Editor and foreign correspondent, *Washington Post*.

81. Fay, Paul B., Jr. Fragmentary materials of Kennedy's close friend and Undersecretary of the Navy (1961-63).

82. Feild, John G. Executive Director, President's Commission on Equal Employment Opportunity (1961-63).

83. Fenn, Dan H. Tariff commissioner, later became director of the John F. Kennedy Library.

84. Fowler, Henry H. Undersecretary of the Treasury (1961-63).

85. Fredericks, Jacob Wayne. Deputy Assistant Secretary of State for African Affairs (1961-63).

86. Freeman, Orville L. Secretary of Agriculture, Freeman's papers include a detailed diary.

87. Galbraith, John Kenneth. Kennedy's ambassador to India and one who had his attention on many matters.

88. Gatov, Elizabeth R. Treasurer of the United States (1961-62).

89. Gessell, Gerhard. Director of President's Committee on Equal Opportunity in the Armed Forces (1962-63).

90. Gilpatric, Roswell L. Deputy Secretary of Defense (1961-63).

91. Goldberg, Arthur J. Copies of materials of Kennedy's Secretary of Labor (1961-62).

92. Goodwin, Doris Kearns. Research materials and manusript drafts of her *The Fitzgeralds and the Kennedys* (1987).

93. Goodwin, Richard N. Assistant Special Counsel to the President (1961), Deputy Assistant Secretary of State for Inter-American Affairs (1961-62), and director of International Peace Corps Secretariat (1962-63).

94. Gordon, Kermit. Member of the Council of Economic Advisers (1961-62) and director, Bureau of the Budget (1962-63).

95. Gordon, Lincoln. Ambassador to Brazil (1961-63).

96. Hackett, David L. Presidential campaign staff and later director of the President's Committee on Juvenile Delinquency (1961-62).

97. Hamilton, Milo Fowler. Administrator of the Agency for International Development (1961-62).

98. Hamilton, Nigel. Research material of his *JFK: Reckless Youth* (1992). Hamilton recently moved his papers to the Massachusetts Historical Society.

99. Hanify, Edward. Attorney for John F. Kennedy, Inc. and the John F. Kennedy Library Foundation.

100. Harllee, John. Chairman of the Federal Maritime Commission (1963).

101. Harris, Seymour E. A small collection of an economic adviser to Kennedy.

102. Hartigan, William J. Special assistant to Kennedy (1961-62) and the Assistant Postmaster General (1963).

103. Hays, Brooks. Kennedy's colorful special assistant (1961-63).

104. Hays, Samuel P. Consultant to the Peace Corps (1961-63).

105. Heller, Walter W. Chairman of the Council of Economic Advisers (1961-63).

106. Henderson, Deirdre. Research assistant in John Kennedy's Boston office (1959-60) and 1960 campaign aide.

107. Henderson, Douglas. Counsel at the U.S. Embassy, Peru (1961-63) and ambassador to Bolivia (1963).

108. Henry, Laurin. Public administrator (1960-61).

109. Higginbothom, A. Leon. Commissioner of the Federal Trade Commission (1962-63).

110. Hilsman, Roger. Director of Intelligence and Research, Department of State (1961-1963) and Assistant Secretary of State for Far Eastern Affairs (1963).

111. Hodges, Luther. Secretary of Commerce (1961-63).

112. Holcombe, Arthur. Professor of Government, Harvard University, when John Kennedy was a student.

113. Horne, John E. Chairman, Federal Home Loan Bank Board (1962-63).

114. Huntley, Chester R. (Chet). Correspondence of a broadcast journalist relating to the coverage of the assassination and funeral of President Kennedy.

115. Jones, Roger W. Deputy Undersecretary of State for Administration (1961-1962) and senior consultant and special assistant to the director, Bureau of the Budget (1962-63).

116. Josephson, William H. General counsel, Peace Corps (1961-63).

117. Kapenstein, Ira. The special assistant to the Postmaster General (1963).

118. Karnow, Stanley. His research material on China.

119. Katzenbach, Nicholas. Deputy Attorney General (1961-62). Katzenbach played a key role in civil rights matters.

120. Kaysen, Carl. Deputy Special Assistant to the President for National Security Affairs (1961-63).

121. Kennedy, Edward Moore. Voluminous papers of the president's brother and Massachusetts senator.

122. Kennedy, Joseph Patrick. Closed papers of the father of the president.

123. Kennedy, Robert Francis. The brother of the president served as campaign manager in 1960 and Attorney General (1961-63). This collection is partly closed.

124. Kennedy, Rose Fitzgerald. The closed papers of the mother of the president, including invaluable material on the family during the 1930s and 1940s.

125. Keppel, Francis. Commissioner of Education, Department of Health, Education, and Welfare (1963).

126. Klotz, Herbert. The Assistant Secretary of Commerce for administration (1962-63).

127. Knapp, Daniel. Research material on his *Scouting the War on Poverty* (1971).

128. Koskoff, David E. Research materials on his *Joseph P. Kennedy: A Life and Times* (1974).

129. Lincoln, Evelyn. Draft materials and draft manuscript of *My Twelve Years with John F. Kennedy* (1965) by Kennedy's personal secretary.

130. Lord, Walter. Research materials on his *The Past That Would Not Die* (1965), which deals with civil rights in Mississippi.

131. Macdonald, Torbert H. Papers of a close friend of the president and U.S. Representative from Massachusetts (1961-63).

132. McMurrin, Sterling M. Commissioner of Education, Department of Health, Education, and Welfare (1961-62).

133. McShane, James P. Chief U.S. marshal (1962-63); his papers include material on the integration of the University of Mississippi.

134. Mankiewicz, Frank. Peace Corps director, Peru (1962-63).

135. Marshall, Burke. Assistant Attorney General, Civil Rights Division, Department of Justice (1961-63).

136. Martin, Edwin. Assistant Secretary of State for Economic Affairs (1960-62) and Assistant Secretary of State for Inter-American Affairs (1962-63).

137. Millikan, Max. Correspondence with President Kennedy on the presidential transition and other subjects.

138. Mitchell, George. Member and consultant to the Board of Governors of the Federal Reserve System.

139. Morris, Thomas D. Assistant Secretary of Defense (1961-63).

140. Moscoso, Teodoro. Ambassador to Venezuela (1961) and U.S. coordinator for the Alliance for Progress, Agency for International Development (1961-63).

141. Murphy, Robert T. Vice chairman, Civil Aeronautics Board (1961-73).

142. Navasky, Victor. Research materials on his *Kennedy Justice* (1971).

143. Nestingen, Ivan. The Undersecretary of Health, Education, and Welfare (1961-63).

144. Neustadt, Richard E. Papers of the author of *Presidential Power* (1960); a consultant to President Kennedy, to the Bureau of the Budget, and to the Atomic Energy Commission (1962-63).

145. Newman, John M. Research materials on his *JFK and Vietnam* (1992).

146. Nunnerly, David. Research materials on his *Kennedy and Britain* (1972).

147. Oberdorfer, Louis F. Assistant Attorney General, Tax Division, Department of Justice (1961-63).

148. O'Brien, Dorothy G. Chairwoman, Illinois Democratic party, Northern District (1959-60).

149. O'Brien, Lawrence F. Papers of the Special Assistant to the President for Congressional Relations and Personnel (1961-63).

150. O'Donnell, Kenneth P. A small collection of an intimate adviser of the president who served as appointment secretary (1961-63).

151. Onassis, Jacqueline Kennedy. Sixteen feet of condolence letters, tributes, requests for photographs or mass cards.

152. Orrick, William H. Orrick served as Assistant Attorney General, Civil Division (1961-62), Antitrust Division (1963), Department of Justice; acted also as Deputy

Undersecretary of State for Administration (1962-63).

153. Palfrey, John. Commissioner, Atomic Energy Commission (1962-63).

154. Peace Corps Collection. Donations by private individuals documenting personal experiences while serving in the Peace Corps.

155. Peterson, Esther. Assistant Secretary of Labor for Labor Standards; member, President's Commission on the Status of Women.

156. Phillips, Franklyn W. Assistant to the administrator, National Aeronautics and Space Council (1960-61) and director, Northeast Office (1962-63).

157. Poullada, Leon B. Ambassador to Togo (1961-63).

158. Powers, David F. Friend and political aide of Kennedy since 1946 who was accorded the title of Special Assistant to the President (1961-63).

159. Ramey, James T. Commissioner, Atomic Energy Commission (1962-63).

160. Reardon, Timothy. A longtime aide who became Administrative Assistant to President Kennedy (1961-63) and Special Assistant to the President for Cabinet Affairs (1961-63).

161. Reese, Matthew A. Campaign adviser to John Kennedy (1960).

162. Reilly, John R. Assistant to the Deputy Attorney General, Department of Justice (1961-63).

163. Renne, Roland. Speeches and publications of the Assistant Secretary of Agriculture for International Affairs (1963).

164. Reuter, Richard W. Director, Food for Peace (1962-63).

165. Rivkin, William R. Ambassador to Luxembourg (1962-63).

166. Roberts, Chalmers M. Chief diplomatic correspondent, *Washington Post.*

167. Roosa, Robert V. Copies of the personal office files of the Undersecretary of the Treasury for Monetary Affairs (1961-63).

168. Rusk, Dean. Copies of appointment books of the Secretary of State.

169. Sanjuan, Pedro A. Assistant Chief of Protocol (1961-63) and director of Special Protocol Services (1963), Department of State.

170. Saxon, James. Comptroller of the Currency (1961-63).

171. Schlesinger, Arthur M., Jr. An extensive and significant collection of a liaison to the intellectual community. As Special Assistant to the President, Schlesinger also served as a speechwriter and adviser on Latin American affairs (1961-63).

172. Schwartz, Abba P. Administrator, Bureau of Security and Consular Affairs, State Department (1962-63).

173. Seaborg, Glenn T. Chairman, Atomic Energy Commission (1961-63).

174. Sheridan, Walter. The papers of an organized crime investigator for the Department of Justice (1961-63).

175. Shriver, Eunice, and R. Sargent Shriver. President Kennedy's sister who was involved in mental retardation and his brother-in-law who directed the Peace Corps (1961-63).

176. Slayton, William L. Commissioner, Urban Renewal Administration, Housing and Home Finance Agency (1961-63).

177. Smith, Benjamin A. Friend of Kennedy and senator from Massachusetts (1961-63).

178. Smith, Frank E. Director, Kennedy-Johnson National Advisory Committee (1960).

179. Smith, Stephen E. The brother-in-law of the president, this small collection deals with political activities relating to the planned 1964 presidential campaign.

180. Sorensen, Theodore C. Special Counsel to the President, perhaps Kennedy's most important domestic agent and his key speechwriter (1961-63).

181. Sprecher, Drexel A. Deputy chairman, Democratic National Committee (1957-60).

182. Staats, Elmer B. Deputy director, Bureau of the Budget (1961-63).

183. Stahr, Elvis. Secretary of the Army (1961-62).

184. Stern, Philip M. Deputy Assistant Secretary of State for Public Affairs (1961-62).

185. Stillman, John S. Deputy to the Undersecretary of Commerce (1961-63) and deputy to the Secretary of Commerce for Congressional Liaison (1963).

186. Surrey, Stanley S. Assistant Secretary of the Treasury for Tax Policy (1961-63).

187. Szulc, Tad. Research materials of journalist who wrote a book about Fidel Castro.

188. Thomson, James C. Special assistant to the Undersecretary of State (1961); special assistant to the President's Special Representative for Africa, Asia, and Latin America (1961-63); and special assistant to the Assistant Secretary of State for Far Eastern Affairs (1963).

189. Tobin, James. Member of the Council of Economic Advisers.

190. Tucker, William H. Commissioner, Interstate Commerce Commission (1961-63).

191. Tyroler, Charles. Director, National Democratic Advisory Committee (1956-61).

192. U.S. Agency for International Development. Records, 1961-63.

193. U.S. Arms Control and Disarmament Agency. Records, 1961-63.

194. U.S. Bureau of the Budget. Records, 1961-63.

195. U.S. Central Intelligence Agency. Printed Materials, 1961-63. U. S. Civil Aeronautics Board. Records, 1961-63.

196. U.S. Civil Service Commission. Records, 1961-63.

197. U.S. Commission of Fine Arts. Records, 1961-63.

198. U.S. Commission on Civil Rights. Records, 1961-63.

199. U.S. Council of Economic Advisers. Records, 1961-63.

200. U.S. Department of the Army. Records relating to Kennedy's funeral, 1963.

201. U.S. Department of State Mission to the United Nations. Records, 1961-63.

202. U.S. District of Columbia Government. Records, 1961-63.

203. U.S. Farm Credit Administration. Records, 1961-63.

204. U.S. Federal Aviation Agency. Records, 1961-63.

205. U.S. Federal Communications Commission. Records, 1961-63.

206. U.S. Federal Maritime Commission. Records, 1961-63.

207. U.S. Federal Mediation and Conciliation Service. Records, 1961-63.

208. U.S. Federal Power Commission. Records, 1961-63.

209. U.S. Federal Trade Commission. Records, 1961-63.

210. U.S. General Services Administration. Records, 1961-63.

211. U.S. Housing and Home Finance Agency. Records, 1961-63.

212. U.S. Inaugural Committee. Records, 1960-61.

213. U.S. Information Agency. Records, 1961-63.

214. U.S. Interstate Commerce Commission. Records, 1961-63.

215. U.S. National Aeronautics and Space Administration. Records, 1961-63.

216. U.S. National Aeronautics and Space Council. Records, 1961-63.

217. U.S. National Labor Relations Board. Records, 1961-63.

218. U.S. National Mediation Board. Records, 1961-63.

219. U.S. National Science Foundation. Records, 1961-63.

220. U.S. Office of Emergency Planning. Records, 1961-63.

221. U.S. Office of Science and Technology. Records, 1961-63.

222. U.S. Peace Corps. Records, 1961-63.

223. U.S. Presidential Railroad Commission. Records, 1961-62.

224. U.S. President's Advisory Commission on Narcotics and Drug Abuse. Records, 1962-63.

225. U.S. President's Boeing Aerospace Board. Records, 1962-63.

226. U.S. President's Commission on the Status of Women. Records, 1961-63.

227. U.S. Secret Service. Records, 1961-63.

228. U.S. Securities and Exchange Commission. Records, 1961-63.

229. U.S. Selective Service System. Records, 1961-63.

230. U.S. Small Business Administration. Records, 1961-63.

231. U.S. Smithsonian Institution. Records, 1961-63.

232. U.S. Tariff Commission. Records, 1961-63.

233. U.S. Tennessee Valley Authority. Records, 1961-63.

234. U.S. Veterans Administration. Records, 1961-63.

235. Wallace, Robert A. Assistant Secretary of the Treasury (1961-63).

236. Webb, James E. Administrator, National Aeronautics and Space Administration (1961-63).

237. Welsh, Edward C. Executive secretary, National Aeronautics and Space Council (1961-63).

238. Welsh, Richard J. Executive secretary, National Aeronautics and Space Council.

239. White, Theodore H. Research materials of noted author and journalist.

240. Wiesner, Jerome B. Special Assistant to the President for Science and Technology (1961-63).

241. Wirtz, W. Willard. Undersecretary of Labor (1961-62) and Secretary of Labor (1962-63).

242. Yarmolinsky, Adam. The Special Assistant to the Secretary of Defense (1961-63.

E. UNPUBLISHED PERSONAL PAPERS OF PRESIDENTIAL ASSOCIATES IN OTHER LIBRARIES

243. Acheson, Dean. Harry S. Truman Library. Truman's Secretary of State served as foreign policy adviser on such matters as Berlin.

244. Alsop, Joseph and Stewart. Manuscript Division, Library of Congress. Key journalists close to the president.

245. Bell, David E. Lyndon B. Johnson Library. The papers of Kennedy's Budget Director.

246. Bergquist, Laura. Boston University. A journalist closely tied to the Kennedys.

247. Berle, Adolph A. Diary. Franklin D. Roosevelt Library. A relic of Roosevelt's New Deal, Berle served as JFK's Latin American affairs adviser.

248. Blair, Joan, and Clay Blair, Jr., American Heritage Center, University of Wyoming. Contains materials on John Kennedy relating to the Blairs's *The Search for JFK*.

249. Bohlen, Charles. Manuscript Division, Library of Congress. Ambassador to the Soviet Union during the Truman presidency, Bohlen was an adviser to JFK on Soviet matters and became ambassador to France, 1962-63.

250. Bowles, Chester. Sterling Memorial Library, Yale University. Controversial Undersecretary of State whom Kennedy removed in 1962,

251. Byrd, Harry F. University of Virginia. Reactionary chairman of the Senate Finance Committee.

252. Capehart, Homer. Indiana State Library, Indianapolis. Republican senator who led the attack against the Kennedy administration.

253. Celler, Emanuel. Manuscript Division, Library of Congress. In 1963 Celler played an important role regarding civil rights as chairman of the House Judiciary Subcommittee.

254. Dirksen, Everett. Dirksen Congressional Leadership Research Center, Pekin, Ill. Dirksen was the Senate minority leader who managed to retain a good working relationship with Kennedy.

255. Douglas, Paul H. Chicago Historical Society. A liberal Democratic senator from Illinois.

256. Dulles, Allen. Seeley Mudd Library, Princeton University. Controversial head of the Central Intelligence Agency, who lost his job after the 1961 Bay of Pigs fiasco.

257. Eisenhower, Dwight D. Dwight D. Eisenhower Library. Republican former president consulted with Kennedy particularly in crisis situations. His papers also convey his private views regarding the Kennedy presidency.

258. Fay, Paul B., Jr. Department of Special Collections, Stanford University Library. Longtime Kennedy friend and Undersecretary of the Navy.

259. Flanders, Ralph. Syracuse University Library. Vermont senator who led the early opposition to Senator Joseph McCarthy.

260. Forrestal, James. Seeley Mudd Library, Princeton University. Kennedy knew Navy Secretary Forrestal during World War II.

261. Freeman, Orville. Minnesota Historical Society. Secretary of Agriculture.

262. Fulbright, J. William. University of Arkansas. Chairman of the Senate Foreign Relations Committee whom JFK seriously considered for Secretary of State.

263. Halleck, Charles A. Indiana University. Overly partisan Republican House of Representative leader who nonetheless cooperated with the Kennedy administration on civil rights legislation in 1963.

264. Harriman, W. Averell. Manuscript Division, Library of Congress. Former Roosevelt and Truman adviser who became Kennedy's "roving ambassador" and engineered the Laotian settlement in 1962; became Assistant Secretary of State for the Far East in 1963.

265. Humphrey, Hubert H. Minnesota Historical Society. Humphrey led the liberal wing of the Democratic party in the Senate.

266. Johnson, Lyndon Baines. Lyndon B. Johnson Library. Voluminous papers of Kennedy's vice president.

267. Kefauver, Estes. University of Tennessee Library. Independent Democratic senator from Tennessee.

268. Kennedy, Joseph P. File. Federal Bureau of Investigation. Freedom of Information Act Reading Room, FBI Headquarters, Washington. J. Edgar Hoover's file on the president's father; recently available on microfilm from Scholarly Resources, Inc.

269. Kennedy, Robert F. File. Federal Bureau of Investigation. Freedom of Information Act Reading Room, FBI Headquarters, Washington. J. Edgar Hoover's file on the president's brother; recently available on microfilm from Scholarly Resources, Inc.

270. Kerr, Robert. Bizzell Memorial Library, University of Oklahoma. A key Democratic powerbroker who chaired the Senate Space Committee.

271. King, Martin Luther, Jr. Boston University. The most important civil rights leader of the Kennedy era.

272. Knebel, Fletcher. Boston University. Journalist, Cowles Publications.

273. Kohler, Foy D. University of Toledo Library. Partial papers of the Assistant Secretary for European Affairs (1961-62) and ambassador to the Soviet Union (1962-63).

274. Krock, Arthur. Seeley Mudd Library, Princeton University. Once a former close friend of the Kennedy family, Krock of the *New York Times* found his friendship tested during the Kennedy presidency.

275. Lippmann, Walter. Sterling Memorial Library,Yale University. One of the leading syndicated columnists of the Kennedy period.

276. Luce, Henry R. Manuscript Division, Library of Congress. Partial collection of the publisher of *Time* magazine, a close family friend.

277. McCloy, John J. Amherst College, Amherst, Massachusetts. JFK's Special Assistant on Disarmament.

278. McCormack, John. Boston University. McCormack, the Democratic Speaker of the U. S. House of Representatives from Massachusetts, cared little for Kennedy because of past intraparty battles.

279. Martin, John Bartlow. Seeley Mudd Library, Princeton University. Writer and biographer of Adlai Stevenson, and JFK's ambassador to the Dominican Republic.

280. Mitchell, Hugh Burnton. University of Washington. Senator from Washington.

281. Nixon, Richard M. National Archives, Laguna Niguel, Calif., and National Archives, Alexandria, Va. Eisenhower's former vice president remained politically active during the Kennedy presidency.

282. Palmer, Paul. Yale University Library. Journalist and editor.

283. Rayburn, Sam. Sam Rayburn Library, Bonham, Tx. The Speaker of the House of Representatives.

284. Roosevelt, Eleanor. Franklin D. Roosevelt Library. FDR's liberal wife had early misgivings about JFK but served as chair of the President's Commission on the Status of Women.

285. Rusk, Dean. University of Georgia. Secretary of State.

286. Russell, Richard B. Richard B. Russell Memorial Library, University of Georgia. Chairman of the Senate Armed Forces Committee; opposed Kennedy on civil rights and on other matters.

287. Schary, Dore. State Historical Society of Wisconsin. Playwright and producer.

Schary produced a film, *The Pursuit of Happiness*, narrated by JFK, which was shown at the 1956 Democratic National Convention.

288. Smathers, George. University of Florida. A conservative Senator, Smathers had an exceedingly close personal relationship with JFK that went back to their days in the House of Representatives.

289. Smith, Howard W. University of Virginia. The reactionary Democratic chairman of the House of Representatives Committee on Rules.

290. Spence, Brent. University of Kentucky Library. Representative from Kentucky.

291. Stevenson, Adlai. Seeley Mudd Library, Princeton University. Voluminous papers of a former Democratic presidential nominee (1952 and 1956) who served as JFK's ambassador to the U.N.

292. Truman, Harry S. Harry S. Truman Library. The elderly former president remained in touch with President Kennedy.

F. UNPUBLISHED ADMINISTRATIVE PAPERS OF KENNEDY CABINET ASSOCIATES IN THE NATIONAL ARCHIVES

293. Agriculture
Attorney General
Commerce
Defense
Health, Education, and Welfare
Interior
Labor
Post Office
State
Treasury

These collections contain various subsidiary groupings that facilitate their use. The Department of State uses a decimal file system that indicates the relations of the United States with every nation. Under Labor, there are, for example, the General Correspondence of the Secretary of Labor, RG 174; the Records of the Bureau of Labor Statistics, RG 257; the Records of the Women's Bureau, RG 86; and the Records of the Bureau of Labor Standards, RG 100.

Selected microfilmed or paper copies of these and other department and agency records were made following JFK's death for inclusion in the Kennedy Library. Some of these collections including Agriculture; Health, Education, and Welfare; Interior; and Labor are open for research. Others--particularly those dealing with national security, foreign relations, defense, and legal cases--are mostly closed. The records of the departments of Defense, State, Treasury, and Justice (at 728 microfilm rolls the largest collection) are completely closed.

G. UNPUBLISHED ADMINISTRATIVE PAPERS OF OTHER KENNEDY ASSOCIATES AND AGENCIES IN THE NATIONAL ARCHIVES

294. Agency for International Development. Records. Record Group 286. The AID was established in November 1961 to carry out nonmilitary U.S. foreign assistance programs.

295. Federal Communications Commission. Record Group 173. Covers the years from 1910 through 1964.

296. Federal Mediation and Conciliation Service. Record Group 280. Includes the Kennedy period.

297. Government of Samoa. Record Group 284. Contains 155 cubic feet of records between 1889 and 1966.

298. National Mediation Board. Record Group 13. For the Kennedy period, there is only material on a special commission dealing with the disputes in the New York City harbor area.

299. Office of Science and Technology. Record Group 359. Covers the period between 1957 and 1967.

300. Office of the Special Representative for Trade Negotiations. Record Group 364. Consist of reports, correspondence, and a related card index, briefs, transcripts, publications, and press releases.

301. President's Committee on Equal Employment Opportunity. Record Group 220. Includes memorandums, correspondence, and case files for 1963-65.

302. U.S. Bureau of the Budget. Record Group 51. Included are reports, correspondence, memorandums, exhibits, statistical tables, and finding aids related to general administrative and budgetary matters.

303. U.S. Electoral Records, 1888-1968. Certified copies of ascertainments of electors including the election of 1960.

304. U.S. Federal Reserve System. Record Group 82. Records consist of minutes of the Federal Open Market Committee, 1936-65 and its executive committee.

305. U.S. General Services Administration. Record Group 269. Chiefly inventory listings of federal real estate leased by civilian or defense agencies in the United

States, U.S. territories, and other countries.

306. U.S. Indian Claims Commission. Record Group 279. Contains 130 cubic feet of records, mostly case files, between 1947 and 1967.

307. U.S. Veterans Administration. Record Group 15. Administrative and legal records.

H. PUBLISHED COMPILATIONS OF THE PERSONAL AND ADMINISTRATIVE PAPERS OF PRESIDENTIAL ASSOCIATES

308. *Annual Report of the Postmaster General, 1961 [1962, 1963].* Washington: Government Printing Office, 1961-1963. Statistical information on mail service, postal activities, and department financial condition by Kennedy's two postmaster generals, Edward Day and John Gronouski.

309. Galbraith, John Kenneth. *Ambassador's Journal: A Personal Account of the Kennedy Years.* Boston: Houghton, Mifflin, 1969. Witty and perceptive.

310. McLellan, David S., and David C. Acheson, eds. *Among Friends: Personal Letters of Dean Acheson.* New York: Dodd, Mead, 1980. Acheson privately criticized the Kennedy presidency.

311. Stevenson, Adlai. *The Papers of Adlai Stevenson.* Edited by Walter Johnson. 8 vols. Boston: Little Brown, 1972-79. Volume 8 focuses on Stevenson as U.N. ambassador, 1961-63.

312. U.S. Department of Agriculture. *Report of the Secretary of Agriculture, 1961 [1962].* Washington: Government Printing Office, 1961-62. provides an annual general review of the general problems of agriculture by Secretary of Agriculture Orville Freeman as well as a report on various program activities.

313. U.S. Department of Commerce. *Annual Report of the Secretary of Commerce in 1961 [1962, 1963, 1964].* Washington: Government Printing Office, 1961-64. Focuses on economic development, expanding industry and business, transportation policy, science, and various Commerce programs emanating from the departments.

314. U.S. Department of Defense. *Annual Report for Fiscal Year 1961 [1962, 1963, 1964].* Washington: Government Printing Office, 1962-65. Reports of Secretary of Defense Robert McNamara, Secretary of the Army, Secretary of the Navy, and Secretary of the Air Force.

315. U.S. Department of Health, Education, and Welfare. *Annual Report, 1961 [1962, 1963, 1964].* Washington: Government Printing Office, 1962-65. Reports of HEW secretaries Abraham Ribicoff and Anthony Celebrezze as well as those of the Social Security Administration, Public Health Service, Office of Education, Food and Drug Administration, Office of Vocational Rehabilitation, and Saint Elizabeth's Hospital.

316. U.S. Department of the Interior. *Annual Report of the Secretary of the Interior, 1961 [1962, 1963, 1964].* Washington: Government Printing Office, 1962-65. For 1961 and 1962 there are lengthy introductory chapters on the environment and conservation; all volumes contain reports from the various bureaus, offices, and services.

317. U.S. Department of Justice. *Annual Report of the Attorney General of the United States for the Fiscal Year 1961 [1962, 1964].* Washington: Government Printing Office, 1962-63, 1965. Reports from the various divisions and bureaus.

318. U.S. Department of Labor. *Annual Report United States Department of Labor Fiscal Year 1961 [1962, 1963].* Washington: Government Printing Office, 1962-64. Reports of Labor secretaries, Arthur Goldberg and W. Willard Wirtz, the Office of the Secretary, and various bureaus.

319. U.S. Department of State. *Foreign Relations of the United States, 1961 [1962, 1963].* Washington: Government Printing Office, 1988-1995. Thus far four volumes on Vietnam have been published for the Kennedy period, two on the Berlin crisis of 1961-63, and volumes on the Laotian crisis, the Soviet Union, the Kennedy-Khrushchev correspondence, and Eastern Europe, with a total of at least 25 printed volumes and six microfiche supplements planned for the Kennedy years.

320. U. S. Department of the Treasury. *Annual Report of the Secretary of the Treasury on the State of Finances for the Fiscal Year Ended June 30, 1961 [1962, 1963, 1964].* Washington: Government Printing office, 1962-65. Statistics regarding all aspects of the national economy along with administrative reports from the various agencies of Treasury.

I. CONTEMPORARY PRINT MEDIA

321. Few presidents were as popular with the working press. Moreover, few presidents perused newspapers and news magazines as extensively, cultivated and managed journalists as assiduously, and responded to criticism as sensitively as Kennedy. From the beginning of his political career, he could count on the support of Boston-area newspapers such as the *Globe, Herald,* and *Traveler.* In 1952 Kennedy's father even purchased the endorsement of the *Boston Post* during JFK's Senate race against Henry Cabot Lodge, Jr.

Nationally, major newspapers such as the *New York Times, Washington Post, St. Louis Post-Dispatch, Philadelphia Inquirer,* and the *Chicago Daily News* treated Kennedy favorably. JFK's friendship with publishers Philip Graham of the

Washington Post, Arthur H. Sulzberger of the *New York Times*, and Henry Luce of *Time Inc.* especially proved beneficial. Yet the *Times'* occasional critical editorials most bothered the president because of the perceived importance of that newspaper. To researchers, the *New York Times* is particularly important for its coverage on foreign policy, while the *Washington Post* provides inside information on Capitol Hill.

In a period when syndicated columnists were so important with the well informed, JFK received favorable pieces from such leading writers as Joseph and Stewart Alsop, Charles Bartlett, Rowland Evans, James Reston, Tom Wicker, and usually Walter Lippmann.

Among the key anti-Kennedy newspapers included the Republican eastern establishment New York *Herald-Tribune*, which especially criticized Kennedy on domestic issues; the conservative and isolationist *Chicago Tribune*; the right-wing *St. Louis Globe-Democrat;* the Republican *Kansas City Star*; and the Hearst-owned *San Francisco Examiner*. Virtually all the above newspapers are on microfilm.

Of the news magazines, Kennedy rightly believed *Newsweek* the most supportive even though he frequently complained to friend Benjamin Bradlee, head of that magazine's Washington bureau, of inaccuracies in its political gossip columns. Despite the Luce ownership, *Time* magazine became Kennedy's "source of special despair" because of its supposedly slanted and unfair treatment. Kennedy never even bothered to read the conservative *U.S. News and World Report,* which he thought had "little news and less to report." Of the intellectual news weeklies, the liberal *New Republic* and the *Nation* were generally pro-Kennedy and the reactionary *National Review* was almost always anti-Kennedy.

2

Oral Histories

In studying recent American presidents, scholars are increasingly relying on the oral histories of individuals who were close to presidents or served in their administrations. Consequently, presidential libraries and other repositories have been conducting major projects to record and transcribe that sort of testimony.

A. ORAL HISTORIES AT THE JOHN FITZGERALD KENNEDY LIBRARY

There are more than eleven hundred oral histories of people who were involved with the Kennedys. Only those directly connected with JFK are listed below. While these oral histories constitute an invaluable source, some limitations do exist. For example, many oral histories were conducted shortly after Kennedy's assassination, which made the interviewer reluctant to raise tough-minded questions. Some of the early oral histories are so laudatory and amateurishly done that they are virtually useless to researchers. About three hundred interviews are unavailable to scholars as a consequence of deed-of-gift stipulations or because of the failure of the interviewee to complete the paperwork following the interview. The Kennedy Library will make available a list of unprocessed oral histories, enabling researchers to contact the interviewee directly. Most oral histories are available on interlibrary loan.

322. Abel, Elie. Broadcast journalist, National Broadcasting Co. and author of *The Missile Crisis* (1966). 1970. Portions Closed. 42 pp.

323. Acheson, Dean G. Presidential adviser on foreign affairs. Especially valuable on Cuba. 1964. 34 pp.

324. Aiken, Frank. Minister of External Affairs, Ireland. 1966. 30 pp.

325. Aiken, George. Senator from Vermont. 1964. 42 pp.

326. Ailes, Stephen. Undersecretary of the Army. 1968. 63 pp.

327. Akers, Anthony B. Ambassador to New Zealand (1961-76). 1971. 41 pp.

328. Albert, Carl. Representative from Oklahoma (1947-77). 1965. 37 pp.

329. Almond, J. Lindsay. Governor of Virginia. 1968. 25 pp.

330. Alphand, H. E. Hervé. French Ambassador to the United States (1956-65). 1964. 11 pp.

331. Alsop, Joseph. Journalist, author, JFK friend. One of the more invaluable oral histories. 1964. 111 pp.

332. Amory, Robert. Deputy Director, Central Intelligence Agency (1957-62); Chief, International Division, Bureau of the Budget (1962-65). 1966. 153 pp.

333. Amos, John. Democratic National Committeeman from West Virgina (1959-68). 1965. 41 pp.

334. Anderson, Clinton P. Senator from New Mexico (1949-73). 1967. 57 pp.

335. Anderson, Eugenie M. Ambassador to Bulgaria (1962-65). Portions closed. 1973. 64 pp.

336. Anderson, George W. Admiral, U.S. Navy; Chief of Naval Operations, Joints Chiefs of Staff (1961-63). Important regarding the Cuban missile crisis. 1967. 28 pp.

337. Anderson, Glenn M. Lieutenant Governor (1959-67) and Representative (1969-), California. 1970, 1971. 86 pp.

338. Andolsek, Ludwig. Commissioner, Civil Service Commission. 1979. 20 pp.

339. Arata, Lawrence. White House upholsterer (1961-77). 1964. 6 pp.

340. Aspinall, Wayne. Representative from Colorado (1949-73). 1965. 6 pp.

341. Attwood, William. Presidential campaign staff and Ambassador to Guinea (1961-63). 1965. 13 pp.

342. Auchincloss, Janet. Mother-in-law of President Kennedy. Portions closed. 37 pp.

343. Avery, Isaac. White House carpenter. 1964. 22 pp.

344. Aylward, James P. Missouri political figure. 1967. 20 pp.

345. Badeau, John S. Ambassador to the United Arab Republic (1961-64). 1969. 27 pp.

346. Bailey, John M. Chairman, Democratic National Committee (1961-75). 1964. 157 pp.

347. Baker, John A. Assistant Secretary of Agriculture (1962-69). 1964. 27 pp.

348. Baldrige, Letitia. White House social secretary (1961-63). Much of her book, *Of Diamonds and Diplomats*, is a replication of her earlier oral history. (1968). 1964. 126 pp.

349. Baldwin, Charles. Ambassador to Malaysia (1961-64). 1969. 78 pp.

350. Balewa, Alhaji Sir Abubaker Tafawa. Prime Minister, Federal Republic of Nigeria (1957-66). 1964. 4 pp.

351. Banks, James G. Assistant Commissioner for Relocation and Community Organization, Housing and Home Finance Agency. 1966. 28 pp.

352. Barboza, Joanne. Waitress, Stone and Gable Restaurant, Hyannisport (1946-47). 1982. 23 pp. Excellent on John Kennedy and the Kennedy family.

353. Barnes, Donald F. Presidential interpreter, Department of State (1956-66). 1964. 108 pp.

354. Barnett, Ross R. Governor of Mississippi (1960-64). 1969. 24 pp.

355. Barron, William. Attorney General (1956-61), Governor (1961-65), West Virginia. 1965. 14 pp.

356. Barrows, Leland. Ambassador to Cameroon (1960-66). 1971. 21 pp.

357. Bartlett, Charles. Journalist, friend of JFK. 1965. 166 pp.

358. Batt, William L. Administrator, Area Redevelopment Administration, Department of Commerce (1961-65). 1966, 1967. 206 pp.

359. Battle, Lucius. Special assistant to the Secretary and Executive Secretary (1961-62), Consul General (1962), and Assistant Secretary of State for Education and Cultural Affairs (1962-64), Department of State. Portions closed. 1968. 141 pp.

360. Bayley, Edwin R. Director of Public Information, Peace Corps (1961); director, Information Staff, Agency for International Development (1961-63). Portions closed. 1968. 121 pp.

361. Bazelon, David. Member, President's Panel on Mental Retardation (1962-63). 1969. 22 pp.

362. Beale, Sir Howard. Australian Ambassador to the United States (1958-64). 1964. 21 pp.

363. Beasley, D. Otis. Administrative Assistant Secretary, Department of the Interior (1952-65). 1969. 24 pp.

364. Beaty, Orren. Assistant to the Secretary of the Interior (1961-67). 1969, 1970. 333 pp.

365. Begab, Michael J. Executive officer to the Special Assistant to the President for Mental Retardation (1963-64). 1968. 25 pp.

366. Behn, Gerald. Secret Service, special agent in charge of White House detail. 1976. 11 pp.

367. Belen, Fred. Post Office Department employee. 1976. 47 pp.

368. Bell, David E. Director, Bureau of the Budget (1961-62); administrator, Agency for International Development (1963-66). 1964, 1965. 169 pp.

369. Bell, Jack L. Journalist, Associated Press (1937-69). 1966. 71 pp.

370. Ben-Gurion, David. Prime Minister, Israel (1955-63). 1965. 17 pp.

371. Bennett, James V. Director, Bureau of Prisons, Department of Justice (1937-64). 1974. Portions closed. 23 pp.

372. Benson, Marguerite R. Wisconsin political figure. 1965. 21 pp.

373. Benton, William L. Senator from Connecticut (1949-53). Portions closed. 1964. One of the more incisive oral histories on Kennedy. 78 pp.

374. Bergquist, Laura (Knebel). Journalist, *Look*. Portions closed. 1965. Excellent regarding JFK's attitude toward women. 25 pp.

375. Berlin, Sir Isaiah. Kennedy associate; professor of social and political theory, Oxford University (1957-67). Permission required. 1965. 23 pp.

376. Bernhard, Berl I. Staff director, Commission on Civil Rights (1958-63). 1968. 56 pp.

377. Bernhard, Prince. Prince of the Netherlands (1937-). 1964. 4 pp.

378. Bernstein, Leonard. Composer, conductor, New York Philharmonic Orchestra (1957-69). 1965. 15 pp.

379. Bertsch, Howard. Administrator, Farmers Home Administration (1961-69). 1964. 22 pp.

380. Berube, Edward C. Massachusetts political figure. 1967. 45 pp.

381. Biemiller, Andrew John. Director, Department of Legislation, AFL-CIO (1956-82). 1965, 1979. 85 pp.

382. Billings, K. LeMoyne. JFK's close friend since prep school days, later a frequent visitor to the White House. Closed. 1964, 1965, 1966. 810 pp.

383. Bilodeau, Thomas J. Massachusetts political figure; Kennedy family associate. 1964. 11 pp.

384. Bingham, Jonathan. U.S. representative, U.N. Trusteeship Council (1961-62), and Economic and Social Council (1962-63). 1965. 17 pp.

385. Birkhead, Kenneth M. Assistant to the Secretary of Agriculture for Congressional Liaison (1961-66). 1964, 1967. 91 pp.

386. Bissell, Richard M. Deputy director, Central Intelligence Agency (1959-62).

387. Blaik, Earl. Athletic director, United States Military Academy (1949-58); President Kennedy's personal representative, Birmingham, Ala. (1963). 1964. 21 pp.

388. Blair, William. Ambassador to Denmark (1961-64). 1964. 39 pp.

389. Blatnik, John. Representative from Minnesota (1947-74). 1966. 34 pp.

390. Blundell, James. Democratic National Committee member. 1976. 25 pp.

391. Boggs, Elizabeth. Member of the President's Panel on Mental Retardation. 1968, 1969. 69 pp.

392. Boggs, Hale. Representative from Louisiana (1947-72); vice chairman, Democratic National Committee (1956-72); member, Warren Commission, (1963-64). 1964. 39 pp.

393. Bohlen, Charles. Special Assistant to the Secretary of State for Soviet Affairs (1960-62); Ambassador to France (1962-67).

394. Bolling, Jim Grant. Kennedy campaign worker (1960); Department of Health, Education, and Welfare official for Congressional Liaison. 1966. 104 pp.

395. Bolling, Richard. Representative from Missouri (1949-82). 1965. 66 pp.

396. Bookbinder, Hyman. Special Assistant to the Secretary of Commerce (1961-62). 1964. 64 pp.

397. Booker, Simeon. Journalist, Johnson Publishing Co. 1967. Portions closed. 39 pp.

398. Bornstein, Samuel. Journalist; managing editor, *Boston Sunday Advertiser* (1942-71). 1977. 13 pp.

399. Bosch, Juan. President, Dominican Republic (1963). 1964. 23 pp.

400. Bouck, Robert I. Agent, Protective Research, Secret Service. 1976. 16 pp.

401. Bourgiba, Habib Ben Ali. President of Tunisia (1957-88). 1963. 4 pp.

402. Bourgiba, Habib, Jr. Tunisian ambassador to the United States (1961-63). 1964. 13 pp.

403. Boutin, Bernard. Kennedy campaign worker (1960); Administrator, General Service Administration (1961-64). 1964. Portions closed. 56 pp.

404. Bowles, Chester. Platform chairman, Democratic National Committee (1960); Under Secretary of State (1961); President's Special Representative for Asian, African, and Latin American Affairs (1961-63); Ambassador to India (1963-69). 1965, 1970. 107 pp.

405. Boyle, Bernard J. Democratic National Committeeman from Nebraska. 1967. Permission required. 15 pp.

406. Bradley, Don L. California political figure. 1966. 27 pp.

407. Brandon, Henry. Journalist; chief American correspondent, Washington Bureau, *Sunday Times*, London (1939-). 1967. 22 pp.

408. _____. Interview conducted by David Nunnerly for his dissertation on Anglo-American relations during the Kennedy administration. 1970. 14 pp.

409. Brawley, Hiram Wilks. Deputy Postmaster General (1961-62); executive assistant to the chairman, Democratic National Committee (1962-66). 1964. 47 pp.

410. Brennan, James B. Wisconsin political figure. 1965. 21 pp.

411. Bridge, Dinah. Kennedy friend and associate, Great Britain. 1966. Portions closed. 12 pp.

412. Brightman, Samuel C. Deputy chairman, Democratic National Committee. 1964. 19 pp.

413. Broderick, Thomas. Massachusetts political figure. 1964. 72 pp.

414. Brown, Edmund G. Governor of California (1959-66). 1964. 19 pp.

415. Brown, Harold. Director, Defense Research Engineering, Department of Defense (1961-65). Closed. 282 pp.

416. Brown, Winthrop G. Ambassador to Laos (1960-62). 1968. 35 pp.

417. Bruce, Preston. White House doorman. 1964. 21 pp.

418. Bryant, Traphes L. White House electrician. 1964. 17 pp.

419. Bundy, McGeorge. Special Assistant to the President for National Security Affairs (1961-66). Interview conducted by David Nunnerly for his dissertation on Anglo-American relations during the Kennedy administration. 1970. 7 pp.

420. Burke, Arleigh. Admiral, Chief of Naval Operations, Joint Chiefs of Staff (1955-61). 1967. Permission required. 39 pp.

421. Burke, Grace. Secretary in the Kennedy Boston congressional office. 1964. 23 pp.

422. Burke, John T. Liaison at advertising agency used by JFK in the 1952 Senate campaign. 1964. 14 pp.

423. Burke, Kenneth. White House policeman. 1964. 8 pp.

424. Burkhardt, Robert J. New Jersey political figure; Assistant Postmaster General, Bureau of Facilities, Post Office Department (1961-62). 1964. 8 pp.

425. Burkley, George G. Physician to President Kennedy (1961-63). Burkley tells little about Kennedy's health problems. 1967. 24 pp.

426. Burnham, Elaine. Office worker in JFK's 1960 presidential campaign in Oregon. 1966. 6 pp.

427. Burns, James MacGregor. Political scientist, educator, Massachusetts political figure, author, *John F. Kennedy, a Political Profile* (1960). 1965. 54 pp.

428. Burrows, Charles (Robert). Ambassador to Honduras (1960-65). 1969. Portions closed. 54 pp.

429. Byrne, Garrett. Massachusetts political figure. 1967. 46 pp.

430. Cabot, John Moors. Ambassador to Brazil (1959-61); Ambassador to Poland (1962-65). 1977. 27 pp.

431. Calhoun, Stewart A. West Virginia political figure. 1965. 21 pp.

432. Campos, Roberto De Oliveira. Brazilian Ambassador to the United States (1961-63). 1964. 56 pp.

433. Caplin, Mortimer M. Commissioner of Internal Revenue Service (1961-64). Interview conducted for the Internal Revenue Service. 1991. 93 pp.

434. Carey, James B. President, International Union of Electrical, Radio, and Machine Workers (1949-65). 1964. 19 pp.

435. Carr, James K. Undersecretary of the Interior (1961-64). 1970, 1971. 35 pp.

436. Carver, John A. Assistant Secretary of the Interior for Public Lands Management (1961-64). 1968, 1969. Permission required. 484 pp.

437. Casey, Constance. President Kennedy's personal representative, Uganda independence ceremony (1962). 1966. 7 pp.

438. Casey, Joseph E. Massachusetts political figure. 1967. 25 pp.

439. Cass, Millard. Deputy Undersecretary of Labor (1955-71). 1970. 44 pp.

440. Cauley, John. Journalist, foreign affairs editor, Washington bureau, *Kansas City Star* (1957-64). 1966. 15 pp.

441. Cavanaugh, John M. Kennedy family friend, associate; Roman Catholic priest, University of Notre Dame (1946-69). 1966. 21 pp.

442. Celebrezze, Anthony J. Secretary of Health, Education and Welfare (1962-65). 1965. 26 pp.

443. Cerrell, Joseph R. Executive director, California Democratic party (1959). 1969. 37 pp.

444. Chafin, Raymond. West Virginia figure. 1964. 8 pp.

445. Chapin, Arthur A. Staff member, Democratic National Committee; Assistant to the Secretary, U.S. Employment Service, Department of Labor. 1967. 52 pp.

446. Chapman, Alfred F. West Virginia political figure. 1965. 29 pp.

447. Chayes, Abram. Staff director, Democratic Platform Committee (1960); legal adviser, Department of State (1961-64). 1964. Portions closed. 287 pp.

448. Chernenko, John G. West Virginia political figure. 1964. 15 pp.

449. Chiang, Ching-Kuo. Minister without Portfolio, Republic of China (1958-69). 1964. 3 pp.

450. Chiang, Kai-shek. President, Republic of China (1948-75). 1964. 5 pp.

451. Chilton, William. Publisher, *Charlestown Gazette*; West Virginia political figure. 1964. 13 pp.

452. Christie, Alexander. Labor leader. 1966. 30 pp.

453. Christie, Sidney L. West Virginia political figure. 1964. 26 pp.

454. Church, Frank. U.S. Senator from Idaho (1957-81). 1981. 19 pp.

455. Clague, Ewan. Commissioner, Bureau of Labor Statistics, Department of Labor (1946-65). 1966. 73 pp.

456. Clapp, Norman M. Wisconsin political figure; Administrator, Rural Electrification Administration (1961-69). 1964. 15 pp.

457. Clark, Joseph S. Senator from Pennsylvania (1957-69). 1965. 92 pp.

458. Clay, Lucius D. President Kennedy's personal representative in Berlin (1961-62). 1964. 24 pp.

459. _____. Interview conducted by David Nunnerly for his dissertation on Anglo-American relations during the Kennedy administration. 1970. 16 pp.

460. Cleveland, James Harlan. Assistant Secretary of State for International Organization Affairs (1961-65). 1978. 56 pp.

461. Cliff, Edward P. Chief, Forest Service, Department of Agriculture. 1964. 17 pp.

462. Cloherty, Peter. Massachusetts political figure; campaign worker, John F. Kennedy's first congressional campaign (1946); delegate, (1952, 1956), alternate delegate (1960), Democratic National Convention. 1967. 52 pp.

463. Cochrane, Willard. Director, Agricultural Economics, Department of Agriculture (1961-64). 1964. 30 pp.

464. Coffin, Frank M. Deputy Administrator, Agency for International Development (1961-64). 1964. 30 pp.

465. Coggs, Isaac. Wisconsin political figure. 1965. 14 pp.

466. Cogley, John. Journalist, adviser to the 1960 campaign staff. 1968. 55 pp.

467. Cohen, Wilbur. Assistant Secretary of Health, Education, and Welfare (1961-65). 1964, 1971. 80 pp.

468. Coit, Margaret. Author-in-residence, Fairleigh Dickinson University. 1966. Permission required. 40 pp.

469. Colbert, James G. Political editor, *Boston Post.* 1964. 27 pp.

470. Colbert, Mary S. Massachusetts political figure. 1964. 11 pp.

471. Cole, Charles W. Ambassador to Chile (1961-64). 1969. Portions closed. 77 pp.

472. Coleman, Barbara J. Journalist; White House press aide (1961-62). 1968, 1969. Portions closed. 65 pp.

473. Collins, Thomas Leroy. Governor of Florida (1955-60); president, National Association of Broadcasters (1961-64). 1965. 56 pp.

474. Connors, William F. Regional manager, Veterans Administration, Boston. 1964. 22 pp.

475. Cooke, Robert E. Chairman, Medical Advisory Board, Joseph P. Kennedy, Jr. Foundation; member, Science Advisory Council. 1968. Portions closed. 46 pp.

476. Cooper, Chester L. Liaison officer to National Security Council staff from Central Intelligence Agency; staff assistant to Ambassador Harriman at the Geneva conference on Laos (1961-62). 1966. 60 pp.

477. Cosgrave, Liam. Irish political figure. 1966. 5 pp.

478. Costin, Thomas P. Massachusetts political figure. 1976. 53 pp.

479. Council of Economic Advisers. Includes Hugh Gardner Ackley, Kermit Gordon, Walter W. Heller, Joseph A. Pechman, Paul A. Samuelson, James Tobin. 1964. 483 pp.

480. Couve de Murville, Jacques Maurice. French Minister of Foreign Affairs, (1958-68). 1964. 15 pp.

481. Crafts, Edward C. Director, Bureau of Outdoor Recreation, Department of the Interior (1962-69). 1969. 55 pp.

482. Crawford, William A. Minister to Rumania (1961-64). 1971. 37 pp.

483. Crimmins, John H. Deputy director and director, Office of Caribbean and Mexican Affairs, Department of State (1961-63). 1964. 12 pp.

484. Crockett, William. Assistant Secretary of State for Administration (1961-63), Deputy Undersecretary of State for Administration (1963-67). Interview conducted for the Foreign Affairs Oral History Program at Georgetown University. 1990. 162 pp.

485. Cronin, Peter. Reporter, United Press International. Interview about Robert Frost. 1973. 3 pp.

486. Cuban Prisoners Exchange Panel. Participants: John Jones; Louis Oberdorfer; Mitchell Rogovin. 1964. 23 pp.

487. Cull, Richard, et al. Interview with Immigration and Naturalization Service officials about the Cuban prisoners exchange. 1970. 39 pp.

488. Culley, Edward A. West Virginia figure. 1965. 13 pp.

489. Curley, Robert. Circuit court judge, Wisconsin. Permission required. 14 pp.

490. Curname, Joseph. Massachusetts political figure; journalist. 1966. 110 pp.

491. Cushing, Richard Cardinal. Roman Catholic archbishop of Boston and Kennedy family friend (1944-70). 1966. 22 pp.

492. Cutler, Lloyd N. Adviser on Cuban prisoner exchange. 1964. 23 pp.

493. Dalton, John M. Massachusetts political figure. 1964. 32 pp.

494. Daly, Charles U. Staff Assistant to the President for Congressional Liaison (1962-64). 1966. Portions closed. 76 pp.

495. Daniels, Wilbur F. Missouri political figure. 1967. 10 pp.

496. Dantas, Francisco Clementino San Tiago. Brazilian Minister of Foreign Affairs, Minister of Finance. 1964. 7 pp.

497. Darlington, Charles F. Ambassador to Gabon (1961-65). 1971. Portions closed. 16 pp.

498. Davens, Edward. Member, President's Panel on Mental Retardation (1962-63). 1968. 38 pp.

499. Davis, Mary W. Secretary to Representative John F. Kennedy (1947-52). 1976. Portions closed. 41 pp.

500. Dazzi, Andrew, and Harris, John. Journalists, *Boston Globe.* 1964. 26 pp.

501. De Blieux, Joseph Davis. Louisiana political figure. 1967. 22 pp.

502. Debus, Kurt H. Director, Launch Operations Center (1960-63), director, John F. Kennedy Space Center (1963-74), National Aeronautics and Space Administration. 1964. 11 pp.

503. Decker, George H. General, Chief of Staff, U.S. Army (1960-62). 1968. 45 pp.

504. Degugliemo, Joseph. Massachusetts political figure; JFK friend. 1964. 25 pp.

505. Demarco, William. Massachusetts political figure. 1964. 14 pp.

506. Dempsey, John F. Lieutenant, Massachusetts State Police. 1964. 16 pp.

507. Depaulo, J. Raymond. West Virginia political figure. 1965. 23 pp.

508. Desautels, Claude. Special Assistant to the President (1961-66). 1964, 1977. 34 pp.

509. Des Marais, Philip H. Worker, 1960 presidential campaign, Louisiana; Special Assistant to the Assistant Secretary for Legislation, Department of Health, Education, and Welfare. 1966, 1967. 114 pp.

510. De Valera, Eamon. President of Ireland (1959-73). 1966. 8 pp.

511. Dillon, C. Douglas. Secretary of the Treasury (1961-65). 1964. Permission required. Portions closed. 214 pp.

512. Dillon, C. Douglas, and Robert V. Roosa. Roosa was Undersecretary of the Treasury for Monetary Affairs. 1965. Permission required. 15 pp.

513. Dilworth, Richardson. Mayor of Philadelphia (1955-62); co-chairman, Pennsylvania Citizens for Kennedy (1960). 1964. 27 pp.

514. DiSalle, Michael V. Governor of Ohio (1959-63). 1964. 49 pp.

515. Dixon, Margaret. Journalist, managing editor, *Baton Rouge Morning Advocate.* 1967. 14 pp.

516. Dixon, Paul Randall. Associate of Senator Estes Kefauver (1957-61); chairman, Federal Trade Commission (1961-69). 1968. 50 pp.

517. Dobie, Frank E. Massachusetts political figure. 1964. 12 pp.

518. Docking, Robert B. Kansas political figure; chairman, Small Business Advisory Board. 1967. 13 pp.

519. Dodson, James Edward. Administrative Assistant to the Secretary of Labor (1961-62). 1970. 22 pp.

520. Dolan, Joseph F. Assistant Deputy Attorney General (1961-65). 1964. 120 pp.

521. _____. Interview concerning Cuban prisoners exchange. 1964. 16 pp.

522. Donahue, Maurice A. Massachusetts political figure. 1976. 19 pp.

523. Donelan, Paul G. Massachusetts political figure; aide in John F. Kennedy's 1952 Senate campaign. 1964. 9 pp.

524. Dooley, Francis X. Advanced man in Johnson's vice presidential campaign (1960); staff member, Office of Civil and Defense Mobilization and Office of Emergency Planning; director of Congressional, Liaison, Area Development Administration. 1976. 87 pp.

525. Douglas, Paul H. Senator from Illinois (1950-67). 1964. 33 pp.

526. Douglas, William O. Associate Justice, U.S. Supreme Court (1939-75). 1967. 39 pp.

527. Douglas-Home, Sir Alec. British Secretary for Foreign Affairs (1960-63), Prime Minister (1963-64). 1965. 7 pp.

528. _____. Interview conducted by David Nunnerly for his dissertation on Anglo-American relations during the Kennedy administration. 1970. Closed. 11 pp.

529. Douglas-Home, William. Kennedy associate, Great Britain. 1966. 22 pp.

530. Doyle, James E. Wisconsin political figure. 1966. 21 pp.

531. Doyle, Patrick J. Deputy Assistant to the President for Mental Retardation. 1968. 39 pp.

532. Drachnik, Joseph B. Chief, Navy Section, Military Assistance Advisory Group, Vietnam (1961-64). 1970. 19 pp.

533. Dragon, Ed. Advance man for 1960 campaign in North Carolina and Illinois; assistant general counsel, Agency for International Development. 1976. 31 pp.

534. Droney, John J. Massachusetts political figure. 1964. 29 pp.

535. Dryden, Hugh L. Deputy administrator, National Aeronautics and Space Administration (1958-65). 1964. 31 pp.

536. Dugal, Peter. Campaign worker, 1960 presidential campaign, Wisconsin (1960). 1966. 28 pp.

537. Duke, Angier Biddle. Chief of Protocol, White House and State Department (1961-65). 1964. 68 pp.

538. Dulles, Allen. Director, Central Intelligence Agency (1953-61). 1964. 34 pp.

539. Dungan, Ralph A. Staff assistant to Senator Kennedy (1956-60); Special Assistant to the President (1961-63). 1967. Permission required. 125 pp.

540. Dutton, Frederick G. Special Assistant to the President (1961); Assistant Secretary of State for Congressional Relations (1961-64). 1965. 67 pp.

541. Earl, Charles H. Member, Post Office Advisory Board. 1964. 10 pp.

542. Ellender, Allen. Democratic Senator from Louisiana (1937-72). 1967. 50 pp.

543. Ellis, Claude. West Virginia political figure. 1964. 13 pp.

544. Ellis, Clyde T. General Manager, National Rural Electric Cooperative Association (1943-67). 1965. 79 pp.

545. Enthoven, Alain. Deputy Comptroller, Assistant Secretary, Department of Defense (1961-71). 1971. 30 pp.

546. Estes, Thomas S. Ambassador to the Republic of Upper Volta (1961-66). 1971. 23 pp.

547. Evans, Rowland. Journalist, *New York Herald Tribune* (1955-63); syndicated columnist (1963-). 1966. 54 pp.

548. Everton, John S. Ambassador to Burma (1961-63). 1969. 36 pp.

549. Farley, Philip J. Special Assistant to the Secretary of State for Atomic Energy and Outer Space (1961-62); chief, political section, U.S. Mission to the North Atlantic Treaty Organization (1962). 1966. 18 pp.

550. Farmer, James. National director, Congress of Racial Equality (1961-66). 1967. 29 pp.

551. Farrell, James. Sports equipment man, Harvard University (1930s-40s). 1964. 8 pp.

552. Faubus, Orval. Governor of Arkansas (1955-67). 1967. Closed. 36 pp.

553. Fay, Paul B., Jr. Friend of JFK. Undersecretary of the Navy (1961-63). 1971. 350 pp.

554. Feild, John G. Worker, 1960 presidential campaign; executive director, President's Commission on Equal Employment Opportunity (1961-63). 1967. 52 pp.

555. Feldman, Myer. Deputy Special Counsel to the President (1961-64). 1966, 1967, 1968. 693 pp.

556. Fenn, Dan H. Massachusetts political figure. 1968. 25 pp.

557. Fike, Stanley R. Executive director, Symington for President campaign (1960). 1967. 91 pp.

558. Fine, Phil. Deputy administrator, Small Business Administration (1961-62). 1964. 14 pp.

559. Finletter, Thomas K. Ambassador to the North Atlantic Treaty Organization (1961-65). 1965. 13 pp.

560. Fischer, Frank H. West Virginia political figure. 1965. 16 pp.

561. Fisher, Adrian S. Deputy director, Arms Control and Disarmament Agency (1961-69). 1964. 28 pp.

562. Fitzgerald, Ray V. South Dakota political figure; deputy administrator, Agricultural Stabilization and Conservation Service, Department of Agriculture. 1964. 15 pp.

563. Fitzpatrick, Howard. Middlesex, Ma. county sheriff (1949-69). 1967. 19 pp.

564. Flood, Richard. Friend and classmate of Joseph P. Kennedy, Jr. at Harvard (1935-38); worker, John F. Kennedy's congressional campaign (1946) and Senate campaign (1952). 1964. 13 pp.

565. Fogarty, John E. Representative from Rhode Island (1945-67). 1965. 12 pp.

566. Folliard, Edward T. Journalist, *Washington Post*. 1967. 34 pp.

567. Forbes, Fred. 1960 campaign worker. 1966. Portions closed. 70 pp.

568. Forrestal, Michael V. Assistant to the President for Far Eastern Affairs (1962-64); senior staff member, National Security Council (1962-67). 1964. Permission required. 171 pp.

569. Foster, William C. Director, Arms Control and Disarmament Agency (1961-69). 1964. Portions closed. 40 pp.

570. Fox, David. Chairman, 1960 presidential campaign, Cabel County, WV. 1964. 10 pp.

571. Fraleigh, William N. Counselor on political affairs, U.S. Embassay, Madrid (1957-62) and Rome (1962-67). 1966. 19 pp.

572. Frankfurter, Felix. Associate Justice, United States Supreme Court (1939-62). 1964. 75 pp.

573. Frazer, Hugh. Kennedy family friend and associate; British Parliamentary Undersecretary of State for the Colonies (1960-62); Secretary of State for Air (1962-64). 1966. 16 pp.

574. _____. Interview conducted by David Nunnerly for his dissertation on Anglo-American relations during the Kennedy administration. 1970. 18 pp.

575. Freed, Hirsh. Boston political figure. 1964. 31 pp.

576. Freeman, Fulton. Ambassador to Colombia (1961-64), ambassador to Mexico (1964-69). 1969. 51 pp.

577. Freeman, Orville L. Secretary of Agriculture (1961-69). 1964. 45 pp.

578. Frost, Laurence H. Rear admiral, U. S. Navy; director, National Security Agency (1960-62). 1970. Portions closed. 11 pp.

579. Fuchs, Lawrence H. Peace Corps director, Philippines (1961-63). 1966. 57 pp.

580. Fulbright, J. William. Democratic Senator from Arkansas; chairman, Senate Foreign Relations Committee (1959-75). 1964. 163 pp.

581. _____. Interview conducted by David Nunnerly for his dissertation on Anglo-American relations during the Kennedy administration. 1970. 6 pp.

582. Furcolo, Foster. Democratic Governor of Massachusetts (1957-61). 1964. 18 pp.

583. Gabriel, Victor J. West Virginia political figure. 1964. Permission required. 35 pp.

584. Gallagher, Edward M. Kennedy family friend. 1965. 31 pp.

585. Gallucio, Anthony. Massachusetts political figure. 1964. 15 pp.

586. Galvin, John Thomas. Advertising and publicity volunteer for John Kennedy, (1946-58). 1964. 70 pp.

587. Gamarekian, Barbara. Staff assistant, John F. Kennedy's 1960 presidential campaign; staff assistant, transition talent recruitment staff; secretary to the Assistant Press Secretary, White House Press Office (1961-63). 1964. Portions closed. 103 pp.

588. Garabedian, Charles B. Massachusetts political figure. 1964. 19 pp.

589. Garrigues, Antonio. Spanish ambassador to the United States (1962-64). 1966. 16 pp.

590. Gatov, Elizabeth R. Democratic national committeewomen from California (1956-60, 1963-65); Treasurer of the United States (1961-62). 1969. Portions closed. 54 pp.

591. _____. Interview conducted by the Women in Politics Oral History Project, University of California, Berkeley. 1975, 1976. 404 pp.

592. Gaud, William S. Assistant administrator, Bureau for the Near East and South Asia, Agency for International Development (1961-64). 1966. 57 pp.

593. Geoghegan, William A. Worker, John F. Kennedy's presidential campaign, Ohio (1960); Assistant Deputy Attorney General, legislative program, Department of Justice (1961-65). 1966. 99 pp.

594. Gianfala, Evelyn N. Louisiana political figure. 1967. 4 pp.

595. Gilpatric, Roswell L. Deputy Secretary of Defense (1961-64). 1970. Portions closed. 118 pp.

596. Gilruth, Robert R. Director, Manned Spaceflight Center, National Aeronautics and Space Administration (1961-72). 1964. 11 pp.

597. Glenn, John H. Project Mercury astronaut (1959-64). 1964. 32 pp.

598. Godber, Joseph B. British Minister of State for Disarmament, Foreign Office, (1961-63). Interview conducted by David Nunnerly for his dissertation on Anglo-American relations during the Kennedy administration. 1970. 5 pp.

599. Godby, J. Thomas. West Virginia political figure. 1964. 11 pp.

600. Goldfarb, Ronald. Lawyer, Department of Justice, Criminal Division, Organized Crime Section. 1981. 19 pp.

601. Goldwater, Barry M. Republican senator from Arizona (1953-83). 1965. Closed. 27 pp.

602. Goodwin, Robert C. Administrator, Bureau of Employment Security, Department of Labor. 1967. 30 pp.

603. Gordon, Lincoln. Ambassador to Brazil (1961-66). 1964. Portions closed. 144 pp.

604. _____. Interview conducted by Craig Van Grasstek regarding JFK's Task Force on Immediate Latin American Problems. 1980. 42 pp.

605. Gore, Albert. Democratic senator from Tennessee (1953-71). 1964. 13 pp.

606. Gore-Booth, Lord Paul. British High Commissioner, India (1960-65); Permament Undersecretary, Foreign Office, Great Britain (1965-69). Interview conducted by David Nunnerly for his dissertation on Anglo-American relations during the Kennedy administration. 1970. 4 pp.

607. Grace de Monaco. Princess of Monaco. 1965. 10 pp.

608. Gravel, Camille F. Louisiana political figure; member of Democratic National Committee (1954-60). 1967. 77 pp.

609. Green, Edith. Representative from Oregon (1956-74). 14 pp.

610. Grennan, Josephine. Irish cousin of Kennedy. 1966. 9 pp.

611. Gretchen, Michael. West Virginia labor leader. 1965. 27 pp.

612. Grewe, Wilhelm. West German ambassador to the United States (1957-62); West German ambassador to the North Atlantic Treaty Organization (1962-71). 1966. 20 pp.

613. Gudeman, Edward. Undersecretary of Commerce (1961-63). 1964. 27 pp.

614. Gullion, Edmund A. Ambassador to the Republic of the Congo (1961-64). 1964, 1977. Permission required. 17 pp.

615. Guthman, Edwin O. Editor, *Seattle Times* (1947-61); director of Public

Information, Department of Justice (1961-64); press assistant to Robert F. Kennedy (1964-65). 1968. 76 pp.

616. Gwirtzman, Milton S. Presidential adviser. 1966. 47 pp.

617. Hackett, David L. Executive director, President's Committee on Juvenile Delinquency and Youth Crime (1961-62); member, John F. Kennedy's presidential campaign staff (1960). 1970. 116 pp.

618. Hailsham, Lord (Quintin Hogg). Leader of the British House of Lords (1960-63); Minister of Science and Technology (1959-64). 1966. Permission required. 10 pp.

619. Halaby, Najeeb. Administrator, Federal Aviation Agency (1961-65). 1964. 108 pp.

620. Hale, Walter. Wisconsin political figure; chairman, Democratic party, Milwaukee County (1960). 1965. 17 pp.

621. Halle, Kay. Author and Kennedy family friend. 1967. 25 pp.

622. Halleck, Charles. Representative from Indiana (1935-69); House minority leader (1959-65). 1965. 39 pp.

623. Hamilton, Fowler. Administrator, Agency for International Development (1961-62). 1964. 46 pp.

624. Hanford, A. Chester. Professor of Government, Harvard University (1923-75). 1966. 6 pp.

625. Hare, Raymond A. Ambassador to Turkey (1961-65). 1969. 39 pp.

626. Harlech, Lord (William David Ormsby-Gore). British Minister of State for Foreign Affairs (1957-61); ambassador to the United States (1961-65). 1964. Closed. 88 pp.

627. Harllee, John. Kennedy associate; Chairman, Federal Maritime Commission (1963-69). 1964. 17 pp.

628. Harriman, Averell. Ambassador at Large (1961); Secretary of State for Far Eastern Affairs (1961-63); Undersecretary of State for Political Affairs (1963-65), 1964, 1965. 129 pp.

629. Harris, Oren. Representative from Arkansas (1941-66). 1965. 66 pp.

630. Harris, Seymour E. Economic adviser to Senator John Kennedy; senior consultant to the Secretary of the Treasury (1961-68). 1964. 84 pp.

631. Harrison, Gilbert A. Editor and publisher, *New Republic* (1954-74). 1967. 18 pp.

632. Hart, Parker T. Minister to Yemen (1961-63); ambassador to Kuwait (1962-63); ambassador to Saudi Arabia (1961-65). 1969, 1970. 63 pp.

633. Hart, Walter. West Virginia political figure. 1964. 22 pp.

634. Hartigan, William J. Massachusetts political figure; White House staff assistant (1961-62); Assistant Postmaster General (1963-67). 1964. 29 pp.

635. Hartsfield, William. Mayor of Atlanta (1937-61). 1966. 10 pp.

636. Hatcher, Andrew. Assistant press secretary to President Kennedy (1961-63). 1972. 15 pp.

637. Haught, James F. West Virginia political figure. 1964. 18 pp.

638. Hays, Brooks. Assistant Secretary of State for Congressional Relations (1961); Special Assistant to the President (1961-63). 1964. 59 pp.

639. Healey, Joseph P. Campaign worker on John Kennedy's House and Senate campaigns; Massachusetts political figure. 1964. 73 pp.

640. Hearst, Anne. West Virginia political figure. 1964. 17 pp.

641. Hearst, William Randolph. Owner, editor, Hearst Newspapers. 1971. 9 pp.

642. Heath, Kathryn. Assistant for Special Studies, U.S. Office of Education. 1971. 137 pp.

643. Heckscher, August. Special Consultant to the President on the Arts (1962-63). 1965. 79 pp.

644. Hedrich, Robert E. West Virginia political figure; manager, 1960 presidential campaign, Randolph County, WV. 1964. Portions closed. 18 pp.

645. Heinz, Luther C. Admiral, U. S. Navy; Regional Director for the Far East, Office of International Security Affairs, Department of Defense (1960-63). 1970. 55 pp.

646. Henderson, Douglas. Counsel, U.S. Embassy, Peru (1961-63); ambassador to Bolivia (1963-64). 1978. Portions closed. 145 pp.

647. Hennessey, Louella. Kennedy family nurse (1935-63). 1964. 17 pp.

648. Henning, John F. Undersecretary, Department of Labor (1962-67). 1970. Portions closed. 18 pp.

649. Henry, Aaron E. Member, Executive Committee, Democratic party of Mississippi; president, Mississippi State Conference of the NAACP. 1969. 123 pp.

650. Henry, E. William. Staff member, Nationalities Division, Democratic National Committee; commissioner (1962-63), chairman (1963-66), Federal Communications Commission. 1966. 51 pp.

651. Heren, Louis. American editor, *Times* of London. Interview conducted by David Nunnerly for his dissertation on Anglo-American relations during the Kennedy administration. 1970. 4 pp.

652. Herling, John. Publisher, *John Herling's Labor Letter* (1947-). 1966. 48 pp.

653. Hesburgh, Theodore. President, University of Notre Dame (1952-72). 1966. 28 pp.

654. Hickenlooper, Bourke B. Senator from Iowa (1945-69). 1964. 70 pp.

655. Highley, David P. JFK's barber. 1964. 2 pp.

656. Hillenbrand, Martin. Director, Office of German Affairs, Department of State (1958-62); director, Berlin Task Force (1962-63). 1964. 44 pp.

657. Hilsman, Roger. Director, Bureau of Intelligence and Research, Department of State (1961-63); Assistant Undersecretary of State for Far Eastern Affairs (1963-64). 1970. 36 pp.

658. _____. Interview conducted by David Nunnerly for his dissertation on Anglo-American relations during the Kennedy administration. 1970. 13 pp.

659. Hirsh, Jacqueline. French language instructor to JFK's children. 1966. 19 pp.

660. Hobbs, Nicholas. Member, President's Panel on Mental Retardation (1961-62); director of Selection and Research, Peace Corps (1961-62). 1968. 32 pp.

661. Hodges, Luther. Democratic Governor of North Carolina (1954-61), Secretary of Commerce (1961-64). 1964. Portions closed. 117 pp.

662. Hoff, William Bruce. West Virginia political figure. 1964. 33 pp.

663. Hoffman, Harry G. Journalist, editor, *Charleston Gazette*. 1964. 20 pp.

664. Holifield, Chet. Representative from California (1943-75). Interview conducted by the Claremont Graduate School). 1975. 418 pp.

665. Holness, Wilma. White House household staff. 1967. 7 pp.

666. Holt, Pat. Consultant to the Chief of Staff (1950-73), Chief of Staff (1974-77), Senate Foreign Relations Committee. Interview conducted by the U.S. Senate Historical Office. 1980. 311 pp.

667. Holtz, Jackson J. Vice chairman, JFK's Senate campaign (1952). 1964. 13 pp.

668. Hooker, John Jay. Member, Kennedy's presidential campaign staff (1960). 1965. Portions closed. 66 pp.

669. Hooton, Claude E. Staffer, 1960 presidential campaign staff. 1966. Permission required. 35 pp.

670. Hopkins, William J. Executive clerk, White House Office (1943-66). 1964, 1978. 31 pp, 24 pp.

671. Horne, John E. Administrative assistant to Democratic Senator John Sparkman of Alabama (1947-51, 1953-61); Kennedy campaign worker (1960); administrator, Small Business Administration (1961-63). 1967. 107 pp.

672. Horsey, Outerbridge. Minister and Deputy Chief of Mission, U.S. Embassy, Rome (1959-62); ambassador to Czechoslovakia (1963-66). 1971. 17 pp.

673. Horsky, Charles A. Adviser to the president for national capital affairs (1961-65). 1964. 84 pp.

674. Horton, Ralph. Classmate of JFK at Choate School and Princeton University; member of 1960 presidential campaign staff; special assistant, equal opportunity program, Department of the Army (1962-69). 1964. 42 pp.

675. Horwitz, Solis. Staffer, Kennedy's 1960 presidential campaign; director, Office of Organizational and Management Planning, Department of Defense (1961-64). 1966. Portions closed. 31 pp.

676. Houvouras, Andrew J. West Virginia political figure. 1964. 25 pp.

677. Huber, Oscar L. Roman Catholic priest who administered last rites to President Kennedy. 1964. 10 pp.

678. Hughes, Philip S. Assistant Director for Legislative Reference, Bureau of the Budget (1959-67). 1968. 49 pp.

679. Hughes, Sarah T. Judge, Texas district court. Interview conducted by the University of North Texas Oral History Collection. 1969. 30 pp.

680. Hughes-Hallett, John. British Parliamentary Secretary to the Ministry of Transport for Shipping and Shipbuilding (1961-64). Interview conducted by David Nunnerly for his dissertation on Anglo-American relations during the Kennedy administration. 1969. 22 pp.

681. Humphrey, Hubert H. Senator from Minnesota (1949-64), delegate to the United Nations (1956-58); presidential candidate (1960). 1964. 150 pp.

682. Hundley, William G. Chief, Organized Crime and Racketeering Section, Department of Justice. 1970. Permission required. 64 pp.

683. Hurley, Francis T. Roman Catholic monsignor; assistant secretary, National Catholic Welfare Conference (1958-68). 1967. 21 pp.

684. Hurwitch, Robert A. Special Assistant for Cuban Affairs, Department of State (1962-63). 1964, 1967. 221 pp.

685. Hutchinson, Edmond C. Assistant Administrator for Africa and Europe, Agency for International Development (1961-66). 1966. 30 pp.

686. Jackson, Barbara Ward. Economist, author. 1964. 32 pp.

687. Jacobs, William L. West Virginia political figure; Hubert Humphrey campaign worker (1960). 1964. 39 pp.

688. Jacobson, Benjamin A. JFK associate. 1964. 21 pp.

689. Jeffrey, Mildred. Member platform committee, Democratic party (1955-60); delegate, Democratic National Convention (1956, 1960); worker, 1960 presidential campaign. 1970. 54 pp.

690. Jensen, Hans O. Nebraska political figure; area director, Department of Agriculture. 1967. 28 pp.

691. Jernegan, John. Ambassador to Iraq (1958-62). 1969. 34 pp.

692. Johnson, Douglas. Director, Plans and Policy Office, Joint Chiefs of Staff (1960-64). 1970. 22 pp.

693. Johnson, U. Alexis. Deputy Undersecretary of State for Political Affairs (1961-64). 1964. 53 pp.

694. Jones, Howard P. Ambassador to Indonesia (1958-65). 1969. 68 pp.

695. Jones, Robert E. Representative from Alabama (1947-77). 1968. Portions closed. 22 pp.

696. Jones, Roger W. Deputy Undersecretary for Administration, Department of State (1961-62); senior consultant and Special Assistant to the Director, Bureau of the Budget (1962-75). 1967. 103 pp.

697. Josephson, William. General counsel, Peace Corps (1963-66). 1968, 1969. Permission required. 69 pp.

698. Kaiser, Philip M. Ambassador to the Republic of Senegal (1961-64); ambassador to the Islamic Republic of Mauritania (1961-64). 1966. 41 pp.

699. Kamlowsky, John H. West Virginia political figure. 1965. 21 pp.

700. Kapenstein, Ira. Journalist, *Milwaukee Journal* (1956-63). 1965. 29 pp.

701. Kappel, Frederick R. Chairman, American Telephone and Telegraph Co. (1961-67); chairman, Business Council (1963-64). 1965. 28 pp.

702. Karamanlis, Konstantine G. Prime Minister of Greece (1961-63). 1965. 4 pp.

703. Karitas, Joseph J. White House painter. 1964. 25 pp.

704. Kastenmeier, Robert W. Representative from Wisconsin (1959-81). 1965. 18 pp.

705. Katzenbach, Nicholas De B. Assistant Attorney General (1961-62); Deputy Attorney General (1962-64); Attorney General of the United States (1964-66). 1964. 169 pp.

706. _____. Interview conducted for the Robert F. Kennedy Oral History Project. 1969. 79 pp.

707. Kaysen, Carl. Deputy Special Assistant to the President for National Security Affairs (1961-63). 1966. 194 pp.

708. Keel, William A. Research director, Democratic National Committee (1963-64). 1970. Closed. 55 pp.

709. Keenan, Joseph D. Labor adviser to JFK (1960); member, President's Advisory Committee on Labor-Management Policy. 1968. 28 pp.

710. Kellam, Sydney S. Virginia political figure. 1968. 10 pp.

711. Kelly, John M. Assistant Secretary for Mineral Resources, Department of the

Interior (1961-65). 1969, 1970. 56 pp.

712. Kelly, Mary. Oregon political figure. 1966. 27 pp.

713. Kelly, William F. Massachusetts political figure. 1964. 21 pp.

714. Kelso, John H. Journalist, *Boston Post*. 1967. 44 pp.

715. Kennan, George F. Ambassador to Yugoslavia (1961-63). 1965. Portions closed. 141 pp.

716. Kennedy, Robert F. Brother of President Kennedy; Attorney General of the United States (1961-64). 1964, 1965, 1967. Portions closed. 700 pp.

717. Kennedy, Rose Fitzgerald. Wife of Joseph P. Kennedy, mother of President Kennedy. Interview conducted by the Herbert Hoover Library Foundation. 1968. 22 pp.

718. Kennedy's telephone call to King. Interviews concerning John Kennedy's telephone call to Martin Luther King, Jr., during the 1960 presidential campaign. Interviews with Louis Martin, Parren Mitchell, Sam Proctor, Sargent Shriver, Franklin Mitchell, and Harris Wofford. 1988. 110 pp.

719. Kent, Roger. California political figure. 1970. Portions closed. 58 pp.

720. Keppel, Francis. Commissioner of Education, Office of Education, Department of Health, Education, and Welfare (1962-65). 1964. 21 pp.

721. Kety, Seymour S. Member, President's Panel on Mental Retardation (1962-63). 1968. Permission required. 64 pp.

722. Khoman, Thanat. Thai Minister of Foreign Affairs (1959-71). 1964. 8 pp.

723. Khrushchev, Nikita S. Chairman, Council of Ministers, Union of Soviet Socialist Republics (1958-64). 1964. 5 pp.

724. Kiernan, Thomas J. Irish Ambassador to the United States (1961-64). 1966. Portions closed. 26 pp.

725. Kilpatrick, Carroll. Journalist, *Washington Post*. 1966. 19 pp.

726. King, Martin Luther, Jr. Civil rights leader; president, Southern Christian Leadership Conference (1957-68). 1964. 26 pp.

727. Kirkpatrick, Lyman B. Inspector General, Central Intelligence Agency (1953-61). 1967. Permission required. 29 pp.

728. Kirwan, Michael J. Representative from Ohio (1937-70). 1964. 18 pp.

729. Klotz, Herbert W. worker, 1960 presidential campaign; Assistant Secretary of Commerce for Administration (1962-65). 1964. 30 pp.

730. Klutznick, Philip M. U.S. Representative to the United Nations Economic and Social Council (1961-63). 1970. 53 pp.

731. Knebel, Fletcher. Journalist, Cowles Publications, *Look* (1950-64). Portions closed. 1977.

732. Knight, William E. Foreign Service officer, Italian-Austrian Affairs (1961); Deputy Director, Western European Affairs (1961-62), Department of State. 1978. Portions closed. 67 pp.

733. Knox, William E. President, Westinghouse Electric International (1946-63), who met with Khrushchev in Moscow during the Cuban missile crisis, October 1962. 1977. 34 pp.

734. Kohler, Foy D. Assistant Secretary of State for European Affairs (1959-62); ambassador to the USSR (1962-66). 1964. 10 pp.

735. Komer, Robert W. Senior staff member, National Security Council (1961-65). 1964, 1969, 1970. Permission required. 214 pp.

736. Kraft, Joseph. Journalist, syndicated columnist (1963-86). 1967. 31 pp.

737. Krock, Arthur. Journalist, *New York Times* (1927-67); Kennedy family associate. 1964. 27 pp.

738. Krulak, Victor. Lt. General, United States Marine Corps; specialist on counterinsurgency, Office of the Joint Chiefs of Staff (1962-64). 1970. Permission required. 22 pp.

739. Landrum, Phillip. Representative from Georgia (1953-77). 1965. 14 pp.

740. Larrabee, Donald. Journalist, Griffin-Larrabee News Bureau. 1966. 44 pp.

741. Laski, Fridda. Wife of Harold Laski of the London School of Economics. 1966. 4 pp.

742. Lawford, Peter. Actor, brother-in-law of JFK. 1968. 36 pp.

743. Lawrence, David. Democratic Governor of Pennsylvania (1959-63). 1966. 43 pp.

744. Lawrence, William H. Journalist, *New York Times* (1943-61); news commentator, American Broadcasting Company (1961-68). 1966. 28 pp.

745. Lawson, Belford V. District of Columbia political figure; presidential adviser on civil rights. 1966. 23 pp.

746. Lawson, Marjorie McKenzie. Civil rights adviser, 1960 presidential campaign. 1965. 74 pp.

747. Leahy, Joseph F. Massachusetts political figure. 1964. 19 pp.

748. Lee, Robert L. Massachusetts political figure. 1964. 16 pp.

749. Lemass, Sean. Irish Prime Minister (1959-66). No date. 23 pp.

750. Lemnitzer, Lyman L. General, U.S. Army; Supreme Allied Commander, Europe (1963-69). Interview conducted by David Nunnerly for his dissertation on Anglo-American relations. 1970. 21 pp.

751. Lempart, Helen. Secretary, Senator John Kennedy's Washington office and White House. 1966. Portions closed. 65 pp.

752. Lennartson, Roy. Associate administrator, Agricultural Marketing Service (1954-64). 1964. 9 pp.

753. Lesser, Arthur. Head, Children's Bureau, Department of Health, Education and Welfare. 1976. 42 pp.

754. Lester, Richard A. Economic adviser, 1960 presidential campaign; alternate delegate from New Jersey, Democratic National Convention (1960); vice chairman, President's Commission on the Status of Women (1961-63). 1970, 1974. 37 pp.

755. Lewin, Charles J. Editor, general manager, *New Bedford Standard Times*; president *Cape Cod Standard Times*. 1964. 38 pp.

756. Lewis, Anthony L. Journalist, *New York Times*, Washington bureau (1955-64), London bureau (1965-72). Interview conducted for the Robert F. Kennedy Oral History Project. 1970. Portions closed. 20 pp.

757. Lewis, Robert. Director, national headquarters, Farmers for Kennedy-Johnson Committee (1960); deputy administrator for Commodity Operations, Agricultural Stabilization and Conservation Service (1961-64). 1967. 30 pp.

758. Lewis, Roger F. Confidential assistant to the Secretary, Department of Labor (1960-67). 1970. 95 pp.

759. Lewis, Samuel B. Vice president, general manager, Carlyle Hotel, New York. 1965. 15 pp.

760. Lincoln, G. Gould. Journalist, editor, *Washington Star* (1909-74). 1966. 25 pp.

761. Lippmann, Walter. Journalist, *New York Herald Tribune, Newsweek*. 1964. Portions closed. 18 pp.

762. Lisagor, Peter. Journalist, chief, Washington bureau, *Chicago Daily News* (1959-76). 1966. 85 pp.

763. Lodge, Henry Cabot. Republican senator from Massachusetts (1947-53); ambassador to South Vietnam (1963-64, 1965-67). 1965. Portions closed. 36 pp.

764. Loeb, James. Ambassador to Peru (1961-62); ambassador to Guinea (1963-65). 1967, 1968. 74 pp.

765. Loevinger, Lee. Assistant Attorney General, Antitrust Division, Department of Justice (1961-63); commissioner, Federal Communications Commission (1963-68). 1966. 45 pp.

766. Lonesome, William L. West Virginia political figure. 1964. Permission required. 19 pp.

767. Loucheim, Kathleen. Director, women's activities, Democratic National Committee (1953-60); Deputy Assistant Secretary of State for Public Affairs (1966-69). 1968. 76 pp.

768. Love, Charles M. West Virginia political figure. 1964. 20 pp.

769. Loveless, Herschel. Democratic Governor of Iowa (1957-60); national chairman, Farmers for Kennedy-Johnson Committee (1960); member, Renegotiation Board (1961-69). 1967. 46 pp.

770. Lovett, Robert A. Member, General Advisory Committee, Arms Control and Disarmament Agency. 1964. 59 pp.

771. Low, George M. Deputy Director for Programs, Office of Manned Space Flight, National Aeronautics and Space Administration (1963-64). 1964. 32 pp.

772. Luce, Henry R. Founder and publisher, Time, Inc.; editor-in-chief, *Time* (1923-64). 1965. 42 pp.

773. Lucey, Patrick J. Chairman, Democratic party of Wisconsin (1957-63). 1964. 50 pp.

774. Luns, Joseph M. A. H. Dutch Foreign Minister (1956-71). 1965. 49 pp.

775. Lytton, Bart. Finance chairman, California Deomocratic State Committee (1958-60). 1966. 49 pp.

776. McCarthy, Eugene. Representative (1949-58); senator from Minnesota (1958-70). 1964. Closed. 31 pp.

777. McClure, Stewart E. Chief clerk, Committee on Labor, Education, and Public Welfare, U. S. Senate (1955-69, 1971-73). Interview conducted by the U. S. Senate Historical Office. 1982, 1983. 292 pp.

778. McCormack, Edward J. Massachusetts political figure; candidate for the U.S. Senate (1962). 1967. 38 pp.

779. McCormack, Francis X. Wisconsin political figure. 1965. 13 pp.

780. McCormack John W. Representative from Massachusetts (1928-71); Speaker of the House of Representatives (1962-71). 1977. 41 pp.

781. McCulloch, Frank W. Chairman, National Labor Relations Board (1961-70). 1967. 40 pp.

782. McDermott, Edward. Director, Office of Emergency Planning (1962-65); member, National Security Council (1962-65). 1967. 40 pp.

783. McDermott, Geoffrey. British diplomat in Berlin (1961-62). Interview conducted by David Nunnerly for his dissertation on Anglo-American Relations during the Kennedy administration. 1967. 30 pp.

784. McDonald, David. President, United Steelworkers of America (1952-65). 1966. 27 pp.

785. McDonough, Robert. Director, 1960 presidential primary in West Virginia primary (1960). 1964, 1965. Portions closed. 64 pp.

786. McGhee, George. Undersecretary of State for Political Affairs (1961-63); ambassador to West Germany (1963-68). 1964. 24 pp.

787. McGill, Ralph. Publisher, *Atlanta Constitution*. 1966. 25 pp.

788. McGovern, George. Director, Food for Peace (1961-62); Senator from South Dakota (1963-81). 1964. 51 pp.

789. McGuire, Marie C. Commissioner, Public Housing Administration (1961-66). 1967. 51 pp.

790. Mackenzie, Vernon G. Chief, Division of Air Pollution, Public Health Service. 1967. 24 pp.

791. McLaughlin, Edward F. JFK associate during World War II; Massachusetts political figure. 1964. Permission required. 20 pp.

792. McNamara, Robert S. Secretary of Defense (1961-68). 1964. Portions closed. 29 pp.

793. _____. Interview, conducted by David Nunnerly for his dissertation on Anglo-American relations during the Kennedy administration. 1970. Portions closed. 6 pp.

794. McNaughton, John T. Assistant Secretary of Defense for International Security Affairs. 1964. Closed. 50 pp.

795. McNeely, Mary. Massachusetts political figure. 1964. 16 pp.

796. McShane, James J. P. Chief U. S. Marshal, Department of Justice (1962-68). 1966. 34 pp.

797. Macomber, William. Ambassador to Jordan (1961-64). 1969. 29 pp.

798. Macy, John W. Chairman, Civil Service Commission (1961-69), 1964, 1968. 104 pp.

799. Mahoney, William P. Arizona political figure; Ambassador to Ghana (1962-66). 1975. 161 pp.

800. Makarios III. Archbishop and head of state of Cyprus (1960-74). 1964. 9 pp.

801. Manatos, Mike. Administrative assistant to the president (1961-63). 1970. 18 pp.

802. Manchin, A. James. JFK worker, 1960 primary campaign in West Virgina; state director, Farmer's Home Administration (1961-70). 1964. 19 pp.

803. Manley, Norman W. Premier of Jamaica (1959-62). 1964. 11 pp.

804. Mann, Thomas. Assistant Secretary of State for Inter-American Affairs (1960-61); Ambassador to Mexico (1961-63). 1968. 58 pp.

805. Manning, Robert. Assistant Secretary of State for Public Affairs (1962-64); editor, *Atlantic Monthly*. 1967. 23 pp.

806. Mannix, Jean McGonigle. Secretary to Senator John F. Kennedy (1952-54). 1966. 25 pp.

807. Mansfield, Mike. Senator from Montana (1953-77); Senate majority leader (1961-77). 1964. 46 pp.

808. Marcy, Carl M. Chief of Staff, U.S. Senate Committee on Foreign Relations (1955-73). Interview conducted by the U.S. Senate Historical Office. 1983. 284 pp.

809. Marshall, Burke. Assistant Attorney General, Civil Rights Division, Department of Justice (1961-64). 1964. 112 pp.

810. Marshall, Thurgood. Director, counsel, NAACP Legal Defense and Education Fund (1940-61); U.S. circuit judge, Second Circuit Court of Appeals (1961-65). 1964. 24 pp.

811. Martin, Clarence. West Virginia legislator. 1965. 27 pp.

812. Martin, Edwin. Assistant Secretary of State for Economic Affairs (1960-62); Assistant Secretary of State for Inter-American Affairs (1962-63). 1964. Permission required. 115 pp.

813. Martin, Louis. Deputy chairman of Democratic National Committee (1961-69). 1966. Portions closed. 130 pp.

814. Mayo, Leonard W. Chairman, President's Panel on Mental Retardation (1961-62); executive director, Association for the Aid of Crippled Children (1949-65). 1968. 50 pp.

815. Mboya, Thomas Joseph. Kenyan Minister of Labor (1962-63); Minister of Justice and Constitutional Affairs (1963-64). 1968. 8 pp.

816. Meany, George. President, American Federation of Labor-Congress of Industrial Organization. (1955-79). 1964. 53 pp.

817. Merchant, Livingston. Undersecretary of State for Political Affairs (1958-61); Ambassador to Canada (1961-62). 1965. Portions closed. 194 pp.

818. Meredith, James H. Missouri political figure; associate of Senator Stuart Symington. 1967. 14 pp.

819. Merrick, Samuel V. Special Assistant to the Secretary, Director, Office of Legislative Liaison, Department of Labor (1962-68). 1966. 129 pp.

820. Meyner, Robert B. Governor of New Jersey (1954-62). 1964. 16 pp.

821. Miller, George P. Representative from California (1945-53); chairman, House Science and Astronautics Committee (1961-73). 1964. 11 pp.

822. Miller, Herbert John. Assistant Attorney General, Criminal Division, Department of Justice (1961-65). 1971. Portions closed. 76 pp.

823. Mills, Wilbur. Representative from Arkansas (1939-77); chairman, House Ways and Means Committee (1957-74). 1967. 18 pp.

824. Minihan, Andrew. Irish cousin of JFK who was mayor of New Ross. 1966. 11 pp.

825. Minow, Newton. Chairman of the U.S. Communications Commission (1961-63). 1964. 77 pp.

826. Mitchell, Clarence M. Director, Washington bureau, National Association for the Advancement of Colored People (1950-78). 1967. 47 pp.

827. Monagan, John. Representative from Connecticut (1959-71). 1966. 23 pp.

828. Monfils, Owen F. Wisconsin political figure. 1966. 31 pp.

829. Monroney, Michael. Adlai Stevenson campaign worker (1960); Executive Assistant to the Postmaster General (1961-66). 1967. 27 pp.

830. Morgan, Edward P. News commentator, American Broadcasting Co., Washington (1955-67). 1967. 37 pp.

831. Morrison, Frank B. Governor of Nebraska (1961-67). 1968. 23 pp.

832. Morrissey, Francis X. Massachusetts judge, Kennedy family friend. 1964. 82 pp.

833. Morton, Thruston B. Senator from Kentucky (1957-68); chairman, Republican National Committee (1959-61). 1964. 25 pp.

834. Moss, John. Representative from California (1953-78). 1965. 19 pp.

835. Muccio, John J. Ambassador to Guatemala (1959-61). 1971. 13 pp.

836. Mulkern, Patrick J. Massachusetts political figure. 1964. 79 pp.

837. Muñoz Marin, Luis. Governor of Puerto Rico (1952-65). 1965. 17 pp.

838. Munroe, Patrick. Navy friend of JFK. 1982. Portions closed. 21 pp.

839. Murphy, Charles S. Undersecretary of Agriculture (1961-65). 1964. 31 pp.

840. Murphy, James M. Massachusetts political figure. 1964. 23 pp.

841. Muskie, Edmund S. Senator from Maine (1959-80). 1966. 111 pp.

842. Myers, Robert. West Virginia political figure. 1964. 22 pp.

843. Nash, Philleo. Commissioner, Bureau of Indian Affairs, Department of the Interior (1961-66). 1966, 1971. 68 pp.

844. Nathan, Robert. Chairman, National Executive Committee, Americans for Democratic Action (1957-59). 1967. 29 pp.

845. Neely, W. Walter. West Virgina political figure. 1964. 9 pp.

846. Nelson, Gaylord. Governor (1959-63); senator from Wisconsin (1963-81). 1964. Portions closed. 15 pp.

847. Neuberger, Maurine. Senator from Oregon (1960-67). 1970. 33 pp.

848. Newsom, Herschel D. Master, National Grange (1950-68). 1967. 27 pp.

849. Nicholson, Norman Edwin. Member, President's Commission on the Status of Women (1962); member, Citizen's Advisory Council to the Interdepartmental Commission on the Status of Women (1963-66). 1970. 52 pp.

850. Nitze, Paul. Assistant Secretary of Defense for International Security Affairs (1961-63); Secretary of the Navy (1963-67). 1964. Permission required. 30 pp.

851. Nix, Edmund. Wisconsin political figure. 1966. 34 pp.

852. Nogueira, Alberto Franco. Portugese Minister of Foreign Affairs (1961-69). 1966. 7 pp.

853. Nolan, John E. Department of Justice lawyer involved in Cuban prisoner exchange (1962-63). 1967. 28 pp.

854. _____. Interview conducted for the Robert F. Kennedy Oral History Program. 1970, 1971, 1972. 207 pp.

855. Nolting, Frederick E. Ambassador to South Vietnam (1961-63). 1966, 1970. 149 pp.

856. Norberg, Donald A. Chairman, Iowa Democratic party; Department of Agriculture official for congressional relations. 1967. 27 pp.

857. Norodom, Sihanouk. Cambodian Head of State (1960-70). 1964. 3 pp.

858. Norton, Clement A. Massachusetts political figure. 1964. 11 pp.

859. Notti, Robert W. Democratic campaign organizer (1960); Regional Director of Administration, Housing and Home Finance Agency. 1967. 33 pp.

860. Oberdorfer, Louis F. Assistant Attorney General, Tax Division, Department of Justice (1961-65). 1964. 34 pp.

861. O'Brien, Daniel F. Massachusetts political figure. 1964. 11 pp.

862. O'Connor, Frank. Massachusetts political figure. 1964. 11 pp.

863. Oehmann, Andrew F. Executive assistant to the Attorney General (1961-64). 1970. 16 pp.

864. Oettinger, Katherine B. Chief, Children's Bureau (1957-68); Deputy Assistant Secretary (1968-69), Department of Health, Education, and Welfare. Interview conducted by the Women in the Federal Government Project, Schlesinger Library, Radcliffe College. 1985. 432 pp.

865. O'Ferrall, Frank. Kennedy family friend in London. 1966. 20 pp.

866. Ong, Tan Sri. Malaysian Ambassador to the United States (1962-72). 1970. 28 pp.

867. Orlich, Jose Francisco. President of Costa Rica (1962-66). 1964. 3 pp.

868. Orrick, William H. Assistant Attorney General, Civil Division (1961-62), Antitrust Division (1963-65), Department of Justice; Deputy Undersecretary for Administration, Department of State (1962-63). 1970. Portions closed. 118 pp.

869. Pahlavi, Mohammad-Reza. Emperor of Iran (1941-79). 1964. 27 pp.

870. Palmer, Williston B. Director of Military Assistance, Department of Defense (1960-73). 1970. 19 pp.

871. Parsons, J. Graham. Ambassador to Laos (1956-58); Assistant Secretary of State for Far Eastern Affairs (1959-61). 1969. 42 pp.

872. Patterson, Bradley H. Assistant to the secretary of President Eisenhower's Cabinet (1955-61); Executive Secretary, Peace Corps; National Security Affairs Adviser, Department of the Treasury. 1968. 57 pp.

873. Patterson, John. Governor of Alabama (1959-63). 1967. Portions closed. 46 pp.

874. Pattison, Thomas R. Wisconsin political figure. 1966. 32 pp.

875. Paul VI, Pope. Leader of the Roman Catholic Church (1963-78). 1964. 4 pp.

876. Pell, Claiborne. Senator from Rhode Island (1961-). 1967. 50 pp.

877. Pereira, Pedro. Portugese Ambassador to the United States (1961-63). 1966. 33 pp.

878. Perez, Leander. Louisiana political figure. 1967. 10 pp.

879. Peters, Charles G. West Virginia political figure; director, Division of Evaluation, Peace Corps (1962-68). 1964. 45 pp.

880. Peters, Esther. Chairperson, Women for Kennedy, West Virginia (1960). 1964. 15 pp.

881. Peterson, Esther. Assistant Secretary for Labor Standards (1961-69); director, Women's Bureau (1961-64), Department of Labor; executive vice chairperson, President's Commission on the Status of Women (1961-63). 1966, 1970. 96 pp.

882. Phillips, Vel. 1960 presidential campaign worker in Wisconsin. 1966. 9 pp.

883. Piemonte, Gabriel. Massachusetts political figure. 1964. 6 pp.

884. Pierce, Nelson. White House usher. 1964. 11 pp.

885. Pittman, Steuart. Assistant Secretary of Defense for Civil Defense (1961-64). 1970. 20 pp.

886. Plimpton, Francis T. P. Deputy U.S. representative to the United Nations (1961-65). 1969. 73 pp.

887. "Poverty and Urban Policy" (Brandeis University Conference). Participants: David Austin, Raymond Bauer, Richard Boone, William Cannon, William Capron, Richard Cloward, Henry Cohen, Dan H. Fenn, Arnold Gurin, David Hackett, Frederick O. Hayes, David Hunter, Daniel Knapp, Sanford Kravitz, Lloyd E. Ohlin, Frances Fox Piven, Martin Rein, and Adam Yarmolinsky. 1973. 423 pp.

888. Powers, David F. Kennedy friend and associate; Special Assistant to the President (1961-63). Interview conducted for the Robert F. Kennedy Oral History Project. 1969. 22 pp.

889. Press Panel. Interview with White House correspondents: George Herman, Peter Lisagor, and Mary McGrory. 1964. Portions closed. 184 pp. A revealing account of Kennedy's press relations.

890. Prettyman, E. Barrett, Jr. White House aide for transportation matters (1962-63) 1969. Portions closed. 33 pp.

891. Proxmire, William. Republican senator from Wisconsin (1957-88). 1966. 17 pp.

892. Pryor, Ralph. Judge, West Virginia. 1964. 15 pp.

893. Pusey, Nathan M. President, Harvard University (1953-71). 1967. 36 pp.

894. Quigley, James M. Representative from Pennsylvania (1959-61); Assistant Secretary, Department of Health, Education, and Welfare (1961-66). 1967. 55 pp.

895. Quigley, Thomas J. Director, outpatient clinic, Veterans Administration Hospital, Boston, Ma. 1964. 7 pp.

896. Quimby, Thomas H. E. Michigan political figure; director of Public Affairs (1961-62); director of Peace Corps, Liberia (1961-68). 1968. 60 pp.

897. Randolph, Jennings. Senator from West Virginia (1958-65). 1965. 15 pp.

898. Rashish, Myer. Deputy Special Assistant to the President for International Trade Policy (1961-63). 1967. 39 pp.

899. Rauh, Joseph. Vice chairman, District of Columbia Democratic Committee (1952-64); vice chairman, Americans for Democratic Action (1957-   ). 1965. 114 pp.

900. Ray, David B. Member, Office of the Special Assistant to the President for Mental Retardation. 1968. 32 pp.

901. Raywid, Alan. Special Assistant to Assistant Attorney General, Civil Division. 1974. 34 pp.

902. Read, Benjamin. Special Assistant to the Secretary and Executive Secretary, Department of State (1963-69). 1966, 1969. 52 pp.

903. "Recruitment during the Kennedy Administration." Panel interview with: Richard Barrett, John Clinton, Dan H. Fenn, David C. Jelinek, Terrence Scanlon, and Edward L. Sherman. 1964? Portions closed. 137 pp.

904. Redmayne, Lord Sir Martin. British government chief whip (1959-64). 1969. 22 pp.

905. Reed, James A. Massachusetts political figure; Special Assistant to the Attorney General for Bank Mergers (1961); Assistant Secretary of the Treasury

(1961-65). 1964. Portions closed. 82 pp.

906. Reed, Robert S. Assistant to the Secretary of Agriculture. 1964. 13 pp.

907. Rees, Thomas. Representative from California (1965-76). 1969. 27 pp.

908. Reese, Matthew A. Organizer in 1960 presidential primary in West Virginia. 1964. 32 pp.

909. Reeves, Frank D. Civil rights activist; Special Assistant to the President (1961). 1967. 31 pp.

910. Reggie, Edmund M. JFK worker in 1960 presidential primary in Louisiana. 1967. 103 pp.

911. Regulatory Agencies Panel. Participants: Alan S. Boyd, William L. Cary, Newton N. Minow, Joseph C. Swidler, and William H.Tucker. 1964. Portions closed. 187 pp.

912. Reid, Warren. Assistant to Senator Warren Magnuson of Washington (1949-81). Interview conducted by the U.S. Senate Historical Office. 1981. 190 pp.

913. Reilly, James. District of Columbia political figure; member, Post Office Advisory Board. 1964. 7 pp.

914. Reilly, Sir Patrick. British Undersecretary, Foreign Office (1960-64). Interview conducted by David Nunnerly for his dissertation on Anglo-American relations during the Kennedy administration. 1969. 10 pp.

915. Reinhardt, G. Frederick. Ambassador to Italy (1961-68). 1966. 12 pp.

916. Reinsch, J. Leonard. Executive director, Democratic National Convention (1960, 1964); media consultant, 1960 presidential campaign. 1966. 59 pp.

917. Reis, Harold. Lawyer, Office of Legal Counsel, Department of Justice. 1974, 1975. Portions closed. 45 pp.

918. Reischauer, Edwin O. Ambassador to Japan (1961-66). 1966. 51 pp.

919. Reston, James. Journalist, editor, *New York Times.* Interview conducted by David Nunnerly for dissertation on Anglo-American relations during the Kennedy administration. 1970. 6 pp.

920. Reuss, Henry. Representative from Wisconsin (1955-83). 1965. 97 pp.

921. Reuter, Richard W. Executive director, CARE (1955-62); director, Food for Peace (1962-65). 1964. 27 pp.

922. Reynolds, James J. Assistant Secretary of Labor for Labor-Management Relations (1961-67). 1970. 55 pp.

923. Rice, Cyrus F. Journalist, *Milwaukee Sentinel.* 1965. 17 pp.

924. Richardson, William H. West Virginia political figure. 1964. 43 pp.

925. Rickover, Hyman G. Chief, Bureau for Nuclear Propulsion, Bureau of Ships, U. S. Navy (1947-81); Chief, Naval Reactors Branch, Atomic Energy Commission (1953-81). 1964. 12 pp.

926. Riggins, William J. Worker, 1960 presidential primary in Wisconsin. 1965. 14 pp.

927. Riley, Arch W. West Virginia political figure. 1965. 52 pp.

928. Ringler, Paul. Journalist, *Milwaukee Journal.* 1965. 11 pp.

929. Rinke, Kenneth. Staff member, Kennedy for President Committee of Oregon (1960). 1966. 21 pp.

930. Roberts, Chalmer M. Journalist, *Washington Post* (1949-71). 1977. Portions closed. 37 pp.

931. Roberts, Charles. Contributing editor, *Newsweek.* 1966. Portions closed. 58 pp.

932. Rogers, Paul G. Representative from Florida (1955-79). 1968. 14 pp.

933. Roncalio, Teno. Wyoming political figure. 1965. 65 pp.

934. Rose, Donald. Democratic county chairman, Los Angeles County. (1954-62). 1969. 172 pp.

935. Rosetti, Joseph E. Campaign worker, JFK's 1946 congressional campaign; staff member, Boston office of Representative Kennedy (1947-51); investigator, chief, Department of Security (1961-62); Chief, Domestic Operations, Department of State (1962-66). 1967. 172 pp.

936. Rostow, Walt W. Deputy Special Assistant to the President for National Security Affairs (1961); chairman, Policy Planning Council, Department of State (1961-66). 1964. Portions closed. 157 pp.

937. Rothschild, Robert. Deputy chief, Belgian Diplomatic Mission to the Republic of the Congo (1960). 1966. 32 pp.

938. Runge, Carlisle P. Assistant Secretary of Defense for Manpower (1961-62). 1971. 45 pp.

939. Rusk, Dean. Secretary of State (1961-1969). 1969, 1970. Portions closed. 401 pp.

940. _____. Interview conducted by David Nunnerly for his dissertation on Anglo-American relations during the Kennedy administration. 1970. 4 pp.

941. Russell, Francis H. Ambassador to Ghana (1960-62). 1972, 1973. 63 pp.

942. Russo, Joseph. Massachusetts political figure. 1964. 8 pp.

943. Salinger, Pierre. Press secretary to the President (1960-64). 1965. 206 pp.

944. Saltonstall, John. Massachusetts political figure; member, Democratic state committee; delegate at large, Democratic National Convention (1960). 1969. 16 pp.

945. Saltonstall, Leverett. Senator from Massachusetts (1945-67). 1964, 1965. 72 pp.

946. Sanders, Carl. Governor of Georgia (1963-67). 1967. 26 pp.

947. Sanford, Terry. Governor of North Carolina (1961-65). 1970. 55 pp.

948. Sanjuan, Pedro A. Assistant Chief of Protocol, Department of State (1961-63). 1969. Permission required. 161 pp.

949. Santos, Charles. Campaign worker for JFK in Lowell, Ma., 1952 and 1960. 1979. 15 pp.

950. Satterthwaite, Joseph C. Ambassador to South Africa (1961-65). 1971. 21 pp.

951. Sayre, Francis B. Dean of Washington Cathedral; chairman, U.S. Committee for Refugees (1958-61). 1964. 17 pp.

952. Scali, John. Journalist, Associated Press and ABC News. 1982. 14 pp.

953. Schary, Dore. Playwright, motion picture producer. 1967. 17 pp.

954. Schlei, Norbert A. Assistant Attorney General, Office of Legal Counsel, Department of Justice (1962-66). 1968. 62 pp.

955. Schlesinger, Arthur M., Jr. Special Assistant to the President (1961-64).

Interview conducted by David Nunnerly for his dissertation on Anglo-American relations during the Kennedy administration. 1970. 3 pp.

956. Seamans, Robert. Associate Administrator, National Aeronautics and Space Administration (1960-65). 1964. 46 pp.

957. Seigenthaler, John. Administrative Assistant to the Attorney General (1961). 1964, 1966. Portions closed. 568 pp.

958. Semer, Milton P. General Counsel, Housing and Home Finance Agency (1961-66). 1968. 94 pp.

959. Senghor, Leopold Sedar. President, Senegal Republic. (1960-80). 1964. 6 pp.

960. Sharkey, Joseph T. New York political figure; active in 1960 campaign. 1967. 71 pp.

961. Sharon, John H. Democratic party campaign organizer (1960); presidential adviser on foreign affairs. 1967. 35 pp.

962. Shaw, Maud. Kennedy family governess (1957-63). 1965. 26 pp.

963. Shea, Maurice. Contemporary of JFK at Choate School. 1966. 16 pp.

964. Shea, Robert. Vice president, American Red Cross, involved in the Cuban prisoners exchange. 1964. 28 pp.

965. Sheble, Walter F. Advance man, 1960 presidential campaign; consultant to the president (1961-63); investigator of stockpiling of materials for national emergency (1962). 1976. 16 pp.

966. Shepard, Alan B. Project Mercury astronaut, National Aeronautics and Space Administration (1959-65). 1964. 21 pp.

967. Shepard, Tazewell. Naval aide to JFK (1961-63). 1964, 1968. 90 pp.

968. Shermarke, Abdi Rashid Ali. Somali Prime Minister (1960-64). 1965. Portions closed. 21 pp.

969. Shoup, David M. Commandant of the Marine Corps. 1967. 47 pp.

970. Shriver, Eunice Kennedy. Sister of President Kennedy; executive vice president, Joseph P. Kennedy, Jr. Foundation (1950-). 1968. 30 pp.

971. Shuman, Howard E. Legislative and administrative assistant to Senator Paul Douglas of Illinois and William Proxmire of Wisconsin. Interview conducted by the

U. S. Senate Historical Office. 1987. 631 pp.

972. Sidey, Hugh. Journalist, *Time, Life* (1955-). 1964. 53 pp.

973. Silberling, Edwyn. Assistant Attorney General for Organized Crime and Racketeering. 1971. 68 pp.

974. Simkin, William E. Director, Federal Mediation and Conciliation Service (1961-69). 1967, 1969. 66 pp.

975. Sitrin, Gloria. Secretary to Theodore C. Sorensen. 1966. 39 pp.

976. Skinner, Carlton. Financial vice president, Fairbanks-Whitney Corporation (1958-63). 1970. 65 pp.

977. Slayton, William L. Commissioner, Urban Renewal Administration (1961-66). 1967. 47 pp.

978. Slim, Mongi. Tunisian Ambassador to the United States (1955-61); President, United Nations General Assembly (1961-62); Tunisian Secretary of State for Foreign Affairs (1962-64). 1965. 19 pp.

979. Smathers, George A. Senator from Florida (1951-69). 1964. Portions closed. 68 pp.

980. Smith, Hulett C. State chairman, West Virginia Democratic party (1956-61). 1965. 40 pp.

981. Solins, Samuel. West Virginia political figure. 1965. 22 pp.

982. Sorensen, Theodore C. Staff assistant, speechwriter to Senator Kennedy (1952-61), Special Counsel to the President (1961-64). 1964. Portions closed. 169 pp.

983. Southwick, Paul. Deputy administrator, Area Redevelopment Administration (1962-63). 1970. 29 pp.

984. Spalding, Charles. JFK friend and campaign aide. 1968. Portions closed. 110 pp.

985. Sparkman, John J. Senator from Alabama (1947-79). 1978. 30 pp.

986. Spolar, Walter. Campaign organizer, John F. Kennedy's presidential campaign (1960); congressional relations official for the Post Office Department. 1966. 20 pp.

987. Sprecher, Drexel A. Deputy chairman, Democratic National Committee (1957-60). 1972. 102 pp.

988. Sprouse, Philip D. Ambassador to Cambodia (1962-64). 1969. 88 pp.

989. Staats, Elmer B. Deputy director, Bureau of the Budget (1958-66). 1964. 36 pp.

990. Staebler, Neil. Chairman, President's Commission on Campaign Costs (1961-62). 1964. 10 pp.

991. Stahr, Elvis. Secretary of the Army (1961-62). 1964. 136 pp.

992. Stakem, Thomas E. Chairman, U.S. Maritime Commission (1961-63). Interview conducted by David Nunnerly for his dissertation on Anglo-American relations during the Kennedy administration. 1970. 11 pp.

993. Stanley, Miles C. President, West Virginia Labor Federation, AFL-CIO (1957-74). 1964. 24 pp.

994. Stedman, Donald. Associate director for research, Joseph P. Kennedy, Jr., Foundation. 1968. 41 pp.

995. Steeves, John M. Assistant Secretary of State for Far Eastern Affairs (1959-62); Ambassador to Afghanistan (1962-66). 1969, 1970. Closed. 80 pp.

996. Steiner, Richard M. Minister, First Christian Church, Portland, Oregon (1960). 1966. 6 pp.

997. Stevens, George. Motion picture director. Interview concerning the film *PT-109*. 1980. 3 pp.

998. Stevenson, William. Ambassador to the Phillipines (1961-64). 1969. 136 pp.

999. Stikker, Dirk U. Secretary-General, North Atlantic Treaty Organization (1961-64). 1965. Permission required. 76 pp.

1000. Stout, Benjamin B. West Virginia political figure. 1964. 15 pp.

1001. Stringham, Luther. Program analysis officer, Department of Health, Education, and Welfare (1956-63); consultant on mental retardation, member, President's Committee on Employment of the Handicapped (1963-68). 1968. 28 pp.

1002. Sukarno, Achmed. Head of State, Republic of Indonesia (1949-65). 1964. 15 pp.

1003. Sullivan, William H. United Nations adviser, Bureau of Far Eastern Affairs, Department of State (1960-64); Special Assistant to the Undersecretary of State for Political Affairs (1963-64). 1970. 48 pp.

1004. Sundquist, James L. Member, Democratic National Committee Platform Committee (1960); staff member, 1960 presidential campaign; Deputy Undersecretary of Agriculture (1963-65). 1965. 17 pp.

1005. Sutton, William. JFK associate, Boston. 1964. 20 pp.

1006. Swainson, John B. Governor of Michigan (1961-63). 1970. 18 pp.

1007. Swig, Benjamin H. California political figure; delegate, Democratic National Convention (1956, 1960); member, President's Committee for Traffic Safety (1961-63). 1970. 7 pp.

1008. Swope, Gordon. Labor chairman, Kennedy for President Committee, Oregon (1960). 1966. 9 pp.

1009. Sylvester, Arthur. Assistant Secretary of Defense for Public Affairs (1961-1967). 1977. Portions closed. 56 pp.

1010. _____. Interview conducted by Lawrence Suid. 1973, 1974. 39 pp.

1011. Symington, James W. Missouri political figure; deputy director, Food for Peace (1961-62). 1968. 31 pp.

1012. Symington, Stuart. Senator from Missouri (1953-77). 1964. 54 pp.

1013. Talmadge, Herman. Senator from Georgia (1957-81). 1966. 38 pp.

1014. Tames, George. Photographer, Washington bureau, *New York Times* (1945-85). Interview conducted by the U.S. Senate Historical Office. 1988. 198 pp.

1015. Tawes, J. Millard. Governor of Maryland (1959-67). 1968. 17 pp.

1016. Taylor, George. John F. Kennedy's valet and chauffer, Boston. 1964. 21 pp.

1017. Taylor, Hobart. Executive vice chairman, President's Panel on Equal Employment Opportunity (1962-65); Special Assistant to the Vice President (1963). 1967. 35 pp.

1018. Taylor, Maxwell D. General, U.S. Army; military representative of the President (1961-62); chairman, Joint Chiefs of Staff (1962-64). 1964. Portions closed. 80 pp.

1019. Telles, Raymond L. Ambassador to Costa Rica (1961-67). 1970. 90 pp.

1020. Terry, Luther L. Surgeon General of the United States; Public Health Service, Department of Health, Education, and Welfare (1961-65). 1970. 80 pp.

1021. Thant, U. Secretary General of the United Nations (1962-65). 1964. 19 pp.

1022. Thaw, William. West Virginia political figure. 1964. 11 pp.

1023. Thaxton, Cordenia. White House maid. 1965. 15 pp.

1024. Thompson, Arthur T. Administrative assistant to Governor Herschel Loveless of Iowa (1959-61); director, Grain Policy Staff, Agricultural Stabilization and Conservation Service (1961-68). 1964. 28 pp.

1025. Thompson, Frank. Representative from New Jersey (1955-80); chairman, National Voters Registration Committee (1960). 1965. 22 pp.

1026. Thompson, Llewellyn E. Ambassador to the U.S.S.R. (1957-62), U.S. Ambassador-at-Large (1962-66). 1964, 1966. 62 pp.

1027. Thompson, Robert E. Press secretary, John F. Kennedy's Massachusetts senatorial reelection campaign (1958); Washington correspondent, *Los Angeles Times* (1962-66); author, *Robert F. Kennedy: The Brother Within* (1962). 1965. 35 pp.

1028. Thorneycroft, Lord Peter. British Minister of Aviation (1960-62); Minister of Defence (1962-64). 1966. Portions closed. 23 pp.

1029. _____. Interview conducted by David Nunnerly for his dissertation on Anglo-American relations during the Kennedy administration. 1969, 1970. 48 pp.

1030. Thurston, Raymond L. Alternate representative, U. S. delegation to the North Atlantic Treaty Organization (1961); Ambassador to Haiti (1961-63). 1970. 49 pp.

1031. Tierney, Lawrence. West Virginia labor and political figure. 1964. 11 pp.

1032. Tinker, Harold. Teacher, Choate School. 1977. 9 pp.

1033. Titler, George. West Virginia political figure. 1965. 10 pp.

1034. Tobriner, Walter. Commissioner, District of Columbia (1961-67). 1964. 6 pp.

1035. Tracy, Ambrose. Wisconsin political figure. 1966. 17 pp.

1036. Travell, Janet G. Physician to President Kennedy (1961-63). 1966. Permission required. 30 pp.

1037. Tree, Marietta. New York political figure; member, Democratic Advisory Council (1956-60); member, New York Citizens for Kennedy (1960); delegate to the Human Rights Commission, United Nations (1961-67). 1969, 1971. 49 pp.

1038. Tretick, Stanley. Photographer, United Press International, *Look*. 1964. 50 pp.

1039. Trevelyan, Sir Humphrey. British Deputy Undersecretary, Foreign Office (1962); British Ambassador to Iraq (1958-61) and to the U.S.S.R. (1962-65). 1967. 13 pp.

1040. Trimble, William. Ambassador to Cambodia (1959-62). 1969. Portions closed. 60 pp.

1041. Tubby, Roger. Assistant Secretary of State for Public Affairs (1961-62); Ambassador to the European office of the United Nations and other international organizations, Geneva (1962-69). 1967. Permission required. 73 pp.

1042. Tubridy, Dorothy. Irish friend of the Kennedy family. 1966. 38 pp.

1043. Tucker, Herbert E. Massachusetts political figure; chairman, NAACP, Boston; worker in JFK's 1952 and 1958 Senate campaigns and 1960 presidential campaign. 1967. 49 pp.

1044. Tucker, William H. Commissioner, Interstate Commerce Commission (1961-67). 1967. 25 pp.

1045. Tydings, Joseph D. Senator from Maryland (1965-71). 1971, 1973. 23 pp.

1046. Tyler, William R. Deputy Assistant (1961-62) and Assistant Secretary of State for European Affairs (1962-65). 1964. 40 pp.

1047. Udall, Stewart. Secretary of the Interior (1961-69). 1970. 173 pp.

1048. Ulen, Harold S. JFK's Harvard swimming coach. 1964. 7 pp.

1049. Valenti, Jack. Motion picture executive. 1982. 15 pp.

1050. Van Roijen, J. Herman. Dutch Ambassador to the United States (1950-64). 1966. 19 pp.

1051. Vandiver, S. Ernest. Governor of Georgia (1959-63). 1967. 70 pp.

1052. Vance, Cyrus. General Counsel, Department of Defense (1961); Secretary of the Army (1961-63). 1971, 1973. 51 pp.

1053. Vander Zee, Rein J. Assistant to the Senate Democratic Whip and assistant secretary of the majority (1961-64). Interview conducted by the U. S. Historical Office. 1992.

1054. Vaugh, Wilton. Massachusetts political figure. 1965. 25 pp.

1055. Verkler, Jerry T. Senate Interior and Insular Affairs Committee; staff assistant, 87th Congress. 1970. 31 pp.

1056. Vickers, Carl B. West Virginia political figure. 1965. 39 pp.

1057. Vogelsinger, Sue Mortensen. Secretary to JFK (1958-63). 1964. 27 pp.

1058. Von Braun, Wernher. Director, George C. Marshall Space Flight Center, National Aeronautics and Space Administration (1960-72). 1964. 20 pp.

1059. Wade, Richard. Campaigner for John and Robert Kennedy. 1973, 1974. Interview done for the Robert F. Kennedy Oral History Project.

1060. Wallace, Robert A. Assistant to Secretary of the Treasury (1961-63), Assistant Secretary of the Treasury (1963-69). 1968 and 1972. 105 pp.

1061. Wallick, Franklin. Editor, *Wisconsin CIO News*; Wisconsin political figure. 1966. 91 pp.

1062. Warren, Ernest. Reporter, Associated Press. 1968. 25 pp.

1063. Warren, Stafford L. Special Assistant to the President for Mental Retardation (1962-63). 1966. 46 pp.

1064. Watkinson, Viscount. British Minister of Defence (1959-62). 1970. Closed. 22 pp.

1065. Watson, Thomas J. Vice chairman, Business Advisory Council; chairman, International Business Machines Corporation (1961-71); member, Labor-Management Relations Committee (1961-69). 1965. 26 pp.

1066. Watt Ruth Young. Chief clerk, Senate Permanent Subcommittee on Investigations (1948-79). Interview conducted by the U.S. Senate Historical Office. 1979. 315 pp.

1067. Weaver, George. Special Assistant to the Secretary of Labor (1961); Assistant Secretary for International Affairs and director, Bureau of International Labor Affairs, Department of Labor (1961-69). 1964. 25 pp.

1068. Weaver, Robert C. Administrator, Housing and Home Finance Agency (1961-66). 1964. Permission required. 246 pp.

1069. _____. Interview conducted by Morton J. Schussheim. 1985. 33 pp.

1070. Weber, Stanley E. Journalist, *Oregon Journal*. 1966. 34 pp.

1071. Welsh, Edward C. Executive secretary, National Aeronautics and Space Council. 1964. 51 pp.

1072. Werts, Leo R. Administrative Assistant to the Secretary, Department of Labor (1961-64); Assistant Secretary of Labor for Administration. 1970. 21 pp.

1073. West, J. Bernard. White House chief usher. 1967. 13 pp.

1074. West, Marshall G. Co-chairman, Hubert Humphrey's West Virginia primary campaign (1960). 1964. 14 pp.

1075. Wheeler, Earle. General, U.S. Army; director, Joint Chiefs of Staff (1960-62); commanding general, European command (1962); Chief of Staff, U. S. Army (1962-64). 1964. 72 pp.

1076. "White House Staff Reflections on the New Frontier" Conference. Participants: Charles U. Daly, Claude J. Desautels, Richard K. Donahue, Robert J. Donovan, Ralph A. Dungan, Frederick G. Dutton, William J. Hartigan, Robert Healey, Charles A. Horsky, Carl Kaysen, Godfrey T. McHugh, John J. McNally, Michael N. Manatos, Richard W. Reuter, Walt W. Rostow, Arthur M. Schlesinger, Jr., Tazewell Shepard, Theodore C. Sorensen, Lee C. White, Tom Wicker. 1981. Portions closed. 204 pp.

1077. White, Lee C. Assistant Special Counsel to the President (1961-63). 1964, 1970. 386 pp.

1078. Wicker, Tom. Journalist and author. 1966. 239 pp.

1079. Wild, Payson S. Professor of government, Harvard University (1935-49). 1968. 18 pp.

1080. Wilkins, Fraser. Ambassador to Cyprus (1960-64). 1971. 19 pp.

1081. Wilkins, Roy. Executive secretary of the NAACP (1955-64). 1964. 29 pp.

1082. Williams, Donald A. Administrator, Soil Conservation Service. 1964. 23 pp.

1083. Williams, G. Mennen. Assistant Secretary of State for African Affairs (1961-66). 1970. 81 pp.

1084. Williams, Irwin M. White House gardener. 1965. 23 pp.

1085. Williams, Murat. Ambassador to El Salvador (1961-64). 1970. 48 pp.

1086. Williams, Walter. Associate director, Manned Space Flight Center, National Aeronautics and Space Administration. 1964. 25 pp.

1087. Wilson, Donald M. Member, John F. Kennedy's presidential campaign staff (1960); deputy director, U.S. Information Agency (1961-65), 1964, 1972. 87 pp.

1088. Wine, James. Member, John F. Kennedy's presidential campaign staff (1960); Ambassador to Luxembourg (1961-62); Ambassador to the Republic of the Ivory Coast (1962-67). 1967. 81 pp.

1089. Winship, Thomas. Journalist; Washington correspondent (1945-56); editor, *Boston Globe*. 1964. 71 pp.

1090. Wofford, Harris. Assistant to Senator John F. Kennedy (1960); Special Assistant to the President for Civil Rights (1961-62); Special Representative for Africa, Peace Corps (1962-64). 1965, 1968. 158 pp.

1091. Wolfbein, Seymour. Deputy Assistant Secretary of Labor (1959-62); Deputy Manpower Administrator for Planning, Research, and Evaluation, Department of Labor (1962-65). 1966. 34 pp.

1092. Wolfe, Thomas W. Regional director for Sino-Soviet Affairs, Department of Defense (1961-62). 1970. 25 pp.

1093. Wood, Robert C. Educator, presidential adviser. 1968. 36 pp.

1094. Woodcock, Leonard. International vice president, United Auto Workers Union (1955-70). 1970. 25 pp.

1095. Woodward, Robert F. Ambassador to Chile (1961; Assistant Secretary of State for Inter-American Affairs (1961-62); Ambassador to Spain (1962-65). 1970. 26 pp.

1096. Wright, Dick. West Virginia political figure. 1965. 11 pp.

1097. Wright, Sir Michael. British delegate to the Geneva disarmament talks (1960, 1962-63). Interview conducted by David Nunnerly for his dissertation on Anglo-American relations during the Kennedy administration. 1969. 27 pp.

1098. Yarmolinsky, Adam. Special Assistant to the Secretary of Defense (1961-65). 1964. 77 pp.

1099. Yasko, Karel. Architect and special assistant to the Commissioner, Public Building Service, General Services Administration (1961-69). 1966. 124 pp.

1100. York, Herbert. Member, General Advisory Committee, Arms Control and Disarmament Agency (1962-69). 1964. Portions closed. 28 pp.

1101. Yost, Charles. Ambassador to Morocco (1958-61); U.S. deputy to the U.N. (1961-66). 1978. 50 pp.

1102. Zablocki, Clement. Representative from Wisconsin (1949-83). 1965. 50 pp.

1103. Zack, Albert J. Director of public relations, AFL-CIO (1957-80). 1967. 32 pp.

1104. Ziffren, Paul. Democratic National Committeeman from California (1953-60). 1970. 32 pp.

1105. Zuckerman, Eugene M. Chief science adviser to the British Secretary of State for Defence (1960-66). 1966. 29 pp.

1106. Zuckert, Eugene M. Secretary of the Air Force (1961-65). 1964. 151 pp.

B. ORAL HISTORIES RELATING TO KENNEDY AT THE LYNDON B. JOHNSON LIBRARY

1107. Adair, E. Ross. Representative from Indiana. 1969. Permission required. 30 pp.

1108. Aiken, George D. Senator from Vermont. 1968. 30 pp.

1109. Albert, Carl. Congressman from Oklahoma; majority leader. 1969. Permission required. 1969. Four interviews: 24, 16, 14, and 27 pp.

1110. Allen, Robert S. Columnist; former partner of Drew Pearson. 1969. 28 pp.

1111. Almond, J. Lindsay, Jr. Congressman from Virginia; Attorney General and Governor of Virginia. 1969. 27 pp.

1112. Alsop, Joseph W. Columnist. 1969. Closed. 19 pp.

1113. Alsop, Stewart J. Columnist. 1969. 19 pp.

1114. Bachelder, Toinette. Career White House secretary. 1969. 34 pp.

1115. Bartlett, Charles L. Journalist. 1969. 45 pp.

1116. Beirne, Joseph A. President, Communications Workers of America; vice president, AFL-CIO. Contains information on the assassination. 1969. 29 pp.

1117. Billings, William F. Supervisor, Washington headquarters of the FBI. Contains information on the assassination. 1969. 20 pp.

1118. Birkhead, Kenneth M. Assistant to the Secretary of Agriculture. 1970. Three interviews: 35, 39, and 8 pp.

1119. Blackman, Herbert N. Administrator, Bureau of International Labor Affairs, Department of Labor. 1969. 42 pp.

1120. Boggs, Hale. Congressman from Louisiana; majority whip. 1969. Two interviews: 22, 17 pp.

1121. Bowles, Chester. Longtime government official; U.S. Ambassador to India (1963-69). Contains information on the assassination. 1969. 67 pp.

1122. Brown, Edmund G. Governor of California. Contains information on Kennedy assassination. 1969, 1970. Two interviews: 19, 34 pp.

1123. Burkley, George G. White House physician. Better on JFK's health than Burkley's oral history at Kennedy Library. Contains information on the assassination. 1968. 25 pp.

1124. Carpenter, Elizabeth. Journalist; executive assistant to Vice President Johnson. 1968-1971. Five interviews: 37, 38, 47, 46, and 33 pp.

1125. Carter, Hodding, Jr. Newspaper editor, *Delta Democrat-Times*, Greenville, Miss.; active in the civil rights movement and the War on Poverty. 1968. 30 pp.

1126. Carter, Joseph H. Speechwriter for Lyndon Johnson. Contains information on the assassination. 1968. 24 pp.

1127. Christian, George E. LBJ Press Secretary and Special Assistant (1966-69). 1968-1971. Five interviews: 14, 39, 27, 43, and 31 pp.

1128. Clark, Ramsey. Assistant U.S. Attorney General and Attorney General (1961-69). Contains information on the assassination. 1968, 1969. Five interviews: 30, 31, 20, 30, and 29 pp.

1129. Clifford, Clark. Secretary of Defense (1968-69); Kennedy family attorney. 1969, 1970. Nine interviews: 30, 27, 35, 36, 26, 12, 21, 6, and 11 pp.

1130. Cohen, Sheldon. Commissioner of Internal Revenue. Permission required. 1968. Four interviews: 5, 48, 6, and 42 pp.

1131. Cohen, Wilbur. Assistant Secretary of Health, Education, and Welfare (1961-65). 1968, 1969. Three interviews: 38, 31, and 38 pp.

1132. Costello, William A. Journalist; White House correspondent, Mutual

Broadcasting System (1958-68). Contains information on the assassination. 1968. 30 pp.

1133. Curry, Jesse E. Dallas police chief at the time of the assassination. 1969. 13 pp.

1134. Deason, Willard. Longtime personal friend of LBJ. Contains information on the assassination. 1965, 1969, 1978. Five interviews: 19, 28, 36, 27, 33, and 30 pp.

1135. Dillon, C. Douglas. Secretary of the Treasury (1961-65). 1969. 29 pp.

1136. DiSalle, Michael V. Governor of Ohio (1959-63). 1969. 34 pp.

1137. Dungan, Ralph A. Special Assistant to Presidents Kennedy and Johnson. 1969. 38 pp.

1138. Dutton, Frederick G. Special Assistant to JFK; organizing director of JFK Oral History Project. Contains information on the assassination. 1969. 33 pp.

1139. Eastland, James O. Democratic senator from Mississippi. Contains information on the assassination. 1971. 24 pp.

1140. Edwards, India. Director of Women's Division, Democratic National Committee. 1969. 49 pp.

1141. Ellender, Allen J. Senator from Louisiana. 1969. 19 pp.

1142. Farley, James A. U.S. Postmaster General (1933-40); chairman, Democratic National Committee (1933-40). 1968. 47 pp.

1143. Farmer, James. Civil rights activist; national director, Congress of Racial Equality (1961-65). 1969, 1971. Two interviews: 16, 33 pp.

1144. Finletter, Thomas K. Ambassador to North Atlantic Treaty Organization (1961-65). 1968. 35 pp.

1145. Fortas, Abe. Longtime friend and adviser to LBJ; Associate Justice, U.S. Supreme Court (1965-69). 1969. 37 pp.

1146. Fowler, Henry. Investment banker. 1969. Four interviews: 39, 30, 35, and 13 pp.

1147. Fox, Sanford. Administrative officer of the White House Social Entertainment Office. 1968. 31 pp.

1148. Frankel, Max. Editor, *New York Times*. Permission required. 1969. 49 pp.

1149. Freeman, Orville. Secretary of Agriculture (1961-69). 1969. 102 pp.

1150. Gaud, William S. Deputy administrator, Agency for International Development. 1968. 48 pp.

1151. Godfrey, Horace D. Administrator, Agricultural Stabilization and Conservation Service, Department of Agriculture. 1968. 41 pp.

1152. Goodpaster, Andrew J. General, U S. Army; Defense liaison officer and staff secretary to the president (1954-61); supreme allied commander, Europe. Contains information on the assassination. 1971. 47 pp.

1153. Graham, Katharine. Publisher, *Washington Post*. 1969. 38 pp.

1154. Halleck, Charles A. Congressman from Indiana; majority and minority leader, 80th-88th Congresses. Contains information on the assassination. 1968. 31 pp.

1155. Harris, Oren. Congressman from Arkansas. No date. 47 pp.

1156. Hays, Wayne L. Congressman from Ohio. 1969. 15 pp.

1157. Helms, Richard. Director, Central Intelligence Agency (1966-73). 1969, 1981. Two interviews: 37, 29 pp.

1158. Hesburgh, Theodore. President of the University of Notre Dame; member of U.S. Commission on Civil Rights. 1971. 38 pp.

1159. Hickenlooper, Bourke B. Republican Senator from Iowa. 1968. 25 pp.

1160. Hilsman, Roger. Director of Bureau of Intelligence and Research, Department of State (1961-63); Assistant Secretary of State for Far Eastern Affairs (1963-64). 1969. 44 pp.

1161. Hodges, Luther H., Sr. Secretary of Commerce (1961-65). Contains information on the assassination. 1968. 32 pp.

1162. Holcomb, Luther. Baptist minister, Equal Employment Opportunity Commission. Contains information on the assassination. 1969. Three interviews: 26, 25, and 19 pp.

1163. Holleman, Jerry. Assistant Secretary of Labor. 1971. 61 pp.

1164. Horne, John E. Executive director, Citizens for Kennedy-Johnson, 1960. 1969. 38 pp.

1165. Hughes, Phillip S. Deputy director, Bureau of the Budget. 1969. 29 pp.

1166. Hughes, Sarah T. Judge, U.S. District Court, Dallas; administered oath of office to President Johnson. 1968. 32 pp.

1167. Humphrey, Hubert. Democratic Senator from Minnesota. 1971, 1977. Three interviews: 45, 17, and 28 pp.

1168. Huntley, Chet R. NBC news commentator. Contains information on the assassination. 1969. 31 pp.

1169. Hutchinson, Everett. Commissioner and chairman of the Interstate Commerce Commission (1955-65). Contains information on the assassination. 1969. 36 pp.

1170. Ink, Dwight A. Assistant director, Office of Management and Budget. 1969. 41 pp.

1171. Jaworski, Leon. Special assistant, U.S. Attorney General (1962-65). Contains information on the assassination. 1968. 36 pp.

1172. Jordan, Robert E., III. Staff director, President's Commission on Equal Opportunity in the Armed Forces. 1969. Portions closed. Three interviews: 42, 40, and 5 pp.

1173. Katzenbach, Nicholas. Assistant Attorney General (1961-62), Deputy Attorney General (1962-64). 1968. 90 pp.

1174. Kennedy, Edward M. Democratic Senator from Massachusetts. 1969, 1970. Restricted. Three interviews: 11, 15, and 17 pp.

1175. Kinch, Sam, Sr. Journalist, *Fort Worth Star-Telegram*. Contains information on the assassination. 1970. 25 pp.

1176. Krock, Arthur. Columnist, author. 1968. 32 pp.

1177. Lincoln, Gould. Journalist, *Washington Evening Star* (1909-67). Contains information on the assassination. 1968. 23 pp.

1178. Locke, Eugene M. Deputy ambassador to South Vietnam (1967-68). 1969. 34 pp.

1179. McCloy, John J. Coordinator, U.S. Disarmament Activities (1961-63); member, Warren Commisssion; adviser to presidents. 1969. 21 pp.

1180. McCone, John. Director of the CIA (1961-65). Contains information on the the assassination. 1970. 29 pp.

1181. McCormack, John. Congressman from Massachusetts; Speaker of the House

(1961-72). Contains information on the assassination. 1968. 55 pp.

1182. McGee, Gale. Democratic Senator from Wyoming. 1968. Two interviews: 50, 23 pp.

1183. McGhee, George C. Ambassador to the Federal Republic of Germany (1963-68). 1969. 23 pp.

1184. McGovern, George. Democratic Senator from South Dakota. 1969. 32 pp.

1185. McPherson, Harry C., Jr. Associate counsel, Senate Democratic Policy Committee (1959-61); Deputy Undersecretary of the Army for International Affairs (1963-64). 1968, 1969. Five interviews: 80, 38, 40, 63, and 63 pp.

1186. Macomber, William B., Jr. Ambassador to Jordan (1961-64). 1968. 42 pp.

1187. Marshall, Burke. Assistant Attorney General, Civil Rights Division, Department of Justice (1961-65). Contains information on the assassination. 1968. 40 pp.

1188. Marshall, Thurgood. Associate Justice, U.S. Supreme Court. 1969. 20 pp.

1189. Meany, George. President, AFL-CIO. Contains information on the Kennedy assassination. 1969. 22 pp.

1190. Menzies, Sir Robert. Prime Minister of Australia (1949-66). Contains information on the Kennedy assassination. 1969. 16 pp.

1191. Mitchell, Clarence M., Jr. Director, Washington bureau of the NAACP. 1969. 71 pp.

1192. Monroney, A. S. Democratic Senator from Oklahoma. 1969. Three interviews: 28, 32, and 32.

1193. Mooney, Booth. Author, Senate aide of LBJ. Contains information on the assassination. 1969, 1971. Two interviews: 48, 29 pp.

1194. Nichols, Dorothy J. Longtime secretary to Johnson. Contains information on the Kennedy assassination. 1968, 1974. Two interviews: 35, 31 pp.

1195. Nolting, Frederick. Ambassador to South Vietnam (1961-63). 1982. 34 pp.

1196. O'Donnell, Kenneth P. Appointments Secretary to JFK. 1969. 111 pp.

1197. Onassis, Jacqueline Kennedy. First Lady (1961-63). Contains information on the assassination. 1974. 19 pp.

1198. O'Neill, Thomas P. Democratic Congressman from Massachusetts. 1976. 33 pp.

1199. Owings, Nathaniel. Architect; chairman, Temporary Commission on Pennsylvania Avenue (1964-73). 1970. 33 pp.

1200. Payne, Harvey O. Director of Public Relations, State Bar of Texas. 1968. 25 pp.

1201. Pearson, Drew. Author, columnist. 1969. 27 pp.

1202. Pechman, Joseph A. Executive director, Studies on Government Finance, Brookings Institution (1960-69); consultant, Council of Economic Advisers (1961-68). Contains information on the assassination. 1969. 27 pp.

1203. Pierson, W. DeVier. Special Counsel to the President. 1969. Three interviews: 31, 35, and 13 pp.

1204. Pryor, Richard S. KTBC announcer and TV personality. Contains information on the assassination. 1968. 27 pp.

1205. Quie, Albert H. Republican Congressman from Minnesota. 1969. 32 pp.

1206. Randolph, A. Philip. President, Brotherhood of Sleeping Car Porters; civil rights leader. 1968. 30 pp.

1207. Reedy, George E., Jr. Journalist; member of LBJ's staff (1951-65, 68). Contains information on the assassination. 1968-1984. Sixteen interviews: 135, 42, 68, 40, 34, 64, 41, 134, 75, 32, 51, 59, 38, 70, 35, and 79 pp.

1208. Roberts, Chalmers. Journalist, *Washington Post* (1949-71). 1969. 34 pp.

1209. Robertson, A. Willis. Democratic Senator from Virginia. 1968. 39 pp.

1210. Rowley, James J. Supervising agent, Secret Service (1946-61); director, Secret Service. Contains information on the assassination. 1969. 22 pp.

1211. Russell, Harold J. Chairman, President's Committee on Employment of the Handicapped. 1968. 44 pp.

1212. Saltonstall, Leverett. Republican Senator from Massachusetts (1945-67). 1968. 31 pp.

1213. Schlesinger, Arthur M., Jr. Historian, Special Assistant to the President (1961-64). Contains information on the assassination. 1971. 36 pp.

1214. Schnittker, John A. Undersecretary of Agriculture (1965-69). Contains information on the assassination. 1968. 64 pp.

1215. Skelton, Byron G. Democratic party leader in Texas; judge, U. S. Court of Claims. 1968. 62 pp.

1216. Stennis, John C. Democratic Senator from Mississippi. 1972. 27 pp.

1217. Taylor, Hobert, Jr. Executive vice chairman, President's Commission on Equal Employment Opportunity (1962-65); Special Assistant to the Vice President (1963). 1972. 43 pp.

1218. Taylor, Maxwell D. Military representative to the President (1961-62); chairman, Joint Chiefs of Staff (1962-64). 1981. Four interviews: 22, 26, 42, and 13 pp.

1219. Thomas, Lera. Wife of Democratic Congressman Albert Thomas from Texas. Contains information on the assassination. 1968. 32 pp.

1220. Thompson, Clark Wallace, and Libbie Moody Thompson. Democratic Congressman from Texas. 1968. 35 pp.

1221. Udall, Stewart L. Secretary of the Interior (1961-69). 1969-1972. Five interviews: 43, 40, 43, 21, and 31 pp.

1222. Valenti, Jack. Special Assistant to the President (1963-66). Contains information on the assassination. 1969-1973. Five interviews: 29, 46, 12, 33, and 35 pp.

1223. Warren, Earl. Chief Justice, U.S. Supreme Court (1953-69). Contains information on the assassination. 1971. 36 pp.

1224. Weaver, George L. P. Assistant Secretary of Labor for International Affairs. 1969. 29 pp.

1225. Weaver, Robert C. Administrator of the Housing and Home Finance Agency (1961-66). Contains information on the assassination. 1968. Three interviews: 49, 21, and 12 pp.

1226. Webb, James E. NASA administrator (1961-68). Excellent on the Kennedy space program. 1969. 55 pp.

1227. Weisl, Edwin L. Counsel, House Committee on Space and Astronautics. Contains information on the assassination. 1969. 44 pp.

1228. Welsh, Edward C. Executive secretary, President's Aeronautics and Space

Council (1961-69). 1969. 36 pp.

1229. White, Lee C. Assistant Special Counsel to President Kennedy (1961-63); Associate Counsel to President Johnson (1963-66). Contains information on the assassination. 1970-1971. Five interviews: 31, 33, 44, 20, and 27 pp.

1230. Wilkins, Roy. Executive director, NAACP. 1969. 24 pp.

1231. Wood, Robert C. Undersecretary and Secretary of the Department of Housing and Urban Development (1966-69). 1968. 34 pp.

1232. Woodward, Robert F. Ambassador to Spain; Undersecretary of State for Latin American Affairs. 1968. 37 pp.

1233. Young, Andrew J., Jr. Civil rights activist; administrator, Southern Christian Leadership Conference (1961-64). 1970. 29 pp.

1234. Youngblood, Rufus. Secret Service agent, White House detail. Contains information on the assassination. 1968. 45 pp.

C. ORAL HISTORIES RELATING TO KENNEDY AT THE HARRY S. TRUMAN LIBRARY

Only those oral histories having at least three pages devoted to Kennedy are listed below.

1235. Andrews, Stanley. Administrator, Technical Cooperation Administration (1951-53). 1970. 192 pp.

1236. Babcock, Gaylon. Banker. 1964. 115 pp.

1237. Bell, David E. Administrative Assistant to the President (1951-53). 1968. 212 pp.

1238. Bell, Jack L. Chief of the U.S. Senate staff of the Associated Press (1940-69). 1971. 80 pp.

1239. Biemiller, Andrew J. Congressman from Wisconsin (1945-47 and 1949-51). 1974. 117 pp.

1240. Brandt, Raymond P. Chief, Washington Bureau, *St. Louis Post-Dispatch* (1934-61). 1970. 98 pp.

1241. Brightman, Samuel. Director of publicity, Democratic National Committee (1952-57). 1966. 143 pp.

1242. Bruce, David K. E. Undersecretary of State (1952-53). 1972. 49 pp.

1243. Clifford, Clark M. Special Counsel to the President (1946-50). 1971, 1972, 1973. 483 pp.

1244. Cole, David L. Director, Federal Mediation and Conciliation Service (1952-53). 1972. 103 pp.

1245. Daniel, E. Clifton. Chief, Washington bureau, *New York Times* (1973-77) and son-in-law of Harry S. Truman. 1972. 77 pp.

1246. Davidson, C. Girard. Assistant Secretary of the Interior (1946-50). 1972. 225 pp.

1247. Edwards, India. Vice chairman, Democratic National Committee (1950-56). 1967, 1975. 137 pp.

1248. Edwards, Willard A. Washington correspondent, *Chicago Tribune*. 1988. 67 pp.

1249. Elsey, George M. Administrative Assistant to the President (1949-51); Assistant to the director, Mutual Security Agency (1951-53). 1964, 1965, 1969, 1970. 477 pp.

1250. Ensley, Grover W. Executive director, Joint Economic Committee, U.S. Congress (1949-57). 1977. 91 pp.

1251. Evans, Tom L. Kansas City businessman. 1962, 1963. 771 pp.

1252. Feinberg, Abraham. Business executive and philanthropist; friend of Harry S. Truman, active in the creation of the State of Israel (1945-48). 1973. 68 pp.

1253. Folliard, Edward T. White House correspondent, *Washington Post* (1943-54). 1970. 80 pp.

1254. Friedman, Monroe. Chairman, Alameda County (Calif.) Democratic Central Committee (1948). 1970. 55 pp.

1255. Gilpatric, Roswell L. Undersecretary of the Air Force (1951-53). 1972. 48 pp.

1256. Jessee, Randall S. Kansas City friend of Harry S. Truman. 1975. 53 pp.

1257. Jones, Marvin. Chief judge, U.S. Court of Claims (1947-64). 1970. 397 pp.

1258. Judd, Walter H. Republican Congressman from Minnesota (1943-62). 1970, 1976. 123 pp.

1259. Keyserling, Leon H. Chairman, Council of Economic Advisers (1950-53). 1971. 208 pp.

1260. Loeb, James I. National director, Americans for Democratic Action (1947-51). 1970. 232 pp.

1261. MacDonald, Donald J. Naval officer; commander of the presidential yacht, USS *Williamsburg* (1948-51). 1970. 78 pp.

1262. McEnery, John P. Vice chairman, California State Democratic Central Committee (1946-48). 1970. 273 pp.

1263. McGowan, Carl. Member of the staff of Illinois Governor Adlai E. Stevenson (1949-53). 1970. 89 pp.

1264. McKim, Edward D. Chief Administrative Assistant to the President (1945). 1964. 177 pp.

1265. Mann, Thomas C. Deputy Assistant Secretary of State for Inter-American Affairs (1950-51). 1974. 99 pp.

1266. Morison, H. Graham. Assistant Attorney General, Antitrust Division, Department of Justice (1950-52). 1972. 451 pp.

1267. Murphy, Charles S. Special Counsel to the President (1950-53). 1963, 1969, 1970. 549 pp.

1268. Nixon, Robert G. Washington correspondent, International News Service (1944-58). 1970. 1057 pp.

1269. Porter, James Woodrow. Reporter, *Kansas City Star* (1944-73). Interview conducted by the William Jewell College Oral History Project. 1975. 42 pp.

1270. Reinsch, J. Leonard. White House radio adviser (1945-52). 1967. 147 pp.

1271. Rigdon, William M. Assistant naval aide to the President (1942-53). 1970. 65 pp.

1272. Riggs, Robert L. Chief, Washington bureau, *Louisville Courier-Journal* (1942-67). 1971. 50 pp.

1273. Salant, Walter S. Economist, Council of Economic Advisers (1946-52). 1970. 98 pp.

1274. Service, John Stewart. Foreign Service officer. Interview conducted by the Regional Oral History Office, University of California, Berkeley. 1977. 522 pp.

1275. Slater, Harold M. City editor, *St. Joseph News-Press* (1927-79). 1982. 74 pp.

1276. Steelman, John R. Assistant to the President (1946-53). 1963. 65 pp.

1277. Strout, Richard L. Reporter, Washington bureau, *Christian Science Monitor* (1925-84). 1971. 69 pp.

1278. Symington, Stuart. Democratic Senator from Missouri. 1981. 86 pp.

1279. Tames, George. Photographer for the *New York Times* (1945-85). 1980, 1988. 73 pp.

1280. Tannenwald, Theodore, Jr. Assistant director and chief of staff to the director, Mutual Security Agency (1951-53). 1969. 84 pp.

1281. Trohan, Walter. Chief, Washington bureau of the *Chicago Tribune* (1949-69). 1970. 129 pp.

1282. Truman White House: Joint interview with Charles S. Murphy, Special Counsel to the President (1950-53); Richard E. Neustadt, Special Assistant in the White House Office (1950-53); David H. Stowe, Administrative Assistant to the President (1949-53); and James E. Webb, Director of the Bureau of the Budget (1946-49). Interview conducted by the National Academy of Public Administration. 1980. 104 pp.

1283. Vaughan, Harry H. Military aide to President Truman (1945-53). 1963, 1976. 157 pp.

1284. Walsh, Robert K. Reporter, *Washington Evening Star* (1946-69). 1970. 208 pp.

1285. Wilcox, Francis O. Chief of staff, U.S. Senate Foreign Relations Committee (1947-55). Interview conducted by the U.S. Senate Historical Office. 1984. 240 pp.

D. ORAL HISTORIES RELATING TO KENNEDY IN THE COLUMBIA ORAL HISTORY COLLECTION

1286. The published guide is *The Oral History Collection of Columbia University*, edited by Elizabeth B. Mason and Louis M. Starr. New York Research Office, 1979. It is incomplete on Kennedy-related oral histories. The Oral History Research Office has an in-house comprehensive master list containing Kennedy references, however. Information on individual interviews can be obtained from the on-line catalog on RLIN (Research Libraries Information Network). Only oral histories having at least three pages devoted to JFK are listed below.

1287. Abel, Elie. Journalist. 1970. 45 pp.

1288. Alcorn, Hugh Meade, Jr. Lawyer and Republican politician. 1967. 159 pp.

1289. Alsop, Joseph Wright. Journalist. In Eisenhower Administration Project. 1972. 19 pp.

1290. Anderson, Dillon. Lawyer. 1969. 130 pp.

1291. Annis, Edward Roland. President of the AMA (1963-64). 1967. 84 pp.

1292. Arvey, Jacob M. Politician. In Adlai Stevenson Project. 1967. 59 pp.

1293. Attwood, Simone. Wife of Ambassador-publisher William Attwood. 1975. 136 pp.

1294. Attwood, William. Publisher and ambassador. In Adlai Stevenson Project. 1967. 33 pp.

1295. Bacall, Lauren. Actress. In Adlai Stevenson Project. 1968. 76 pp.

1296. Badeau, John. Ambassador to Egypt (1961-64). 1979. 461 pp.

1297. Baldwin, Roger. Head of the American Civil Liberties Union. 1975. 106 pp.

1298. Ball, Robert M. Government official. In Social Security Project. Permission required. 1968. 84 pp.

1299. Barco, James William. Diplomat. 1963. 1061 pp.

1300. Beale, Betty. Newspaper columnist. In Adlai Stevenson Project. 1969. 36 pp.

1301. Bedini, Silvio. Museum curator. 1982. 391 pp.

1302. Bell, Jack L. Journalist. In Eisenhower Administration Project. 1972. 31 pp.

1303. Benjamin, Robert S. Lawyer and film executive. In Adlai Stevenson Project. 1968. 39 pp.

1304. Benton, William. Democratic Senator from Connecticut. 1968. 213 pp.

1305. _____. In Adlai Stevenson Project. 40 pp.

1306. Bergland, Robert. Farm policy expert. 1982. 635 pp.

1307. Berman, Howard. In Allard Lowenstein Project. 1990. Closed. 33 pp.

1308. Berrigan, Philip. Peace activist. 1985. 232 pp.

1309. Biemiller, Andrew John. Lobbyist. In Social Security Project. 1966. 49 pp.

1310. Bingham, Barry. Editor. 1969. 117 pp.

1311. Blair, William McCormick, Jr. Adlai Stevenson adviser. 1969. Permission required. 94 pp.

1312. Blough, Roger M. Chairman, U.S. Steel (1942-69). 1975. 316 pp.

1313. Bolster, Archie. U.S. diplomat in Iran. 1988. 244 pp.

1314. Bowles, Chester. Diplomat, Government official. 1963. 866 pp.

1315. Bray, Howard. Assisted Democratic Senator Clinton Anderson. In Social Security Project. 1966. 112 pp.

1316. Briggs, Ellis O. Ambassador to Greece (1959-61). 1972. 139 pp.

1317. Browning, Gordon. Tennessee political leader. 1965. 144 pp.

1318. Bush, Prescott. Senator from Connecticut. 1966. 454 pp.

1319. Cabot, Paul Codman. Financier, investment banker. 1980. 206 pp.

1320. Campbell, Loraine L. Lobbyist. In Women's History and Population Issues Project. 1974. 93 pp.

1321. Carlton, Winslow. In Social Security Project. No date. 55 pp.

1322. Carstenson, Blue. Executive director, National Council of Senior Citizens (1961-65). 1966. 227 pp.

1323. Chatelain, Nicolas. U.S. correspondent for *Le Figaro*. 1961. 55 pp.

1324. Cherne, Leo. Economist and political analyst. 1961. Closed until death. 590 pp.

1325. Clark, Joseph James. Naval officer. 1962. Permission required. 840 pp.

1326. Clark, Kenneth Bancroft. Black psychologist and educator. 1976. Closed. 407 pp.

1327. Clay, Lucius D. Army general and JFK's personal representative in Berlin. 1971. 1101 pp.

1328. Clayton, William Lochhart. Government official. 1962. 235 pp.

1329. Cochran, Jacqueline. Aviator and executive. In Eisenhower Administration Project. 1973. 257 pp.

1330. Cohen, Wilbur J. Assistant Secretary, Health, Education, and Welfare (1961-68). 1974. 191 pp.

1331. Cook, Charles D. Eisenhower diplomat. 1964. Permission required. 658 pp.

1332. Cott, Ted. Radio and television executive. 1961. 297 pp.

1333. Craig, William. In Lowenstein Project. 1988. 50 pp.

1334. Cruikshank, Nelson Hale. Labor economist. 1967. 506 pp.

1335. Daly, Charles U. Government official. In Social Security Project. 1967. 27 pp.

1336. Davidson, Ben. New York State politician. 1978. 857 pp.

1337. Davies, Richard T. Diplomat, Soviet expert. 1980. 514 pp.

1338. Dent, Albert W. In United Negro College Fund Project. 1980, 1981. Two interviews: 92, 26 pp.

1339. Dick, Jane W. Adlai Stevenson friend. 1969. 102 pp.

1340. Dillon, C. Douglas. JFK's Secretary of the Treasury. 1972. 94 pp.

1341. Donahue, Richard. Kennedy's congressional liaison staff. In Social Security Project. Closed until death. 1967. 74 pp.

1342. Donovan, Robert. Journalist. 1968. 51 pp.

1343. Drew, Robert. Documentary filmmaker. 1980. 431 pp.

1344. Drummond, Roscoe. Columnist. 1967. 32 pp.

1345. Edelman, John W. Labor representative. 1957. 247 pp.

1346. Eisenhower, Dwight David. Army officer and president. 1967. 114 pp.

1347. Eisenhower, Milton S. Government official. 1967. 115 pp.

1348. Eliot, Theodore L. U.S. diplomat in Iran. 1986. 88 pp.

1349. Elman, Philip. Member, Federal Trade Commission. 1984. 405 pp.

1350. Esselstyn, Caldwell. Physician. In Social Security Project. 1966. 43 pp.

1351. Evans, Carol. Secretary to Adlai Stevenson. In Adlai Stevenson Project. 1971. 46 pp.

1352. Evans, Luther Harris. Educator and librarian. 1965. 844 pp.

1353. Fair, Clinton. In Social Security Project. Closed until death. 1965. 75 pp.

1354. Feldman, Justin N. New York City Democratic politician. 1968. Closed until death. 330 pp.

1355. Fenwick, Millicent. Civil rights activist. 1981. 546 pp.

1356. Field, Ruth. A close friend of Stevenson. In Adlai Stevenson Project. 1967. Permission required. 26 pp.

1357. Finch, Robert. Republican leader. 1967. Permission required. 69 pp.

1358. Folsom, Marion Bayard. Social Security. 1965. 207 pp.

1359. Foner, Moe. Labor union organizer. 1986. 836 pp.

1360. Forand, Aime Joseph. Legislator. In Social Security Project. 1965. 77 pp.

1361. Fritchey, Clayton. Columnist. In Adlai Stevenson Project. 1968. 27 pp.

1362. Gates, Thomas S., Jr. Member, Eisenhower administration. 1967. 59 pp.

1363. Gibbons, Katherine Clark. In Adlai Stevenson Project. 1969. Permission required. 73 pp.

1364. Goin, Lauren J. Office of Public Safety. 1990. 33 pp.

1365. Gore, Albert A. Senator from Tennessee. 1976. 103 pp.

1366. Granger, Lester B. Civil rights activist. 1960. 326 pp.

1367. Gray, Gordon. Government official. 1967. Permission required. 338 pp.

1368. Guinzburg, Thomas H. Publisher. 1980. 612 pp.

1369. Hagerty, James C. Journalist and Eisenhower's press secretary. 1968. Permission required. 569 pp.

1370. Harr, Karl. Eisenhower Administration official. 1967. Permission required. 41 pp.

1371. Harriman, W. Averell. Government official, presidential adviser (1943-69). 1969. Permission required. 353 pp.

1372. Harrington, Donald. Minister and political activist. 1977. Permission required. 319 pp.

1373. Heckscher, August. New York City official and journalist. 1978. 78 pp.

1374. Henry, Emil William. Lawyer. In Federal Communications Commission Project. 1978. 53 pp.

1375. Henry, Ray. Social Security advocate. 1966. Closed until death. 135 pp.

1376. Higgins, Juanda. In Adlai Stevenson Project. 1966. Partly closed until 2017. 41 pp.

1377. Hightower, John M. Newspaperman. 1968. 41 pp.

1378. Hilsman, Roger. Assistant Secretary for Far Eastern Affairs (1963-64). 1981. 152 pp.

1379. Hockwalt, Fredreick G. Catholic priest. 1962. 47 pp.

1380. Hodges, Luther Hartwell. Secretary of Commerce (1961-65). 1968. 39 pp.

1381. Hoegh, Leo Arthur. Iowa Republican leader and director of Civil and Defense Mobilization (1958-61). 1968. 95 pp.

1382. Houghton, Amory. Diplomat. 1968. Permission required. 96 pp.

1383. Hutton, William R. Public relations, Social Security. 1966. 113 pp.

1384. Ianni, Francis A. J. Educator. 1967. 66 pp.

1385. Irwin, Leo. Lawyer and judge. In Social Security Project. 1966. 76 pp.

1386. Ives, Elizabeth Stevenson. Sister of Adlai Stevenson. 1969. 309 pp.

1387. John F. Kennedy Project. Interviews with friends and associates of JFK, conducted during the preparation of Herbert Parmet's biography. 1976. 443 pp.

1388. Johnson, Walter. Historian and Adlai Stevenson adviser. 1976. 191 pp.

1389. Jones, Roger. Government official. 1967. 73 pp.

1390. Judd, Walter H. Congressman from Minnesota. 1970. 149 pp.

1391. Kaul, Brij Mohan. Chief of the General Staff, Indian Army (1961-62). 1964. Permission required. 445 pp.

1392. Kazan, Abraham. Labor leader. 1968. 554 pp.

1393. Keating, Sean. Government official. 1974. 67 pp.

1394. Kellerman, Henry Joseph. Government official. In Eisenhower Administration Project. 1971. 23 pp.

1395. Keyserling, Leon H. Democratic economist. 1969. 65 pp.

1396. Killian, James R., Jr. Scientist. 1970. 375 pp.

1397. Kimball, Arthur A. Government official. 1967. 104 pp.

1398. Kimball, Lindsley Fiske. In United Negro College Fund Project. 1980. 78 pp.

1399. Knowland, William F. Republican Senator from California. 1970. 170 pp.

1400. Kristeller, Paul Oskar. Professor at Columbia University. 1981. Closed until death of interviewee. 1080 pp.

1401. Kunzig, Robert Lowe. Judge. In Eisenhower Administration Project. 1972. 40 pp.

1402. Kuralt, Charles. Journalist. 1989. 31 pp.

1403. Lahey, Edwin A. Columnist. 1959. 161 pp.

1404. Landis, James McCauley. Intimate Kennedy family associate. 1964. 685 pp.

1405. Lasker, Mary. Philanthropist. 1965. Closed until five years after death. 1157 pp.

1406. Lazarus, Fred, Jr. Merchandising executive. 1965. Permission required. 1039 pp.

1407. Lesser, Allen. Government official. In Social Security Project. 1966. 46 pp.

1408. Lewis, Mort. Author. 1970. Permission required. 110 pp.

1409. Lowry, W. McNeil. Vice president, humanities and the arts, Ford Foundation. 1967. Permission required. 297 pp.

1410. Luce, Clare Boothe. Government official. 1968. 108 pp.

1411. Lundahl, Arthur C. Head of National Photographic Interpretation Center during Cuban Missile Crisis. 1981. 499 pp.

1412. Lyons, Eugene J. Government official. In Eisenhower Administration Project. 1976. 90 pp.

1413. McCabe, Edward Aeneas. Eisenhower administration official. 1967. 171 pp.

1414. McDougal, Katherine. In Adlai Stevenson Project. 1967. 42 pp.

1415. McGowan, Carl. Judge. 1969. 252 pp.

1416. Manatos, Michael N. Congressional liasion staff. In Social Security Project. 1967. 41 pp.

1417. Mann, Thomas Clifton. Ambassador to Mexico (1961-63). 1968. Permission required. 1968.

1418. Matthews, Thomas Stanley. Editor, *Time*. 1959. 136 pp.

1419. Mayo, Leonard W. Educator. In Association for the Aid of Crippled Children Project. 1972. 71 pp.

1420. Merriam, Robert Edward. Business executive. 1969. 209 pp.

1421. Meyer, Armin Henry. Member of Kennedy Task Force on Iran. 1985. 57 pp.

1422. Mickelson, Sig. Journalist and broadcasting executive. 1961. 122 pp.

1423. Midgley, Lester. Journalist covering the assassination. 1988. 293 pp.

1424. Miklos, Jack C. U.S. diplomat in Iran. 1986. 248 pp.

1425. Minow, Newton N. Chairman of the Federal Communications Commission (1961-63). 1969. 122 pp.

1426. Mitchell, Clarence Maurice. Civil rights activist. 1981. 72 pp.

1427. Mitchell, Stephen Arnold. National leader, Democratic party. 1967. Permission required. 173 pp.

1428. Monroney, Almer Stillwell Mike. Senator from Oklahoma. 1969. Permission required. 128 pp.

1429. _____. In Adlai Stevenson Project. 1969. 50 pp.

1430. Moon, Henry Lee. African American journalist. 1980. Closed. 559 pp.

1431. Motley, Constance Baker. Civil rights leader. 1978. 801 pp.

1432. Myers, Robert Julius. Actuary, Social Security program. 1967. 94 pp.

1433. Nelson, Richard. Executive. In Adlai Stevenson Project. 1969. 79 pp.

1434. Nestingen, Ivan Arnold. Government official. 1965. 109 pp.

1435. Neustadt, Richard Elliott. Adviser to JFK. 1961. Permission required. 77 pp.

1436. Novak, Robert. Journalist. In Social Security Project. 1966. Closed. 46 pp.

1437. O'Brien, James C. Social Security. 1966. 220 pp.

1438. Odell, Charles. Social Security. 1966. 117 pp.

1439. O'Donnell, Kenneth P. Appointment Secretary to JFK; politician. In Social Security Project. 1966. 40 pp.

1440. Paepcke, Elizabeth. In Adlai Stevenson Project. 1967. Closed until 2027. 46 pp.

1441. Parton, James. Editor, publisher. 1959. 24 pp.

1442. Patterson, Bradley H., Jr. Government official. In Eisenhower Administration Project. 1968. 65 pp.

1443. Patterson, Frederick Douglass. In United Negro College Fund Project. 1980, 1981. Two interviews: 94, 46 pp.

1444. Pennebaker, D. A. Documentary filmmaker. 1981. 777 pp.

1445. Peterson, Esther. Assistant Secretary of Labor (1961-58). 1983. 321 pp.

1446. Plimpton, Francis Taylor Pearsons. A longtime friend of Stevenson. In Adlai Stevenson Project. 1967. 74 pp.

1447. Poletti, Charles. Lawyer and politician. 1978. 677 pp.

1448. Pollack, Jerome. In Social Security Project. 1966. 47 pp.

1449. Potofsky, Jacob Samuel. Union official. 1965. 833 pp.

1450. Powledge, Fred. Journalist covering the assassination. 1987. 94 pp.

1451. Price, Hollis. In United Negro College Fund Project. 1981. 110 pp.

1452. Rabb, Maxwell M. Government official. 1970. 38 pp.

1453. Ramey, Estelle. Endocrinologist and women's rights activist. 1980. 98 pp.

1454. Rawalt, Marguerite. Women's rights advocate. 1980. 1097 pp.

1455. Reidy, William. Health insurance adviser. Social Security. 1966. 101 pp.

1456. Reston, James. In Journalism Lectures. 46 pp.

1457. Reynolds, William A. Administrative assistant. In Social Security Project. 1967. 61 pp.

1458. Rice, Edward E. State Department official. In Eisenhower Administration Project. 1972. 73 pp.

1459. Roberts, Charles Wesley. Journalist. In Eisenhower Administration Project. 1972. Permission required. 35 pp.

1460. Roberts, Clifford. Business executive. 1972. Closed until 1997. 878 pp.

1461. Roosa, Robert V. Economist. In Eisenhower Administration Project. 1972. 153 pp.

1462. Rovere, Richard Halworth. Writer and editor. 1968. 44 pp.

1463. Saltonstall, Leverett. Republican Senator from Massachusetts. 1967. 151 pp.

1464. Samuels, Cynthia. Journalist. In Allard Lowenstein Oral History Project. 1990. 38 pp.

1465. Sanford, Terry. Governor of North Carolina (1961-65). 1976. 173 pp.

1466. Saunders, Harold. In Iranian-American Relations Oral History Project. 1987. 153 pp.

1467. Scherer, Raymond Lewis. Journalist. 1968. 54 pp.

1468. Schlesinger, Arthur, Jr. Historian and Kennedy aide. In Adlai Stevenson Project. 1967. 43 pp.

1469. Schorr, Lisbeth Bamberger. Active in Social Security program. 1967. 105 pp.

1470. Schultz, John C. Film editor. 1980. 88 pp.

1471. Schulz, Robert L. Military aide to Eisenhower. 1968. 293 pp.

1472. Seigenthaler, John Lawrence. Newspaper editor and administrative assistant to Attorney General Robert Kennedy. 1974. 121 pp.

1473. Sevareid, Eric. Journalist. In Adlai Stevenson Project. 1967. 47 pp.

1474. Sharon, John. Adlai Stevenson associate. 1969. 149 pp.

1475. Sheldon, James. State government official. 1972. 186 pp.

1476. Shepley, James Robinson. Journalist. 1967. 39 pp.

1477. Sheppard, Harold. Government executive. In Social Security Project. 1967. 104 pp.

1478. Shikler, Aaron. Painter. 1977. 160 pp.

1479. Shor, Bernard ("Toots"). Restaurateur. 1975. 216 pp.

1480. Siciliano, Rocco. Government official. In Eisenhower Administration Project. 1968. 91 pp.

1481. Singer, Arthur. Carnegie Corporation official. 1969. Permission required. 138 pp.

1482. Smith, Blackwell. Expert on Third World economic development. 1987. 140 pp.

1483. Smith, Howard K. Journalist. 1968. 44 pp.

1484. Smylie, Robert E. Republican governor of Idaho. In Eisenhower Administration Project. 1975. 72 pp.

1485. Snyder, Murray. Eisenhower administration official. 1967. 66 pp.

1486. Somers, Herman Miles. Economist involved with Social Security. 1968. 199 pp.

1487. Sonosky, Jerome N. Assistant to the Assistant Secretary of Health, Education, and Welfare. 1974. 82 pp.

1488. _____. In Abraham Ribicoff Staff Oral History Project. 1989. 117 pp.

1489. Spector, Sidney. In Social Security Project. 1966. 57 pp.

1490. Spingarn, Arthur B. An NAACP founder. 1966. 101 pp.

1491. Sprague, Mansfield Daniel. Eisenhower administration official. 1968. 57 pp.

1492. Staats, Elmer Boyd. Eisenhower administration official. 1967. 59 pp.

1493. Steffen-Fluhr, Nancy. In Allard Lowenstein Project. 1988. Closed. 69 pp.

1494. Stetler, C. Joseph. Pharmacutical executive. In Social Security Project. 1967. 58 pp.

1495. Stevenson, Adlai III. Stevenson's oldest son. In Adlai Stevenson Project. 1967. 75 pp.

1496. Stevenson, John Fell. Stevenson's youngest son. In Adlai Stevenson Project. 1966. Permission required. 28 pp.

1497. Storey, Robert Gerald. Lawyer. In Eisenhower Administration Project. 1971. 65 pp.

1498. Straus, Roger W. Publisher. 1979. 1173 pp.

1499. Summerfield, Arthur. Government official. In Eisenhower Administration Project. 1970. Permission required. 93 pp.

1500. Talmadge, Herman Eugene. Democratic Senator from Georgia. 1975. 132 pp.

1501. Tally, Joseph. Stevenson political supporter. In Adlai Stevenson Project. 1966. 13 pp.

1502. Tatum, Wilbert. Newspaper publisher. 1987. 80 pp.

1503. Teller, Ludwig. New York politician. 1962. 571 pp.

1504. Thomas, Evan Welling II. Editor and publisher who worked on *Profiles in Courage* and other Kennedy books. 1974. 313 pp.

1505. Thompson, Frank, Jr. Congressman from New Jersey. 1967. Permission required. 138 pp.

1506. Tree, Marietta. Adlai Stevenson associate, diplomatic representative. 1967. 161 pp.

1507. Trent, William. Executive Director, United Negro College Fund Oral History Project. 1980. 125 pp.

1508. Twining, Nathan Farragut. Air Force officer. 1967. 250 pp.

1509. Vanden Heuvel, William. Diplomat. 1982. 30 pp.

1510. Wagner, Robert F. Mayor of New York City (1954-65). 1979. Permission required. 1263 pp.

1511. Ware, Caroline. In Women in the Federal Government Project. 1982. 160 pp.

1512. Warne, Colston Estey. Economist, consumer adviser. 1981. 801 pp.

1513. Weber, Palmer. Civil rights activist. 1985. 368 pp.

1514. Weeks, Edward. Editor, *Atlantic Monthly*. 1981. 31 pp.

1515. Wheaton, Anne W. Eisenhower administration official. 1968. 178 pp.

1516. Wickenden, Elizabeth. Consultant on health insurance. 1966. 211 pp.

1517. Willcox, Alanson. Lawyer active with Social Security. 1966. 140 pp.

1518. Williams, Murat Willis. Alliance for Progress. 1979. 40 pp.

1519. Williamson, Kenneth. Adviser on Social Security. 1967. 240 pp.

1520. Wirtz, William Willard. Kennedy's Secretary of Labor. In Adlai Stevenson Project. 1969. 87 pp.

1521. Wolkstein, Irwin. Assistant chief, Coverage and Disability Branch, Social Security. 1968. 255 pp.

1522. Wood, Lee B. Executive editor, *New York World-Telegram*. 1980. 85 pp.

1523. Wright, Stephen J. In United Negro College Fund Project. 1981. 122 pp.

1524. Wyatt, Wilson Watkins. Adlai Stevenson associate. 1969. 161 pp.

3
Writings of John F. Kennedy

Many of Kennedy's books and articles involved the research and writing of others. For example, Professor Jules Davids of Georgetown University and Theodore C. Sorensen, Kennedy's senatorial administrative assistant, did most of the work on *Profiles in Courage*. The compilation below excludes JFK's published speeches and newspaper articles.

1525. Kennedy, John F. "Ahead of the Game." *Field and Stream* 65 (January 1961): 6. President-elect Kennedy expresses a concern over pollution of recreational areas.

1526. _____. "The Algerian Crisis: A New Phase?" *America* 98 (October 5, 1957): 15-7.

1527. _____. *As We Remember Joe.* Privately printed by the University Press, Inc., Cambridge, Ma. A memorial honoring JFK's brother, Joe Jr., who died in World War II.

1528. _____. "Brothers, I Presume?" *Vogue* 127 (April 1, 1956): 117, 142-44. Kennedy writes of the parallels between literature and politics.

1529. _____. "The Challenge of Political Courage." *New York Times Magazine* (December 18, 1955). pp. 13, 32, 34, 36. Based on *Profiles in Courage*, this article discusses the importance of political courage.

1530. _____. "Citizenship and Politics." *Kiwanis Magazine* 58 (February 1958): 11. Senator Kennedy hopes negative attitudes toward politicians changes.

1531. _____. "Congress: How It Works toward a More Organized Defense Effort." *General Electric Defense Quarterly* 2 (January/March 1959): 19-21. There are five ways in which Congress exercises its constitutional control over defense policies.

1532. _____. "Congressional Lobbies: A Chronic Problem Re-examined."

Georgetown Law Journal 54 (Summer 1957): 535-67. Senator Kennedy advocates passage of the Legislative Activities Disclosure Act to alleviate some of the problems of the 1946 Lobbying Act.

1533. _____. "Creative America: The Arts in America." *Look* 26 (December 1962): 104-10. Based on Kennedy's essay in the book, *Creative America*, he argues that both Lincoln and Franklin Roosevelt understood that the life of the arts is very close to the center of a nation's purpose.

1534. _____. "The Crisis in Foreign Affairs." *AFL-CIO American Federationist* 67 (November 1960): 7-11. Concentrates on six crisis areas: Cuba, Ghana, Japan, Laos, Poland, and India.

1535. _____. "A Day I'll Remember." *Look* 24 (September 13, 1960): 51-4. Covers Kennedy's nomination.

1536. _____. "A Democrat Looks at Foreign Policy." *Foreign Affairs* 36 (October 1957): 44-59. The United States foreign policy must reflect the changes in the world since World War II.

1537. _____. "A Democrat Says Party Must Lead--Or Get Left." *Life* 42 (March 11, 1957): 164-66, 171-79. Senator Kennedy presents guidelines to ensure party victory in 1960.

1538. _____. "Disamament Can Be Won." *Bulletin of the Atomic Scientists* 16 (June 1960): 217-19. The United States must adopt positive proposals.

1539. _____. "The Education of an American Politician." *National Parent Teacher* 51 (May 1957): 10-12. The popular image of the political profession needs to be improved.

1540. _____. "Ellsworth, Oliver." *Encyclopedia Britannica*. Vol. 8. Chicago: William Benton, Publisher, 1959. One of Connecticut's delegates to the Constitutional Convention.

1541. _____. "Every Citizen Holds Office." *NEA Journal* 50 (October 1961): 18-20. On the importance of every American's participation in government.

1542. _____. "The Fate of the Nation." *NEA Journal* 47 (January 1958): 10-11. Focuses on the need to improve public education.

1543. _____. "Floor Beneath Wages Is Gone." *New Republic* 128 (July 20, 1953): 14-15. Kennedy advocates the strengthening of the Walsh-Healey Act.

1544. _____. "Foreign Policy Is the People's Business." *New York Times Magazine* (August 8, 1954), pp. 5, 28, 30, 32. Only by joining informed public opinion to firm leadership can we dispel the myths that befog our policies.

1545. _____. "General Gavin Sounds the Alarm." *Reporter* 19 (October 30, 1958): 35-6. A favorable review of Gavin's *War and Peace in the Space Age.*

1546. _____. "A Great Day in American History." *Colliers* 136 (November 25, 1955): 40-2, 44, 46. Kennedy writes of Daniel Webster's unpopular decision to support the Clay Compromise.

1547. _____. "How Should Cadets Be Picked?" *New York Times Magazine* (August 19, 1951), pp. 16, 44-5. Kennedy proposes reforms of the selection process.

1548. _____. "If India Falls" *Progressive* 22 (January 1958): 8-11. Concerned that India's Second Five-Year Plan might fail, Senator Kennedy urges possible legislation to assist this financially strapped nation.

1549. _____. "If the Soviets Control Space--They Can Control Earth." *Missiles and Rockets* 7 (October 10, 1960): 12-3, 50. Kennedy calls for national recognition of the strategic space race with Russia, reorganization of U.S. defenses, and immediate acceleration of ICBM programs.

1550. _____. "If the World Knows Us Better." *New York Times Book Review* (February 8, 1959), pp. 1, 22. Kennedy takes issue with Arthur Larson's book, *What We Are For,* on whether our real concern should be the image the U.S. projects abroad.

1551. _____. "Labor Racketeers and Political Pressure." *Look* 23 (May 12, 1959): 17-21. Labor racketeers, and the political pressure they exert, is the reason for pending legislation.

1552. _____. "Let's Get Rid of College Loyalty Oaths!" *Coronet* 47 (April 1960): 88-94. Kennedy proposed legislation to repeal such oaths.

1553. _____. *A Nation of Immigrants.* New York: Harper and Row, 1964. Brief history of immigration and immigration policy in America.

1554. _____. "New England and the South." *Atlantic Monthly* 193 (January 1954): 32-6. Kennedy's concerns regarding industry migration to the South.

1555. _____. "The New Frontier." *Recreation* 53 (December 1960): 459. Resource conservation is our New Frontier.

1556. _____. "The Next Twenty-Five Years." *Look* 26 (January 16, 1962): 17. On the eve of *Look*'s twenty-fifth anniversary, JFK expressed the hope that in the next twenty-five years world peace would be achieved and unemployment and illness would be greatly reduced in America.

1557. _____. "Physical Fitness: A Report of Progress." *Look* 27 (August 13, 1963): 82-3. Kennedy is concerned about our nation's youth because of a perceived correlation between physical fitness and a nation's strength.

1558. _____. "President-elect Kennedy Talks about Our Children." *Parents' Magazine* 36 (January 1961): 35. More attention must be given to children.

1559. _____. *Profiles in Courage*. New York: Harper and Row, 1956. An anthology of political statesmen from Daniel Webster to Robert Taft who put aside personal, political concerns for the national interest; this book won the Pulitzer Prize for biography.

1560. _____. A Review of *Al Smith and His America* by Oscar Handlin. *Washington Post* (March 30, 1958), p. E6. As an emerging presidential candidate, Kennedy curiously avoided mentioning Smith's Catholicism and its impact on the 1928 campaign but praised Smith for his "unusual capacity to face and absorb facts and to mobilize talents from the professions," a trait others thought a Kennedy strength.

1561. _____. A Review of *Deterrent or Defense* by B. H. Lindell Hart. *Saturday Review* 43 (September 3, 1960): 17-18. A favorable review of Hart's book advocating the use of conventional forces to combat the threat of communism.

1562. _____. A Review of *Senator Joe McCarthy* by Richard Rovere. *Washington Post* (June 28, 1959), p. E6. In his brief evaluation of Rovere's scathing critique of McCarthy, Kennedy stayed clear of his own personal position on McCarthy while praising Rovere for combining "sympathy with condemnation."

1563. _____. "Ross of Kansas." *Harper's Magazine* 211 (December 1955): 40-4. Kennedy profiles the courage of Senator Edmund G.Ross.

1564. _____. "Search for the Five Greatest Senators." *New York Times Magazine* (April 14, 1957). pp. 14-6, 18-9. Kennedy chairs Senate committee to select the five top Senators.

1565. _____. "Senator Kennedy's Resolution." *Nation* 185 (July 20, 1957): 21.

1566. _____. "The Shame of the States." *New York Times Magazine* (May 18, 1958), pp. 12, 37-8, 40. Advocates fair representation for cities in the state legislatures is crucial.

1567. _____. "Social Security: Constructive if not Bold." *New Republic* 130 (February 8, 1954): 14-15. Eisenhower's proposed reforms do not go far enough.

1568. _____. "Speaking of Living." *Living for Young Homemakers* 78 (August 1957): 31, 92. At age 40, Kennedy discusses the role young people should play in government.

1569. _____. "Special Statement Prepared for the NEA Journal." *National Education Association Journal* 49 (October 1960): 10. Kennedy claims that education is in a crisis.

1570. _____. "The Spirit of One Man's Independence." *Reader's Digest* 73 (July 1958): 104-06. Kennedy writes of the courage of John Adams on the 132nd anniversary of his death.

1571. _____. "Sport on the New Frontier: The Soft American." *Sports Illustrated* 13 (December 26, 1960-January 2, 1961): 14-17. The president-elect bemoans the decline of fitness in America.

1572. _____. "The Strength and Style of Our Navy Tradition." *Life* 51 (August 10, 1962): 79, 83-6. Centers on Franklin Roosevelt's collection of naval art.

1573. _____. "Take the Academics Out of Politics." *Saturday Evening Post* 228 (June 2, 1956): 36-7, 46, 49-50. Kennedy argues that congressmen place too much emphasis on academics when nominating students to military academies.

1574. _____. "Three Women of Courage." *McCall's* 85 (January 1958): 36-7, 54-5. Anne Hutchinson, Jeanette Rankin, and Prudence Crandell.

1575. _____. "To Keep the Lobbyist within Bounds." *New York Times Magazine* (February 19, 1956), pp. 11, 40, 42, 44, 47. On the weaknesses of the 1946 lobbying law.

1576. _____. "Vigor We Need." *Sports Illustrated* 17 (July 16, 1962): 12-14. The physical unfitness of young Americans represents a national problem; Kennedy looks to the President's Council on Youth Fitness for assistance.

1577. _____. "The Voters' Choice in the Bay State." *New York Review of Books* 47 (September 20, 1959): 31. A favorable review of *Massachusetts People and Politics, 1919-1933* by J. Joseph Huthmacker, which deals with the evolution of the modern Democratic coalition in Massachusetts.

1578. _____. "We Must Climb to the Hilltop." *Life* 49 (August 22, 1960): 70-2, 76-7. The need for Americans to think in an idealistic way about America's future.

1579. _____. "What Business Can Do for America." *Nation's Business* 51 (September 1963): 29-31, 60. Includes an appeal for equal opportunity and his attempt to sell his tax cut proposal to business.

1580. _____. "What Should the United States Do in Indochina?" *Foreign Policy Bulletin* 33 (May 15, 1954): 4, 6. Kennedy favors supporting the Associated States of Indochina.

1581. _____. "What's the Matter with New England?" *New York Times Magazine* (November 8, 1953), pp. 12, 28, 30, 32. Kennedy proposes a forty-point plan to assist the region.

1582. _____. "What's Wrong with Social Security." *American Magazine* 156 (October 1953): 19, 109-12. Kennedy suggests reforms to correct inequities in the law.

1583. _____. "When the Executive Fails to Lead." *Reporter* 19 (September 1958): 14-17. The chief executive must display leadership in the area of foreign policy.

1584. _____. "Where We Stand." *Look* 27 (January 13, 1963): 18, 20. Communism is threatening the free world, and so we must not relax our efforts.

1585. _____. *Why England Slept.* New York: Wilfred Funk, 1940. Kennedy's Harvard senior thesis, polished by Arthur Krock and others, was a timely focus on the inherent handicaps of a democracy to mobilize society against a totalitarian danger.

1586. _____. "Why Go Into Politics." In *Politics U.S.A.: A Practical Guide of Public Office.* Edited by James M. Cannon. Garden City, NY: Doubleday, 1960. A family tradition.

4

Biographical Publications

A. JOHN F. KENNEDY

1587. Armbuster, Maxim E. *The Presidents of the United States and Their Administrations from Washington to Reagan.* 7th rev. ed. New York: Horizon Press, 1982. pp. 331-36. Mixed review of Kennedy as president.

1588. Bartlett, Charles. "Portrait of a Friend." In *The Kennedy Presidency: Seventeen Intimate Perspectives of John F. Kennedy.* Edited by Kenneth W. Thompson. Lanham, Md.: University Press of America, 1985, pp. 1-18. Bartlett's reminiscences of JFK.

1589. Bassett, Margaret. *Profiles and Portraits of American Presidents and Their Wives.* New York: David McKay, 1976, pp. 201-09. A dated and an otherwise unsatisfactory profile.

1590. Bergquist, Laura, and Stanley Tretick. *A Very Special President.* New York: McGraw Hill, 1965. Bergquist, an insightful *Look* magazine writer, and Tretick, a *Look* photographer, combined in this early effort.

1591. Bernstein, Irving. "John F. Kennedy." In *Encyclopedia of the American Presidency.* Vol. 3. Edited by Leonard Levy and Louis Fisher. New York: Simon and Schuster, 1994, pp. 916-23. Highlights the major events of the Kennedy presidency.

1592. _____. *Promises Kept: John F. Kennedy's New Frontier.* New York: Oxford University Press, 1991. A very charitable view of President Kennedy's domestic successes and dryly written, but nevertheless, this is an important study because it is grounded in extensive primary sources on such topics as Medicare and federal aid to education.

1593. Blair, Joan, and Clay Blair, Jr. *The Search for JFK.* New York: Berkley Medallion Books, 1976. The Blairs were relentless in tracking down information on Kennedy prior to 1950; much of what we first knew of Kennedy's medical history and early personal life came from their efforts.

1594. Brauer, Carl M. "John F. Kennedy." In *The Presidents: A Reference History.* Edited by Henry F. Graff. New York: Charles Scribner's Sons, 1984, pp. 573-94. Thoughtful and judicious essay.

1595. _____. "John F. Kennedy: The Endurance of Inspirational Leadership." In *Leadership in the Modern Presidency.* Edited by Fred I. Greenstein. Cambridge: Ma.: Harvard University Press, 1988, pp. 108-33. Kennedy was inspirational in a way that few presidents have been.

1596. Burner, David. *John F. Kennedy and a New Generation.* Glenview, Ill.: Scott Forseman, 1988. Brief and balanced.

1597. Burns, James MacGregor. *John Kennedy: A Political Profile.* New York: Harcourt Brace Jovanovich, 1960. A model campaign biography, Burns was the first to use Kennedy's congressional correspondence in a work that retained its mild criticism of Kennedy's liberalism despite pressure to alter that interpretation.

1598. Carr, William H. A. *JFK: A Complete Biography, 1917-1963.* New York: Lancer Books, 1968. A superficial popular biography that focuses on the pre-presidential period.

1599. Contosta, David R. "John F. Kennedy 1917-1963." In *The Research Guide to American Historical Biography.* Edited by Robert Muccigrosso. 3 vols. Washington: Beacham Publishing, 1988, 3:868-874. A review of Kennedy's life, with a bibliography of published and manuscript sources.

1600. Cronin, Thomas E. "John F. Kennedy: President and Politician." In *John F. Kennedy: The Promise Revisited.* Edited by Paul Harper and Joan P. Krieg. Westport, Ct.: Greenwood Press, 1988, pp. 1-21. Kennedy's greatness lies less in what he accomplished than in what he proposed and began.

1601. David, Lester, and Irene David. *JFK: The Wit, the Charm, the Tears: Remembrances from Camelot.* New York: Paperjacks, 1988. Based on some primary sources, this brief biography was written for the general audience.

1602. Fairlie, Henry. *The Kennedy Promise: The Politics of Expectation.* Garden City, N.Y.: Doubleday, 1973. A popular revisionist work of the 1970s.

1603. Ferris, Robert G., ed. *The Presidents: Historic Places Commemorating the Chief Executive of the United States.* Washington: U.S. Department of the Interior, National Park Service, 1976, pp. 286-93. Brief sketch plus illustrations.

1604. Freidel, Frank. *Our Country's Presidents.* 8th ed. Washington: National

Geographic Society, 1979, pp. 225-33. Uncritical account with innumerable illustrations.

1605. Giglio, James N. *The Presidency of John F. Kennedy.* Lawrence: University Press of Kansas, 1991. A balanced effort to separate image from reality and to deal comprehensively with President Kennedy's responses to major issues and problems.

1606. Graham, Hugh Davis. "John F. Kennedy, 1961-1963." In *The American Presidents: The Office and the Men.* 3 vols. Pasadena, Ca.: Salem Press, 1986, 3:691-711. An even-handed account.

1607. Hamilton, Nigel. *JFK: Reckless Youth.* New York: Random House, 1992. Although very critical of Kennedy's parents, this work deals with the young John Kennedy fairly and empathetically and with considerable additional source material; this is the most detailed study of Kennedy's early years.

1608. Hilty, James. "John F. Kennedy: An Idealist without Illusions." *Forum Series.* St. Louis: Forum Press, 1976. Any attempt to understand Kennedy is difficult because of a series of contradictions.

1609. "Kennedy, John Fitzgerald." *National Cyclopedia of American Biography.* New York: James T. White, 1970, 52:1-22. Favorable and factual.

1610. Lasky, Victor. *JFK, the Man and the Myth: A Critical Portrait.* New York: Macmillan, 1963. A cutting, right-wing account.

1611. Leuchtenburg, William E. *In the Shadow of FDR: From Harry Truman to Ronald Reagan.* Ithaca, NY: Cornell University Press. Leuchtenburg provides a perceptive biograpahical essay.

1612. Lorant, Stefan. *The Glorious Burden: The American Presidency.* New York: Harper and Row, 1968, pp. 811-867. Some very interesting illustrations.

1613. Martin, Ralph G. *A Hero for Our Times: An Intimate Story of the Kennedy Years.* New York: Macmillan, 1983. A popular biography by a contemporary containing material not found elsewhere.

1614. Miroff, Bruce. *Pragmatic Illusions: The Presidential Politics of John F. Kennedy.* New York: McKay, 1976. An insightful revisionist study on Kennedy based largely on secondary sources.

1615. Paper, Louis J. *The Promise and the Performance: The Leadership of John F. Kennedy.* New York: Crown, 1975. One of several revisionist works published during the 1970s.

1616. Parmet, Herbert. *Jack: The Struggles of John F. Kennedy.* New York: Dial

Press, 1980. First volume of an important and balanced biography that carries Kennedy to the 1960 presidential campaign.

1617. _____. *JFK: The Presidency of John F. Kennedy*. New York: Dial Press, 1983. The first "outside" scholar to use Kennedy's papers, Parmet views Kennedy as a "moderate conservative" domestically and a Wilsonian in foreign policy who sought to make the world safe for diversity.

1618. Randall, Marta. *John F. Kennedy*. New York: Chelsea House Publishers, 1988. Based on secondary sources, it provides a succinct overview and contains many illustrations.

1619. Reeves, Richard. *President Kennedy: Profile of Power*. New York: Simon and Schuster, 1993. Viewing Kennedy as a pragmatic cold warrior, Reeves provides a detailed, intimate, and telling account of what it was like to be president.

1620. Reeves, Thomas C. *A Question of Character: A Life of John F. Kennedy*. New York: Macmillan, 1991. An overly damning portrayal of Kennedy's character based largely on secondary sources.

1621. Schlesinger, Arthur, Jr. "A Biographer's Perspective." In *The Kennedy Presidency*. Edited by Kenneth W. Thompson, pp. 19-40. No. **1588**. Discusses his personal impressions of Kennedy.

1622. _____. "John Fitzgerald Kennedy." In *Dictionary of American Biography*. Edited by John A. Garraty. New York: Charles Scribner's Sons, 1981, Supplement 7, pp. 418-27. A favorable summation of Kennedy's life by a prominent historian who served as JFK's administrative assistant.

1623. _____. *A Thousand Days: John F. Kennedy in the White House*. Boston: Houghton Mifflin, 1965. An impressive work that puts Kennedy into the context of his times while revealing the people who most influenced him.

1624. Schoor, Jean. *Young Jack Kennedy*. New York: Harcourt, Brace and World, 1963. To Kennedy's presidential election; intended for young readers.

1625. Sorensen, Theodore C. *Kennedy*. New York: Harper and Row, 1965. A personal biography by Kennedy's senate administrative assistant and the president's special counsel that provides the Kennedy position on the major issues of his presidency; this is the closest thing there is to a Kennedy memoir.

1626. Strober, Gerald S., and Deborah H. Strober. *"Let Us Begin Anew": An Oral History of the Kennedy Presidency*. New York: Harper Collins, 1993. Between 1989 and 1992 the authors interviewed more than 120 former Kennedy associates on the man and the presidency.

1627. Weinstein, Lewis H. "John F. Kennedy: A Personal Memoir, 1946-1963." *American Jewish History* 75 (September 1985): 5-30. Recounts the author's close personal and political association with JFK.

1628. Whitney, David C. *The American Presidents*. Garden City, NY.: Doubleday, 1975, pp. 321-332. A dated account.

1629. Whitney, David C., and Robin Vaughn Whitney. *The American Presidents*. 7th ed. New York: Prentice Hall, 1990, pp. 302-13. Borders on advocacy.

1630. Wilson, Vincent, Jr. *The Book of the Presidents*. Silver Spring, Md: American History Research Associates, 1962, pp. 74-5. Cursory treatment.

1631. *World Book of America's Presidents*. Chicago: World Book, 1988, pp. 206-13. Brief commentary with illustrations.

B. THE KENNEDY FAMILY AND FAMILY MEMBERS

1632. Adler, Bill. *The Kennedy Children: Triumphs and Tragedies*. New York: Franklin Watts, 1980. A popular account of Joe and Rose's grandchildren.

1633. Burner, David, and Thomas R. West. *The Torch Is Passed: The Kennedy Brothers and American Liberalism*. St. James, NY: Brandywine Press, 1984 [first published by Atheneum in 1984]. The evolution of the Kennedy brothers' liberalism.

1634. Burns, James MacGregor. *Edward Kennedy and the Camelot Legacy*. New York: W. W. Norton, 1976. A popular account of John Kennedy's youngest brother.

1635. Cameron, Gail. *Rose: A Biography of Rose Fitzgerald Kennedy*. New York: Putnam, 1971. Stresses the religious faith and devotion which have sustained John Kennedy's mother.

1636. Cassidy, Bruce, and Bill Adler. *RFK: A Special Kind of Man*. Chicago: Playboy Press, 1977. A popular biography based on secondary sources.

1637. Clinch, Nancy Gager. *The Kennedy Neurosis*. New York: Grosett and Dunlap, 1973. A much criticized family psychobiography.

1638. Collier, Peter, and David Horowitz. *The Kennedys: An American Drama*. New York: Warner Books, 1984. An unflattering view of the Kennedys.

1639. Davis, John H. *The Kennedys: Dynasty and Disaster, 1848-1984*. New York: McGraw Hill, 1984. An insightfully critical study by Jacqueline Kennedy's cousin.

1640. De Toledano, Ralph. *RFK: The Man Who Would Be President*. New York: Putnam, 1967. A scathing, unscholarly attack.

1641. Dinneen, Joseph F. *The Kennedy Family*. Boston: Little, Brown, 1959. Former *Boston Globe* reporter who provides little insight into the Kennedy family.

1642. Gager, Nancy. *Kennedy Wives, Kennedy Women*. New York: Dell, 1976. An undocumented popular account based on secondary sources.

1643. Goodwin, Doris Kearns. *The Fitzgeralds and the Kennedys*. New York: Simon and Schuster, 1987. Based on the Kennedy family papers, which other scholars have been unable to use, this is an empathetic and balanced biography that reaches back into the nineteenth century for the rise and eventual merger of two important Irish families of Boston.

1644. Guthman, Edwin O., and Jeffrey Shulman. eds. *Robert Kennedy in His Own Words, the Unpublished Recollections of the Kennedy Years*. New York: Bantam, 1988. Based on the voluminous Kennedy oral history at the Kennedy Library.

1645. Halberstam, David. *The Unfinished Odyssey of Robert Kennedy*. New York: Random House, 1968. An uncharacteristically sloppy effort by a former *New York Times* correspondent who agrees with Kennedy's hostility to the Vietnam war.

1646. Hess, Stephen. *America's Political Dynasties: From Adams to Kennedy*. Garden City, NY: Doubleday, 1966. Kennedy chapter is based on published sources.

1647. Kennedy, Rose. *Times to Remember*. Garden City, NY: Doubleday, 1974. A less than candid memoir from John Kennedy's mother.

1648. Koskoff, David S. *Joseph P. Kennedy: A Life and Times*. Englewood Cliffs, NJ: Prentice Hall, 1974. A critical, well-researched assessment of the paterfamilias.

1649. Lasky, Victor. *Robert Kennedy: The Myth and the Man*. New York: Trident Press, 1968. A polemical right-wing work reminiscent of his 1963 study on JFK.

1650. Leamer, Laurence. *The Kennedy Women: The Saga of an American Family*. New York: Villard Books, 1994. A serious and detailed book that looks at the family through five generations with emphasis on feminine concerns.

1651. Lenrow, Adele Levine. "A Toulmin Analysis of the Argumentation Patterns in Selected Speeches of Joseph Kennedy, John Kennedy, Robert Kennedy, and Edward Kennedy." Ed.D. diss., Columbia University, 1971. Uses the Toulmin analysis to examine the speeches of four Kennedys and analyzes the personal values upon which each based his reasoning.

1652. McCarthy, Joe. *The Remarkable Kennedys*. NY: Popular Library, 1960. Essentually a campaign portrait of the Kennedy family, lacking the thoroughness of James Macgregor Burns's effort.

1653. McTaggart, Lynne. *Kathleen Kennedy: Her Life and Times*. Boston: Houghton Mifflin, 1983. A biography of John Kennedy's sister who lost her life in an airplane crash in 1948.

1654. Newfield, Jack. *Robert Kennedy: A Memoir*. New York: Dutton, 1969. An intimate, favorable view of the changes in Robert's thought and style since his brother's assassination.

1655. Quirk, Lawrence. *Robert Francis Kennedy: The Man and the Politician*. Los Angeles: Holloway House Publishing Co., 1968. A favorable journalistic biography written for the 1968 campaign.

1656. Rachlin, Harvey. *The Kennedys: A Chronological History, 1823-Present*. New York: World Almanac, 1986. A compilation of important events of family members with John Kennedy the primary focus.

1657. Russell, Francis. *The President Makers: From Mark Hanna to Joseph P. Kennedy*. Boston: Little, Brown, 1976. Contains a sprightly written essay on Joe Kennedy, "the dynast from East Boston."

1658. Saunders, Frank. *Torn Lace Curtain*. New York: Holt, Rinehart and Winston, 1982. An intimate view of the Kennedy clan by the family chauffeur.

1659. Schlesinger, Arthur, Jr. *Robert Kennedy and His Times*. Boston: Houghton Mifflin, 1978. A extremely favorable but noteworthy biography grounded in extensive primary sources, some of which are still unavailable to other scholars.

1660. Searls, Hank. *The Lost Prince: Young Joe, the Forgotten Kennedy*. New York: World Publishing, 1969. A readable, well-researched study of John Kennedy's oldest brother by a former World War II navy pilot.

1661. Shannon, William Vincent. *The Heir Apparent: Robert Kennedy and the Struggle for Power*. New York: Macmillan, 1967. A competent journalistic account that places Kennedy in political context.

1662. Sorensen, Theodore C. *The Kennedy Legacy*. New York: Macmillan, 1969. The legacy of John and Robert Kennedy lives on.

1663. Stein, Jean, and George Plimpton, eds. *American Journey: The Times of Robert Kennedy*. New York: Harcourt Brace Jovanovich, 1970. Contains invaluable recollections of contemporaries who had contacts with Robert during the Kennedy presidency.

1664. Sulzberger, C. L. *Fathers and Children*. New York: Arbor House, 1987. Contains a somewhat disappointing essay by a journalist who knew Joseph and John Kennedy personally.

1665. Thompson, Robert E., and Hortense Myers. *Robert F. Kennedy: The Brother Within*. New York: Macmillan, 1962. An early portrait of Robert Kennedy after a year as attorney general.

1666. Whalen, Richard J. *The Founding Father: The Story of Joseph P. Kennedy*. New York: New American Library, 1964. The first major work on Kennedy's father, it is based largely on published sources.

1667. Wills, Garry. *The Kennedy Imprisonment: A Meditation on Power*. Boston: Little, Brown, 1981. A perceptive but overly critical account on the Kennedys.

5

Childhood and Early Years, 1917–1946

A. ROOTS AND CHILDHOOD

1668. Cutler, John Henry. *"Honey Fitz": Three Steps to the White House*. Indianapolis: Bobbs-Merrill, 1962. A biography of John Kennedy's maternal grandfather.

1669. Curtis, John. *History of the Town of Brookline*. Boston: Houghton Mifflin, 1933. History of John Kennedy's birthplace.

1670. Flood, Richard T. *The Story of Noble and Greenough School, 1886-1966*. Dedham, Ma.: Noble and Greenough School, 1966. John Kennedy attended this private Brookline school from the third into the sixth grade.

1671. Goodwin, Doris Kearns. *The Fitzgeralds and the Kennedys*. No. **643**. Excellent on John Kennedy's early family relationships.

1672. _____. "The Fitzgeralds and the Kennedys: Reflections of a Biographer." *Prologue: Quarterly of the National Archives* 22 (Summer 1990): 115-27. Some of this deals with John Kennedy's upbringing.

1673. Handlin, Oscar. *Boston's Immigrants: A Study in Acculturation*. Cambridge: The Belknap Press of Harvard University Press, 1959. Essential background material for any biography on Kennedy.

1674. Hennessy, Maurice N. *I'll Come Back in The Springtime: John F. Kennedy and the Irish*. New York: Ives Washburn, 1966. A brief history of the Kennedy and Fitzgerald families in Ireland.

1675. McCaffery, Lawrence. *The Irish Diaspora in America*. Bloomington: Indiana University Press, 1976. Provides insights into Kennedy's Irish heritage.

1676. _____. *Textures of Irish America*. Syracuse: Syracuse University Press, 1992. Interprets the Irish journey in America from the working-class ghettos to the middle class suburbs as a success story.

1677. Maguire, John. *The Irish in America*. New York: Arno Press.

1678. O'Connor, Edwin. *The Last Hurrah*. Boston: Little, Brown, 1956. Fictional work patterned after James Michael Curley, long-time mayor of Boston.

1679. Parmet, Herbert. *Jack: The Struggles of John F. Kennedy*. No. **1616**.

1680. Russell, Francis. "Honey Fitz." *American Heritage* 19 (August 1968): 28-31, 76-80. Analyzes the political career of Boston's John Francis Fitzgerald, grandfather of John Kennedy.

1681. Shannon, William V. *The American Irish*. New York: Macmillan, 1963. A journalistic account of the history of the Catholic Irish in America.

1682. Wayman, Dorothy. *Cardinal O'Connell of Boston*. New York: Farrar Straus and Young, 1955. The Cardinal during Kennedy's youth.

1683. Whitehill, Walter Muir. *Boston in the Age of JFK*. Norman: University of Oklahoma Press, 1966. This book contains little information on John Kennedy.

B. EARLY LIFE

1684. Buchan, John. *Pilgrim's Way*. Boston: Houghton Mifflin, 1940. A favorite of Kennedy's, it is essential reading for an understanding of him.

1685. Damore, Leo. *The Cape Cod Years of JFK*. Englewood Cliffs, NJ.: Prentice Hall, 1967. Written by a longtime resident of Cape Cod, it focuses on Kennedy's forty years of summer activities there.

1686. Donovan, Robert J. *PT 109: John F. Kennedy in World War II*. New York: McGraw Hill, 1961. President Kennedy read the galleys of the work of this sympathetic journalist who researched much of it in the Solomon Islands.

1687. Hamilton, Nigel. *JFK: Reckless Youth*. No. **1607**. Superb on the health problems of a young Kennedy, his early relationships, and his service experience.

1688. Hersey, John. "Survival." *New Yorker* 20 (June 17, 1944): 31-43. [Republished in condensed form in *Reader's Digest*, August 1944, pp. 75-80]. Kennedy's story on surviving the ramming of PT-109.

1689. Hirsch, Phil, ed. *The Kennedy War Heroes*. New York: Pyramid Books, 1962.

Fourteen World War II heroes, including New Frontiersmen Orville Freeman, Kenneth O'Donnell, George McGovern, and Arthur Goldberg.

1690. Michaelis, David. *The Best of Friends: Profiles of Extraordinary Friendships.* New York: William Morrow, 1983. Includes a chapter on the lifelong friendship of Choate Academy roommates, John Kennedy and K. LeMoyne Billings.

1691. _____. "The President's Best Friend." *American Heritage* 34 (June/July 1983): 12-27. On K. LeMoyne Billings.

1692. Muheim, Harry. "When JFK Was Rich, Young and Happy," *Esquire* 66 (August 1966): 65-6, 132-33. A favorable first-hand account of Kennedy's brief stay at Stanford University.

1693. "Pre-presidential." *New Yorker* 37 (April 1, 1961): 26-7. Explores the longtime friendship of K. LeMoyne Billings and John Kennedy.

1693a. Richardson, Nan, ed. *The Billings Collection.* Boston: John F. Kennedy Foundation, 1991. (Privately printed limited edition of 300 copies). Memorial essays by friends, family, and associates of Lem Billings, illustrated with "Lemorabilia," photographs, and facsimiles from Billings's papers.

1694. *The Spee Club of Harvard University.* Lunenberg, Vt: Stinehour Press, 1968. Kennedy was a member.

1695. Tregaskis, Richard. *John F. Kennedy and PT 109.* New York: Random House, 1962. A former Harvard classmate of JFK and an International News Service correspondent in the South Pacific, he devoted only three of eleven chapters to the ramming of PT 109.

1696. _____. *John F. Kennedy: War Hero.* New York: Dell Publishing, 1962. A slightly expanded version of Tregaskis's Random House book.

1697. Waldrop, Frank C. "JFK and the Nazi Spy." *The Washingtonian* 10 (April 1975): 89-91. Kennedy's affair with Inga Arvad who was wrongly accused of being a Nazi spy.

1698. Walker, Gerald, and Donald A. Allan. "Jack Kennedy at Harvard." *Coronet* 50 (May 1961): 83-95. A personal account by Kennedy's roommates, instructors, and close friends.

1699. Whipple, Chandler. *Lt. John F. Kennedy--Expendable.* New York: Universal Publishing and Distributing Corporation, 1962. A popular account of Kennedy's PT-109 service.

6

The Congressional Years, 1947–1960

1700. Bayley, Edwin R. "Kennedy Warms Up Wisconsin Democrats." *New Republic* 138 (June 2,1958): 9. Kennedy woos Wisconsin Democrats for 1960.

1701. Blagden, Ralph M. "Cabot Lodge's Toughest Fight." *Reporter* 7 (September 1952): 10-11. The 1952 senatorial race in Massachusetts.

1702. Bowles, Chester. "The Foreign Policy of Senator Kennedy." *America* 104 (October 15, 1960): 67-73. A Kennedy associate, Bowles mirrors Kennedy's views.

1703. Burns, James MacGregor. *John Kennedy: A Political Profile.* No. **1597**. Excellent on Kennedy's congressional career.

1704. "Can the Catholic Vote Swing an Election?" *U.S. News and World Report* 41 (August 10, 1956): 41-6. Concerns itself with the so-called Bailey Memorandum, secretly written by Theodore Sorensen, which suggested that Stevenson would need a Catholic vice presidential running mate in 1956.

1705. Cater, Douglass. "The Cool Eye of John F. Kennedy." *Reporter* 21 (December 10, 1959): 27-32. Kennedy represents a different breed of Irish politician.

1706. Chaples, Ernest A. "The Voting Behavior of United States Senators for Four Selected Issues, 1943-1964." Ph.D. diss., University of Kentucky, 1969. The select issues are agriculture, foreign policy, public works and resources, and welfare and labor.

1707. Clancy, John Patrick. "Adlai Ewing Stevenson and the Bureaucracy of the Democratic Party in the 1950s." Ph.D. diss., United States International University, 1975. The Democratic presidential nominee of 1952 and 1956.

1708. Clemens, Cyril. "My Visit with John F. Kennedy." *Hobbies* 72 (April 1967):

109, 116. The founder of the Mark Twain Society remembers his visit to Senator Kennedy's office.

1709. Coffin, Tristram. *Senator Fulbright: Portrait of a Public Philosopher*. New York: E. P. Dutton, 1966. Fulbright, the Democratic senator from Arkansas from 1945-1975, chaired the Senator Foreign Relations Committee at the time of Kennedy's membership.

1710. _____. "John Kennedy: Young Man in a Hurry." *Progressive* 23 (December 1959): 10-8. Probing analysis of a presidential candidate.

1711. Crosby, Donald F. *God, Church, and Flag: Senator Joseph R. McCarthy and the Catholic Church, 1950-1957*. Chapel Hill: University of North Carolina Press, 1978. McCarthy remained a Kennedy dilemma.

1712. Dallek, Robert. *Lone Star Rising: Lyndon Johnson and His Times, 1908-1960*. New York: Oxford University Press, 1991. As senate majority leader, Johnson worked closely with Senator Kennedy.

1713. Diamond, Sigmund. "On the Road to Camelot." *Labor History* 21 (Spring 1980): 279-90. Suggests that Congressman Kennedy tried to link the 1946-47 Allis-Chalmers strike in Milwaukee, Wisconsin, to the Communist party.

1714. Douglas, Paul H. *In the Fullness of Time*. New York: Harcourt Brace Jovanavich, 1971. Democratic senator from Illinois.

1715. Evans, Rowland, and Robert Novak. *Lyndon B. Johnson: The Exercise of Power--A Political Biography*. New York: New American Library, 1966. Study is based on their personal observations as reporters as well as on over 200 interviews.

1716. Fischer, John. "Hard Questions for Senator Kennedy." *Harper's* 220 (April 1960): 16, 21-3. A favorable assessment.

1717. Fontaine, Andre. "Senator Kennedy's Crisis." *Redbook* 113 (November 1957): 49-51, 119-122. Focuses on the conflict between Kennedy's ideals and his presidential ambitions.

1718. Fontenay, Charles L. *Estes Kefauver: A Biography*. Knoxville: University of Tennessee Press, 1981. Tennessee senator from 1949-63 who ran against Kennedy for the 1956 vice presidential nomination.

1719. Fuchs, Lawrence H. "The Senator and the Lady." *American Heritage* 25 (October 1974): 57-61, 81-3. John Kennedy and Eleanor Roosevelt.

1720. Gorman, Joseph B. *Kefauver: A Political Biography*. New York: Oxford University Press, 1971. Covers Kennedy's 1956 vice presidential bid.

1721. Gray, Charles H. "Coalition, Consensus, and Conflict in the United States Senate (1957-1960)." Ph.D. diss., University of Colorado, 1962. Includes Kennedy's years in the Senate.

1722. _____. "A Scale Analysis of the Voting Records of Senators Kennedy, Johnson, and Goldwater, 1957-1960." *American Political Science Review* 59 (1965): 615-21. Senator Kennedy emerged as a strong supporter of liberal labor, housing, and welfare programs, a moderately strong backer of public power programs, an advocate of high agricultural price supports, a recent convert to civil rights legislation, a moderately strong defender of foreign military aid, and a firm internationalist.

1723. Griffith, Robert W. *The Politics of Fear: Joseph R. McCarthy and the Senate.* Lexington: University of Kentucky Press, 1970. Kennedy was the only Democratic senator who failed to vote or pair against McCarthy.

1724. Hardeman, D. B., and Donald C. Bacon. *Rayburn: A Biography.* Austin: Texas Monthly Press, 1987. Rayburn was the speaker of the House of Representatives during the 1950s.

1725. Harris, Eleanor. "The Senator is in a Hurry." *McCall's* 84 (August 1957): 44-5, 118-19, 123, 125. A personal profile of a future presidential candidate.

1726. Hasenfus, William Albert. "Managing Partner: Joseph W. Martin, Jr. Republican Leader of the United States House of Representatives, 1939-1959." Ph.D. diss., Boston College, 1986. This Republican leader from Massachusetts served in the House with Kennedy.

1727. Healy, Paul F. "Galahad in the House." *The Sign* 29 (July 1950): 9-11. One of the Kennedy family's many promotional efforts, emphasizing Jack Kennedy's successes in the House of Representatives.

1728. _____. "The Senate's Gay Young Bachelor." *Saturday Evening Post* 225 (June 13, 1953): 26-7, 123-24, 126-27, 129. Full of misconceptions.

1729. "A Kennedy Runs for Congress: The Boston-Bred Scion of a Former Ambassador is a Fighting Conservative." *Look* 10 (June 11, 1946): 32-6. Focuses on war record and family background of one whom *Look* assumed would adopt his father's political positions.

1730. "Kennedy's Reform." *New Republic* 140 (March 2, 1959): 5. Kennedy's proposed revisions of the McCarran-Walter Act.

1731. Knebel, Fletcher. "Democratic Forecast: A Catholic in 1960." *Look* 23 (March 3, 1959): 13-17. Political observers believe the Democratic party will nominate a

Catholic presidential candidate in 1960.

1732. Lachman, Seymour P. "The Cardinal, the Congressmen, and the First Lady." *Journal of Church and State* 7 (Winter 1965): 35-66. Federal aid to education bills in 1949 involved Eleanor Roosevelt, Francis Cardinal Spellman, and John Kennedy who played important roles in the unsuccessful efforts.

1733. Landis, Mark L. "Personality and Style in the United States Senate." Ph.D. diss., Columbia University, 1973. Modeled on James David Barber's work, the active-positive Kennedy is one of the senators studied.

1734. Lash, Joseph. *Eleanor Roosevelt: The Years Alone*. New York: W. W. Norton, 1972. Deals with Eleanor's mistrust of Kennedy.

1735. Latham, Earl. *Massachusetts Politics*. New York: Citizenship Clearing House, undated. Covers the Kennedy congressional years.

1736. Lemke, William Edgar. "The Political Thought of John F. Kennedy: To the Inaugural Address." Ph.D. diss., University of Maine, 1975. Argues that many of the ideas and attitudes of Joseph Kennedy were often present in John Kennedy's thinking.

1737. Lenchner, Paul. "Senate Voting Patterns and American Politics, 1945-1965." Ph.D. diss., Cornell University, 1973. Roll calls studied includes the 1957 session, the only one involving JFK in this study.

1738. Levine, Erwin L. *Theodore Francis Green: The Washington Years, 1937-1960*. Providence: Brown University Press, 1971. The Democratic senator from Rhode Island from 1937 to 1961 had a liberal voting record and was a staunch internationalist.

1739. "*Life* Goes Courting with a U.S. Senator." *Life* 35 (July 20, 1953): 96-9. The courtship of John Kennedy and Jacqueline Bouvier.

1740. Lincoln, Evelyn. *My Twelve Years with John F. Kennedy*. New York: David McKay, 1965. Lincoln served as Kennedy's personal secretary since the senatorial period.

1741. Lodge, Henry Cabot, Jr. *As it Was: An Inside View of Politics and Power in the 50's and 60's*. New York: W. W. Norton, 1976. Although Lodge was Kennedy's opponent in the 1952 Senate race, he only devotes two pages to that contest.

1742. Luhning, Donavon L. "Prelude to Power: John F. Kennedy and the Democratic Convention of 1956." M.A. thesis, Vanderbilt University, 1991. Argues that JFK began earlier and worked more extensively for the 1956 vice-presidential nomination than was generally acknowledged.

1743. Mallan, John P. "Massachusetts: Liberal and Corrupt." *New Republic* 127 (October 13, 1952): 10-12. Mallan expresses reservations about Kennedy's senatorial candidacy.

1744. Martin, John Bartlow. *Adlai Stevenson and the World*. Garden City, NY: Doubleday, 1977. Covers Stevenson's life from 1952 to 1965.

1745. Marwell, Gerald. "Party, Region, and the Dimensions of Conflict in the House of Representatives, 1949-1954." *American Political Science Review* 61 (1967): 380-99. Analyzes the 81st through the 83rd congresses and identifies three major influences on congressional voting behavior.

1746. Miller, William J. *Henry Cabot Lodge*. New York: James H. Heineman, 1967. Authorized biography of Kennedy's 1952 senate race opponent.

1747. Murphy, Paul I. "Kennedy, Our Next President?" *Padre* 6 (March 1955): 108-11. A promotional piece on John Kennedy.

1748. _____. "Unmarried Millionaires: Jack Kennedy." *American Weekly* 10 (May 30, 1948): 14-15. Full of fluff.

1749. Nurse, Ronald J. "America Must Not Sleep: The Development of John F. Kennedy's Foreign Policy Attitudes, 1947-1960," Ph.D. diss., Michigan State University, 1971. Focuses on three Kennedy foreign policy themes during the congressional years: military preparedness, anti-colonialism, and technical assistance to Third World countries.

1750. _____. "Critic of Colonialism: JFK and Algerian Independence." *Historian* 39 (February 1977): 307-26. In Third World countries such as Algeria, Senator Kennedy was perceptively aware of the near futility of a Western power combating a popular national drive for independence.

1751. O'Brien, Lawrence F. *No Final Victories: A Life in Politics--From John F. Kennedy to Watergate*. NY: Doubleday, 1974. O'Brien played a key role in Kennedy's senatorial campaigns.

1752. O'Donnell, Kenneth, and David Powers. *"Johnny, We Hardly Knew Ye": Memories of John Fitzgerald Kennedy*. Little, Brown, 1972. Personal story of a seventeen-year friendship that began with the political campaigns of the late 1940s.

1753. Parmet, Herbert S. *The Democrats: The Years after FDR*. New York: Oxford University Press, 1976. Coverage of Kennedy during the 1950s.

1754. Phillips, Cabel. "Case History of a Senate Race," *New York Times Magazine*

(October 26, 1952), pp. 10-11, 49-51. Kennedy's approaching upset election victory against Henry Cabot Lodge.

1755. _____. "Two Candidates on the Road." *New York Times Magazine* (October 25, 1959), pp. 24, 48, 50, 52, 55. Kennedy and Hubert Humphrey seeking the Democratic presidential nomination.

1756. Reichard, Gary W. "Divisions and Dissent: Democrats and Foreign Policy, 1952-1956." *Political Science Quarterly* 93 (Spring 1978): 51-72. Kennedy in concert with Adlai Stevenson and Chester Bowles in opposing colonialism.

1757. Roosevelt, Eleanor. "On My Own: Of Stevenson, Truman, and Kennedy." *Saturday Evening Post* 230 (March 8, 1958): 32-3, 72-5. Eleanor Roosevelt takes a dim view of Kennedy.

1758. Ross, Irwin. "The Senator Women Elected." *Cosmopolitan* 135 (December 1953): 81-5. A personal profile of Kennedy, including his strong appeal to women, which enabled him to defeat Lodge in 1952.

1759. Rovere, Richard. "Kennedy's Last Chance to Be President." *Esquire* 26 (April 1959): 61-7. Rovere sees Kennedy's youth, vigor, freshness, and supposed innocence as assets.

1760. Scharf, Lois. *Eleanor Roosevelt: First Lady of American Liberalism.* Boston: Twayne Publications, 1987. Roosevelt questioned Kennedy's liberalism during the 1950s.

1761. Schary, Dore. *Heyday: An Autobiography.* Boston: Little, Brown, 1979. Covers Kennedy and the 1956 Democratic national convention.

1762. Shaffer, William R. "Senator John F. Kennedy and the Liberal Establishment: Presidential Politics and Civil Rights Legislation in 1957." In *John F. Kennedy.* Edited by Paul Harper and Joann P. Krieg, pp. 225-35. No. **1600.** Based on his voting record, Senator Kennedy should not be classified as a liberal on civil rights.

1763. Sink, George T. "John F. Kennedy's Road to the White House." M.A. thesis, Western Michigan University, 1970. Examines the forces, especially Kennedy's father, that drove John Kennedy to the White House.

1764. Smith, Jean Edward. "Kennedy and Defense: The Formative Years." *Air University Review* 18 (March 1967): 39-54. A thoughtful essay that refutes the allegation that Kennedy was a cold warrior.

1765. Solberg, Carl. *Hubert Humphrey.* New York: W. W. Norton, 1984. A leader in the Senate during Kennedy's senatorial career.

1766. Spiering, Frank. "John F. Kennedy, Patriot of the Year." *Notre Dame Scholastic* 97 (November 30, 1956): 17, 32. Based on an annual award given by the senior class at Notre Dame.

1767. Steinberg, Alfred. *Sam Rayburn: A Biography*. New York: Hawthorne Books, 1975. Better on Kennedy for the 1950s than Hardeman and Bacon.

1768. "This is John Fitzgerald Kennedy." *Newsweek* 51 (June 23, 1958): 29-30, 33-4. A positive assessment of the personality and recent record of a probable presidential candidate.

1769. Thomson, C. A. H., and F. M. Shattuck. *The 1956 Presidential Campaign*. Washington: Brookings Institution, 1960. Covers Kennedy's vice presidential candidacy.

1770. Turner, Russell. "Senator Kennedy: The Perfect Politician." *American Mercury* 84 (March 1957): 33-40. Although Kennedy insists he will not be a presidential candidate in 1960, the beginning of the buildup is under way.

1771. Uslaner, Eric M. "Conditions for Party Responsibility: Partisanship in the House of Representatives, 1947-1970." Ph.D. diss., Indiana University, 1973. Covers Kennedy's years in the House.

1772. Van Camp, John. "What Happened to the Labor Reform Bill?" *Reporter* 19 (October 2, 1958): 24-8. On the death of the Kennedy-Ives labor-reform bill.

1773. Waldron, James R. *8818*. New York: Pageant Press, 1965. On the efforts of Senator John Kennedy to reinstate a discharged army officer.

1774. Zane, Maitland. "Joan Hitchcock's Evenings with JFK." *Oui* (July 15, 1976), pp. 77, 116. Joan Hitchcock, a former airline hostess, claimed to have an affair with Kennedy from 1956 to 1960 which resulted in an abortion.

7

The Election of 1960

A. CANDIDATES AND CAMPAIGNS

1775. Alexander, Herbert E. *Financing the 1960 Election*. Citizen's Research Foundation, Study No. 5, 1962. An expanded and revised version of a chapter written for *The Presidential Election and Transition, 1960-1961*.

1776. Ambrose, Stephen E. *Nixon: The Education of a Politician, 1913-1962*. New York: Simon and Schuster, 1987. A superb analysis of Nixon and Kennedy as candidates in 1960.

1777. Anderson, Totten J. "The Political West in 1960." *Western Political Quarterly* 14 (1961): 287-99. Covers thirteen-state area.

1778. Arnett, Nancy Carol. "John F. Kennedy's 1960 Presidential Campaign: Rhetorical Strategies and Image Projection." Ph.D. diss., Florida State University, 1983. Explores how Kennedy's liabilities, especially his religion, were managed through speeches.

1779. Barrett, Patricia. *Religious Liberty and the American Presidency: A Study in Church-State Relations*. New York: Herder and Herter, 1963. The religious issue in the 1960 campaign.

1780. Blanshard, Paul. *Personal and Confidential: An Autobiography*. Boston: Beacon, 1973. Blanshard was personally involved with Kennedy and the 1960 campaign.

1781. Boller, Paul F., Jr. *Presidential Campaigns*. New York: Oxford University Press, 1984. A popular account.

1782. Bradford, Richard. "John F. Kennedy and the 1960 Presidential Primary in West Virginia." *South Atlantic Quarterly* 75 (Spring 1976): 161-72. Kennedy's victory is tied to campaigning from Franklin Roosevelt, Jr., a superior campaign organization, effective use of television, appeals to the poor and unemployed, and reverse psychology on the Catholic issue.

1783. Bruno, Jerry. *The Advance Man.* New York: Morrow, 1971. Includes Bruno's work for Kennedy in 1960.

1784. Burns, James MacGregor. "John F. Kennedy, Candidate on the Eve: Liberalism without Tears." *New Republic* 143 (October 31, 1960): 14-16. Kennedy is committed to a liberalism that works, not to one of lost causes.

1785. Carney, Francis M., and Frank H. Way, Jr. eds. *Politics.* San Francisco: Wadsworth, 1960. An anthology focusing on the events of the 1960 election year.

1786. Chamberlain, John. "The Chameleon Image of John F. Kennedy." *National Review* 8 (April 23, 1960): 41-50. A conservative writer, in a leading conservative publication, charges Kennedy with adopting conflicting positions on domestic and foreign issues.

1787. Cosman, Bernard. "Presidential Republicanism in the South, 1960." *Journal of Politics* 24 (May 1962): 303-22. Nixon generally sustained the largest losses relative to Eisenhower (1956) in cities where black registrants and Catholics were numerous.

1788. Crews, James McRae, Jr. "J.F.K. and the Mountaineers: John F. Kennedy's Rhetoric in the 1960 West Virginia Presidential Primary." Ph. D. diss., Florida State University, 1980. Focuses on Kennedy's speeches and the religious issue.

1789. David, Paul T., et al. *The Presidential Election and Transition, 1960-1961.* Washington: Brookings Institution, 1961. Studies by eleven political scientists of the nominations, conventions, campaign, and presidential transition.

1790. De Sola Pool, Ithiel, et al. *Candidates, Issues, and Strategies: A Computer Simulation of the 1960 Presidential Election.* Cambridge: MIT Press, 1964. A description of the election project done for the Democratic party by the Simulmatics Corporation.

1791. Divine, Robert A. *Foreign Policy and U.S. Presidential Elections, 1952-1960.* New York: New Viewpoints, 1974. Contains two chapters on the 1960 election.

1792. Dorough, C. Dwight. *Mr. Sam.* New York: Random House, 1962. Deals with Kennedy-Rayburn conversation regarding Johnson's vice presidential nomination.

1793. Foley, Michael. "From Mighty Oaks to Little Acorns: The Problems of the Presidential Timber Business." *Journal of American Studies* 24 (April 1990): 85-92. By his primary successes in 1960, Kennedy contributed to the weakening of the party power brokers, leading to disarray in the selection of presidential nominees.

1794. Fuchs, Lawrence H. *John F. Kennedy and American Catholicism.* New York: Meredith Press, 1967. Includes attitudes toward Catholicism during the 1960 campaign and election.

1795. Fuller, Sharon. "The Candidate as Commodity: An Examination of the Penetration of the Political Arena by Marketplace Discourse." M.A. thesis, Simon Fraser University, 1990. Explores how four presidents, including Kennedy, used the commercial marketplace to project their image.

1796. Gacek, Christopher M. "Contending Approaches to the Use of Force: The 'Never Again' and 'Limited War' Schools in American Foreign Policy." Ph.D. diss., Stanford University, 1989. Kennedy was exposed to both politico-military concepts following the Korean War.

1797. Hajda, Joseph. "Choosing the 1960 Democratic Candidate: The Case of the Unbossed Delegation." *Kansas Quarterly* 8 (1976): 71-87. Recollections from a Kansas delegate.

1798. Hudson, W. Gail. "The Role of Humor in John F. Kennedy's 1960 Presidential Campaign." Ph.D. diss., Southern Illinois University, 1979. Explores how Kennedy used humor in 1960 and humor's contextual validity.

1799. "It Will Be a Different Kind of President in 1961." *U.S. News and World Report* 49 (August 15, 1960): 40-1. No matter who wins, Kennedy or Nixon will differ greatly from any recent president.

1800. Kemper, Deane Alwyn. "John F. Kennedy Before the Greater Houston Ministerial Association, September 12, 1960: The Religious Issue." Ph.D. diss., Michigan State University, 1968. An analysis and evaluation of Kennedy's appearance before the Houston clergy, which supposedly eliminated religion as a respectable campaign issue.

1801. Knebel, Fletcher. "Pulitzer Prize Entry: John F. Kennedy." In *Candidates, 1960: Behind the Headlines in the Presidential Race.* Edited by Eric Sevareid. New York: Basic Books, 1959, pp. 181-215. Knebel captures some of the stronger flavor of Kennedy's earlier campaigns and of Massachusetts politics in general.

1802. Kraus, Sidney. *The Great Debates: Kennedy v. Nixon, 1960.* Bloomington: Indiana University Press, 1977. First published in 1962, it contains the complete texts of the four debates.

1803. Land, Guy Paul. "John F. Kennedy's Southern Strategy, 1956-1960." *North Carolina Historical Review* 56 (1979): 41-63. Even though courting southern leaders since 1956, Kennedy was viewed less favorably in the South by the time of the 1960 National Convention.

1804. Lang, Kurt and Gladys Engel Lang. "Ordeal by Debate: Viewer Reactions." *Public Opinion Quarterly* 25 (Summer 1961): 277-88. The impact of the presidential debates more favored Kennedy than Nixon.

1805. Lasky, Victor. *John F. Kennedy: What's Behind the Image?* Washington: Free World Press, 1960. The predecessor of Lasky's scorching *JFK: The Man and the Myth.*

1806. Lisle, Teddy David. "The Canonical Impediment: John F. Kennedy and the Religious Issue during the 1960 Presidential Campaign." Ph.D. diss., University of Kentucky, 1982. A discussion of how Kennedy, the Catholic hierarchy, and the Protestant clergy handled the Catholic issue.

1807. _____. "Southern Baptists and the Issue of Catholic Autonomy in the 1960 Presidential Campaign." In *John F. Kennedy.* Edited by Paul Harper and Joann P. Krieg, pp. 273-85. No. **1600.** Southern Baptists were sincere in their fears.

1808. Longley, Lawrence D., and Alan G. Braun. *The Politics of Electoral Reform.* New Haven: Yale University Press, 1972. Focuses on the presidential campaign and the operation of the electoral college system.

1809. McGrory, Mary. "Man Out Front." *America* 104 (November 5, 1960): 167. Kennedy campaign surging.

1810. Mailer, Norman. "Superman Comes to the Supermarket." *Esquire* 54 (November 1960): 119-27. A perceptive portrait of Kennedy, a man of "a dozen faces," following the Democratic National Convention.

1811. Martin, Ralph G., and Ed Plaut. *Front Runner, Dark Horse.* Garden City, NY: Doubleday, 1960. John Kennedy and Stuart Symington are seen as "contrasting prototypes--front runner and dark horse."

1812. Meadow Robert G., and Marilyn Jackson-Beeck. "Issue Evaluation: A New Perspective on Presidential Debates." *Journal of Communication* 28 (1978): 84-92. A comparison of the debates of 1960 and 1976.

1813. Melton, Thomas Ronald. "The 1960 Election in Georgia." Ph.D. diss., University of Mississippi, 1985. Kennedy was more successful in appealing to diverse elements than any of his opponents.

1814. Michener, James A. *Report of the County Chairman.* New York: Random House, 1961. The account of a Bucks County, Pennsylvania, campaign worker for Kennedy.

1815. Mickelson, Sig. *The Electric Mirror: Politics in an Age of Television*. New York: Dodd, Mead, 1972. Contains a chapter on the presidential debates.

1816. Middleton, Russell. "The Civil Rights Issue and Presidential Voting among Southern Negroes and Whites." *Social Forces* 40 (March 1962): 209-15.

1817. Morgan, Thomas B. "Madly for Adlai." *American Heritage* 35 (1984): 49-64. Stevenson's candidacy for the presidential nomination in 1960.

1818. Nixon, Richard M. *Six Crises*. New York: Doubleday, 1962. Nixon's sixth crisis was the campaign of 1960.

1819. Norden, Martin F. "Sunrise at Campobello and 1960 Presidential Politics." *Film and History* 16 (1986): 2-8. Dore Schary released the film version of his play "Sunrise at Campobello" to help the Democratic party in 1960.

1820. Osborne, John. "The Economics of the Candidates." *Fortune* 42 (October 1960): 136-41, 277-78, 283-84, 288, 290. Osborne provides a reasonably objective analysis of what might be expected of Kennedy or Nixon as president.

1821. Pike, James A. *A Roman Catholic in the White House*. New York: Doubleday, 1960. The extent to which the views of the Catholic Church can weigh on Catholic candidates.

1822. Pomper, Gerald M. *Nominating the President: The Politics of Convention Choice*. Evanston, Il.: Northwestern University Press, 1963. Kennedy and 1960, including the campaign.

1823. Powell, James Grant. "An Analytical and Comparative Study of the Persuasion of Kennedy and Nixon in the 1960 Campaign." Ph.D. dissertation, University of Wisconsin, 1963. An analysis of the campaign speeches of the two candidates and the audience's reaction to them.

1824. Reinsch, J. Leonard. *Getting Elected: From Radio and Roosevelt to Television and Reagan*. New York: Hippocrene, 1988. Kennedy's media consultant includes chapters on JFK's use of the media in 1960.

1825. Rossman, Jules. "*Meet the Press* and National Elections: The Candidates and the Issues, 1952-1964." Ph.D. diss., Michigan State University, 1968. Contends that Kennedy's and Nixon's linguistic styles were similar in their lack of warmth, humor, or colorful language.

1826. Sarbaugh, Timothy Jerome. "John Fitzgerald Kennedy, the Catholic Issue, and Presidential Politics, 1959-1960." Ph.D. diss., Loyola University of Chicago, 1988. Sarbaugh contends that the Catholic Church and press followed a neutral policy toward the two major candidates in the election of 1960.

1827. Sather, Lawrence Arne. "Biography as Rhetorical Criticism: An Analysis of John F. Kennedy's 1960 Presidential Campaign by Selected Biographers." Ph.D. diss., Washington State University, 1974. Examines several biographical accounts of Kennedy's 1960 presidential campaign.

1828. Schlesinger, Arthur M., Jr. *Kennedy or Nixon: Does It Make Any Difference?* New York: Macmillan, 1960. Schlesinger's contribution to Kennedy's presidential effort.

1829. Sevareid, Eric, ed. *Candidates 1960: Behind the Headlines in the Presidential Race*. New York: Basic Books, 1959. Journalist Fletcher Knebel wrote the chapter on Kennedy.

1830. Silvestri, Vito Nicholas. "John F. Kennedy: His Speaking in the Wisconsin and West Virginia Primaries 1960." Ph.D. diss., Indiana University, 1966. In Wisconsin Kennedy relied on logical reasoning; in West Virginia, on strong emotional appeals.

1831. Smith, David S. "Alfred E. Smith and John Kennedy: The Religious Issue during the Presidential Campaigns of 1928 and 1960." Ph.D. diss., Southern Illinois University, 1964. Kennedy's handling of the religious issue was far superior than Smith's approaches.

1832. Sorensen, Theodore C. "Election of 1960." In *History of American Presidential Elections, 1789-1968*. Edited by Arthur M. Schlesinger, Jr. 9 vols. New York: Chelsea House, 1985, 9:3449-3569. Sorensen blames Kennedy's narrow victory on his Catholicism, which cost him the votes of Protestant Democrats.

1833. *The Speeches, Remarks and Press Conferences of Senator John F. Kennedy and Vice President Richard M. Nixon*. U. S. Congress, Senate Subcommittee on Communications of the Committee on Commerce, Report 994, 87th Congress, 1st Session. Part I: The Campaign Speeches of John F. Kennedy: Part II: The Campaign Speeches of Richard M. Nixon; Part III: The Televised Debates. Washington: Government Printing Office, 1961-1962.

1834. Spragens, William C. "Kennedy Era Speechwriting, Public Relations and Public Opinion." *Presidential Studies Quarterly* (Winter 1984): 78-86. Examines the pioneering public opinion monitoring in 1960 by Kennedy's "Cambridge Group" and other associates, which influenced the speechwriting.

1835. Stelznew, Hermann G. "Humphrey and Kennedy Court West Virginia, May 3, 1960." *Southern Speech Communication Journal* 37 (Fall 1971): 21-33. The deceptive use of language by the candidates in the West Virginia primary race.

1836. Tillet, Paul, ed. *Inside Politics: The National Conventions, 1960*. St. Dobbs Ferry, NY: Oceana Publications, 1962. Political scientists focus on the composition of the state delegations to the conventions, campaign organizations, and nominations.

1837. Vanocur, Sander. "Humphrey v. Kennedy: High Stakes in Wisconsin." *Reporter* 22 (March 17, 1960): 28-30. Kennedy's gamble in entering the Wisconsin primary.

1838. White, Theodore H. *The Making of the President, 1960.* New York: Atheneum, 1967. The best of White's presidents books, he argues that Kennedy ran a brilliant campaign.

1839. Wolfe, James S. "Exclusion, Fusion, or Dialogue: How Should Religion and Politics Relate?" *Journal of Church and State* 22 (Winter 1980): 89-105. Discusses religion and its relation to politics by contrasting the place of religion in the Kennedy and Jimmy Carter presidential campaigns of 1960 and 1976.

1840. _____. "The Religion of and about John F. Kenndey." In *John F. Kennedy.* Edited by Paul Harper and Joann P. Krieg, pp. 287-99. No. **1600.** Kennedy's religion was comprised of Catholicism, humanism, and patriotism.

1841. _____. "The Religious Issue Revisited: Presbyterian Responses to Kennedy's Presidential Campaign." *Journal of Presbyterian History* 57 (Spring 1979): 1-18. Presbyterians focused more on Kennedy's character, record, and policy positions than they did on the religious issue.

1842. Young, William Lewis. "The John F. Kennedy Library Oral History Project: The West Virginia Democratic Presidential Primary, 1960." Ph.D. diss., Ohio State University, 1982. Based on interviews by the author of forty-eight West Virginians who participated in the 1960 Democratic primary, this study summarizes their views on various issues of the campaign.

B. ELECTION RESULTS AND THE TRANSITION

1843. "An Advance Glimpse of Kennedy's Ideas." *U.S. News and World Report* 49 (November 28, 1960): 40-1. New ideas and proposed changes in government.

1844. "After the Election." *Commonweal* 73 (November 18, 1960): 187-88. Anticipates a change of mood and direction in the management of the country's affairs.

1845. Ascoli, Max. "The Inaugural Address." *Reporter* 24 (February 2, 1961): 10, 12. Kennedy's address failed to impress Ascoli.

1846. Beck, Kent M. "Necessary Lies, Hidden Truths: Cuba in the 1960 Campaign." *Diplomatic History* 8 (1984): 37-59. Cuba failed to have a crucial impact because the campaign produced no clear-cut difference between Kennedy and Nixon on that issue.

1847. Bone, Hugh A. "The 1960 Election in Washington." *Western Political Quarterly* 14 (1961): 373-82. Washington state narrowly voted for Richard Nixon.

1848. Brauer, Carl M. *Presidential Transitions: Eisenhower through Reagan.* New York: Oxford University Press, 1986. Comparative analysis of the period between the election and the inauguration.

1849. Burns, James MacGregor. "How Kennedy as President Will Differ from Eisenhower." *U. S. News and World Report* 50 (January 30, 1961): 31. In an interview, Burns suggests Kennedy will be much more of a political president.

1850. _____. "Size-up of Kennedy." *U.S. News and World Report* 49 (November 28, 1960): 72-6. In an interview, Burns predicts Kennedy will be a strong legislative leader, a strong party leader, and a strong chief of state.

1851. Converse, Philip E., et al. "Stability and Change in 1960: A Reinstating Election." *American Political Science Review* 55 (June 1961): 269-80. Blames Kennedy's narrow victory on his Catholic religion.

1852. Dawidowicz, Lucy S., and Leon J. Goldstein. *Politics in a Pluralist Democracy: Studies of Voting in the 1960 Election.* New York: Institute of Human Relations Press, 1963. Studies the effects of religion and ethnic origin on the 1960 presidential election.

1853. "Decisions Press on Kennedy." *Business Week* (November 26, 1960), pp. 25-7. Laying plans for the new administration.

1854. Driggs, Don W. "The 1960 Election in Nevada." *Western Political Quarterly* 14 (1961): 347-49. Nevada narrowly went to Kennedy.

1855. "A Family Man with a Big New Job to Do." *Life* 49 (November 21, 1960): 32-5. Focusing on election night activities and the days ahead.

1856. "First Week with Kennedy." *U.S. News and World Report* 49 (November 28, 1960): 37-9. Focusing on Kennedy's busy transition schedule.

1857. "Flying High." *Time* 76 (November 28, 1960): 16-7. Meetings with Richard Nixon and Lyndon Johnson.

1858. Folliard, Edward T. "How Kennedy Views Nation's Mood." *Nation's Business* 48 (December 1960): 27-8. Kennedy believes the nation is ready to move.

1859. Hahn, Dan F. "Ask Not What a Youngster Can Do For You: Kennedy's

Inaugural Address." *Presidential Studies Quarterly* 12 (Fall 1982): 610-14. Kennedy had to overcome his liabilities of his youthfulness, which he began to do in his inaugural address.

1860. "Inauguration: 1961." *Commonweal* 73 (Februrary 3, 1961): 471-72. The inauguration of Kennedy represents one of the most dramatic political events of this century.

1861. Irion, Frederick C. "The 1960 Election in New Mexico." *Western Political Quarterly* 14 (1961): 350-54. New Mexico barely went to JFK.

1862. Jeffries, John W. "The 'Quest for National Purpose' of 1960." *American Quarterly* 30 (1978): 451-70. Kennedy capitalized on the supposed lack of national purpose.

1863. Johnson, Gerald W. "Ben Hur Made It." *New Republic* 143 (December 26, 1960): 10. Kennedy's success in getting first-class men to accept second-class jobs.

1864. Jonas, Frank H. "The 1960 Election in Utah." *Western Political Quarterly* 14 (1961): 365-72. Nixon carried Utah.

1865. Kallina, Edmund, F., Jr. *Courthouse Over White House: Chicago and the Presidential Election of 1960.* Orlando: University of Central Florida Press, 1988. Vote fraud in Illinois.

1866. _____. "The State's Attorney and the President: The Inside Story of the 1960 Presidential Election in Illinois." *Journal of American Studies* 11 (1978): 147-60. Election day fraud in Cook County.

1867. _____. "Was Nixon Cheated in 1960?" *Journalism Quarterly* 62 (1985): 138-40. Nonpartisan special prosecutor found no evidence of ballot manipulation in Chicago in 1960, at least not based on Earl Mazo's charges.

1868. "Kennedy, Mystery Man to the Rest of World." *U. S. News and World Report* 49 (November 21, 1960): 82-4. World leaders expect changes but nobody is sure the direction they will take.

1869. "The Kennedy Strategy: Clues to the Next Four Years." *U.S. News and World Report* 49 (December 19, 1960): 38-41. Predictions of rapid change are being revised.

1870. Key, V. O., Jr., and Milton C. Cummings, Jr. *The Responsible Electorate: Rationality in Presidential Voting, 1936-1960.* Cambridge: Harvard University Press, 1966. An analysis of aggregate voting behavior.

1871. Lee, Eugene C., and William Buchanan. "The 1960 Election in California."

Western Political Quarterly 14 (1961): 309-26. The campaign resulted in a close victory for Nixon.

1872. "Let Us Begin: Reflections on the Inaugural Address." *New Republic* 144 (January 30, 1961): 3-4. The tired have retired and the men of energy and boundless self-confidence are in charge.

1873. McGrory, Mary. "Flying Start and Notable Agility." *America* 104 (February 4, 1961): 585. A coverage of JFK during the inaugural weekend.

1874. Margolis, Howard. "John Kennedy's New Frontier: The Margin was Narrow but the Responsibility is Clear." *Science* 132 (November 18, 1960): 1472-73. The challenge of passing education and scientific research measures.

1875. Martin, Boyd A. "The 1960 Election in Idaho." *Western Political Quarterly* 14 (1961): 339-42. A victory for Nixon.

1876. Martin, Curtis. "The 1960 Election in Colorado." *Western Political Quarterly* 14 (1961): 327-30. Nixon won in Colorado.

1877. Medhurst, Martin Jay. "'God Bless the President': The Rhetoric of Inaugural Prayer." Ph.D. diss., Pennsylvania State University, 1980. A critical study of the role played by clergymen in the inauguration of the president, including how the issue of Kennedy's Catholicism affected the inaugural prayers.

1878. Neustadt, Richard E. "Approaches to Staffing the Presidency: Notes on FDR and JFK." *American Political Science Review* 57 (December 1963): 855-62. In late 1960 Professor Neustadt sent JFK a report on the staffing problems facing a new president; Kennedy was fascinated by the way Franklin Roosevelt solved his staffing problems.

1879. Payne, Thomas. "The 1960 Election in Montana." *Western Political Quarterly* 14 (1961): 343-46. Kennedy carried Montana.

1880. "President-elect: Answers and Questions." *Time* 76 (November 21, 1960): 17-18. Kennedy's first press conference includes the announcement of his first administrative appointments.

1881. "President-elect: Boundless and Endless." *Time* 77 (January 2, 1961): 13-14. Meetings at Palm Beach and more announced administrative appointments.

1882. "President-elect: 'Daddy' Was a Busy Man." *Newsweek* 57 (January 9, 1961): 20-3. The interruption of Kennedy's daughter, the release of the economic task force report, and cabinet level appointments.

1883. "Ring Up the Curtain." *New Republic* 144 (January 9, 1961): 2. Because of a lack of a national emergency, Kennedy's task is more difficult than Franklin Roosevelt's.

1884. Roper, Elmo. "Polling Post Mortem." *Saturday Review* 43 (November 26, 1960): 10-12. This study indicated a significant shift of Eisenhower Catholic voters to Kennedy.

1885. Rovere, Richard. "Letter from Washington." *New Yorker* 36 (November 19, 1960): 203-10. Kennedy will begin from a position of weakness.

1886. Schnapper, B. N., ed. *New Frontiers of the Kennedy Administration: The Texts of the Task Force Reports Prepared for the President.* Washington: Public Affairs Press, 1961. A compilation of the various task force reports, written by distinguished authorities and public figures at Kennedy's request either during the transition period or the early days of the administration.

1887. Slotnik, Herman E. "The 1960 Election in Alaska." *Western Political Quarterly* 14 (1961): 300-04. Nixon narrowly carried Alaska.

1888. "A Staff Size-up of Two Presidents: Eisenhower and Kennedy." *U.S. News and World Report* 50 (January 30, 1961): 38-9. Written by the staff of *U.S. News and World Report* who see significant differences between the two presidents.

1889. Strauss, William L. "The 1960 Election in Arizona." *Western Political Quarterly* 14 (1961): 305-08. A landslide victory for Nixon.

1890. Swarthout, John M. "The 1960 Election in Oregon." *Western Political Quarterly* 14 (1961): 355-64. Nixon won Oregon.

1891. Sweeney, James R. "Whispers in the Golden Silence: Harry F. Byrd, John F. Kennedy, and Virginia Democrats in the 1960 Presidential Election." *Virginia Magazine of History and Biography* 99 (January 1991): 3-44. Conservative Democratic Senator Harry Byrd worked behind the scenes against Kennedy.

1892. Trachsel, Herman H. "The 1960 Election in Wyoming." *Western Political Quarterly* 14 (1961): 383-87. Another win for Nixon.

1893. "Transition from Ike to JFK." *Senior Scholastic* 77 (November 30, 1960): 18-20. Includes an analysis of the presidential election.

1894. Tuttle, Daniel W., Jr. "The 1960 Election in Hawaii." *Western Political Quarterly* 14 (1961): 331-38. A very narrow win for Nixon.

1895. "What Kennedy Will Be Like as President." *U.S. News and World Report* 50 (January 30, 1961) 28-30. A contrasting with Eisenhower's presidency.

1896. "What Kennedy Will Do as President." *U.S. News and World Report* 49 (November 21, 1960): 40-4. Strategy is to move fast before the flush of victory wears off.

1897. Webster, Daniel Charles. "The Taking of the Fifth: The Contested 1960 Election in the Indiana Fifth Congressional District." Ed.D. diss., Ball State University, 1986. A rare congressional election study in a pivotal election year.

8
The Kennedy Administration, 1961–1963

A. GENERAL WORKS

1898. Adler, Bill. *Do You Remember the '60s?* New York: Avon Books, 1992. A question and answer book on the 60s.

1899. *Americans in the 1960's: A Study of Public Attitudes.* New York: Yankelovich, Skelly and White, prepared for the John F. Kennedy Library, 1978.

1900. Bailey, Blake. *The 60s.* New York: Mallard Press, 1992. An oversized book that includes many illustrations.

1901. Bernstein, Irving. *Promises Kept: John F. Kennedy's New Frontier.* No. 1592. Only covers the domestic side but in detailed, up-to-date fashion.

1902. Braden, William. *The Age of Aquarius: Technology and the Cultural Revolution.* Chicago: Quadrangle Books, 1970. A synthesis focusing on the struggle between the humanists and the technologists.

1903. Bradlee, Benjamin C. *Conversations with Kennedy.* New York: W. W. Norton, 1975. Bradlee of *Newsweek* provides an intimately revealing account.

1904. Brooks, John. *The Great Leap: The Past Twenty-Five Years in America.* New York: Harper and Row, 1966. Covers social trends into the 1960s.

1905. Chalmers, David M. *And the Crooked Places Made Straight: The Struggle for Social Change in the 1960s.* Baltimore: Johns Hopkins University Press, 1991. A thoughtful survey of the 60s.

1906. Collier, Peter, and David Horowitz. *Destructive Generation: Second Thoughts about the Sixties.* New York: Summit Books, 1989. Critical view of the New Left.

1907. Cowan, Paul. *The Making of an Un-American: A Dialogue with Experience.* New York: Viking Press, 1970. A personal account by a former Peace Corps member.

1908. Dickstein, Morris. *Gates of Eden: American Culture in the Sixties.* New York: Basic Books, 1977. Excellent on the relationship between culture and radicalism.

1909. Drake, Nicholas. *The Sixties: A Decade in Vogue.* New York: Prentice Hall, 1988. Striking illustrations.

1910. Ferber, Michael, and Staughton Lynd, eds. *The Resistance.* Boston: Beacon Press, 1971. An empathetic view of the anti-war movement.

1911. Gelfand, Mark I. *A Nation of Cities: The Federal Government and Urban America, 1933-1965.* New York: Oxford University Press, 1975. Excellent study of national policy.

1912. Giglio, James N. *The Presidency of John F. Kennedy.* No. **1605.** Synthesis of domestic and foreign policy.

1913. Gitlin, Todd. *The Sixties: Years of Hope, Days of Rage.* New York: Bantam Books, 1987. Written by a 60s activist, this is probably the most detailed social account of that decade, focusing on the New Left and counterculture.

1914. Goldstein, Toby. *Working from the Dream: America in the Sixties.* New York: J. Messner, 1988. An impressionistic memoir that touches on such issues as civil rights, Vietnam, and the women's movement.

1915. Goodman, Mitchell, ed. *The Movement toward a New America: The Beginning of a Long Revolution.* Philadelphia: Pilgrim Press, 1971. A collection of underground press articles.

1916. Goodwin, Richard N. *Remembering America: A Voice from the Sixties.* Boston: Little, Brown, 1988. Written by an insider who views Kennedy as maturing at the time of his assassination.

1917. Gottlieb, Annie. *Do You Believe in Magic? The Second Coming of the Sixties Generation.* New York: Times Books, 1987. Recollections of the Sixties.

1918. Grant, R. G. *The 1960s.* New York: Mallard Press, 1990. A coffee table account.

1919. Hamby, Alonzo L. *Liberalism and Its Challengers: FDR to Reagan.* New York: Oxford University Press, 1985. Includes a chapter on "From the Old Politics to the New: John and Robert Kennedy."

1920. Harris, David. *Dreams Die Hard*. New York: St. Martin's, 1982. A portrait of three individuals involved in the student movement, including Allard K. Lowenstein.

1921. Hayden, Tom. *Reunion: A Memoir*. New York: Collier Books, 1989. One of the founders of the SDS, Hayden provides his impressions of the Kennedy brothers.

1922. Heath, Jim F. *Decade of Disillusionment: The Kennedy-Johnson Years*. Bloomington: Indiana University Press, 1975. Decade began with high optimism and ended tragically, told in a straightforward fashion.

1923. Hoffman, Abbie. *Revolution for the Hell of It*. New York: Dial Press, 1968. The convicted leader of the antiwar Youth International Party who sought revolution through political comedy.

1924. Issel, William. *Social Change in the United States, 1945-1983*. New York: Schocken Books, 1985. Effects of capitalism on American society.

1925. Isserman, Maurice. *If I Had a Hammer: The Death of the Old Left and the Birth of the New Left*. New York: Basic Books, 1987. Examines continuities between the Old Left and early New Left.

1926. Jackson, Kenneth T. *Crabgrass Frontier: The Suburbanization of America*. New York: Oxford University Press, 1985. Focuses on one of the significant migrations in American history, which especially occurred during Kennedy's public life.

1927. Jencks, Christopher, and David Riesman. *The Academic Revolution*. Garden City, NY: Doubleday, 1968. A sociological and historical analysis of American higher education.

1928. Kaiser, Charles. *1968 in America: Music, Politics, Chaos, Counterculture, and the Shaping of a Generation*. New York: Weidenfeld and Nicolson, 1988. Written by a strong admirer of John Kennedy and a close friend of Theodore White.

1929. Keefe, Robert. "On Cowboys and Collectives: The Kennedy-Nixon Generation." *Massachusetts Review* 21 (Fall 1990): 551-60. Examines Kennedy's *Profiles in Courage* (1956) and Richard Nixon's *Six Crises* (1962) with the idea that their writings have something to say about their fantasy worlds.

1930. Kelman, Steven. *Push Comes to Shove: The Escalation of Student Protest*. Boston: Houghton Mifflin, 1970. Focuses on student unrest at Harvard University.

1931. Keniston, Kenneth. *Youth and Dissent: The Rise of a New Opposition*. New York: Harcourt Brace Jovanovich, 1971. Psychological approach to student dissent during the 1960s.

1932. Knight, Douglas M. *Street of Dreams: The Nature and Legacy of the 1960s.* Durham: Duke University Press, 1989. Much of this insightful personal history focuses on Duke University.

1933. Koerselman, Gary H. *The Lost Decade: A Story of America in the 1960s.* New York: Peter Lang, 1987. Even though Kennedy's policies would have little lasting effect, his political style did.

1934. Kraft, Joseph. *Profiles in Power: A Washington Insight.* New York: New American Library, 1966. Includes portraits of Kennedy, Robert McNamara, and McGeorge Bundy.

1935. Kuklick, Bruce. *The Good Ruler: From Herbert Hoover to Richard Nixon.* New Brunswick, NJ: Rutgers University Press, 1988. Kuklick evaluates presidents on the basis of how Americans feel about them, making Kennedy a successful chief executive.

1936. Leary, Timothy. *Flashbacks: An Autobiography.* Los Angeles: J. P. Tarcher, 1983. An oblique reference to Kennedy supposedly experimenting with LSD.

1937. Lee, Martin, and Bruce Schlain. *Acid Dreams: the CIA, LSD and the Sixties Rebellion.* New York: Grove Press, 1985. The impact of LSD on both the politics of the 1960s and on the CIA.

1938. Light, Paul. *The President's Agenda: Domestic Policy Choice from Kennedy to Carter.* Baltimore: Johns Hopkins University Press, 1983. General coverage of Kennedy's domestic agenda.

1939. Mangano, Joseph J. *Living Legacy: How 1964 Changed America.* Lanham, Md.: University Press of America, 1993. Contains scattered references to Kennedy.

1940. Matusow, Allen J. *The Unraveling of America: A History of Liberalism in the 1960s.* New York: Harper and Row, 1984. A beautifully written critique of liberalism from a New Left perspective, Matusow covers Kennedy's domestic policies.

1941. Miller, James. *"Democracy is in the Streets": From Port Huron to the Siege of Chicago.* New York: Simon and Schuster, 1987. About the origins and early years of the New Left when students launched "America's last great experiment in democratic idealism."

1942. Morgan, Edward P. *The 60s Experience: Hard Lessons about Modern America.* Philadelphia: Temple University Press, 1991. An excellent scholarly effort by an academic participant.

1943. Morrison, Joan, and Robert K. Morrison. *From Camelot to Kent State: The*

Sixties Experience in the Words of Those Who Lived It. New York: Times Books, 1987. The recollections of fifty-nine men and women who lived through the 60s.

1944. Mowry, George, and Blaine A. Brownell. *The Urban Nation, 1920-1980*. New York: Hill and Wang, 1981. Good on the 1960s.

1945. Mueller, John. "Presidential Popularity from Truman to Johnson." *American Political Science Review* 64 (March 1970): 18-34. The popular decline of Presidents Truman and Johnson was quite steep while President Kennedy seems to have been somewhat better at maintaining his popularity.

1946. O'Brien, Geoffrey. *Dream Time: Chapters from the Sixties*. New York: Viking Press, 1988. A collection of reflections on American culture in the 1960s.

1947. O'Neill, William L. *Coming Apart: An Informal History of America in the 1960's*. Chicago: Quadrangle Books, 1971. A comprehensive popular history of the 60s focusing more on the culture and intellectual side, concluding that Kennedy left a mediocre record.

1948. Opotowsky, Stan. *The Kennedy Government*. New York: Popular Library, 1961. A preview for the general public of the cabinet officers, the Congress, and the regulatory agencies at the beginning of the new administration.

1949. Parmet, Herbert. *JFK: The Presidency of John F. Kennedy*. No. **1617**.

1950. Pope, Harrison, Jr. *Voices from the Drug Culture*. Boston: Beacon Press, 1971. Published senior thesis at Harvard University that benefited from the assistance of Erik Erikson and others.

1951. Reeves, Thomas, ed. *John F. Kennedy: The Man, the Politician, the President*. Malabar, Fl.: Robert E. Krieger Publishing, 1990. An anthology of selections from published works.

1952. _____. *A Question of Character: A Life of John F. Kennedy*. No. **1620**.

1953. Reich, Charles. *The Greening of America: How the Youth Revolution is Trying to Make America Livable*. New York: Random House, 1970. A favorable view of the supposed new American revolution.

1954. Roland, Charles P. *The Improbable Era: The South since World War II*. Lexington: University of Kentucky Press, 1975. World War II changed the South almost as much as the Civil War--a major theme in this gracefully written book.

1955. Rorabaugh, W. J. *Berkeley at War*. New York: Oxford University Press, 1989. Berkeley students turned away from Kennedy after the Cuban missile crisis.

1956. Roszak, Theodore. *The Making of a Counter Culture: Reflections on the Technocratic Society and its Youthful Opposition*. Garden City, NY: Doubleday, 1969. A standard work that praises the counterculture's rejection of rationality and technology.

1957. Sale, Kirpatrick. *SDS*. New York: Random House, 1973. An early work on the Students for a Democratic Society.

1958. Schlesinger, Arthur M., Jr. *The Cycles of American History*. Boston: Houghton Mifflin, 1986. Springled with innumerable references to the Kennedy presidency.

1959. _____. *A Thousand Days: John F. Kennedy in the White House*. No. **1624**. A detailed, thoughtful account from an administration insider.

1960. Shachtman, Tom. *Decade of Shocks: Dallas to Watergate, 1963-1974*. New York: Poseidon Press, 1983. A penetrating examination of the myths and assumptions Americans held about their society that were challenged and even altered by the "decade of shocks."

1961. Slater, Philip. *The Pursuit of Loneliness: American Culture at the Breaking Point*. Boston: Beacon Press, 1970. An excellent assessment of those who joined the counterculture.

1962. Sorensen, Theodore C. *Decision-making in the White House: The Olive Branch or the Arrows*. New York: Columbia University Press, 1963. Cogently analyzes the process of presidential decisions.

1963. _____. *Kennedy*. No. **1625**. For the Kennedy administration position.

1964. Steinem, Gloria. *Outrageous Acts and Everyday Rebellions*. New York: Holt, Rinehart, and Winston, 1983. A strong admirer of Kennedy, Steinem was a frequent visitor to the White House in the fall of 1963.

1965. Tanzer, Lester, ed. *The Kennedy Circle*. Washington: Robert B. Luce, 1961. Washington reporters write biographical essays of Kennedy administration officials in the White House and cabinet.

1966. Tichler, Barbara L., ed. *Sights on the Sixties*. New Brunswick, NJ: Rutgers University Press, 1992. A diverse anthology on the 1960s that includes essays on films, antiwar dissent in the college press, and humanistic psychology.

1967. Unger, Irwin. *The Movement: A History of the American New Left, 1959-1972*. New York: Dodd, Mead, 1974. The rejection of liberalism.

1968. Viorist, Milton. *Fire in the Streets: America in the 1960s*. New York: Simon and Schuster, 1979. Excellent on social disorder from Greensboro in 1960 to Kent State University in 1970.

1969. Von Hoffman, Nicholas. *We Are the People Our Parents Warned Us Against.* Chicago: Quadrangle Books, 1968. Centers on the Haight-Ashbury section of San Francisco.

1970. Warhol, Andy, and Pat Hackett. *POPism, The Warhol '60's.* New York: Harcourt Brace Jovanovich, 1980. Warhol's personal view of the Pop phenomenon in New York.

1971. Wattenberg, Ben J. *This U.S.A.: An Unexpected Family Portrait of 194,067,296 Americans Drawn from the Census.* Garden City, NY: Doubleday, 1965. From the 1960 decennial census and subsequent census data through 1965.

1972. Wofford, Harris. *Of Kennedys and Kings: Making Sense of the Sixties.* New York: Farrar, Straus, Giroux, 1980. An important and provocative overview of liberalism by a Kennedy administration member.

1973. Wolfe, Tom. *The Electric Kool-Aid Acid Test.* New York: Farrar, Straus, and Giroux, 1968. Drugs and the counterculture.

B. CONTEMPORARY ASSESSMENTS OF KENNEDY AS PRESIDENT

1974. Alsop, Joseph. "Legacy of John F. Kennedy: Memories of an Uncommon Man." *Saturday Evening Post* 237 (November 21, 1964): 15-19. Kennedy will be remembered as a great president.

1975. Alsop, Stewart. "How's Kennedy Doing?: The President's 'Report Card' to Date." *Saturday Evening Post* 234 (September 16, 1961): 44-5, 101-04, 106. Kennedy is a tough and intelligent guy who learns quickly.

1976. "Are You Satisfied?" *New Republic* 144 (May 29, 1961): 2. Debits and assets of Kennedy's presidential performance.

1977. Bergquist, Laura. "JFK One Year Later." *Look* 26 (January 2, 1962): 44-5. The same nagging problems are around, only more so.

1978. "Birch View of JFK." *Newsweek* 63 (February 24, 1964): 29-30. The ultra-right-wing organization views Kennedy as an agent of the international Communist conspiracy.

1979. Brandon, Donald. "Kennedy's Record in Foreign Affairs." *Catholic World* 195

(July 1962): 219-27. Kennedy initially demonstrated a lack of understanding and skill in foreign affairs.

1980. "British View of Kennedy Rule: Disarray on Higher Levels." *U.S. News and World Report* 51 (July 10, 1961): 51. The London *Times* finds confusion and shortcomings in U.S. policy on vital issues.

1981. Burns, James MacGregor. "The Four Kennedys of the First Year." *New York Times Magazine* (January 14, 1962), pp. 9, 70, 72. The first Kennedy was preoccupied with foreign affairs; the second was a policy liberal having difficulties with a conservative Congress; the third, a fiscal moderate; and the fourth, a conservative regarding organization and institutions.

1982. _____. "The Legacy of the 1,000 days." *New York Times Magazine* (December 1, 1963), pp. 27, 118, 120. Burns's appraisal: "I believe [Kennedy] did make a complete political and intellectual commitment to his policies and programs. It will never be known whether he ultimately would have made a commitment of the heart."

1983. _____. "New Size-up of the President." *U.S. News and World Report* 51 (December 4, 1961): 44-6, 49. Burns contends that Kennedy has made the White House the center of action; in foreign policy, he is cautious; domestically, he has an "economy streak."

1984. Carleton, William Graves. "Kennedy in History: An Early Appraisal." *Antioch Review* 24 (Fall 1964): 277-99. Carleton doubts whether Kennedy would have been more successful in a second term; he argues that Kennedy "needlessly fanned the flames of the Cold War."

1985. Cater, Douglass. "A New Style, A New Tempo." *Reporter* 24 (March 16, 1961): 28-30. The new look of the Kennedy administration includes a take-charge president and a reduction of formal organizational structures.

1986. "As Changes Start under Kennedy. . . ." *U.S. News and World Report* 50 (February 6, 1961): 31-3. Kennedy's early take-charge actions intermixed with caution.

1987. Cogley, John. "Kennedy the Catholic." *Commonweal* 79 (January 10, 1964): 422-24. Kennedy's performance as a Catholic president is reviewed by a Catholic viewpoint.

1988. Collins, Frederic W. "The Mind of John F. Kennedy." *New Republic* 144 (May 8, 1961): 15-20. A good preliminary assessment of the Kennedy presidency.

1989. "Criticisms of Kennedy." *New Republic* 148 (May 18, 1963): 2. Kennedy seems unable to get the country moving again.

1990. Crown, James Tracy, and George P. Penty. *Kennedy in Power*. New York: Ballantine, 1961. An analysis of Kennedy's first year as president.

1991. Fairlie, Henry. "He Was a Man of Only One Season." *New York Times Magazine* (November 21, 1965), p. 28-9, 129-31. The British political writer contends that Kennedy's vision of politics left no clear sense of direction.

1992. "For a Year's Foreign Policy: 'A' for JFK." *Life* 54 (April 13, 1962): 4. The nation has regained its confidence in JFK and in itself.

1993. Frankfurter, A. "Kennedy Pro Arte . . . Et Sequitur?" *Art News* 62 (January 1964): 23, 46-7, 60-1. Kennedy's presidency had a positive effect on the arts in America.

1994. Greenberg, D. S. "John F. Kennedy: The Man and His Meaning." *Science* 142 (November 29, 1963): 1151-52. Kennedy brought the academies, the literati, and the scientists into the nation's capital as workers, guests, and companions.

1995. Griffiths, Eldon. "Kennedy's Image Abroad, Free-World Leaders Speak Their Minds." *Newsweek* 57 (April 3, 1961): 42-4, 46. Countries include Britain, France, Italy, Lebanon, Iran, Pakistan, India, Hong Kong, and Japan.

1996. Hagan, Roger. "Between Two Eras." *Correspondent* (January-February 1964), pp. 33-42. Hagan argues that Kennedy's greatest failure was his inability to move beyond a bipolar world.

1997. Halle, Louis J. "Appraisal of Kennedy as World Leader." *New York Times Magazine* (June 16, 1963), pp. 7, 40, 42. JFK receives mixed reviews from Europeans.

1998. _____. "The Proper Washingtonian." *New Republic* 145 (December 11, 1961): 9-10. Halle draws a parallel between Kennedy and Lincoln.

1999. Hazlitt, Henry. "First 100 Days." *Newsweek* 57 (May 15, 1961): 90. The unfolding Kennedy domestic program is one of inflation and welfare-statism; the Bay of Pigs is his greatest foreign policy failure.

2000. "How Kennedy Looks to the World Now." *U.S. News and World Report* 51 (September 18, 1961): 64-8. Kennedy is evaluated in various foreign nations.

2001. "How Kennedy Runs the White House." *U.S. News and World Report* 51 (November 13, 1961): 54-7. After ten months in office Kennedy's lines of authority are more obvious.

2002. "How Rest of the World Sees President Kennedy." *U.S. News and World Report* 50 (January 30, 1961): 45-6. A country-by-country appraisal.

2003. Hughes, H. Stuart. "A Most Unstuffy Man." *Nation* 197 (December 14, 1963) 408-11. A history professor at Harvard evaluates the loss of a childhood friend and speculates on President Johnson's political fortunes.

2004. Hyman, Sidney. "How Mr. Kennedy Gets the Answers." *New York Times Magazine* (October 20, 1963), pp. 17, 104-05. An examination of Kennedy's formal and informal sources of information.

2005. "An Intelligent, Courageous Presidency." *Life* 55 (November 29, 1963): 4. Kennedy's legacy was intelligence and grace in action.

2006. "It's One Year after JFK: The Changes." *U.S. News and World Report* 57 (November 23, 1964): 60-6. Includes an interview with Kennedy biographer James MacGregor Burns.

2007. "JFK: Reflections a Year Later." *Life* 57 (November 20, 1964): 4. A favorable evaluation.

2008. "JFK on the First Hundred Days." *Newsweek* 57 (May 8, 1961): 23-4. The heady optimism following the inauguration has long vanished.

2009. "JFK and His Critics." *Newsweek* 60 (July 16, 1962): 15-19. Not since the days of FDR and the New Deal has an attack on a president seemed so heated.

2010. Johnson, Gerald W. "What is Kennedy?" *New Republic* 145 (July 24, 1961): 14. At the completion of the first six months, the administration's character is not yet clearly apparent.

2011. "Kennedy as Target." *New Republic* 148 (June 1, 1963): 3-5. Kennedy's performance is less impressive than his style.

2012. "Kennedy's First Eighteen Months, the Record." *U.S. News and World Report* 53 (July 23, 1962): 39-43. Kennedy still faces most of the problems that he inherited.

2013. Kluckhohn, Frank L. *America Listen! An Up to the Minute Report on the Chaos in Today's Washington. The Fumblings of the Kennedy Administration, The Search for Power, The Wielding of Influence over Business and the Press.* Derby, Ct: Monarch Books, 1963. An ultra-conservative diatribe.

2014. Kraft, Joseph. "John F. Kennedy: Portrait of a President." *Harper's* 228 (January 1964): 96, 98, 100. A description of Kennedy's personal and public characteristics.

2015. Lasky, Victory. *JFK: The Man and the Myth.* No. **1610.** A negative appraisal.

2016. Lawrence, David. "After Two Years--." *U.S. News and World Report* 54 (January 28, 1963): 100. If the election were held at this time, Kennedy would win a second term largely because of Republican ineptitude in exposing the administration's shortcomings.

2017. "Lessons to Learn from a Faltering Start." *Business Week* (January 13, 1962), p. 118. The irresolution of the administration made for a mixed first-year performance.

2018. Lippmann, Walter. "Kennedy at Mid-term." *Newsweek* 61 (January 21, 1963): 24-6, 29. The narrow 1960 election victory has restrained Kennedy's efforts domestically; Kennedy is facing a world which is less dangerous than it seemed to be in 1961.

2019. "Looking Back, Looking Forward: Kennedy's First Two Years." *U.S. News and World Report* 52 (January 8, 1962): 59-61. Like the first year, the pattern for the second suggests some new disappointments and some fresh successes.

2020. "Man of the Year: A Way with People." *Time* 79 (January 5, 1962): 9-14. Includes the controversial cover portrait by Pietro Annigoni which aroused Kennedy's anger.

2021. Moley, Raymond. "FDR-JFK: A Brain Truster Compares Two Presidents, Two Programs." *Newsweek* 57 (April 17, 1961): 32-4, 37. An excellent essay by Franklin Roosevelt's former brain trust chief.

2022. "Mr. Kennedy Today, the Change in Him." *Newsweek* 57 (January 23, 1961): 16-20. Much of the brashness of the cock-sure candidate has vanished.

2023. Muggeridge, Malcolm. "Kennedy the Man and the Myth." *Maclean's Magazine* 79 (April 1966), 14-15. Sees Kennedy as a product of his staff.

2024. Neustadt, Richard E. "Kennedy in the Presidency: A Premature Appraisal." *Political Science Quarterly* 79 (September 1964): 321-54. Neustadt gives Kennedy high marks for his understanding of the presidency, his "feel" for the exercise of power, and his judgment regarding priorities.

2025. _____. *Presidential Power: The Politics of Leadership, with Reflections on Johnson and Nixon.* rev. ed. New York: John Wiley, 1964. The president must wage eternal war to keep from becoming clerk instead of leader in his own office--a conclusion Kennedy strongly accepted.

2026. Nixon, Richard Milhous. *Six Crises*. No. **1818**. An understandably critical appraisal of President Kennedy's first year by his 1960 opponent.

2027. Percy, Charles H., and Chester Bowles. "Promises and Performances: Two

Views of the Kennedy Record." *U.S. News and World Report* 53 (October 29, 1962): 112-18. Percy, chairman of the 1960 Republican Platform Committee, sees Kennedy's talk as "unrelated to action; Bowles, chairman of the 1960 Democratic Platform Committee, argues that Kennedy's record is one of "substantial progress."

2028. Rayburn, Sam. "The Speaker Speaks of Presidents." *New York Times Magazine* (June 4, 1961), pp. 34, 37, 39, 42, 44. In commenting on the eight presidents he served, House Speaker Sam Rayburn is reserved about Kennedy.

2029. Robertson, Archie. "From 'Bully!' to 'Vigah!'" *Horizon* 5 (November 1963): 68-71. There are differences as well as similarities between Theodore Roosevelt and Kennedy.

2030. "Second 100 Days: Education of a President." *U.S. News and World Report* 50 (May 29, 1961): 53-5. New ideas for running the government are colliding with hard realities when put in operation.

2031. Shannon, William V. "The Kennedy Administration: The Early Months." *American Scholar* 31 (Autumn 1961): 481-88. Journalist Shannon contends that Kennedy's advisers' "first criterion on every important problem is, how will this help 'the boss' get reelected in 1964?"

2032. _____. "The New What?" *Commonweal* 77 (February 1, 1963): 481-2. Kennedy's use of the "politics of personality" succeeds at the expense of the "politics of program."

2033. Sutherland, John P. "How Kennedy Differs from Ike." *U.S. News and World Report* 50 (May 1, 1961): 68-70. A very precise comparison of Eisenhower's and Kennedy's first eighty days in office.

2034. "The Two Sides of the U.S. Presidency." *Business Week* (July 8, 1961), p. 116. An evaluation of Kennedy's first six months in office.

2035. Walsh, John. "John F. Kennedy: Policy and Legacy." *Science* 142 (November 29, 1963): 1152-53. On federal policy on science and education, Kennedy evinced a more sytematic understanding and active concern than any of his predecessors in office.

2036. "The White House Years." *Newsweek* 62 (December 2, 1963): 45-8. An evaluation of the Kennedy years one week after the assassination.

2037. Wicker, Tom. "Kennedy without Tears." *Esquire* 61 (June 1964): 108-11, 138-41. A perceptive appraisal by the *New York Times* journalist that focuses on Kennedy's human and political side.

2038. Wiesner, Jerome B. "John F. Kennedy: A Remembrance." *Science* 142

(November 29, 1963): 1147-50. Kennedy's respect for science as an instrument of good was one of his distinctive qualities.

2039. "The Worst and the Best." *New Republic* 144 (May 1, 1961): 2. The Bay of Pigs in the midst of domestic successes.

2040. "A Year after the Assassination the U.S. Recalls John F. Kennedy." *Newsweek* 64 (November 30, 1964): 26-7. The personal qualities of Kennedy are remembered.

2041. "Young Man in a Hurry." *Nation* 192 (April 22, 1961): 333-34. Kennedy is ahead of the liberal shift slated for 1962 or later, if one accepts Arthur Schlesinger's pendulum theory of history.

C. POLITICS OF THE KENNEDY ERA

Political Ideologies

2042. Allet, Patrick Nicholas. "Catholic Lay Intellectuals in the American Conservative Movement, 1950-1980." Ph.D. diss., University of California, 1986. Roman Catholic laymen became leaders in the new conservative movement.

2043. Annunziata, Frank. "The New Left and the Welfare State: The Rejection of American Liberalism." *Southern Quarterly* 15 (1976): 35-56. An excellent exposition of how New Left criticism of statism differs from right-wing conservatism.

2044. Bell, Daniel, ed. *The Radical Right*. Garden City, NY: Doubleday, 1964. Essays by historians and sociologists on various conservative movements and organizations in the 1950s and 1960s.

2045. Brock, Clifton. *Americans for Democratic Action: Its Role in National Politics*. Washington: Public Affairs Press, 1962. A liberal organization dedicated to supporting liberal candidates and policies regardless of party.

2046. Cottrell, Robert Charles. "Wielding the Pen as a Sword: The Radical Journalist, I. F. Stone." Ph.D. diss., University of Oklahoma, 1983. Stone was one of the most persistent critics of cold war liberalism.

2047. Crawford, Kenneth. "Kennedy on Kennedy." *Newsweek* 59 (January 15, 1962): 27. Kennedy considers himself a moderate progressive.

2048. Crick, Bernard. "The Strange Quest for an American Conservatism." *Review of Politics* 17 (1975): 359-76. Crick defines a conservative ideology in contemporary America.

2049. Diggins, John P. "Buckley's Comrades: The Ex-Communist as Conservative." *Dissent* 22 (1975): 370-86. The ex-radicals and ex-Communists who turned conservative and joined William F. Buckley's *National Review* from the 1950s through the 1970s.

2050. Forster, Arnold, and Benjamin R. Epstein. *The Radical Right*. New York: Random House, 1967. Focuses on the John Birch Society and its allies.

2051. Galbraith, John Kenneth. *A Life in Our Times: Memoirs*. Boston: Houghton Mifflin, 1981. A liberal view of the Kennedy era written with grace and humor.

2052. Gillon, Stephen Michael. *Politics and Vision: The ADA and American Society*. New York: Oxford University Press, 1987. Analyzes why the Americans for Democratic Action failed to organize a unified liberal coalition.

2053. "Is Kennedy Shifting His Course?" *U. S. News and World Report* 51 (October 9, 1961): 45-8. After nine months in office Kennedy is becoming more conservative.

2054. Kazin, Alfred. "The President and Other Intellectuals." *American Scholar* 31 (Autumn 1961): 498-516. Kazin concludes that Kennedy's "most essential quality is that of the man who is always remaking himself."

2055. "Kennedy and the Clergy." *Newsweek* 59 (January 22, 1962): 48. Kennedy has lost ground with Catholics but has gained with Protestants.

2056. Kraft, Joseph. "Kennedy and the Intellectuals." *Harper's* 227 (November 1963): 112, 114-17. Kennedy's relationship with intellectuals inside and outside his administration.

2057. Lewis, Ted. "Kennedy: Profile of a Technician." *Nation* 196 (February 2, 1963): 92-4. Kennedy's leadership techniques are more evident than the direction of his policies.

2058. Meyer, Frank S. "Which Way for JFK?" *National Review* 10 (February 11, 1961): 81. An early conservative critique of Kennedy.

2059. Nash, George. *The Conservative Intellectual Movement in America since 1945*. New York: Basic Books, 1976. Focuses on well-known conservatives such as William Buckley and Russell Kirk as well as lesser knowns like Willmoore Kendall.

2060. Schlesinger, Arthur M., Jr. *The Vital Center: The Politics of Freedom*. Boston: Houghton Mifflin, 1949. The bible of cold war liberalism.

2061. Troy, Ekard Vance, Jr. "Ideology and Conflict in American Ultraconservatism,

1945-1960." Ph.D. diss., University of Oregon, 1965. Ultraconservatives shifted their loyalty from propaganda organizations to politically active organizations such as the John Birch Society.

2062. Unger, Irwin. *The Movement: A History of the American New Left, 1959-1972*. No. **1967**.

2063. Voegelli, William John, Jr. "Postwar American Liberalism and the Welfare State." Ph.D. diss., Loyola University of Chicago, 1984. The liberal goal of greater economic equality was less easily formulated and conveyed during the postwar era.

2064. "Where Kennedy Is Changing Course." *U.S. News and World Report* 55 (November 4, 1963): 31-2. Kennedy shifts policy toward the center in a number of different areas.

2065. "Why Are Some 'Liberals' Cool to the Kennedy Administration?" *Newsweek* 59 (April 16, 1962): 29-31. Liberals criticize Kennedy's domestic and foreign policies.

Political Parties

2066. Brown, Roger Glenn. "Partisanship and Party Leadership in the Contemporary Presidency." Ph.D. diss., Johns Hopkins University, 1983. Includes an evaluation of how Kennedy exercised partisanship and party leadership as president.

2067. Burns, James MacGregor. *The Deadlock of Democracy*. Englewood, NJ: Prenctice Hall, 1963. Burns contends that four political parties exist, two within the Republican and two within the Democratic parties.

2068. Camp, Helen Collier. "'Gurley'" A Biography of Elizabeth Gurley Flynn, 1890-1964." Ph.D. dissertation, Columbia University, 1980. In 1961 Flynn became the first woman to become chairman of the American Communist party.

2069. Cater, Douglass. "What's Happening to the Democratic Party?" *Reporter* 26 (May 10, 1962): 23-6. Kennedy's attachment to Republican Senator Everett Dirksen sparks rumors of party infidelity during a presidential election year.

2070. Cooper, James Pershing, Jr. "The Rise of George C. Wallace: Alabama Politics and Polity, 1958-1966." Ph.D. diss., Vanderbilt University, 1987. Wallace helped destroy the solid South by challenging the Democratic national leadership.

2071. Fisher, Joel Marshall. "The Role of the National Party Chairman in American Politics." Ph.D. diss., Claremont Graduate School, 1969. Fisher employs six case studies, including one of Paul Butler, to analyze the role of party chairmen.

2072. Louchheim, Katie. *By the Political Sea.* Garden City, NY: Doubleday, 1970. Louchheim was vice chairman of the Democratic National Committee and Special Assistant to Under Secretary of State Chester Bowles.

2073. Mayer, George H. *The Republican Party, 1854-1966.* 2nd ed. New York: Oxford University Press, 1967.   Covers Republican activities during the Kennedy era.

2074. Parmet, Herbert S. *The Democrats.* No. **1753.**   Particularly good in capturing the political environment from which Kennedy emerged and also covers the New Frontier.

2075. Reinhard, David W. *The Republican Right since 1945.* Lexington: University Press of Kentucky, 1983.   Coverage of the right wing of the Republican party.

2076. Renner, Tari. "Partisan Dealignment and the Emergence of Southern Republicanism." Ph.D. diss., American University, 1985.   The upper South exhibited much greater continuity in partisan voting patterns from 1954 to 1980 than did the rest of the South.

2077. Scheele, Henry Z. "The Kennedy Era: A Retrospective View of the Opposition Party." In *John F. Kennedy: Person, Policy, Presidency.* Edited by J. Richard Snyder. Wilmington, De.: Scholarly Resources, 1988, pp. 55-63.   Focuses on the Joint Senate-House Republican Leadership press conferences, a creation of the television age.

2078. Stadther, Dennis George. "The Rise of Southern Republicanism, 1956-1976." Ph.D. diss., University of Pittsburgh, 1981.   Voters since 1964 have shown a greater willingness to support the GOP than older voters.

2079. Stennett, Ronald F. *Democrats, Dinners, and Dollars: A History of the Democratic Party, Its Dinners, Its Rituals.* Ames: Iowa State University Press, 1967. A history of the Democratic party's sponsorship of dinners to raise campaign funds.

2080. Sundquist, James L. *Dynamics of the Party System: Alignment and Realignment of Political Parties in the United States.*   Washington: Brookings Institution, 1973.   Alludes to Kennedy.

2081. _____. *Politics and Policy: The Eisenhower, Kennedy, and Johnson Years.* Washington: Brookings Institution, 1968.   Argues that the national government alternates between spurts of creative energy and longer periods of deadlock and relative inaction.

2082. Thielemann, Gregory Scott. "The Reality of Realignment in the Post-World War II South." Ph.D. dissertation, Rice University, 1988.   Political change is overstated in the South.

Congress

2083. Amlund, Curtis Arthur. "Executive-Legislature Imbalance: Truman to Kennedy." *Western Political Quarterly* 18 (September 1965): 640-45. No evidence exists to support a thesis that the legislative role disproportionately declined from that of the president from 1945 to 1963.

2084. Baker, Robert. *Wheeling and Dealing: Confessions of a Capitol Hill Operator.* New York: W. W. Norton, 1978. An inside viewpoint by the colorful secretary of Senate Democrats.

2085. Burke, Vincent, and Frank Eleazer. "How Kennedy Gets What He Wants." *Nation's Business* 49 (September 1961): 96-102. The ploys Kennedy uses to influence Congress.

2086. Covington, Cary R. "Congressional Support for the President: The View from the Kennedy/Johnson White House." *Journal of Politics* 48 (August 1986): 717-28. Office of Congressional Relations statistics compiled by the White House during the Kennedy and Johnson administrations have more accurately measured congressional support of administration positions than have those compiled by *Congressional Quarterly*.

2087. Cummings, Milton C. *Congressmen and the Electorate: Elections for the U.S. House and the President, 1920-1964.* New York: Free Press, 1966. Cummings seeks to assess the presidential coattail effect on congressional elections in presidential election years.

2088. Dameron, Kenneth, Jr. "President Kennedy and Congress: Process and Politics." Ph.D. diss., Harvard University, 1975. Indispensable on Kennedy's relationship with Congress.

2089. Edwards, George C. III. *Presidential Influence on Congress.* San Francisco: Freeman, 1980. Much on Kennedy by a political scientist.

2090. Fox, Douglas M., and Charles H. Clapp. "The House Rules Committee and the Programs of the Kennedy and Johnson Administrations." *Midwest Journal of Political Science* 14 (November 1970): 667-72. Examines the effect of the House Rules Committee on the legislative programs of Kennedy and Johnson.

2091. Fuller, Helen. "Kennedy's Problem: Could He Get More From Congress?" *New Republic* 148 (March 9, 1963): 12-14. Concludes that Kennedy has proved a sporadic and impersonal explainer to the public on matters he considers vital.

2092. Greenfield, Meg. "Why Are You Calling Me, Son?" *Reporter* 21 (August 16,

1962): 29-31. A summary of charges of inept congressional liaison committed by the Kennedy administration.

2093. Hacker, Andrew. "When the President Goes to the People." *New York Times Magazine* (June 10, 1962), pp. 13, 61-2. Hacker analyzes the methods used by Woodrow Wilson and Franklin Roosevelt to get their legislation passed and the applicability of these methods for Kennedy.

2094. Hart, John. "Staffing the Presidency: Kennedy and the Office of Congressional Relations." *Presidential Studies Quarterly* 13 (Winter 1983): 101-10. Examines the president's development of the White House Office of Congressional Relations, which was institutionalized in the Kennedy period.

2095. Holtzman, Abraham. *Legislative Liaison: Executive Leadership in Congress.* Chicago: Rand McNally, 1970. Good on White House lobbying efforts orchestrated by Larry O'Brien.

2096. "How Congress Sizes Up President Kennedy." *U.S. News and World Report* 52 (February 26, 1962): 50-60. An anonymous poll conducted by *U. S. News and World Report* that evaluates Kennedy and members of his cabinet.

2097. Hyman, Sidney. "Presidential Popularity Is Not Enough." *New York Times Magazine* (August 12, 1962): 10, 64, 66. Kennedy is urged to forget his popular appeal with voters and concentrate on other approaches with legislators.

2098. "Kennedy Sets New Course in Congress." *U.S. News and World Report* 54 (January 14, 1963): 33-4. On Kennedy's plan for working with the 88th Congress.

2099. "Kennedy Takes His Case to the Country." *U.S. News and World Report* 51 (October 23, 1961): 37-8. In an effort to garner more support with the Congress, Kennedy is taking his message to the people.

2100. "Kennedy's Next Job: Congress." *Business Week* (January 7, 1961), pp. 17-19. Kennedy prepares to meet the 87th Congress.

2101. Kilpatrick, Carroll. "The Kennedy Style and Congress." *Virginia Quarterly Review* 39 (Winter 1963): 1-11. Instead of using the presidency as an educational forum, he has sought compromises with congressmen.

2102. Lester, Robert Leon. "Developments in Presidential-Congressional Relations: Franklin D. Roosevelt-John Kennedy." Ph.D. diss., University of Virginia, 1969. Kennedy's legislative liaison operation made relations between Congress and the presidency stronger.

2103. Lewis, Ted. "Congress versus Kennedy." *Nation* 195 (July 14, 1962): 4-6. A critical view of Kennedy's relationship with Congress.

2104. Livingston, William S., Lawrence C. Dodd, and Richard L. Schott, eds. *The Presidency and the Congress*. Austin: Lyndon Baines Johnson School of Public Affairs, 1979. Contains scattered references to the Kennedy presidency.

2105. Orfield, Gary. *Congressional Power: Congress and Social Change*. New York: Harcourt Brace Jovanovich, 1975. Congress is more important and less conservative than is generally believed.

2106. Renka, Russell D. "Comparing Presidents Kennedy and Johnson as Legislative Leaders." *Presidential Studies Quarterly* 15 (Fall 1985): 806-25. Judges Johnson the more skilled and effective legislative leader despite parity on the roll call count.

2107. "What They Say about JFK: Congressmen Tell What's On Their Minds." *U.S. News and World Report* 53 (July 30, 1962): 31-4. Expressions against Kennedy's domestic program.

2108. "Why Kennedy's Program Is in Trouble with Congress." *U.S. News and World Report* 53 (September 17, 1962): 62-9. An interview with Senate Majority Leader Mike Mansfield.

2109. "Why Congress Doesn't Give JFK What He Wants." *U.S. News and World Report* 54 (March 18, 1963): 38-42. Some congressmen claim that Kennedy is out of tune with the people; others suggest he does not fight hard enough for his program.

2110. Wicker, Tom. *JFK and LBJ: The Influence of Personality upon Politics*. New York: Morrow, 1968. Excellent on Kennedy's legislative program and his dealings with Congress.

2111. _____. "'A Total Political Animal.'" *New York Times Magazine* (April 15, 1962), pp. 26, 128-30. Concentrates on Kennedy's power of persuasion with legislators.

2112. Williams, Robert J., and David A. Kershaw. "Kennedy and Congress: The Struggle for the New Frontier." *Political Studies* 27 (September 1979): 390-404. Focuses on Kennedy's relations with Congress and on the difficulty of reconciling his reputation as a skillful politician with his legislative disappointments.

D. DOMESTIC ISSUES

Agriculture

2113. "Abundance Abated." *Nation* 196 (June 15, 1963): 497-98. Critically evaluates the wheat farmers' rejection of mandatory controls.

2114. "Agriculture: A Hard Row to Hoe." *Time* 81 (April 5, 1963): 21-5. Cover story on Orville Freeman and the challenges of the Department of Agriculture.

2115. "An Awakening for Orville." *Life* 51 (July 7, 1961): 48. Political failure of the 1961 farm bill.

2116. "Another Try at the Farm Problem: Here's the Kennedy Approach." *U. S. News and World Report* 50 (January 16, 1961): 84-5. The proposed comprehensive Kennedy farm policy program.

2117. "Behind the Billie Sol Mess." *Newsweek* 59 (May 28, 1962): 25-6, 28-9. A major scandal that implicated some Department of Agriculture officials.

2118. Bird, John. "Farmers Face Their Toughest Choice." *Saturday Evening Post* 23 (May 18, 1963), 74-6. Subsidies require toughest controls ever.

2119. Cochrane, Willard, and Mary E. Ryan. *American Farm Policy, 1948-1973*. Minneapolis: University of Minnesota Press, 1976. Co-authored by Cochrane, Secretary of Agriculture Freeman's economic adviser, it is excellent on the Kennedy period.

2120. "Controls Rejected." *Commonweal* 78 (June 7, 1963): 293. The Farm Bureau Federation led the fight against mandatory controls for wheat farmers.

2121. "Cleaning Up the Farm Mess." *Fortune* 68 (July 1963): 132, 279. The wheat farmers' defeat of strict production controls.

2122. "Death of the Farm Bill: Inside Story of a White House Defeat." *U.S. News and World Report* 53 (July 9, 1962): 46-7. Congressional defeat of the supply management plan that would have placed tight controls on wheat and feed grains.

2123. "Drowning, But Bravely." *Time* 79 (April 6, 1962): 18. Criticism of the feed-grain program.

2124. "Farm Message." *Reporter* 26 (February 15, 1962): 14, 16. The problems of farm surpluses and price supports.

2125. "Farm Scandal." *Time* 77 (May 19, 1961): 21-2. Congressional opposition to Kennedy's omnibus farm bill.

2126. "Farmers Say No." *New Republic* 148 (June 1, 1963): 6. The defeat of the wheat referendum.

2127. Fite, Gilbert. *American Farmers: The New Minority*. Bloomington: Indiana University Press, 1981. An exellent survery of the agricultural situation during the 1950s and 1960s.

2128. "Freeman on Kennedy's Farm Plan." *U.S. News and World Report* 50 (June 12, 1961): 84. A detailed account of the administration's comprehensive farm bill.

2129. "Get Off That Tiger." *Time* 80 (December 21, 1962): 21. The approaching wheat referendum.

2130. Giglio, James N. "New Frontier Agricultural Policy: The Commodity Side, 1961-1963." *Agricultural History* 61 (Summer 1987): 53-70. Grounded in the primary sources of the Kennedy Library.

2131. Hadwiger, Don F., and Ross B. Talbot. *Pressures and Protests: The Kennedy Farm Program and the Wheat Referendum of 1963.* San Francisco: Chandler Publishing, 1965. Provides a broader coverage than the title suggests.

2132. Heinz, Jack. "Those Annoying Farmers: Impossible But Not Really Serious." *Harpers' Magazine* 227 (July 1963): 61-8. Impasse on farm legislation is due to the fragmentation of farmers' political power.

2133. Kerr, Norwood. "Drafted into the War on Poverty: USDA Food and Nutrition Programs, 1961-1969." *Agricultural History* 64 (Spring 1990): 154-66. Focuses on Secretary of Agriculture Orville Freeman's efforts to use surplus farm goods to help improve the diets of poor Americans, especially children.

2134. McGovern, George. *Grassroots: The Autobiography of George McGovern.* New York: Random House, 1977. Deals with Food for Peace.

2135. McGrory, Mary. "Trouble on the New Frontier: Estes Scandal." *America* 107 (June 9, 1962): 371. Secretary Orville Freeman lost control of the Estes affair.

2136. "Nibbled to Bits." *New Republic* 145 (July 10, 1961): 3-4. Kennedy's failure to get a comprehensive farm bill.

2137. "Now, A Hope of Farm Sanity." *Life* 54 (June 7, 1963): 4. In a nationwide referendum, wheat farmers vote down mandatory acreage controls.

2138. "Paying the Farmers." *New Republic* 148 (May 18, 1963): 7. An assessment of the farm situation prior to the wheat referendum.

2139. "Politics and Farmers." *New Republic* 144 (April 10, 1961): 3-4. Kennedy seeks to shift the formulation of production control and price support legislation from the Congress to the farmers involved.

2140. "'Regulated Peasantry'--Fate of Farmers under Kennedy Plan?" *U. S. News and World Report* 50 (June 12, 1961): 80-5. An interview with Charles B. Shuman, president of the American Farm Bureau.

2141. "Secretary Freeman Explains His Proposed 1961 Feed Grain Program." *Successful Farming* 59 (December 21, 1961): 42. Brief interview of Freeman.

2142. Schapsmeier, Edward L., and Frederick H. Schapsmeier. *Ezra Taft Benson and the Politics of Agriculture: The Eisenhower Years, 1953-1961.* Danville, Il.: Interstate Printers and Publishers, 1975. Provides background material.

2143. "The Story of a Fight." *Farm Journal* 86 (July 1962): 21, 40. Farmers do not want compulsory government controls.

2144. Toma, Peter A. *The Politics of Food for Peace: Executive-Legislative Interaction.* Tucson: University of Arizona Press, 1967. Discusses how the Kennedy administration used agricultural surpluses to assist Third World nations.

2145. "Wheat Farmers Revolt." *U.S. News and World Report* 55 (June 3, 1963): 40-2. Wheat farmers rejected White House plans for tighter controls.

2146. "Wheat Vote: Against Freeman's Program." *Time* 81 (May 31, 1963): 13-14. Farm Bureau's slogan was "Freedom v. Freeman."

Business

2147. Banks, Louis. "What Kennedy's Free Trade Program Means to Business." *Fortune* 65 (March 1962): 102-04, 206, 208, 213-14, 216, 218, 220. Should help to hold down wages and prices and lead to government encouragement of new investment.

2148. Barber, Richard J. "Mergers: Threat to Free Enterprise?" *Challenge* 11 (March 1963): 6-10. Barber believes that new legislation is necessary to deal with the problem of diversified giants.

2149. _____. *The Politics of Research.* Washington: Public Affairs Press, 1966. On the relationship between government and the defense industry.

2150. Barber, William J. "The Kennedy Years: Purposeful Pedagogy." In *Exhortation and Controls: The Search for a Wage-Price Policy, 1945-1971.* Edited by Craufurd D. Goodwin. Washington: Brookings Institution, 1975. Includes the steel crisis of 1962.

2151. Blough, Roger Miles. "My Side of the Steel Price Story, as Told to Eleanor Harris." *Look* 27 (January 29, 1963): 19-23. Blough professed to be surprised at Kennedy's hostile reaction to the increase in steel prices.

2152. _____. *The Washington Embrace of Business.* New York: Distributed by Columbia University Press, 1975. Blough defends his increasing steel prices in 1962.

2153. "Business Against Kennedy: A One-Sided Hostility." *Round Table* 52 (September, 1962): 355-60. Kennedy faces a combination of fanaticism and obstinacy from business.

2154. Cheit, Earl F., ed. *The Business Establishment.* New York: Wiley, 1964. Includes six essays presented at a University of California workshop ranging from what happened to the antitrust movement to an evolution of an American creed by Richard Hofstadter.

2155. Cherington, Paul W., and Ralph L. Gillen. *The Business Representative in Washington.* Washington: Brookings Institution, 1962. Good on the changing relations between business and government.

2156. Crandall, Robert W. *The U.S. Steel Industry in Recurrent Crises: Policy Options in a Competitive World.* Washington: Brookings Institution, 1981. Puts the steel crisis into a broader perspective.

2157. Deakin, James. *The Lobbyists.* Washington: Public Affairs Press, 1966. Deals with the contemporary period and business interests.

2158. Folliard, Edward T. "Business' Place in Kennedy Plans." *Nation's Business* 49 (January 1961): 23-4. Presents Kennedy's views on business.

2159. Galbraith, John Kenneth. *The New Industrial State.* New York: 1967. Boston: Houghton Mifflin, 1967. The state becomes an instrument of the industrial system and industry becomes an arm of the state.

2160. Godden, Richard, and Richard Maidment. "American Language and Politics: John F. Kennedy and the Steel Crisis." *Presidential Studies Quarterly* 10 (Summer 1980): 317-31. A reinterpretation of Kennedy's behavior during the steel crisis.

2161. Harris, Richard. *The Real Voice.* New York: Macmillan, 1964. A colorful description of the passage of the drug bill in 1962.

2162. Heath, Jim F. *John F. Kennedy and the Business Community.* Chicago: University of Chicago Press, 1969. More of an economic history of the New Frontier with a focus on the relationship between free enterprise and government.

2163. Hodges, Luther. *The Business Conscience.* Englewood Cliffs, NJ: Prentice-Hall, 1963. Firsthand account by Kennedy's commerce secretary on the textile business.

2164. Hoopes, Roy. *The Steel Crisis.* New York: John Day, 1963. Partly because he received greater cooperation from government sources, Hoopes's comments lean more toward the government case.

2165. "JFK in a Truce with Business?" *U.S. News and World Report* 54 (June 3, 1963): 35-6. Kennedy adopts a friendlier approach to business.

2166. "Kennedy--Business Feud Nears Peril Point." *Business Week* (July 7, 1962), pp. 92-3, 96-7. The fears and anxieties of the business community toward the administration are genuine and deep.

2167. Kefauver, Estes. *In a Few Hands; Monopoly Power in America.* New York: Pantheon Books, 1965. Among the industries treated are the drug and pharmaceutical, automobile, and bakery.

2168. Loevinger, Lee. "Antitrust in 1961 and 1962." *Antitrust Bulletin* 8 (May-June 1963): 349-79. A former Humphrey associate from Minnesota, Loevinger argued that antitrust action was inherently pro-business; he lasted as head of the antitrust division until early 1963.

2169. _____. "Recent Developments in Antitrust Enforcement." *Antitrust Bulletin* 6 (January-February 1961): 3-7. Loevinger promises vigorous and uncompromising enforcement of the antitrust laws.

2170. McConnell, Grant. *Steel and the Presidency, 1962.* New York: W. W. Norton, 1963. Largely based on confidential interviews, McConnell claims that Kennedy gave a "virtuoso performance" during the steel crisis.

2171. McQuaid, Kim. *Big Business and Presidential Power: From FDR to Reagan.* New York: William Morrow, 1982. Following the steel crisis, Kennedy courted the business community and acted like a conservative whenever possible.

2172. Matusow, Allen. *The Unraveling of America.* No. **1940.** See chapter 3 for Kennedy and the corporations.

2173. Nossiter, Bernard. *The Mythmakers: An Essay on Power and Wealth.* Boston: Houghton Mifflin, 1964. The first two chapters are on the Kennedy administration.

2174. Oberdorfer, Don, and Walter Pincus. "Businessmen in Politics: Luther Hodges and Edward Day." In *The Kennedy Circle.* Edited by Lester Tanzer. Washington: Robert B. Luce, 1961, pp. 237-54. Hodges was Kennedy's secretary of commerce and Edward Day was postmaster general.

2175. "A Question of National Interest." *Newsweek* 59 (April 23, 1962): 17-22. Detailed coverage of the Kennedy-U.S. Steel confrontation.

2176. Rowen, Hobart. *The Free Enterprisers: Kennedy, Johnson and the Business*

Establishment. New York: G. P. Putnam's Sons, 1964. The standard work on Kennedy and business.

2177. _____. "Keys to the Economy--Steel and Blough." *Newsweek* 59 (January 22, 1962): 69-74. Article speculates on potential problems ahead.

Civil Rights and Race Relations

2178. Anderson, Jarvis. *A. Philip Randolph: A Biographical Portrait.* New York: Harcourt Brace Jovanovich, 1972. Randolph, who organized the proposed March on Washington in 1941, remained active in the civil rights movement in the Kennedy era, including the March on Washington in 1963.

2179. Anderson, Robert Lee. "Negro Suffrage in Relation to American Federalism, 1957-1963." Ph.D. diss., University of Florida, 1965. Focuses on the expanding role of the federal government in intervening through the use of the Fourteenth and Fifteenth amendments.

2180. Barnes, Catherine A. *Journey from Jim Crow: The Desegregation of Southern Transit.* New York: Columbia University Press, 1983. A balanced approach to the Kennedy administration's handling of the desegregation of interstate transportation.

2181. Barrett, Russell H. *Integration at Ole Miss.* Chicago: Quadrangle, 1965. Written by a participant and political science professor at Ole Miss who advised James Meredith.

2182. Belknap, Michael. *Federal Law and Southern Order: Racial Violence and Constitutional Conflict in the Post-Brown South.* Athens: University of Georgia Press, 1987. Despite the Kennedy administration moving against civil rights injustices, it did not make it safe to exercise constitutional rights in the South.

2183. Bernstein, Irving. *Promises Kept.* No. **1592**. Two chapters of favorable coverage on Kennedy's civil rights program.

2184. Bickel, Alexander M. "Civil Rights and the Congress." *New Republic* 149 (August 3, 1963): 14-16. Discusses the constitutional questions associated with civil rights legislation.

2185. Blumberg, Rhoda Lois. *Civil Rights: The 1960s Freedom Struggle.* Boston: Twayne, 1984. In her brief coverage of Kennedy, Blumberg contributes no new insights or knowledge.

2186. Booker, Simeon. "How JFK Surpassed Abraham Lincoln." *Ebony* 19 (February 1964): 25, 27-8, 30, 32-4. Kennedy did more than any other president toward integrating blacks.

2187. _____. "What Negroes Can Expect from Kennedy." *Ebony* 16 (January 1961): 33-6, 38. Black supporters expect a new era of racial and social progress.

2188. Bork, Robert. "Civil Rights--A Challenge." *New Republic* 149 (August 31, 1963): 21-4. Criticizes civil rights legislation for trying to legislate morality and imposing the morals of the majority upon the minority.

2189. Bradley, Pearl Garrett. "A Criticism of the Modes of Persuasion Found in Selected Civil Rights Addresses of John F. Kennedy, 1962-1963." Ph.D. diss., Ohio State University, 1967. An analysis of speech techniques employed by Kennedy.

2190. Branch, Taylor. *Parting the Waters: America in the King Years, 1954-1963*. New York: Simon and Schuster, 1988. Places Martin Luther King, Jr., within the larger black religious culture.

2191. Brauer, Carl M. *John F. Kennedy and the Second Reconstruction*. New York: Columbia University Press, 1977. Well-grounded in primary sources, it does an excellent job of showing the external and internal constrains regarding Kennedy's civil rights efforts.

2192. Carmichael, Stokely, and Charles V. Hamilton. *Black Power: The Politics of Liberation in America*. New York: Vintage Books, 1967. The classic work on the development of black power.

2193. Carson, Clayborne. *In Struggle: SNCC and the Black Awakening of the 1960s*. Cambridge: Harvard University Press, 1981. A reliable, fair-minded study.

2194. "Caught in Crossfire: Halleck on Civil Rights." *U. S. News and World Report* 55 (November 11, 1963): 24. Covers attacks on House Republican leader Charles Halleck for helping President Kennedy get a moderate civil rights bill approved by the House Judiciary Committee.

2195. Chafe, William H. "Kennedy and the Civil Rights Movement." In *John F. Kennedy*. Edited by J. Richard Snyder, pp. 65-74. No. **2077**. Chafe sees Kennedy as a reactor who responded to the collective forces from below rather than being a heroic initiator from above.

2196. "Civil Rights--A Reply." *New Republic* 149 (August 31, 1963): 24. The editors of the *New Republic* refute some of Robert Bork's criticism of civil rights legislation (see **2188**).

2197. "The Civil Rights Bill." *Reporter* 29 (July 18, 1963): 12, 16. Analyzes the position and statements of both sides of the civil rights bill in Congress.

2198. Clark, Wayne Addison. "An Analysis of the Relationship between Anti-Communism and Segregationist Thought in the Deep South, 1948-1964." Ph.D.

diss., University of North Carolina, 1976. Segregationist groups in the South promoted a variation of McCarthyism against the civil rights movement.

2199. Colburn, David R. *Racial Change and Community Crisis: St. Augustine, Florida, 1877-1980*. New York: Columbia University Press, 1985. Ably surveys the matter of race and the impact that the civil rights movement had on the community.

2200. Collins, Frederic. "Senator Russell 'in the Last Ditch.'" *New York Times Magazine* (October 20, 1963), pp. 16, 74, 76, 79-80. A profile of Senator Richard Russell of Georgia and his leadership against civil rights legislation.

2200a. Culpepper, Clark E. *The Schoolhouse Door: Segregation's Last Stand at the University of Alabama*. New York: Oxford University Press, 1993. Praised John and Robert Kennedy for their political courage.

2201. Danigelis, Nicholas L. "Race and Political Activity in the United States, 1948-1968: A Trend Analysis." Ph.D. diss., Indiana University, 1973. Danigelis attempts to explain the reasons behind the variation in political activity among Black Americans between 1948 and 1963.

2202. Dittmer, John. "The Politics of the Mississippi Movement, 1954-1964." In *The Civil Rights Movement in America*. Edited by Charles Eagles. Jackson: University Press of Mississippi, 1986, pp. 65-93. Focuses on black Mississippians struggling for political liberation.

2203. Dorman, Michael. *We Shall Overcome*. New York: Dial Press, 1964. Dorman covers the civil rights revolution in the South for *Newsday*, a Long Island newspaper.

2204. Dulles, Foster Rhea. *The Civil Rights Commission: 1957-1965*. East Lansing: Michigan State University Press, 1968. Covers the first eight years of the commission's activities based on the commission's records.

2205. Elliff, John T. "Aspects of Federal Civil Rights Enforcement: The Justice Department and the FBI, 1939-1964." *Perspectives in American History* 5 (1971): 605-73. Over the years the FBI was both a stubborn obstacle and an indispensable resource in the development of a comprehensive federal civil rights program that made full use of civil remedies, administrative action, and criminal enforcement.

2206. "An End and a Beginning." *Newsweek* 61 (June 24, 1963): 29-34. In less than a day the University of Alabama is desegregated and civil rights leader Medgar Evers is killed.

2207. Eskew, Glenn Thomas. "But for Birmingham: The Local and National Movements in the Civil Rights Struggle." Ph. D. diss., University of Georgia, 1993. The civil rights movement in Birmingham convinced a reluctant Kennedy administration to open the system to African Americans, but while some blacks achieved access, others remained shut out.

2208. Fairelough, Adam. *To Redeem the Soul of America: The Southern Christian Leadership Conference*. Athens: University of Georgia Press, 1987. A thoughtful study of King and the organization he led.

2209. Farmer, James. *Lay Bare the Heart: An Autobiography of the Civil Rights Movement*. New York: Arbor House, 1985. Farmer provides a moving account of the organization he helped to found.

2210. _____. *The Making of Black Revolutionaries*. New York: Macmillan, 1972. Farmer served as executive secretary of Congress of Racial Equality (CORE) during the 1961 Freedom Rides.

2211. Frady, Marshall. *Wallace*. New York: New American Library, 1968. An excellent biography by a Southern journalist that includes Wallace's confrontation with the Kennedy administration during the summer of 1963.

2212. Garrow, David J. *Bearing the Cross: Martin Luther King, Jr., and the Southern Christian Leadership Conference*. New York: William Morrow, 1986. Prodigiously researched, this Pulitzer-Prize-winning work represents the major statement on Martin Luther King, Jr.

2213. _____. *The FBI and Martin Luther King: From "Solo" to Memphis*. New York: W. W. Norton, 1981. The Kennedy administration accepted the FBI's allegation that King's key adviser, Stanley Levison, was a Communist, which led to the authorized wiretapping of King.

2214. Gentile, Thomas. *March on Washington, August 28, 1963*. Washington: New Day, 1983. A descriptive account of the March.

2215. Golden, Harry. *Mr. Kennedy and the Negroes*. Cleveland and New York: World Publishing, 1964. Golden labels Kennedy the second emancipator president.

2216. Graham, Hugh Davis. *The Civil Rights Era: Race, Gender, and National Policy, 1960-1972*. New York: Oxford University Press, 1990. Graham identifies two distinct phases in civil rights policy: the attack on racial discrimination before 1965 and the effort thereafter to remedy past discrimination through affirmative action.

2217. Guthman, Edwin O. *We Band of Brothers*. New York: Harper and Row, 1971. In charge of public information in Robert Kennedy's Justice Department, Guthman concedes that the department had underestimated civil rights problems in the South.

2218. Guthman, Edwin O. and Jeffrey Shulman, eds. *Robert Kennedy in His Own*

Words. No. **1644**. Excellent on Robert Kennedy's viewpoints on racial matters.

2219. Hamilton, Charles V. *The Bench and the Ballot: Southern Federal Judges and Black Voters.* New York: Oxford University Press, 1973. Examines the advantages and disadvantages of a policy that relied on the courts to register black citizens.

2220. Hart, John. "Kennedy, Congress and Civil Rights." *Journal of American Studies* 13 (August 1979): 165-78. Kennedy cajoled and bargained with an unreceptive Congress until his moderate and pragmatic civil rights proposals were headed for congressional approval by the time of his death.

2221. Harvey, James C. *Civil Rights during the Kennedy Administration.* Hattiesburg, Ms.: University and College Press, 1971. A brief account that argues that Kennedy had placed himself at the head of the civil rights movement at the time of his death.

2222. Jacoway, Elizabeth, and David R. Colburn, eds. *Southern Businessmen and Desegregation.* Baton Rouge: Louisiana State University Press, 1982. Original essays on fourteen communities concentrating on the diverse relationships between civil rights activists and Southern white business leaders.

2223. Johnson, Dennis William. "Friend of the Court: The United States Department of Justice as *Amicus Curiae* in Civil Rights Cases before the Supreme Court, 1947-1971." Ph.D. diss., Duke University, 1972. The Justice Department's participation as friend of the court in the Supreme Court is a significant but little recognized aspect of the federal government's civil rights enforcement activities.

2224. Katzenbach, Nicholas. "Origins of Kennedy's Civil Rights." In *The Kennedy Presidency.* Edited by Kenneth W. Thompson, pp. 49-64. No. **1588**. Kennedy's former assistant attorney general recalls the administration's early struggles over civil rights.

2225. Kempton, Murray. "The March on Washington." *New Republic* 149 (September 14, 1963): 19-20. An insightful article about the March on Washington and the relationship of blacks and whites.

2226. Kennedy, Robert F., Jr. *Judge Frank M. Johnson: A Study in Integrity.* New York: Putnam, 1978. Written by the attorney general's son, Kennedy focuses on a federal district judge for the middle district of Alabama since 1955 who extended the constitution to blacks in several of his decisions.

2227. Kilpatrick, James Jackson. "Civil Rights and Legal Wrongs." *National Review* 15 (September 24, 1963): 231-36. Analyzes the seven main provisions of Kennedy's civil rights bill and explains why it is a bad bill.

2228. King, Coretta Scott. *My Life with Martin Luther King, Jr.* New York: Holt,

Rinehart and Winston, 1969. The widow of Martin Luther King, Jr., covers their life together from 1953 until his assassination.

2229. King, Martin Luther, Jr. "Equality Now: The President Has the Power." *Nation* 192 (February 4, 1961): 91-5. King focuses on the opportunity of Kennedy to adopt a radically different civil rights approach.

2230. _____. "Fumbling on the New Frontier." *Nation* 194 (March 3, 1962): 190-93. Despite some praiseworthy achievements, Kennedy, according to King, hesitates to push civil rights legislation because it might undermine other legislative proposals.

2231. _____. "It's a Difficult Thing to Teach a President." *Look* 28 (November 17, 1964): 61, 64. King believes Kennedy grew until the day of his assassination.

2232. King, Mary. *Freedom Song: A Personal Story of the 1960s Civil Rights Movement.* New York: William Morrow, 1987. A former activist, King argues that the word failure should never be applied to SNCC, given its vision and the overwhelming issues it tackled.

2233. Krislov, Samuel. *The Negro in Federal Employment.* Minneapolis: University of Minnesota Press, 1967. Deals with Kennedy's Committee on Equal Employment Opportunity.

2234. Lawson, Steven F. *Black Ballots: Voting Rights in the South, 1944-1969.* New York: Columbia University Press, 1976. The process by which blacks gained the vote in the South in the post-World War II period.

2235. _____. "'I Got It from the New York Times': Lyndon Johnson and the Kennedy Civil Rights Program." *Journal of Negro History* 67 (Summer 1982): 159-72. Based on a lengthy telephone transcription of June 3, 1963 between Vice President Johnson and Theodore Sorensen, a top Kennedy aide.

2236. _____. *Running for Freedom: Civil Rights and Black Politics in America Since 1941.* New York: McGraw Hill, 1991. Contains a brief, judicious summation of the Kennedy administration's commitment to civil rights.

2237. Lewis, Anthony, and the *New York Times. Portrait of a Decade: The Second American Revolution.* New York: Random House, 1964. Based on excerpts of news articles and stories from the *New York Times*, Lewis and other authors focus on the major events of the civil rights movement.

2238. Lewis, David L. *King: A Critical Biography.* New York: Praeger, 1970. The early standard work on King.

2239. Lichtman, Allan. "The Federal Assault against Voting Discrimination in the Deep South, 1957-1967." *Journal of Negro History* 54 (1969): 346-67. The author examines the work of four assistant attorneys general during the first ten years of the Civil Rights Division of the Department of Justice.

2240. Lord, Walter. *The Past That Would Not Die*. New York: Harper and Row, 1965. A well-written account of the Kennedy administration's efforts to desegregate the University of Mississippi in 1962.

2241. Lyttle, Clifford M. "The History of the Civil Rights Bill of 1964." *Journal of Negro History* 51 (October 1966): 275-96. Superficially done by a former official of the Community Relations Service, an agency created by the act.

2242. McAdam, Doug. *Freedom Summer*. New York: Oxford University Press, 1988. McAdam, a sociologist, alludes to Kennedy's inspirational impact on young volunteers engaged in voter registration in Mississippi.

2243. McMillen, Neil R. *The Citizen's Council: Organized Resistance to the Second Reconstruction, 1954-64*. Urbana: University of Illinois Press, 1971. The citizen councils of the South sought to resist implementation of the Supreme Court's desegregation ruling of 1954.

2244. Manning, Marable. *Race, Reform, and Rebellion: The Second Reconstruction in Black America, 1945-1982*. Jackson: University Press of Mississippi, 1984. Provides a provocative and informative synthesis of the struggle for black freedom.

2245. "The March." *New Yorker* 39 (September 7, 1963) 30-1. A first-person account of the sights and sounds of the civil rights March on Washington on August 28, 1963.

2246. Marshall, Burke. "Congress, Communications and Civil Rights." In *The Kennedy Presidency*. Edited by Kenneth W. Thompson, pp. 65-81. No. **1588**. Based on an interview with the assistant attorney general in charge of the Division of Civil Rights.

2247. _____. *Federalism and Civil Rights*. New York: Columbia University Press, 1964. Marshall presents the Kennedy administration viewpoint regarding the enforcement of civil rights in the South.

2248. _____. "Federal Protection of Negro Voting Rights." *Law and Contemporary Problems* 27 (Summer 1962): 455-67. Voting rights violations occur in sections of eight states, leading to a Justice Department commitment against this discrimination.

2249. Martin, John F. *Civil Rights and the Crisis of Liberalism: The Democratic Party, 1945-1975*. Boulder, Co.: Westview Press, 1979. An unsuccessful attempt to explain postwar liberalism and the civil rights struggle.

2250. Martin, Louis. "Organizing Civil Rights." In *The Kennedy Presidency*. Edited by Kenneth W. Thompson, pp. 83-100. No. **1588**. An interview with the deputy chairman of the Democratic National Committee from 1961 to 1969 who in effect was an assistant on minority affairs in the Kennedy-Johnson administrations.

2251. Meier, August, and Elliott Rudwick. *CORE: A Study in the Civil Rights Movement, 1942-1968*. New York: Oxford University Press, 1973. Covers CORE activities in the Kennedy era.

2252. Meredith, James. *Three Years in Mississippi*. Bloomington: Indiana University Press, 1966. Meredith's personal account of the University of Mississippi crisis of 1962.

2253. Moore, Jesse Thomas, Jr. "The Urban League and the Black Revolution, 1941-1961: Its Philosophy and Its Policies." Ph.D. diss., Pennsylvania State University, 1971. The Urban League adopted a different approach from other civil rights organizations.

2254. "More Light on the 'Freedom Rides.'" *U.S. News and World Report* 51 (October 30, 1961): 70-1. Robert Kennedy's involvement is discussed.

2255. Morgan, Ruth. *The President and Civil Rights: Policy-Making by Executive Order*. New York: St. Martin's, 1970. The civil rights policies of presidents from Franklin Roosevelt to Lyndon Johnson are compared.

2256. Morris, Aldon. *Origins of the Civil Rights Movement*. New York: Free Press, 1984. A sociological study of the civil rights movement from 1953 to 1963.

2257. Muse, Benjamin. *Ten Years of Prelude: The Story of Integration since the Supreme Court's 1954 Decision*. New York: Viking, 1964. Muse provides a short, succinct, and accurate summary of events minus perceptive analysis.

2258. Navasky, Victor S. *Kennedy Justice*. New York: Atheneum, 1971. An indispensable, penetrating, and fair-minded evaluation of the civil rights actions of Robert Kennedy's Justice Department.

2259. "Nine Young Men in Charge of Integrating America." *U. S. News and World Report* 55 (July 29, 1963): 55, 58-61. This pictorial account decribes the staff of the civil rights division of the Department of Justice.

2260. O'Reilly, Kenneth. *"Racial Matters": The FBI's Secret File on Black America, 1960-1972*. New York: Free Press, 1989. Based on thousands of pages of FBI documents, this study contends that Kennedy, Johnson, and Nixon failed to control the agency and thus must bear ultimate moral responsibility for its often illegal violent attempts to destroy the civil rights movement.

2261. Oates, Stephen. *Let the Trumpet Sound: The Life of Martin Luther King, Jr.* New York: Harper and Row, 1982. A subjective approach which restricts adequate discussion of King's limitations as a leader.

2262. Oppenheimer, Martin. "Institutions of Higher Learning and the 1960 Sit-ins: Some Clues for Social Action." *Journal of Negro Education* 32 (1963): 286-88. The sit-ins in the South occurred mostly in urban areas with a black college and with a low concentration of blacks in the community.

2263. Peck, James. *Freedom Ride.* New York: Simon and Schuster, 1962. A riveting account by a participant.

2264. "Politics: JFK's Lost Votes." *Newsweek* 62 (October 21, 1963): 55-6. Kennedy loses some voter support over his civil rights commitment.

2265. "Poll Puzzler." *Newsweek* 62 (July 8, 1963): 21-2. Kennedy mentions an unnamed poll that shows a drastic loss of support because of his civil rights policy.

2266. Raines, Howell. *My Soul Is Rested: Movement Days in the Deep South Remembered.* New York: G. P. Putnam, 1977. A revealing collection of interviews with prominent and lesser leaders and opponents of the civil rights movement.

2267. Riccards, Michael P. "Rare Counsel: Kennedy, Johnson and the Civil Rights Bill of 1963." *Presidential Studies Quarterly* 11 (Summer 1981): 395-98. Excellent on Johnson's advice to Kennedy on the Civil Rights Bill of 1963.

2268. Rovere, Richard H. "Letter from Washington." *New Yorker* 39 (June 1, 1963): 100-04, 107-08 and (June 22, 1963): 90-2, 94, 96-8. Essays on the judicial and social context of Kennedy's civil rights policy.

2269. Rowan, Carl T. *Breaking Barriers: A Memoir.* Boston: Little, Brown, 1991. An African American journalist and Kennedy's ambassador to Finland contributes some personal anecdotes on Kennedy and civil rights.

2270. Schlesinger, Arthur, Jr. *Robert Kennedy and His Times.* No. **1659.** Treats the Kennedy administration's civil rights commitment favorably and in considerable detail.

2271. Seigenthaler, John. "Civil Rights in the Trenches." In *The Kennedy Presidency.* Edited by Kenneth W. Thompson, pp. 101-26. No. **1588.** As Robert Kennedy's personal assistant, Seigenthaler was active in the administration's early civil rights actions.

2272. Sellers, Cleveland. *The River of No Return: The Autobiography of a Black*

Militant and the Life and Death of SNCC. New York: William Morrow, 1973. An intimate, moving account of a black activist.

2273. Shull, Steven A., and Albert Ringelstein. "Presidential Attention, Support, and Symbolism in Civil Rights, 1953-1984." *Social Science Journal* 26 (January 1989): 45-54. Kennedy is one of seven recent presidents whose views are compared and analyzed.

2274. Silver, James W. *Mississippi: The Closed Society*. New York: Harcourt, Brace and World, 1963. Written by an Ole Miss history professor, this book deals in a broader context with the controversy over the desegregation of the University of Mississippi.

2275. Sinsheimer, Joseph. "COFO and the 1963 Freedom Vote: New Strategies for Change in Mississippi." *Journal of Southern History* 55 (May 1989): 217-44. Discusses perceptively community organizing and political development relating to symbolic mock elections.

2276. Sitkoff, Harvard. "The Second Reconstruction." *Wilson Quarterly* 8 (1984): 49-59. The impact of the civil rights movement of the 1950s on the Civil Rights Act of 1964.

2277. _____. *Struggle for Black Equality, 1954-1980*. New York: Hill and Wang, 1981. Sitkoff contends that Kennedy was a pragmatist who hoped to better the life of African-Americans, but slowly and at the proper time.

2278. Smith, James George. "Presidential Elections and Racial Discrimination: Campaign Promises, Presidential Performance, and Democratic Accountability, 1960-1980." Ph.D. diss., Indiana University, 1981. Includes an evaluation of Kennedy's campaign promises and presidential performances regarding racial discrimination in voting rights, education, housing, and employment.

2279. Smith, Thomas G. "Civil Rights on the Gridiron: The Kennedy Administration and the Desegregation of the Washington Redskins." *Journal of Sport History* 14 (Summer 1987): 189-208. Focuses on the Kennedy administration pressuring the Redskins to desegregate their NFL football club.

2280. Stanley, Harold Watkins. "The Political Impact of Electoral Mobilization: The South and Universal Suffrage, 1952-1980." Ph.D. diss., Yale University, 1981. The southern voter turnout increase during the 1960s and 1970s contrasts sharply with the national decline.

2281. Stein, Jean, and George Plimpton, eds. *American Journey*. No. **1663**. Contains fascinating reminiscences of those close to the civil rights activities of the Kennedy presidency.

2282. Stern, Mark. "Calculating Visions: Civil Rights Legislation in the Kennedy and Johnson Years." *Journal of Policy History* 5 (2 1993): 231-47. Examines the civil rights strategies of Presidents Kennedy and Johnson as they dealt with what became the Civil Rights Act of 1964 and Voting Rights Act of 1965.

2283. _____. *Calculating Visions: Kennedy, Johnson, and Civil Rights.* New Brunswick, NJ: Rutgers University Press, 1992. Sees Kennedy as a moderate with a highly pragmatic viewpoint on policy.

2284. _____. "John F. Kennedy and Civil Rights: From Congress to the Presidency." *Presidential Studies Quarterly* 19 (Fall 1989): 797-823. Kennedy viewed civil rights strictly from the perspective of a politician.

2285. Sullivan, Donald Francis. "The Civil Rights Program of the Kennedy Administration: A Political Analysis." Ph.D. diss., University of Oklahoma, 1965. Sullivan sees the civil rights actions of the Roosevelt, Truman, and Eisenhower administrations as influences on Kennedy.

2286. Walker, Eugene Pierce. "A History of the Southern Christian Leadership Conference, 1955-1965: The Evolution of a Southern Strategy." Ph.D. diss., Duke University, 1978. The experience of SCLC leaders sheds light on both the larger civil rights movement and on American society itself.

2287. Wasserman, Lois Diane. "Martin Luther King, Jr.: The Molding of Nonviolence as a Philosophy and Strategy, 1955-1963." Ph.D. diss., Boston University, 1972. An analysis of King's commitment to nonviolence and his civil rights strategy as he emerged as the movement's leader.

2288. Watters, Pat, and Reese Cleghorn. *Climbing Jacob's Ladder: The Arrival of Negroes in Southern Politics.* New York: Harcourt, Brace and World, 1967. A critical account of Kennedy's implementation of voting rights program.

2289. Whalen, Charles, and Barbara Whalen. *The Longest Debate: A Legislative History of the Civil Rights Act of 1964.* Cabin John, Md: Seven Locks Press, 1985. A scholarly work that covers the activity and contribution of the Kennedy administration.

2290. Wilkins, Roy, and Tom Matthews. *Standing Fast: The Autobiography of Roy Wilkins.* New York: Viking Press, 1982. Wilkins, the executive secretary of the NAACP, had mixed feelings about Kennedy's civil rights actions.

2291. Williams, Carolyn Sue. "The Political Participation of Blacks Compared to Whites, 1952-1968." Ph.D. diss., University of Oregon, 1973. From the 1940s to the mid-1960s, not surprisingly, blacks were much less active politically than whites.

2292. Williams, Juan. *Eyes on the Prize: America's Civil Rights Years, 1954-1965.*

New York: Viking, 1987. Emphasizes the roles played by plain, though extraordinary, people.

2293. Wofford, Harris. *Of Kennedys and Kings*. No. **1972**. Good insights into the Kennedys and civil rights by a key administration official.

2294. Wolk, Allan. *The Presidency and Black Civil Rights: Eisenhower to Nixon*. Rutherford, NJ: Fairleigh Dickinson University Press, 1971. This study is largely outdated for the Kennedy era.

2295. Woodward, C. Vann. *The Strange Career of Jim Crow*. New York: Oxford University Press, 1966. An excellent overview by an eminent scholar.

2296. Young, Roy Earl. "Presidential Leadership and Civil Rights Legislation, 1963-1964." Ph.D. diss., University of Texas, 1969. A case study evaluating the legislative leadership of Presidents Kennedy and Johnson.

2297. Zinn, Howard. *SNCC: The New Abolitionists*. Boston: Beacon, 1964. The historian Zinn served as an adviser to SNCC.

Economic Conditions and Issues

2298. Bronfenbrenner, Martin. "The Kennedy-Johnson CEA." *Public Policy* 18 (Fall 1970): 743-46.

2299. Canterbery, E. Ray. *Economics on a New Frontier*. Belmont, Ca: Wadsworth Publishing, 1968. Kennedy was the first president to use firsthand the economists' tools and language--the first to utilize fully the economists' skills.

2300. _____. *The President's Council of Economic Advisers: A Study of Its Influence on the Chief Executive's Decision*. New York: Exposition Press, 1961. Provides a good background for studying the work of the CEA during the Kennedy presidency.

2301. Clausen, Aage R., and Richard B. Cheney. "A Comparative Analysis of Senate-House Voting on Economic and Welfare Policy, 1953-1964." *American Political Science Review* 64 (1970): 138-52. The Senate and House voting on economic policy is more heavily influenced by partisan differences while constituency restraints more affects welfare policy voting.

2302. Cypher, James Martin. "Military Expenditures and the Performance of the Postwar U.S. Economy, 1947-1971." Ph.D. diss., University of California, 1973. Military expenditures stimulated growth industries during the cold war.

2303. Davis, Amy Elisabeth. "Politics of Prosperity: The Kennedy Presidency and

Economic Policy." Ph.D. diss., Columbia University, 1988. A competent political history of domestic economic policy during the Kennedy presidency.

2304. Dillon, C. Douglas. "The Kennedy Presidency: The Economic Dimension." In *The Kennedy Presidency*. Edited by Kenneth W. Thompson, pp. 127-44. No. **1588**. The recollections of Kennedy's secretary of the treasury.

2305. Flash, Edward S., Jr. *Economic Advice and Presidential Leadership: The Council of Economic Advisers*. New York: Columbia University Press, 1965. A competent work that places Kennedy's CEA in the context of other councils.

2306. Friedlander, Ann F. "Macro Policy Goals in the Post-war Period: A Study in the Revealed Preference." *Quarterly Journal of Economics* 87 (1973): 25-43. Friedlander analyzes the Kennedy/Johnson administrations and their economic policies.

2307. Friedman, Milton. "Has the New Economics Failed?" *Dun's Review* 91 (February 1968): 38-9, 93-6. The conservative economist Friedman is opposed to the New Economics that evolved out of the Kennedy presidency.

2308. Galbraith, John Kenneth. *The Affluent Society*. Boston: Houghton Mifflin, 1958. Even though Galbraith remained a significant force, his economic beliefs failed to win Kennedy's acceptance.

2309. Garraty, John A. *Unemployment in History: Economic Thought and Public Policy*. New York: Harper and Row, 1978. Includes the twentieth-century transformation of the depiction of unemployment from a personal to a social and political problem.

2310. Gebelein, Herb. "Economic Policy in Practice: Perspective on the 1960s." *John F. Kennedy*. Edited by Paul Harper and Joann P. Krieg, pp. 183-92. The differences between the Kennedy-Johnson economic policies and Reaganomics are more of degree rather than of kind.

2311. Gordon, Robert Aaron. *Economic Instability and Growth: The American Record*. New York: Harper and Row, 1974. Chapter six focuses on the New Economics beginning with the Kennedy administration.

2312. Graham, Otis L., Jr. *Toward A Planned Society: From Roosevelt to Nixon*. New York: Oxford University Press, 1976. Kennedy had difficulty with domestic leadership in part because he gave it his second-best effort.

2313. Hargrove, Erwin C., and Samuel A. Morley, eds. *The President and the Council of Economic Advisers: Interviews with CEA Chairmen*. Boulder, Co: Westview Press, 1984. Contains a summary of and an interview with Kennedy's CEA Chairman Walter W. Heller.

2314. Harrington, Michael. "Reactionary Keynesianism." *Encounter* 26 (March 1966): 50-2. The author of the 1962 *The Other America*, an exposé of American poverty, is critical of economic policy coming out of the Kennedy period.

2315. Harris, Seymour E. *Economics of the Kennedy Years and a Look Ahead.* New York: Harper and Row, 1964. An important book by a liberal Harvard economist who advised Kennedy on economic policy since the senatorial years.

2316. _____. "Economic Policies under Kennedy in 1962 and Fiscal Year 1963: Introduction and Summary." *Review of Economics and Statistics* 44 (February 1962): 1-3. Summarizes the views of seven leading economists regarding the needs of the economy in 1962 and fiscal year 1963.

2317. _____. *The Economics of the Political Parties: With Special Attention to Presidents Eisenhower and Kennedy.* New York: Macmillan, 1962. Harris analyzes the ideological differences between the two major parties.

2318. Heath, Jim F. *John F. Kennedy and the Business Community.* No. **2162.** Contains several chapters on economic policy, including the 1963 tax cut.

2319. Heller, Walter W. "John F. Kennedy and the Economy." In *The Kennedy Presidency.* Edited by Kenneth W. Thompson, pp. 145-74. No. **1588.** An interview with Kennedy's chairman of the Council of Economic Advisers.

2320. _____. *New Dimensions of Political Economy.* Cambridge: Harvard University Press, 1966. The former chairman of the Council of Economic Advisers examines the rapid changes occurring during the 1960s in American economic policy.

2321. Kenski, Henry C. "The Impact of Economic Conditions on Presidential Popularity." *Journal of Politics* 39 (1977): 764-73. Includes the Kennedy presidency.

2322. Kraft, Joseph. "Treasury's Dillon--The Conservative Power Center in Washington." *Harper's Magazine* 226 (June 1963): 51-6. An able Republican operator in the Kennedy administration, Dillon was skilled in strangling liberal ideas.

2323. Lekachman, Robert. *The Age of Keynes.* New York: Random House, 1966. Includes Kennedy's acceptance of Keynesian economics in 1962.

2324. Matusow, Allen J. *The Unraveling of America.* No. **1940.** Labeling him a corporate liberal, Matusow argues that Kennedy's Keynesian ideas contributed to the unraveling of liberalism and the economy--and, therefore, the unraveling of America.

2325. Monroe, Kristen R. "Inflation and Presidential Popularity." *Presidential Studies Quarterly* 9 (1979): 334-40. Presidential popularity is affected by a gradual response to inflation.

2326. Norton, Hugh S. *The Council of Economic Advisers: Three Periods of Influence.* Columbia: Bureau of Business and Economic Research, University of South Carolina, 1973. Includes President Kennedy's CEA.

2327. _____. *The Employment Act and the Council of Economic Advisers, 1946-1976.* Columbia: University of South Carolina Press, 1977. Norton surveys the economic policies of the administrations from Truman to Nixon in light of the role played by the Council.

2328. _____. *The Quest for Economic Stability: Roosevelt to Reagan.* Columbia: University of South Carolina Press, 1985. See chapter six, "Kennedy and the Age of the Professional," which deals primarily with the Council of Economic Advisers.

2329. Pechman, Joseph A., and N. J. Simler, eds. *Economics in the Public Service: Papers in Honor of Walter W. Heller.* New York: W. W. Norton, 1982. See Robert Solow's chapter on "Where Have All the Flowers Gone? Economic Growth in the 1960s."

2330. Ratner, Sidney, James H. Soltow, and Richard Sylla. *The Evolution of the American Economy: Growth, Welfare and Decision Making.* New York: Basic Books, 1979. Provides brief coverage of the Kennedy era.

2331. Rowen, Hobart. *The Free Enterprisers: Kennedy, Johnson, and the Business Establishment.* No. **2176.** Half the book is devoted to Kennedy economic policy, which is covered in a readable style.

2332. _____. "Kennedy's Economists." *Harper's* 223 (September 1961): 25-32. Kennedy follows the more conservative Douglas Dillon approach over that of Walter Heller and the Council of Economic Advisers.

2333. Rukeyser, Merryle Stanley. *The Kennedy Recession: Causes of Our Stagnation Economy and Our Loss of World-Wide Prestige.* Derby, Ct: Monarch Books, 1963. A conservative newspaper economic analyst and business consultant argues that Kennedy is trying to overmanage the economy.

2334. Samuelson, Paul A. "Economic Policy for 1962." *Review of Economics and Statistics* 44 (February 1962): 3-6. Argues that it would be tragic if a premature budget balance were to weaken the momentum of the present recovery.

2335. Sommers, Albert T. "A Primer on the New Economics." *Conference Board*

Record 8 (August 1967): 32-52. Much of the new economics of the Kennedy era was not new.

2336. Stein, Herbert. *Presidential Economics: The Making of Economic Policy from Roosevelt to Reagan and Beyond*. New York: Simon and Schuster, 1984. A survey of economic policy over a fifty-year period by a traditional Republican economist who served in the Nixon and Ford administrations.

2337. Tobin, James. *The Intellectual Revolution in U.S. Economic Policy-making*. London: Longmans, 1966. Focuses on his involvement on the Council of Economic Advisers during the Kennedy period.

2338. _____. *National Economic Policy: Essays*. New Haven: Yale University Press, 1966. These essays focus on such topics as economic planning, deficit spending, and the weaknesses of the international monetary system.

2339. Tobin, James, and Murray Weidenbaum, ed. *Two Revolutions in Economic Policy: The First Economic Reports of Presidents Kennedy and Reagan*. Cambridge: MIT Press, 1988. Contains *The American Economy in 1961: Problems and Policies* and the *Economic Report of the President*, January 1962.

2340. Wilkins, Billy Hughel, ed. *The Economists of The New Frontier: An Anthology*. New York: Random House, 1963. A selection of the writings of economists in government service during the Kennedy administration.

Education

2341. Bailey, Stephen K., and Edith K. Mosher. *ESEA: The Office of Education Administers a Law*. Syracuse: Syracuse University Press, 1968. Although focusing on the 1964-1966 years, it often refers to the Kennedy period.

2342. Bernstein, Irving. *Promises Kept*. No. **1592**. Bernstein emphasizes Kennedy's accomplishments in federal aid to education.

2343. Boggs, Timothy J. "An Analysis of the Opinions of the United States Supreme Court Decisions on Religion and Education from 1948-1972." Ed.D. diss., University of Colorado, 1973. Boggs analyzes the ten most important Supreme Court cases on religion and education.

2344. Boutwell, William D. "What's Happening in Education?" *PTA Magazine* 58 (February 1964): 17-18. Presents the pros and cons of several bills passed to aid education.

2345. Brickman, William W. "President Kennedy and Education." *School and Society* 92 (March 7, 1964): 93. An assessment of Kennedy's views on education.

2346. "Catholic Professor Says JFK is 'Politican' on School Aid." *U. S. News and World Report* 53 (July 2, 1962): 82. A reprint of Rev. Virgil Blum's comments, which proposes federal grants to parochical schools, first published in *Our Sunday Visitor*, a Catholic magazine.

2347. "Catholics vs. Kennedy." *Newsweek* 57 (March 20, 1961): 24-5. Deals with the fight in Congress over the president's proposals on federal aid to education which excluded parochical schools.

2348. Chavez, Jose. "Presidential Influence on the Politics of Higher Education: The Higher Education Act of 1965." Ph.D. diss., University of Texas, 1975. The ultimate fruition of Kennedy's proposed higher education reforms.

2349. Citron, Henry. "The Study of the Arguments of the Interest Groups Which Opposed Federal Aid to Education from 1949-1965." Ph.D. diss., New York University, 1977. The Catholic Church and African-Americans were the most vocal opponents of federal aid to education, the latter because of a desire to prohibit federal aid to segregated school districts.

2350. "Current Documents: Administration Memorandum on Federal Aid to Private Schools." *Current History* 41 (July 1961): 49-50, 53. A reprint of the memorandum prepared by the legal staff of HEW and Justice and sent to Congress by HEW Secretary Abraham Ribicoff supporting President Kennedy's position against aid to private schools.

2351. Drinan, Robert F. *Religion, the Courts, and Public Policy.* New York: McGraw-Hill, 1963. Contains a segment on federal aid to education in 1961.

2352. Eidenberg, Eugene, and Roy D. Morey. *An Act of Congress: The Legislative Process and the Making of Education Policy.* New York: W. W. Norton, 1969. A dated account with a brief focus on the Kennedy years.

2353. Finn, Chester E., Jr. *Education and the Presidency.* Lexington, Ma.: D. C. Heath, 1977. Essential to an understanding of presidential politics of education.

2354. "The First Kennedy Budget and Education." *NEA Journal* 51 (March 1962): 12-13. Summary of the proposed 1962 budget which pertained to education.

2355. Folliard, Edward T. "Kennedy's Dilemma: Federal Aid for Parochial Schools." *Saturday Review* 44 (April 15, 1961): 56-7. Explores the pros and cons of federal aid to parochial schools and why Kennedy's decision to oppose it put him in an uncomfortable position.

2356. Graham, Hugh Davis. *The Uncertain Triumph: Federal Education Policy in the Kennedy and Johnson Years.* Chapel Hill: University of North Carolina Press, 1984. The best secondary work on Kennedy and education.

2357. "Is There Really a Crisis in U.S. Schools?" *U.S. News and World Report* 54 (May 20, 1963): 43-5. An explanation of why many congressmen think federal aid to elementary and secondary education is unnecessary.

2358. Jeffrey, Julie Roy. *Education for the Children of the Poor: A Study of the Origins and Implementation of the Elementary and Secondary Education Act of 1965.* Columbus: Ohio State University, 1976. Covers the Kennedy administration's efforts.

2359. "Kennedy's Latest Plan for Aid to Schools." *U.S. News and World Report* 54 (February 11, 1963): 60. An overview of Kennedy's 1963 proposal for federal aid to education and an assessment of how it was being received in Congress.

2360. Keppel, Francis. *The Necessary Revolution in American Education.* New York: Harper and Row, 1966. Written by Kennedy's commissioner of education.

2361. Kizer, George A. "Federal Aid to Education, 1945-1963." *History of Education Quarterly* 10 (1970): 84-102. An overview of federal aid to education during the Truman, Eisenhower, and Kennedy administrations.

2362. Kliener, Douglas E. *The Vocational Education Act of 1963.* Washington: American Vocational Association, 1965. While focusing on vocational education, it covers all education legislation enacted in 1963.

2363. Knebel, Fletcher. "The Bishops vs. Kennedy." *Look* 25 (May 23, 1961): 40-8. Focuses on the rocky relationship of Kennedy with the Catholic hierarchy in the U.S., culminating in the fight over federal aid to parochial schools.

2364. McAndrews, Lawrence J. "The Avoidable Conflict: Kennedy, the Bishops, and Federal Aid to Education." *Catholic Historical Review* 76 (April 1990): 278-94. Concludes that the religious issue was insignificant to the defeat of federal aid to education in 1961.

2365. _____. "Beyond Appearances: Kennedy, Congress, Religion, and Federal Aid to Education." *Presidential Studies Quarterly* 21 (Summer 1991): 545-57. Ideology and partisanship, not religion, killed federal aid to education in 1961.

2366. _____. "Broken Ground: John F. Kennedy and the Politics of Education." Ph.D. diss., Georgetown University, 1985. Explores Kennedy's performance on federal aid to education.

2367. Margolis, Howard. "Kennedy Program." *Science* 133 (February 17, 1961): 448-49. An assessment of how Kennedy's program for education would affect science in the area of grants and research.

2368. _____. "Kennedy's Program for Education: Teachers' Salaries;

Construction; Scholarships." *Science* 133 (February 24, 1961): 566-68. An overview of certain parts of Kennedy's proposed program for federal aid to education.

2369. Meranto, Philip. *The Politics of Federal Aid to Education in 1965: A Study in Political Innovation.* Syracuse: Syracuse University Press, 1967. Contains information on Kennedy's legislative efforts.

2370. Michel, George J. "Success in National Education Policy from Eisenhower to Carter." *Peabody Journal of Education* 57 (1980): 223-32. Deals briefly with Kennedy.

2371. Munger, Frank J., and Richard F. Fenno. *National Politics and Federal Aid to Education.* Syracuse: Syracuse University Press, 1962. Kennedy's Catholicism heightened his administration's vulnerability.

2372. O'Hara, William T. ed. *John F. Kennedy in Education.* No. **30.** Covers Kennedy's role in education from 1947 to 1963.

2373. Pettit, Lawrence W. "The Policy Process in Congress: Passing the Higher Education Facilities Act of 1963." Ph.D. diss., University of Wisconsin, 1965. Based on data from printed materials and interviews conducted in Washington.

2374. "President Kennedy's Task Force on Education Makes Its Report." *Saturday Review* 44 (January 21, 1961): 94-5. A summary of legislative recommendations concerning federal aid to education made by President Kennedy's Task Force on Education.

2375. Price, Hugh Douglas. "Race, Religion, and the Rules Committee: The Kennedy Aid-to-Education Bills." In *The Uses of Power: 7 Cases in American Politics.* Edited by Alan F. Westin. New York: Harcourt, Brace and World, 1962, pp. 1-71. The president was not prepared to jeopardize his whole legislative program--and perhaps his chances for re-election--by a bitter fight for aid to education.

2376. _____. "Schools, Scholarships, and Congressmen." In *The Centers of Power: 3 Cases in American National Government.* Edited by Alan F. Westin. New York: Harcourt, Brace and World, 1964, pp. 53-105. A revised version of Price's 1961 essay.

2377. Ravitch, Diane. *The Troubled Crusade: American Education, 1945-1980.* New York: Basic Books, 1983. An excellent account with scattered references to Kennedy and a useful bibliographic essay.

2378. Rivlin, Alice M. *The Role of the Federal Government in Financing Higher Education.* Washington: Brookings Institution, 1961. This study influenced the Kennedy administration.

2379. Scanlon, John. "Who Killed Federal Aid?" *Saturday Review* 44 (August 19, 1961): 31-2. An assessment of why the president's aid to education bill was defeated in the House.

2380. Sheerin, John B. "Kennedy's Program and Catholic Schools." *Catholic World* 193 (April 1961): 4-7. Cites legal precedents that would allow federal aid to children attending parochial schools.

2381. Smith, R. H. "Federal Aid to Education: Two More Years of Labor." *Publishers' Weekly* 180 (September 25, 1961): 43. An assessment of the Kennedy administration's efforts to get a federal aid to education bill passed.

2382. _____. "A New Effort for Federal Aid to Education." *Publishers' Weekly* 183 (February 25, 1961): 44. An overview of the renewed efforts of the Kennedy administration to pass a federal aid to education bill in 1963.

2383. Spring, Joel. *The Sorting Machine: National Education Policy since 1945*. New York: McKay, 1976. Spring relates the impact of the cold war on educational developments.

2384. Sundquist, James L. *Politics and Policy*. No. **2081**. See chapter five for an excellent survey of the postwar federal aid to education struggle.

2385. Taylor, Arthuryne J. "Federal Financing of Education, 1945-1972." *Current History* 62 (1972): 298-301, 306. Taylor reviews issues that affected federal aid to education from 1945 to 1972.

2386. "Under Catholic Church Fire: Kennedy's School Plan." *U.S. News and World Report* 50 (January 30, 1961): 54-5. The full text of a speech by Francis Cardinal Spellman in which he attacks the Kennedy administration for excluding parochical schools in a federal aid to education proposal.

2387. Whelan, Charles M. "Only Higher Education, Mr. President?" *America* 104 (March 11, 1961): 758-60. Attacks Kennedy's position that federal aid to parochial schools is unconstitutional.

2388. _____. "The President's Brief on Federal Aid." *America* 105 (April 15, 1961): 140-41. Attacks the HEW memorandum on federal aid on education.

2389. _____. "School Question: Stage Two." *America* 105 (April 1, 1961): 17-19. An exploration of the Catholic Church's position on federal aid to education.

2390. "Who Killed the Bill?" *Newsweek* 58 (August 21, 1961): 58-9. Explains why pressures from religious groups defeated the president's education bill.

Federal Bureau of Investigation

2391. Charns, Alexander. *Cloak and Gavel: FBI Wiretaps, Bugs, Informers, and the Supreme Court*. Urbana: University of Illinois Press, 1992. Scattered references to Attorney General Robert Kennedy and wiretapping and bugging.

2392. Demaris, Ovid. *The Director: An Oral Biography of J. Edgar Hoover*. New York: Harper's Magazine Press, 1975. Interviews with Kennedy associates regarding the Kennedys and Hoover.

2393. _____. "Office Politics of J. Edgar Hoover." *Esquire* 82 (November 1974): 142-50, 204-10. Full of anecdotes regarding Hoover's stormy relationship with Attorney General Robert Kennedy.

2394. De Toledano, Ralph. *J. Edgar Hoover: The Man in His Time*. New York: Arlington House, 1973. This journalist is a longtime admirer of Hoover.

2395. Felt, W. Mark. *The FBI Pyramid: From the Inside*. New York: G. P. Putnam's Sons, 1979. An account by a former FBI special agent and executive that provides anecdotal information on the Robert Kennedy--Hoover relationship.

2396. Garrow, David. *The FBI and Martin Luther King*. No. **2214**. Deals well with the Hoover, King, and Kennedy triangle.

2397. Gentry, Curt. *J. Edgar Hoover: The Man and the Secrets*. New York: W. W. Norton, 1991. This massive work, based on extensive interviews and declassified documents, devotes a chapter to the Kennedys.

2398. Halperin, Morton, et al. *The Lawless State: The Crime of the U.S. Intelligence Agencies*. New York: Penguin, 1976. Written by the staff of The Center for National Security Studies and based on congressional hearings reports and secondary sources, this study covers the Kennedy presidency.

2399. "Hoover's Political Spying for Presidents." *Time* 106 (December 15, 1975): 10-12. The Senate Select Committee on Intelligence Activities confirmed that Attorney General Robert Kennedy authorized wiretapping of several Washington journalists, including Hanson Baldwin of the *New York Times*.

2400. Keller, William. *The Liberals and J. Edgar Hoover: Rise and Fall of a Domestic Intelligence State*. Princeton: Princeton University Press, 1989. Deals with Attorney General Robert Kennedy and Hoover on wiretapping.

2401. Marro, A., and P. Goldman. "J. Edgar Hoover's Secret Files." *Newsweek* 85 (March 10, 1975): 16-17. Mentions that Hoover checked out various congressional critics for presidents, including Kennedy.

2402. Messick, Hank. *John Edgar Hoover*. New York: David McKay, 1972. Based largely on secondary sources and contemporary articles, this is a critical examination of Hoover and the FBI.

2403. Nash, Jay Robert. *Citizen Hoover: A Critical Study of the Life and Times of J. Edgar Hoover and His FBI*. Chicago: Nelson-Hall, 1972. A popular account based largely on secondary sources.

2404. Navasky, Victor S. *Kennedy Justice*. No. **2258**. One of the most perceptive statements on Hoover and the FBI during the Kennedy period.

2405. O'Reilly, Kenneth. *Racial Matters*. No. **2260**. Contains information on Kennedy and the FBI.

2406. Ollestad, Norman. *Inside the FBI*. New York: Lancer Books, 1967. A special agent provides some interesting anecdotes involving Robert Kennedy and Hoover in this popular account.

2407. Powers, Richard Gid. *Secrecy and Power: The Life of J. Edgar Hoover*. New York: Free Press, 1987. A well-researched study that includes coverage of the Kennedy-Hoover relationship.

2408. Sullivan, William C. *The Bureau: My Thirty Years in Hoover's FBI*. New York: W. W. Norton, 1979. Written by the assistant director of the intelligence division, Sullivan provides his personal reminiscences of the Kennedy-Hoover relationship.

2409. Summers, Anthony. *Official and Confidential: The Secret Life of J. Edgar Hoover*. New York: G. P. Putnam's Sons, 1993. Richly anecdotal and based on FBI files, Summers writes extensively on the Hoover--Kennedy connection.

2410. Theoharis, Athan. *From the Secret Files of J. Edgar Hoover*. Chicago: Ivan R. Dee, 1991. Copies of FBI memos, letters, and wiretap transcriptions on John F. Kennedy from the Inga Arvad affair in the 1940s to allegations in the 1960s of a previous Kennedy marriage.

2411. _____. *Spying on Americans: Political Surveillance from Hoover to the Huston Plan*. Philadelphia: Temple University Press, 1978. Kennedy shared the cold war consensus that the seriousness of the internal security threat justified radical departures from traditional values.

2412. Theoharis, Athan, and John Stuart Cox. *The Boss: J. Edgar Hoover and the Great American Inquisition*. Philadelphia: Temple University Press, 1988. Excellent on Hoover's suspicions of--and antagonism toward--the Kennedys, which caused him to keep an extensive file on JFK for possible blackmail purposes.

2413. Turner, William W. *Hoover's FBI: The Men and the Myth*. Los Angeles: Sherbourne Press, 1970. A special agent's personal account with occasional references to the Kennedys.

2414. Ungar, Sanford. *FBI*. Boston: Atlantic Monthly Press, 1975. A massive study that contains little information on President Kennedy.

2415. Welch, Neil, and David Marston. *Inside Hoover's FBI: The Top Field Chief Reports*. Garden City, NY: Doubleday, 1984. Contains some interesting anecdotes involving Hoover and Robert Kennedy.

Fiscal and Monetary Policies

2416. Amen, M. Mark. "A Reappraisal of Liberalism in the Kennedy Administration's Economic Policies." *John F. Kennedy*. Edited by Paul Harper and Joann P. Krieg, pp. 207-24. No. **1600**. A reconsideration of the liberal interpretation of Kennedy's fiscal and balance of payments policies.

2417. "As the White House Seeks More Control Over Money." *U.S. News and World Report* 52 (May 7, 1962): 115-17. Kennedy has stirred up a controversy with his proposal to give the White House more influence over the powerful Federal Reserve Board.

2418. Aubrey, Henry C. *The Dollar in World Affairs: An Essay in International Financial Policy*. New York: Harper and Row, 1964.

2419. "'Don't Nudge Too Far,' Fed Warns Kennedy: Hearings, Joint Economic Committee." *Business Week* (June 10, 1961), pp. 28-9. The Federal Reserve Board warned the Kennedy administration that there are limits to their cooperation in lowering long-term interest rates.

2420. Eckstein, Otto. "The Federal Budget: Question Mark for 1962." *Review of Economics and Statistics* 44 (February 1962): 17-20. There is no need for sudden economy measures in the budget, either in defense or in civilian expenditures, nor is there presently any case for tax increases.

2421. "Fed Goes Along With Kennedy." *Business Week* (February 25, 1961), pp. 32, 34. The Federal Reserve Board has cooperated with the Kennedy administration by lowering long-term interest rates.

2422. Friedman, Milton. *Capitalism and Freedom*. Chicago: University of Chicago Press, 1962. See chapter five for a critique of the Kennedy fiscal policies.

2423. _____. *Dollars and Deficits: Living With America's Economic Problems*. Englewood Cliffs, NJ: Prentice-Hall, 1968. Contains essays on the monetary policy and the balance of payments issues of the Kennedy period.

2424. Friedman, Milton, and Walter W. Heller. *Monetary vs. Fiscal Policy*. New York: W. W. Norton, 1969. Heller, a leading neo-Keynesian economist, and Friedman, a leading spokesman for the monetarist school, clash over economic philosophy for the 1960s.

2425. Froyen, Richard T. "Monetarist Econometric Models and the 1964 Tax Cut." *Economic Inquiry* 12 (June 1974): 59-68. Tests whether several monetarist econometric models could have forecast the expansion in economic activity following the 1964 tax cut.

2426. Jacoby, Neil H. "The Fiscal Policy of the Kennedy-Johnson Administration." *Journal of Finance* 19 (May 1964): 353-69. Fiscal performance under the Kennedy administration was more conservative than Democratic orthodoxy.

2427. Jean, William H. "An Empirical Study of Monetary Policy." Ph.D. diss., Purdue University, 1964. Covers the 1953 to 1962 period.

2428. "Kennedy Holds the Line on Monetary Policy: Appointments to Federal Reserve Board." *U. S. News and World Report* 55 (November 11, 1963): 62. In two Federal Reserve appointments in 1963, Kennedy has leaned toward a conservative viewpoint and hard money.

2429. "Kennedy Moves to Lower Long-term Rates." *Business Week* (February 11, 1961), pp. 28-9. Kennedy seeks to narrow the gap between long-term and short-term interest rates by lowering long-term rates.

2430. "Kennedy's Big Week." *U.S. News and World Report* 54 (January 28, 1963): 29-34. Kennedy discusses his proposed tax cut before Congress.

2431. "Kennedy's Plan for Reserve Board." *U.S. News and World Report* 52 (April 30, 1962): 106. Kennedy has asked Congress for the power to appoint a new chairman of the Federal Reserve Board, starting in 1965.

2432. King, Ronald F. "Continuity and Change: Fiscal Policy in the Kennedy Administration." *John F. Kennedy*. Edited by Paul Harper and Joann P. Krieg, pp. 172-82. No. **1600**. The early Kennedy period should be awarded more importance than is found in the historiography of economic policy.

2433. Lammers, Bernard James. "The Role of Congressional Tax Committees in Internal Revenue Legislation, 1953-1964." Ph.D. diss., Columbia University, 1967. An analysis of the external and internal pressures on the three congressional tax committees.

2434. Lewis, Wilfred, Jr. *Federal Fiscal Policy in the Postwar Recessions*.

Washington: Brookings Institution, 1962. Lewis analyzes federal fiscal activity in the recessions of 1953-55, 1957-58, and 1960-62, placing blame on excessive budget tightening.

2435. "More Tax Cuts Coming." *Nation's Business* 52 (May 1964): 38-41, 108, 110, 112, 114, 116, 118. A behind-the-scenes look at how Kennedy's tax cut evolved.

2436. "New Man on Federal Reserve: The Meaning to Money Policy." *U.S. News and World Report* 51 (July 10, 1961): 88. For the first time a Kennedy appointee, George W. Mitchell, serves on the Federal Reserve Board.

2437. Nossiter, Bernard D. "The Day Taxes Weren't Cut." *Reporter* 21 (September 13, 1962): 25-8. Kennedy's decision to delay a tax cut represented a victory for Treasury Secretary Douglas Dillon over Walter Heller of the Council of Economic Advisers.

2438. "Not in Martin's Pocket: Fed's Hard Money Policies." *Business Week* (November 9, 1963), p. 116. J. Dewey Daane's appointment to the Federal Reserve Board knits the Fed closer to the Treasury Department and keeps the Board's firm money policy on track.

2439. Pechman, Joseph. *Federal Tax Policy*. Washington: Brookings Institution, 1966. Centers on Kennedy's tax cut proposal which became the Revenue Act of 1964.

2440. Pluta, Joseph Edward. "Growth and Patterns in U.S. Government Expenditures, 1956-1970." Ph.D. diss., University of Texas, 1972. The trend was for increased expenditures in education, income maintenance, housing, and public health for the 1956-70 period.

2441. Rowen, Hobart. "David Bell and his Budgeteers." *Harper's Magazine* 225 (July 1962): 45-52. Focuses on the power of Kennedy's Director of the Bureau of the Budget.

2442. _____. "Let's Spend More." *New Republic* 148 (May 25, 1963): 13-18. President Kennedy's tax program will not stimulate the kind of economic growth needed by the United States.

2443. Salant, Walter S. *The United States Balance of Payments in 1968*. Washington: Brookings Institution, 1963. Based on a Kennedy request to appraise the balance of payments problem over the next few years.

2444. Schneider, William, Jr. "The Inside Lag in the Monetary Policy of the United States, 1952-1965." Ph.D. diss., New York University, 1968. Measures the temporal response of monetary policy to changes in the United States for the 1952-65 period.

2445. Simpson, Phillip M. "John F. Kennedy and the 1964 Revenue Act: The Politics of Formulation/Legitimation." *John F. Kennedy.* Edited by Paul Harper and Joann P. Krieg, pp. 193-206. No. **1600.** The tax cut was transitional legislation that would have been followed by a major Kennedy commitment to social and economic justice in a second term.

2446. Smith, H. W. "Who Will Make Monetary Policy?" *New Republic* 144 (February 6, 1961): 17-18. Will Kennedy and his economic aides in the Council of Economic Advisers and the Treasury operate on the same wave length with Chairman Martin of the Federal Reserve Board?

2447. Stein, Arthur A. "Balance of Payments Policy in the Kennedy Administration." *Papers of the Peace Science Society (International)* 23 (1974): 113-22. The Kennedy administration abruptly shifted from its original economic game plan in 1963 regarding the balance of payments deficit.

2448. Stein, Herbert. *The Fiscal Revolution in America.* Chicago: University of Chicago Press, 1969. Stein's work includes the Kennedy tax cut implemented in the Johnson presidency.

2449. _____. "Tax Cut in Camelot." *Trans-action* 6 (April 1969): 38-44. Discusses how Kennedy and his economic advisers came to support the tax reductions later enacted in 1964.

2450. Stern, Philip. *The Great Treasury Raid.* New York: Random House, 1964. Deals with the major "loopholes" in the Internal Revenue Service tax code during the Kennedy period.

2451. "Tax Cut Drive Is On." *Business Week* (December 22, 1962), pp. 15-16. Kennedy discusses his proposed tax cut before the Economic Club of New York.

2452. Triffin, Robert. *Gold and the Dollar Crises: The Future of Convertibility.* rev. ed. New Haven: Yale University Press, 1961. Focuses on a problem that concerned Kennedy immensely in 1961.

2453. Von Furstenberg, George M., and James M. Boughton. "Stabilization Goals and the Appropriateness of Fiscal Policy during the Eisenhower and Kennedy/Johnson Administrations." *Public Finance Quarterly* 1 (1973): 5-28. An extremely esoteric study that is of no use to the general scholar.

2454. "Widening the Role of the Federal Reserve." *Business Week* (April 28, 1962), p. 152. Kennedy seeks to make the term of chairman of the Federal Reserve Board coincide with the presidency so that the chief executive could choose his own person for that post.

Labor

2455. Barnard, John. *Walter Reuther and the Rise of the Auto Workers*. Boston: Little, Brown, 1983. Covers Reuther's attitude toward the Kennedy administration policies.

2456. Bellace, Janice R., and Alan D. Berkowitz. *The Landrum-Griffin Act: Twenty Years of Federal Protection of Union Members' Rights*. Philadelphia: University of Pennsylvania Press, 1979. This highly specialized work includes cases and issues from the Kennedy period.

2457. Goldberg, Arthur J. "The Role of Government." *The Annals of the American Academy of Political and Social Science* 340 (March 1962): 110-16. Kennedy's labor secretary discusses the role the federal government must play to achieve high employment and full productivity.

2458. Goldfield, Michael. *The Decline of Organized Labor in the United States*. Chicago: University of Chicago Press, 1987. Unions have declined in membership because of Landrum-Griffin restrictions, employer resistance, and less aggressiveness on the part of union organizers.

2459. Greenstone, J. David. *Labor in American Politics*. New York: Knopf, 1969. Covers the Kennedy era.

2460. Hazlitt, Henry. "Too Much Labor Law." *Newsweek* 58 (July 31, 1961): 70. Criticizes the Kennedy administration's proposals to increase the federal government's powers to intervene in labor-management disputes.

2461. Hills, Roderick M., James Stern, and Joseph Grodin. "A Symposium: Labor Relations and the Kennedy Administration." *Industrial Relations* 3 (February 1964): 5-45. All three essays include an assessment of the National Labor Relations Board during the Kennedy presidency.

2462. "Is 'Kennedy Board' Rewriting Labor Law?" *U. S. News and World Report* 55 (July 8, 1963): 91-2. Criticizes the NLRB during the Kennedy administration for favoring unions at the expense of employers.

2463. Johnson, David B. "The New Frontier Collective Bargaining Policy." *Labor Law Journal* 13 (July 1962): 591-98. Despite increased government intervention, collective bargaining has produced some independent efforts to solve problems.

2464. Kennedy, Robert F. *The Enemy Within*. New York: Harper and Row, 1960. Kennedy, the chief counsel for the McClellan "Rackets" Committee, combats corruption in unions, especially Jimmy Hoffa's Teamsters.

2465. Lee, R. Alton. *Eisenhower and Landrum-Griffin: A Study in Labor-*

Management Politics. Lexington: University Press of Kentucky, 1990. Includes chapters on Senator John Kennedy's role in drafting labor legislation.

2466. "Let's Put Teeth into the Labor Laws." *Life* 52 (June 29, 1962): 4. The editorial urges Kennedy to get tougher on labor unions and strikes and to ask Congress for more power in dealing with labor disputes.

2467. McGuiness, Kenneth C. *The New Frontier NLRB*. Washington: Labor Policy Association, 1963. Written by a former NLRB policy maker, a consultant to Congress, and an impartial arbitrator.

2468. Martin, Harold H. "Big Labor's Big Worry." *Saturday Evening Post* 235 (December 15, 1962): 66-9. An overview of labor and management's opposition to the Kennedy administration's increasing interference in labor disputes.

2469. Mollenhoff, Clark R. *Tentacles of Power: The Story of Jimmy Hoffa*. Cleveland: World, 1965. Mollenhoff, an investigative reporter and lawyer, worked with Robert Kennedy on the McClellan "Rackets" Committee.

2470. Moskow, Michael H., J. Joseph Loewenberg, and E. C. Koziara. *Collective Bargaining in Public Employment*. New York: Random House, 1970. The year 1962 marked a decisive turning point in the policy of the federal government toward collective bargaining by its employees.

2471. Pennington, Ralph A. "The National Labor Relations Board: Three Decades of Operation." Ph.D. diss., Purdue University, 1968. The board experienced a sevenfold increase in the annual caseload during the first thirty years of its operation.

2472. Pierson, Gail. "The Effect of Union Strength on the U.S. 'Phillips Curve.'" *American Economics Review* 58 (1968): 456-67. Analyzes the impact of union strength on the relationship between wage rate changes and unemployment from 1953 to 1966.

2473. Radosh, Ronald. *American Labor and United States Foreign Policy*. New York: Random House, 1969. Organized labor had a major impact on American foreign policy, especially during the cold war when labor adopted a strongly anti-communist position.

2474. Robinson, Archie. *George Meany and His Times: A Biography*. New York: Simon and Schuster, 1981. In a chapter devoted to Kennedy, Robinson quoted Meany that "JFK would have been a great president had he lived."

2475. Rowen, Hobart. "Taft-Hartley: Changes Goldberg Wants." *Newsweek* 58 (July 17, 1961): 63-4. The secretary of labor outlines the Kennedy administration's proposals for new labor legislation to deal with strikes and other work issues.

2476. Sheridan, Walter. *The Rise and Fall of Jimmy Hoffa*. New York: Saturday Review Press, 1972. Written by a former FBI agent and investigative counsel of the McClellan Committee, it focuses on a major Kennedy nemesis.

2477. Slack, Walter H. "Walter Reuther: A Study of Ideas." Ph.D. diss., University of Iowa, 1965. A Kennedy ally, Reuther promoted the right proposals at the right time on aid to education, civil rights, and medical care for the aged.

2478. Stieber, Jack. "The President's Committee on Labor-Management Policy." *Industrial Relations* 5 (February 1966): 1-19. An assessment of the President's Advisory Committee on Labor-Management Policy established by Secretary of Labor Arthur Goldberg in 1961.

2479. "Tests Coming for Kennedy Formula." *Business Week* (May 5, 1962), p. 69. Examines labor and management negotiations and the Kennedy's administration's positions concerning them.

2480. Ulman, Lloyd. "The Labor Policy of the Kennedy Administration." *Institute of Industrial Relations*. Reprint no. 205. Berkeley: University of California, 1963. Kennedy administration sought to provide conditions conducive to collective bargaining and to set limits on the bargaining power of trade unions.

2481. "When a Big Strike Hits--What to Expect from the White House." *U.S. News and World Report* 51 (July 10, 1961): 89-92. Outlines the steps the administration would use to end a major strike.

2482. "White House Labor Policies Face Test." *Nation's Business* 50 (December 1962): 40-1, 59. A preview of what lies ahead in 1963 in labor-management disputes and the Kennedy administration's increased efforts to become involved in them.

2483. "White House Plan to Deal with Labor Problems." *U.S. News and World Report* 50 (February 20, 1961): 94-5. The article focuses on the newly formed President's Advisory Committee on Labor-Management Policy.

2484. "Why Kennedy Holds Back on New Laws to Prevent Strikes." *U.S. News and World Report* 54 (January 28, 1963): 93-5. Because of the opposition of union leaders and management officials, the Kennedy administration resisted the passage of anti-strike and other tough labor legislation.

Media

2485. Aronson, James. *The Press and the Cold War*. Indianapolis: Bobbs-Merrill, 1970. Written by a journalist of the *National Guardian*, it covers all of the major foreign crises of the Kennedy era.

2486. Balutis, Alan P. "The Presidency and the Press: The Expanding Presidential Image." *Presidential Studies Quarterly* 7 (Fall 1977): 244-51. Based on the earlier work of Elmer Cornwell who focused on the 1885-1957 period, Balutis covers the 1958-77 years.

2487. Berry, Joseph P., Jr. *John F. Kennedy and the Media: The First Television President*. Lanham, Md.: University Press of America, 1987. A brief account, ignoring the archival material at the Kennedy Library and postulating that Kennedy was the first president who fully understood and used the media for its political potential.

2488. Bickers, William Patrick Michael. "Robert Kennedy and the American Press." Ph.D. diss., Ball State University, 1984. Included in this study is Robert Kennedy as attorney general and his relationship to the president.

2489. Bingham, Worth, and Ward S. Just. "The President and the Press." *Reporter* 26 (April 12, 1962): 18-23. Kennedy has revolutionized relations between the press and the president.

2490. "Classic Conflict: The President and the Press." *Time* 80 (December 14, 1962): 45-6. One of many stories on Kennedy's manipulation of the press.

2491. Cogley, John. "The Presidential Image." *New Republic* 144 (April 10, 1961): 29-31. Kennedy's appearances on television have been mostly style and little substance.

2492. Cornwell, Elmer E., Jr. *Presidential Leadership of Public Opinion*. Bloomington: Indiana University Press, 1966. Excellent comparative analysis of Kennedy's press conferences and his other relationships with the media.

2493. Curtin, Michael Joseph. "Defining the Free World: Prime-Time Documentary and the Politics of the Cold War, 1960-1964." Ph.D. diss., University of Wisconsin, 1990. Examines the way the documentaries on television promoted government policies, free enterprise, and anti-communism.

2494. Drummond, Roscoe. "Mr. Kennedy's Calculated Risk." *Saturday Review* 44 (February 11, 1961): 82-4. Analyzes how Kennedy will use the live TV press conference as a powerful instrument of presidential leadership.

2495. Fedler, Fred, Ron Smith, and Milan D. Meeske. "*Time* and *Newsweek* Favor John F. Kennedy, Criticize Robert and Edward Kennedy." *Journalism Quarterly* 60 (Autumn 1983): 489-96. The news stories that appeared in *Time* and *Newsweek* were biased in favor of John Kennedy and against his brothers.

2496. Graber, Doris A. *Mass Media and American Politics*. Washington:

Congressional Quarterly Press, 1980. Scattered references to Kennedy's use of the media.

2497. Grossman, Michael Baruch, and Martha Joynt Kumar. *Portraying the President: The White House and the News Media.* Baltimore: Johns Hopkins University Press, 1981. Contains scattered Kennedy references.

2498. Hart, Roderick P. *The Sound of Leadership: Presidential Communication in the Modern Age.* University of Chicago Press, 1987. Study of a new American presidency based on communication which includes Kennedy's use of the media.

2499. Henggeler, Paul R. "Kennedy and the News Media: The Development of President John F. Kennedy's Media Strategy Based on *Time, Newsweek,* and Television." M.A. thesis, Bowling Green University, 1985. By 1963 television eclipsed print journalism as Kennedy's central medium for image-management.

2500. "Historic Conference." *Newsweek* 57 (February 6, 1961): 56-7. President Kennedy's first live television news conference.

2501. Hoover, Judith. "An Early Use of Television as a Political Tool: The 1961 News Conferences of President John F. Kennedy and the Republican Opposition." *Journal of Popular Film and Television* 16 (Spring 1988): 41-8. Kennedy and the Republican congressional leadership used television press conferences to explain their respective party positions on a variety of issues, which provided a dramatic contrast in media style and effectiveness.

2502. "How Much Management of the News?" *Newsweek* 61 (April 8, 1963): 59-63. An assessment of the extent to which Kennedy attempts to manage the news.

2503. "How a President Makes News: Kennedy Adds Some New Twists." *U.S. News and World Report* 50 (March 13, 1961): 102-06. How Kennedy has tried to make press relations more open.

2504. Hutchison, Earl R. "Kennedy and the Press: The First Six Months." *Journalism Quarterly* 38 (Autumn 1961): 453-59. As a result of his first months as president, Kennedy may foster a government-press relationship of unprecedented smoothness.

2505. "JFK Cloying?" *National Review* 10 (April 8, 1961): 207-08. Argues that Kennedy uses his charm and rhetoric to not answer reporters' questions.

2506. Johnson, Miles B. *The Government Secrecy Controversy.* New York: Vantage Press, 1967. News management in the Eisenhower, Kennedy, and Johnson presidencies.

2507. "The Kennedy 'Image'--How It's Built." *U. S. News and World Report* 52

(April 9, 1962): 56-9. Includes Kennedy's massaging the press.

2508. Kern, Montague. "The Presidency and the Press: John F. Kennedy's Foreign Policy Crises and the Politics of Newspaper Coverage." Ph.D. diss., Johns Hopkins University, 1979. This study explores the forces in society that affect newspapers' coverage of crises faced by presidents.

2509. Kern, Montague, Patricia W. Levering, and Ralph B. Levering. *The Kennedy Crises: The Press, the Presidency, and Foreign Policy*. Chapel Hill: University of North Carolina Press, 1983. Centers on the coverage of five important newspapers during four major crises: Laos, Berlin, Cuba, and Vietnam; this is a significant work.

2510. Keyes, Elizabeth Anne. "President Kennedy's Press Conferences as 'Shapers of the News.'" Ph.D. diss., University of Iowa, 1968. A useful early study.

2511. Knebel, Fletcher. "Kennedy vs. the Press." *Look* 26 (August 28, 1962): 17-21. An important article that concludes that Kennedy's honeymoon with the press is over.

2512. Krock, Arthur. *Memoirs: Sixty Years on the Firing Line*. New York: Funk and Wagnalls, 1968. The *New York Times* journalist and Kennedy family friend includes a chapter on Kennedy.

2513. Levering, Ralph B., and Montague Kern. "The News Management Issue and John F. Kennedy's Foreign Policy." In *John F. Kennedy*. Edited by Paul Harper and Joann P. Krieg, 1988, pp. 143-52. No. **1600**. Much of the focus is on the Cuban missile crisis.

2514. Lewis, Ted. "TV Press Conference." *Nation* (February 11, 1961): 112-13. On what happens at a live TV news conference with a comparison of what earlier presidents did before television.

2515. Locander, Robert. "The Adversary Relationship: A New Look at an Old Idea." *Presidential Studies Quarterly* 9 (Summer 1979): 266-74. While Kennedy lived, his antagonism with the press failed to develop into a major war, but the seeds of greater conflict were already planted and about to surface at the time of his assassination.

2516. "Long Time No See." *Newsweek* 58 (November 13, 1961): 93. Criticism of Kennedy for not holding press conferences more often.

2517. McGaffin, William, and Erwin Knoll. *Anything But the Truth: The Credibility Gap--How the News is Managed in Washington*. New York: G. P. Putnam's Sons, 1968. References to Kennedy.

2518. Manheim, Jarol B. "The Honeymoon's Over: The News Conference and the Development of Presidential Style." *Journal of Politics* 41 (February 1979): 55-74. The Kennedy administration and the advent of live television coverage have transformed presidential press conferences.

2519. Markel, Lester. "Management of News." *Saturday Review* 46 (February 9, 1963): 50-1, 61. The Sunday editor of the *New York Times*, Markel is critical of the Kennedy administration's news management policies.

2520. Mendelsohn, Harold A., and Irving Crespi. *Polls, Television, and the New Politics*. Scranton, Pa.: Chandler Publishing, 1970. In sometimes alluding to Kennedy, this book challenges some widely held conceptions about how American politics has been affected by public opinion polls and television.

2521. Minow, Newton, John B. Martin, and Lee Mitchell. *Presidential Television*. New York: Basic Books, 1973. Includes coverage of Kennedy and television.

2522. Nacos, Brigitte L. *The Press, Presidents, and Crises*. New York: Columbia University Press, 1990. Focusing on the Cuban missile crisis, this study confirms Kern's and the Levering's conclusion that during the Kennedy era the press was "reflective" with respect to foreign crises coverage.

2523. Ostman, Ronald E. "Three Major U.S. Newspapers' Content and President Kennedy's Press Conference Statements Regarding Space Exploration and Technology." *Presidential Studies Quarterly* 13 (Winter 1983): 112-20. Examines the media coverage of Kennedy's press conferences concerning the space program.

2524. Ostman, Ronald E., William A. Babcock, and J. Cecilia Fallert. "Relation of Questions and Answers in Kennedy's Press Conferences." *Journalism Quarterly* 58 (Winter 1981): 575-81. A content analysis of Kennedy's 62 press conferences reveals that questioners who followed certain professional rules for asking questions received "better" answers than those who did not.

2525. Pollard, James. *The Presidents and the Press: Truman to Johnson*. Washington: Public Affairs Press, 1964. In press relations, the Kennedy administration enjoyed a degree of warmth, accessibility, and cordiality unmatched by any previous administration.

2526. Rivers, William L. *The Opinionmakers*. Boston: Beacon Press, 1965. This book about modern political journalism focuses on the Kennedy administration.

2527. Rovere, Richard. "Letter from Washington." *New Yorker* 39 (March 30, 1963): 163-69. Rovere defends Kennedy's management of the news.

2528. Sabato, Larry J. *Feeding Frenzy: How Attack Journalism Has Transformed*

American Politics. New York: Free Press, 1991. Covers the press's cover-up of Kennedy's private life.

2529. Salinger, Pierre. *With Kennedy*. Garden City, NY: Doubleday, 1966. An indispensable work by Kennedy's press secretary.

2530. Sharp, Harry Wall, Jr. "The Kennedy News Conference." Ph.D. diss., Purdue University, 1967. Based on a detailed questionnaire distributed to correspondents who participated at Kennedy's press conferences, on a series of interviews with fifty-three correspondents who regularly participated in the conferences, and on interviews with Pierre Salinger and other White House staffers.

2531. _____. "Live From Washington: The Telecasting of President Kennedy's News Conference." *Journal of Broadcasting* 13 (Winter 1968): 23-32. Based on a questionnaire, most correspondents thought the advantages of Kennedy's live telecasts outweighed the disadvantages.

2532. Small, William J. *Political Power and the Press*. New York: W. W. Norton, 1972. Covers the Kennedy era.

2533. _____. *To Kill A Messenger: Television News and the Real World*. New York: Hastings House, 1970. Much on television coverage of Kennedy.

2534. Smith, Carolyn. *Presidential Press Conferences: A Critical Approach*. New York: Praeger, 1990. Smith, the director of political operations with ABC News, deals briefly with the Kennedy press conference.

2535. Sorensen, Theodore. *Kennedy*. No. **1625**. Kennedy's special counsel devotes an entire chapter to press relations.

2536. Stein, M. L. *When Presidents Meet the Press*. New York: Julian Messner, 1969. Contains a short chapter on Kennedy's relationship with Press Secretary Pierre Salinger.

2537. Streitmatter, Rodger. "The Impact of Presidential Personality on News Coverage in Major Newspapers." *Journalism Quarterly* 62 (Spring 1985): 66-73. Deals with three pairs of twentieth-century presidents, including Eisenhower and Kennedy, and concludes that journalists write more stories about presidents with exciting personalities because they make good copy.

2538. Tebbel, John, and Sarah Miles Watts. *The Press and the Presidency: From George Washington to Ronald Reagan*. New York: Oxford University Press, 1985. Kennedy was the first president to recognize that the president could appear on the evening news as a newsmaker even when there was no real news to make.

2539. Wagner, Philip M. "A Better Way with Press Conferences." *Harper's*

Magazine 222 (May 1961): 12, 14. Examines the benefits of Kennedy's wide-open press conference.

2540. Watson, Mary Ann. *The Expanding Vista: American Television in the Kennedy Years.* New York: Oxford University Press, 1990. American television in the Kennedy years was so different from what had come previously and what was to come soon afterward.

2541. _____. "The Kennedy-Television Alliance." In *John F. Kennedy.* Edited by J. Richard Snyder, pp. 45-54. No. **1600.** Watson focuses on the symbiotic bond between Kennedy and television.

2542. White, William S. "Kennedy's Seven Rules for Handling the Press." *Harper's Magazine* 222 (April 1961): 92-7. Focuses on Press Secretary Pierre Salinger and the administration's policies for keeping the press informed.

2543. Wicker, Tom. "Q's and A's about the Press Conference." *New York Times Magazine* (September 8, 1963), pp. 24-5, 120. Both the president and the press corps have reservations about the new, large-sized televised press conference.

2544. "Worse Than Useless." *Newsweek* 61 (January 14, 1963): 68. Kennedy adviser Arthur Schlesinger's recent address is interpreted as an attack on the press.

2545. Wright, Jack, Jr. "A Comparison of the Projected Image of John F. Kennedy in the Mass Media with the Held-Image of a Sample of College Students." Ph.D. diss., Louisiana State University and Agricultural and Mechanical College, 1969. Analyzes the favorable image of John Kennedy projected by seven major magazines and compares that to the image held by students at two Florida universities.

Military Affairs

2546. "Admiral Burke Speaks Out about 'Muzzling' the Military." *U.S. News and World Report* 51 (August 21, 1961): 85-6. Concerns whether military leaders should speak out against communism and support supposed right-wing views.

2547. Aliano, Richard A. *American Defense Policy from Eisenhower to Kennedy: The Politics of Changing Military Requirements, 1957-1961.* Athens: Ohio University Press, 1975. Focuses on the shift from massive retaliation to a flexible response, contributing to eventual massive intervention in Southeast Asia and a missile-gap-in-reverse.

2548. Alsop, Stewart. "Kennedy's Grand Strategy." *Saturday Evening Post* 235 (March 31, 1962): 11-17. Analyzes how Kennedy is challenging Soviet might with his new defense policy.

2549. _____. "Master of the Pentagon." *Saturday Evening Post* 234 (August 5, 1961): 20-1, 45-6. Focuses on McNamara's controversial role as secretary of defense and his strategies and techniques in running the Pentagon.

2550. _____. "Our New Strategy: The Alternatives to Total War." 235 *Saturday Evening Post* (December 1, 1962): 13-19. Critical review of McNamara's possible responses to a Soviet threat.

2551. Art, Robert J. *The TFX Decision: McNamara and the Military*. Boston: Little, Brown, 1968. The controversy swirled around Defense Secretary McNamara's decision to award the TFX fighter-bomber contract to General Dynamics-Grumman instead of Boeing.

2552. Baldwin, Hanson W. "The McNamara Monarchy." *Saturday Evening Post* 236 (March 9, 1963): 8, 11. The military editor of the *New York Times* comments on Robert McNamara's power and influence in the Pentagon.

2553. Ball, Desmond. *Politics and Force Levels: The Strategic Missile Program of the Kennedy Administration*. Berkeley: University of California, 1980. Well-researched history of American strategy and missile deployment in the 1960s.

2554. Barlow, Jeffrey Graham. "President John F. Kennedy and His Joint Chiefs of Staff." Ph.D. diss., University of South Carolina, 1981. This study explores Kennedy's relationship with the Joint Chiefs of Staff, which was often one of mistrust and underutilization.

2555. Barnet, Richard J. *The Economy of Death*. New York: Atheneum, 1969. A leftist attack on the military-industrial complex of the Kennedy era.

2556. Bell, Coral. *Negotiation from Strength: A Study in the Politics of Power*. New York: Knopf, 1963. Briefly treats the Kennedy presidency.

2557. Bernstein, Barton J. "The Challenges and Dangers of Nuclear Weapons: Foreign Policy and Strategy, 1941-1978." *Maryland Historian* 9 (1978): 73-99. Although the arms race continues, nuclear war is unlikely unless an amoral technocrat errs.

2558. Blaufarb, Douglas S. *The Counterinsurgency Era: U.S. Doctrine and Performance, 1950 to the Present*. New York: Free Press, 1977. Written by a former CIA agent, Blaufarb stresses the input of the Kennedy years.

2559. Blechman, Barry M., and Stephen S. Kaplan, eds. *Force without War: U.S. Armed Forces as a Political Instrument*. Washington: Brookings Institution, 1978. Covers the Laotian War of 1962, the Dominican Republic overthrow of 1961, and the Berlin Crisis of 1961.

2560. Bolles, Charles De Vallon Dugas. "The Search for an American Strategy: The Origins of the Kennedy Doctrine, 1936-1961." Ph.D. diss., University of Wisconsin, 1985. Traces the evolution of Kennedy's ideas on defense and the world order and their impact on the Joint Chiefs of Staff and civilian strategists.

2561. Borklund, C. W. *The Department of Defense.* New York: Praeger, 1968. Covers every aspect of the Department of Defense including organizational structure, the role and activities of the secretary of defense, and its interrelationship with other agencies during the McNamara era.

2562. _____. *Men of the Pentagon: From Forrestal to McNamara.* New York: Praeger, 1966. A dated chapter on McNamara.

2563. Bottome, Edgar M. *The Missile Gap: A Study of the Formulation of Military and Political Policy.* Rutherford, NJ: Fairleigh Dickinson University Press, 1971. Traces the development of the belief that the Soviet Union held a superiority in ballistic missiles from 1958 to 1961.

2564. Bowman, Stephen Lee. "The Evolution of United States Army Doctrine for Counterinsurgency Warfare: From World War II to the Commitment of Combat Units in Vietnam." Ph.D. diss., Duke University, 1985. Explores how a program of counterinsurgency warfare was developed during the Kennedy administration.

2565. Briggs, William Donald. "John F. Kennedy and the Formation of Limited War Policy, 1952-1961: 'Outsiders' as a Factor in Decision-making." Ph.D. diss., George Washington University, 1989. Explores how Kennedy developed the policies of limited war and flexible response before he became president.

2566. Bundy, McGeorge. *Danger and Survival: Choices about the Bomb in the First Fifty Years.* New York: Random House, 1988. Written by Kennedy's national security adviser.

2567. _____. "Kennedy and the Nuclear Question." In *The Kennedy Presidency.* Edited by Kenneth W. Thompson, pp. 203-24. No. **1588**. The useful recollections of a Kennedy intimate.

2568. Davis, Vincent. *The Admirals Lobby.* Chapel Hill: University of North Carolina Press, 1967. As a result of Defense Secretary McNamara's policies and procedures, the navy officers remained pessimistic about the long-range future of their service and the strengths of U. S. sea forces.

2569. "A Defense Shake-up? What It Would Mean." *U.S. News and World Report* 49 (December 19, 1960): 42-5. Reviews proposal by Senator Stuart Symington to centralize and change the command structure of the armed forces and speculates on Kennedy's possible response.

2570. Destler, I. M. "National Security Advice to U.S. Presidents: Some Lessons from Thirty Years." *World Politics* 29 (1977): 143-76. An analytical view of the national security system from 1947 to 1977 with special reference to the evolution of the National Security Council and its varied role in each presidential administration.

2571. Dick, James C. "The Strategic Arms Race, 1957-1961: Who Opened a Missile Gap?" *Journal of Politics* 34 (1972): 1062-1110. There were two missile gaps; the first was a short-lived Soviet technological advantage and the second so greatly favored the United States that it caused the Soviets to place missiles in Cuba.

2572. Enthoven, Alain, and K. Wayne Smith. *How Much Is Enough? Shaping the Defense Program, 1961-1969.* New York: Harper and Row, 1971. Written by the chiefs of McNamara's Systems Analysis Office, it centers on the conflicts over the proper roles of the secretary of defense and the joint chiefs of staff, and the controversial technique of systems analysis.

2573. Figliola, Carl L. "Considerations of National Security in the Transfer of Presidential Power: An Analysis of Decision-making, 1960-1968." Ph.D. diss., New York University, 1971. A study of the instability of presidential power during presidential successions with a focus on the 1960 and 1968 transitions.

2574. Firestone, Bernard J. "Defense Policy as a Form of Arms Control: Nuclear Force Posture and Strategy under John F. Kennedy." In *John F. Kennedy.* Edited by Paul Harper and Joan P. Krieg, pp. 57-69. No. **1600**. Kennedy attempted to integrate, albeit imperfectly, containment of Soviet communism and nuclear war avoidance into a single defense and arms control strategy.

2575. Fryklund, Richard. *100 Million Lives: Maximum Survival in a Nuclear War.* New York: Macmillan, 1962. Includes thermonuclear war strategies pursued by the Kennedy administration.

2576. Gallagher, Nancy Woodworth. "The Politics of Verification and the Control of Nuclear Tests, 1945-1980." Ph.D. diss., University of Illinois, 1990. Develops an alternate framework for analysis by examining the politics of verification at two levels.

2577. "General Taylor at Work--Big Change at the White House." *U.S. News and World Report* 50 (August 7, 1961): 35. Kennedy's new military adviser will bring order to military planning and strategy.

2578. "The Grinding Decision--'Built Like Coral.'" *Newsweek* 59 (March 12, 1962): 23-4. On President Kennedy's controversial decision to resume nuclear testing.

2579. Halperin, Morton H. *Limited War in the Nuclear Age.* New York: Wiley, 1963. A contemporary work that touches on the Kennedy administration.

2580. _____. *Nuclear Fallacy: Dispelling the Myth of Nuclear Strategy.* Cambridge, Ma.: Ballinger Publishing Co., 1987. Halperin states that President Eisenhower institutionalized the assumption that nuclear devices are weapons that can be used to fight and end wars, a fallacy that Kennedy failed to overturn.

2581. _____. "The President and the Military." *Foreign Affairs* 52 (1972): 310-24. Presidential relations with the military from Franklin D. Roosevelt to Richard M. Nixon relating to advice, organization, and budget.

2582. Hoag, Malcolm W. "What New Look in Defense?" *World Politics* 22 (1969): 1-28. Eisenhower's New Look defense policy is favorably compared with policies of the Truman, Kennedy, and Johnson administrations.

2583. "How Kennedy Differs from Ike." *U.S. News and World Report* 50 (May 1, 1961): 68-70. The differences occur on how they handle deadlines, staff and cabinet members, Congress, and press briefings.

2584. "How Kennedy Plans to Run Defense and Foreign Policy." *U.S. News and World Report* 50 (January 9, 1961): 38-9. Much of this is a profile of Paul Nitze, the assistant secretary of defense for international security affairs.

2585. "Is World Balance in Missiles Shifting to U.S.? Survey of Latest Information." *U.S. News and World Report* 50 (January 23, 1961): 62-8. Analyzes actual nuclear strength of U.S. in the wake of "missile gap" criticism.

2586. Johnson, Stephen Michael. "The Politics and Economics of American Arms Transfers in the Post-World War II Era." Ph.D. diss., University of Oregon, 1987. Arms transfers must be viewed in the light of a broad understanding of the evolution of American foreign policy and political ideology since World War II.

2587. Kahan, Jerome H. *Security in the Nuclear Age: Developing U.S. Strategic Arms Policy.* Washington: Brookings Institution, 1975. Deals with the Kennedy administration in the context of the Berlin and Cuban missile crises and the missile gap.

2588. Kanter, Arnold. *Defense Politics: A Budgetary Perspective.* Chicago: University of Chicago Press, 1979. Excellent on Kennedy's Defense Department on budgetary matters.

2589. Kaplan, Fred M. *The Wizards of Armageddon.* New York: Simon and Schuster, 1983. Excellent on Robert McNamara and his Whiz Kids--the young, book-smart, Ivy League, think-tank civilian assistants--who sought to alter defense policy.

2590. Kaufmann, William W. *The McNamara Strategy.* New York: Harper and Row, 1964. An apologia by one of Robert McNamara's whiz kids.

2591. Kraft, Joseph."McNamara and His Enemies." *Harper's Magazine* 223 (August 1961): 41-8. Profile of Secretary of Defense McNamara and a review of the policy changes, problems, and the controversies surrounding him.

2592. Licklider, Roy E. "The Missile Gap Controversy." *Political Science Quarterly* 85 (1970): 600-15. Licklider seeks to make sense of the confusing and conflicting claims surrounding the missile gap controversy.

2593. Loeb, Larry M. "Jupiter Missiles in Europe: A Measure of Presidential Power." *World Affairs* 139 (1976): 27-39. Loeb analyzes the roles of Presidents Eisenhower and Kennedy in the deployment of Jupiter missiles in NATO countries from 1957 to 1963.

2594. McClintock, Michael. *Instruments of Statecraft: U.S. Guerrilla Warfare, Counterinsurgency, Counterterrorism, 1940-1990*. New York: Pantheon, 1992. Focuses on how President Kennedy had counterinsurgency redefined.

2595. McNamara, Robert S. *The Essence of Security: Reflections in Office*. New York: Harper and Row, 1968. Not a memoir, but a self-justifying essay on defense policy.

2596. Mandelbaum, Michael. *The Nuclear Question: The United States and Nuclear Weapons, 1946-1976*. New York: Cambridge University Press, 1979. A survey from the end of World War II through the Ford presidency.

2597. Melman, Seymour. *Pentagon Capitalism: The Political Economy of War*. New York: McGraw-Hill, 1970. A New Left attack on the military-industrial complex and American militarism.

2598. Modelski, George. "United States Alliances: Obsolescence of the 'Korean' System?" *World Affairs* 139 (1976): 75-86. After analyzing the U. S. alliance systems from the 1950s and the subsequent changes in world politics, Modelski gives reasons why a global deterrent system is necessary.

2599. Mollenhoff, Clark R. *The Pentagon: Politics, Profits and Plunder*. New York: G. P. Putnam's Sons, 1967. The investigative journalist Mollenhoff focuses on the abuse of power in the Pentagon for which McNamara comes under fire.

2600. Moulton, Harland Buell. "American Strategic Power: Two Decades of Nuclear Strategy and Weapons Systems, 1945-1965." Ph.D. diss., University of Minnesota. 1969. Buell divides his study into four main periods, including "Missile Gap and Cuban Missile Crisis, 1957-1962."

2601. Murphy, Charles J. V. "Now the President Will Decide on His Own." *Life* 52 (February 16, 1962): 70-2, 74, 76, 79-80, 83. Two prominent scientists debate nuclear testing as Kennedy prepares to make a decision.

2602. Newman, James R. "Testing--What Does Kennedy Mean?" *New Republic* 146 (March 26, 1962): 11-13. Takes a negative view of Kennedy's decision to resume nuclear testing.

2603. Noel, J. V., Jr. "The Navy and the Department of Defense." *United States Naval Institute Proceedings*. 87 (November 1961): 23-31. Recent changes include the unification of the armed services and the constant intrusion by the office of the secretary of defense.

2604. Powaski, Ronald E. *March to Armageddon: The United States and the Nuclear Arms Race, 1939 to the Present*. New York: Oxford University Press, 1987. A synthesis that includes a chapter on the Kennedy presidency.

2605. Prados, John. *The Soviet Estimate: U.S. Intelligence Analysis and Russian Military Strength*. New York: Dial Press, 1982. A study of the effectiveness of U.S. intelligence with considerable focus on the Kennedy presidency.

2606. "President's Dilemma." *Nation* (March 17, 1962): 225-26. Kennedy's decision to resume nuclear testing, even though understandable, is questionable.

2607. Quester, George H. *Nuclear Diplomacy: The First Twenty-Five Years*. New York: Dunellen, 1970. Contains a chapter on the Kennedy administration based on published works.

2608. Roherty, James M. *Decisions of Robert S. McNamara: A Study of the Role of the Secretary of Defense*. Coral Gables, Fl.: University of Miami Press, 1970. Under McNamara during the 1960s, "the displacement of political prudence and political process by technical rationality . . . made its farthest advance" in the Department of Defense.

2609. Rosenberg, David A. "Power and Responsibility: Power and Process in the Making of United States Nuclear Strategy, 1945-68." *Journal of Strategic Studies* 9 (March 1986): 43-50. Explores the historical context of the McNamara reforms and the structural constraints which shaped his choices.

2610. Rostow, W. W. *The Diffusion of Power: An Essay in Recent History*. New York: Macmillan, 1972. Written by Kennedy's deputy national security affairs adviser, Rostow includes military and arms control matters.

2611. Ryan, Paul B. *First Line of Defense: The U.S. Navy since 1945*. Stanford: Hoover Institution Press, 1981. See the chapter on "The Navy and the New Frontier," much of which deals with the missile crisis.

2612. Sagan, Scott D. "SIOP-62: The Nuclear War Plan Briefing to President Kennedy." *International Security* 12 (Summer 1987): 22-51. The nuclear war plan in effect under Kennedy.

2613. Schneider, Barry. "Big Bangs from Little Bombs." *Bulletin of the Atomic Scientists* 31 (1975): 24-8. The nuclear arms system from the 1950s to 1975.

2614. Shapley, Deborah. *Promise and Power: The Life and Times of Robert McNamara.* Boston: Little, Brown, 1993. In an excellent biography, Shapley portrays Kennedy's secretary of defense as both manipulator and scout, a devious tactician and a man of sincere and noble goals.

2615. Smith, William Young. "Kennedy, Defense and Arms Control." In *The Kennedy Presidency.* Edited by Kenneth W. Thompson, pp. 271-84. No. **1588.** An interview with an assistant to General Maxwell Taylor, chairman of the Joint Chiefs of Staff, and a member of McGeorge Bundy's staff.

2616. Steinbruner, John D. *The Cybernetic Theory of Decision: New Dimensions of Political Analysis.* Princeton: Princeton University Press, 1974. Applies a cybernetic paradigm to nuclear sharing within the NATO alliance from 1956-1964.

2617. Swartz, James E. "The Professionalization of Pentagon Public Affairs: The Evolution of a Role in the United States Federal Government, 1947-1967." Traces the role of the Defense Department from coordinator to manager spokesman of defense matters during the Kennedy administration.

2618. Symington, Stuart. "Where the Missile Gap Went." *Reporter* 26 (February 15, 1962): 21-3. Examines the discrepancies between what the press, public, and experts perceive about the missile gap and what problems exist in estimating Soviet military strength.

2619. Taylor, Maxwell. *Swords and Plowshares.* New York: W. W. Norton, 1972. Taylor was Kennedy's personal adviser on military affairs and later his chairman of the Joint Chiefs of Staff.

2620. Thompson, Loren B. "The Emergence of American Central Nuclear Strategy, 1954-1984." Ph.D. diss., Georgetown University, 1987. Nuclear strategy is inherently speculative and the search for something better is likely to remain an issue.

2621. "Top Brass vs. 'Whiz Kids' . . . ." *Newsweek* 57 (May 29, 1961): 24-6. Battle between Kennedy's civilian appointments and traditional military leaders over defense policy and decisions.

2622. Trewhitt, Henry L. *McNamara: His Ordeal in the Pentagon.* New York: Harper and Row, 1971. Written by a diplomatic correspondent for *Newsweek*, Trewhitt concludes that McNarmara's supreme achievement was to substitute rational thought for hysteria on the matter of nuclear weapons.

2623. Tucker, Samuel, ed. *A Modern Design for Defense Decision: A McNamara-*

Hitch-Enthoven Anthology. Washington: Industrial College of the Armed Forces, 1966. Partly based on McNamara's testimony on the need for a budgeting system to manage effectively the resources of the Department of Defense.

2624. Wells, Robert Norton, Jr. "Politics and Policy: Shifting American Concepts of the Army Reserve Forces in International Affairs." Ph.D. diss., University of Michigan, 1969. The Kennedy administration proposed to use Army Reserves for rapid mobilization during cold war military crises but the shortcomings of the reserves during the 1961 Berlin mobilization forced the administration to drop the plan.

2625. Westmoreland, William C. *A Soldier Reports*. Garden City, NY: Doubleday, 1976. Contains some interesting Kennedy anecdotes.

2626. "What the President's Speech Means to You." *Life* 51 (August 4, 1961): 36-41. Kennedy increases military personnel by 217,000.

2627. White, Theodore H. "Revolution in the Pentagon." *Look* 27 (April 23, 1963): 31-48. Conflict between McNamara and his defense team and the joint chiefs over military policy.

2628. Yarmolinsky, Adam. *The Military Establishment: Its Impact on American Society*. New York: Harper and Row, 1971. The military establishment pervaded every aspect of national life.

2629. York, Herbert. *Race to Oblivion: A Participant's View of the Arms Race*. New York: Simon and Schuster, 1970. Written by a member of Eisenhower's Science Advisory Committee, it devotes a chapter to the McNamara era.

Organized Crime

2630. Bonanno, Joseph. *A Man of Honor: The Autobiography of Joseph Bonanno*. New York: Simon and Schuster, 1983. Bonanno calls Attorney General Robert Kennedy a demagogue.

2631. Brashler, William. *The Don: The Life and Death of Sam Giancana*. New York: Harper and Row, 1977. The biography of the Chicago mobster who is linked to the Kennedy administration.

2632. Calder, James D. "Presidents and Crime Control: Kennedy, Johnson, and Nixon and the Influence of Ideology." *Presidential Studies Quarterly* 12 (Fall 1982): 574-89. Until the Kennedy administration, no president had made crime control a major active priority.

2633. Davis, John H. *The Kennedys*. No. **1639**.   Good on Kennedy anti-crime program.

2634. _____. *Mafia Kingfish: Carlos Marcello and the Assassination of John F. Kennedy*. New York: McGraw-Hill, 1989.   Attorney General Robert Kennedy made mobster Carlos Marcello one of his major targets.

2635. Demaris, Ovid. *The Last Mafioso: The Treacherous World of Jimmy Fratianno*. New York: Times Books, 1981.   Interesting anecdotes concerning John Roselli and other mafioso and Kennedy's CIA.

2636. Eisenberg, Dennis, Uri Dan, and Eli Lanau. *Meyer Lansky: Mogul of the Mob*. New York: Paddington Press, 1979.   Briefly covers the Cuban connection.

2637. Elliff, John T. *Crime, Dissent, and the Attorney General: The Justice Department in the 1960's*. Beverly Hills, Ca.: Sage Publications, 1971.   Scattered references to Attorney General Robert Kennedy.

2638. Exner, Judith. *My Story*. New York: Grove Press, 1977.   Judith Campbell Exner had an intimate relationship with President Kennedy and mobster Sam Giancana and supposedly served as a courier between the two.

2639. Giancana, Antoinette, and Thomas C. Renner. *Mafia Princess: Growing Up in Sam Giancana's Family*. New York: William Morrow, 1984.   Told by the daughter of Sam Giancana who says little about the Kennedys.

2640. Giancana, Sam, and Chuck Giancana. *Double Cross: The Explosive, Inside Story of the Mobster Who Controlled America*. New York: Warner, 1992.   Written by Sam Giancana's family members, this undocumented story of the Chicago mobster covers the Kennedys's connection with Giancana and includes an unbelievable account of Marilyn Monroe's death and the Kennedy assassination.

2641. Kelley, Kitty. "The Dark Side of Camelot." *People Weekly* 29 (February 29, 1988): 106-14.   Despite previously denying it, Kennedy's former intimate, Judith Campbell Exner, tells of being the president's courier with the mob.

2642. _____. *His Way: The Unauthorized Biography of Frank Sinatra*. New York: Bantam Books, 1986.   Covers the interrelationship of Sinatra, the mob, and John Kennedy.

2643. Kennedy, Robert. *The Enemy Within*. No. **2464**.   An account by Robert Kennedy, the chief counsel of the McClellan Committee, who investigated improper labor activities during the late 1950s.

2644. Messick, Hank. *Lansky*. New York: G. P. Putnam's Sons, 1971.   A disappointing book regarding its coverage of Kennedy's war against organized crime.

2645. Moldea, Dan E. *The Hoffa Wars: Teamsters, Rebels, Politicians, and the Mob.* New York: Paddington, 1978. A conventional account of Jimmmy Hoffa and the Kennedys.

2646. Rappleye, Charles, and Ed Decker. *All-American Mafioso: The Johnny Rosselli Story.* New York: Doubleday, 1991. An investigative account based on interviews and FBI documents that touches on Rosselli's links with the Kennedys.

2647. Reid, Ed. *The Grim Reapers: The Anatomy of Organized Crime in America.* New York: Bantam Books, 1969. Deals briefly with Attorney General Robert Kennedy's efforts against Carlos Marcello.

2648. Roemer, William, Jr. *Roemer: Man Against the Mob.* New York: Donald I. Fine, 1989. Written by a FBI special agent who worked on organized crime investigations, Roemer provides some marvelous anecdotes about Attorney General Robert Kennedy.

Social Welfare

2649. Berkowitz, Edward D. "The Politics of Mental Retardation during the Kennedy Administration." *Social Science Quarterly* 61 (June 1980): 128-43. President Kennedy's special attention to mental retardation legislation culminated in the passage of the mental retardation provisions of 1963.

2650. Bernstein, Irving. *Promises Kept.* No. **1592.** Bernstein uses the materials of the Kennedy library in amply covering and favorably assessing Kennedy's social welfare program.

2651. Brand, H. "Poverty in the United States." *Dissent* 7 (Autumn 1960): 334-54. One of several contemporary articles that alerted Americans to the existing poverty in this country.

2652. Brauer, Carl. "Kennedy, Johnson, and the War on Poverty." *Journal of American History* 69 (June 1982): 98-119. Poverty did not become a focal point of debate or policy during Kennedy's first two years in office.

2653. Campion, Donald R. "Primer on Medicare." *America* 107 (June 9, 1962): 383-85. Explains the major players and positions in the fight to get a medicare bill passed.

2654. Carlson, David B. "The New Look in Public Housing--Too Little and Too Late?" *Architectural Forum* 119 (July 1963): 116-19. Assesses the current public housing program as a failure and discusses changes in the program proposed by the Kennedy administration.

2655. "The Case for Subtlety." *Time* 80 (July 27, 1962): 9-10. An assessment of why Kennedy failed to get the medicare bill passed in the Senate.

2656. Corning, Peter A. *The Evolution of Medicare. . . From Idea to Law.* Washington: Social Security Administration, 1969. Includes Kennedy's unsuccessful efforts.

2657. David, Sheri Iris. "To Lift a Heavy Burden: The Story of the Medicare and Medicaid Law." Ph.D. diss., City University of New York, 1982. This study includes a discussion of the legislative attempts to pass the medicare program during the Kennedy administration.

2658. _____. *With Dignity: The Search for Medicare and Medicaid.* Wesport, Ct.: Greenwood, 1985. Written by a political scientist, David explores the roots of medicare to include a chapter on "Medicare and the New Frontier."

2659. Davidson, Roger H. *Coalition-building for Depressed Areas Bills, 1955-1965.* Bobbs-Merrill, 1966. Includes a short chapter on the Kennedy administration's role in the Area Redevelopment Act.

2660. Douglas, Paul H. *In the Fullness of Time.* New York: Harcourt Brace Jovanovich, 1972. Douglas was a major promoter of social welfare programs.

2661. Duscha, Julius. "Retracing the Unemployed: Little, Late and Limping." *Reporter* 27 (September 27, 1962): 35-7. Kennedy's retraining program is lagging because of faulty staff work within the executive branch and inept Democratic leadership on Capitol Hill.

2662. Feingold, Eugene. *Medicare: Policy and Politics.* San Francisco: Chandler Publishing, 1966. Covers the legislative frustrations of the Kennedy presidency.

2663. "The Fight over Medical Care--Kennedy's Chances." *U.S. News and World Report* 52 (June 4, 1962): 39. Gives the outlook for different proposals on medicare.

2664. Filerman, Gary L. "The Legislative Campaign for the Passage of a Medical Care for the Aged Bill." M.A. thesis, University of Minnesota, 1962. Objective is to highlight decision-making and the roles of special interest groups, findings of which are based on more than fifty interviews with principal participants, interest group files, and periodicals.

2665. Gilbert, Charles E. "Policy-making in Public Welfare: The 1962 Amendments." *Political Science Quarterly* 81 (June 1966): 196-224. The federal welfare amendments of 1962 represent a fundamental change.

2666. Grossman, Jonathan. "Fair Labor Standards Act: Maximum Struggle for a Minimum Wage." *Monthly Labor Review* 101 (1978): 22-30. Grossman surveys the amendments made to the minimum wage law from 1949 to 1977.

2667. Harrington, Michael. *The Other America: Poverty in the United States.* New York: Macmillan, 1962. Despite the prosperity of the 1950s, some 50 million Americans remain poor, a conclusion that troubled Kennedy.

2668. _____. "Our Fifty Million Poor: Forgotten Men of the Affluent Society." *Commentary* 28 (July 1959): 19-27. Harrington's essay, focusing on the hidden poverty in America, had an impact on Kennedy during the presidential campaign of 1960.

2669. Harris, Richard. *A Sacred Trust.* New York: New American Library, 1966. A journalistic account of the history of medicare.

2670. "Home Sweet Home: Kennedy's $6.1 billion Housing Bill." *Time* 77 (June 30, 1961): 12. Details the main provision of the Housing bill and some criticism of it.

2671. Kaun, David E. "Economics of the Minimum Wage: The Effects of the Fair Labor Standards Act, 1945-1960." Ph.D. diss., Stanford University, 1964. The minimum wage adversely affected employment opportunities for blacks, females, and young people.

2672. Keyserling, Leon. "Two-Fifths of a Nation." *Progressive* 26 (June 1962): 11-14. Keyserling, Truman's former CEA chairman, criticized the Kennedy presidency for not addressing the poverty problem.

2673. Knapp, Daniel. *Scouting the War on Poverty: Social Reform in the Kennedy Administration.* Lexington, Ma.: Heath Lexington Books, 1971. An analysis of the forces working for and against the development of a new social policy toward the dispossessed.

2674. Levitan, Sar A. *Federal Aid to Depressed Areas: An Evaluation of the Area Redevelopment Administration.* Baltimore: Johns Hopkins Press, 1964. Provides an evaluation of the activities of the Area Redevelopment Administration from 1961 into 1963.

2675. MacDonald, Dwight. "Our Invisible Poor." *New Yorker* 38 (January 19, 1963): 82-132. An influential essay by a radical critic, MacDonald reaffirms Michael Harrington's contentions that mass poverty still exists in the United States and that it is disappearing more slowly than is commonly thought.

2676. Marmor, Theodore R. "The Congress: Medicare Politics and Policy." In *American Political Institutions and Public Policy: Five Contemporary Studies.* Edited by Allan P. Sindler. Boston: Little, Brown, 1969, pp. 3-66. An excellent early overview of the fight for medicare, including the struggles during the Kennedy presidency.

2677. _____. *The Politics of Medicare.* Chicago: Aldine Publishing, 1970. Includes the Kennedy fight with the American Medical Association over medicare.

2678. Marris, Peter, and Martin Rein. *Dilemmas of Social Reform: Poverty and Community Action in the United States.* Chicago: Aldine Press, 1973. Community action in the sixties including an examination of projects promoted by the Juvenile Delinquency and Youth Offenses Control Act of 1961.

2679. "Medicare Comes Back." *Business Week* (June 8, 1963), p. 25. Details the administration's drive to pass a medicare bill.

2680. Mogull, Robert G. "Determinants of Welfare Spending." *Presidential Studies Quarterly* 20 (1990): 355-71. An examination of federal public welfare appropriations from 1950 through 1984.

2681. Patterson, James T. *America's Struggle Against Poverty, 1900-1985.* Cambridge: Harvard University Press, 1986. Good assessment of the Kennedy presidency commitment.

2682. Piven, Frances Fox, and Richard A. Cloward. *Regulating the Poor: The Functions of Public Welfare.* New York: Pantheon Books, 1971. Covers the 1960s in general fashion.

2683. "The President and the Aged." *New Republic* 144 (February 20, 1961): 4-5. Supports the president's proposals for medical care for the aged.

2684. Rickenbacker, W. F. "Government Medicare v. Public Health." *National Review* 12 (May 22, 1962): 370. Uses the British system of public health to argue against governmental medical programs.

2685. Rothstein, Joan L. "The Government of the United States and the Young Child: A Study of General Child Care Legislation Between 1935-1971." Ph.D. diss., University of Maryland, 1979. An examination of the relationship of the federal government with children under age six through a study of legislation that addresses the problem of child care.

2686. Shank, Alan. *Presidential Policy Leadership: Kennedy and Social Welfare.* Lanham, Md.: University Press of America, 1980. Includes housing, federal aid to education, and medicare in a conceptual framework that does not ignore antecedents or legacy.

2687. Steiner, Gilbert Y. *Social Insecurity: The Politics of Welfare*. Chicago: Rand McNally, 1966. Includes references to the Kennedy administration.

2688. Sundquist, James L. *Politics and Policy*. No. **2081**. One of the most comprehensive studies on social welfare matters during the Kennedy era.

2689. Warner, David C. *Toward New Human Rights: The Social Policies of the Kennedy and Johnson Administration*. Austin: Lyndon B. Johnson School of Public Affairs, University of Texas, 1977. Contains a variety of essays touching on Kennedy's welfare programs.

2690. Weaver, Robert C. "What the Housing Bill Means for the Nation's Cities." *American City* 76 (August 1961): 5. Explains the effect the Housing Act of 1961 will have on urban renewal, city planning, housing, and senior citizens.

2691. Wicker, Tom. *JFK and LBJ*. No. **2110** . Excellent on Kennedy and Congress regarding social welfare legislation.

Space Program

2692. Alibrando, Alfred P. "Kennedy Plan Stirs Attack on Space Funds." *Aviation Week and Space Technology* 79 (October 7, 1963): 29-30. Congress concerned about cost and Kennedy's failure to consult.

2693. _____. "Kennedy's Offer Stirs Confusion, Dismay." *Aviation Week and Space Technology* 79 (September 30, 1963): 26-7. Questions arise about the future of the National Aeronautics and Space Administration (NASA) after Kennedy proposes a joint U.S.-Soviet lunar program.

2694. "An American on the Moon--A $20 Billion Boondoggle?" *U.S. News and World Report* 53 (August 20, 1962): 52-61. Focuses on expenditures, relevance of Project Apollo, and the role of the military.

2695. Baar, James. "Kennedy Faces Decision on Moon Race." *Missiles and Rockets* 8 (May 1, 1961): 12-13. Following the recent Mercury failure and the Soviet Yuri Gagarin's orbit around the earth, Kennedy was ready to accelerate the U.S. program.

2696. Baker, David. *The History of Manned Space Flights*. New York: Crown Publishers, 1982. A popular account that contains chapters on the Kennedy era.

2697. Baker, Leonard. *The Johnson Eclipse: A President's Vice Presidency*. New York: Macmillan, 1966. Contains a chapter on Johnson's involvement in the space program as Kennedy's vice president.

2697a. Breuer, William B. *Race to the Moon: America's Duel with the Soviets.*

Westport, Ct.: Praeger, 1993. Contains nothing new on Kennedy's activities.

2698. Brooks, Courtney G., James M. Grimwood, and Loyd S. Swenson, Jr. *Chariots for Apollo: A History of Manned Lunar Spacecraft.* Washington: NASA, 1979. Based on the extensive primary documentation of the Apollo program.

2699. "Can U.S. Still Catch Up in Space?" *U.S. News and World Report* 51 (August 21, 1961): 37-9. Discusses U.S. plans to surpass the Soviets.

2700. Cox, Donald. *The Space Race: From Sputnik to Apollo--and Beyond.* Philadelphia: Chilton Company, 1962. A contemporary account critical of the Eisenhower and Kennedy administrations for not fashioning an international space agreement in the United Nations.

2701. Diamond, Edwin. *The Rise and Fall of the Space Age.* Garden City, NY: Doubleday, 1964. Space becomes an antidote to economic stagnation and a new form of political pork barrel.

2702. Divine, Robert A. "Lyndon B. Johnson and the Politics of Space." In *The Johnson Years, Volume Two: Vietnam, the Environment, and Science.* Edited by Robert A. Divine. Lawrence: University Press of Kansas, 1987, pp. 217-53. Includes the Kennedy presidency when Vice President Johnson served as head of the Space Council.

2703. Eastman, Ford. "Kennedy Seeks U.S. Space Race Gains." *Aviation Week and Space Technology* 74 (May 1, 1961): 29. Detailed report on Kennedy's orders for enhanced space program.

2704. Elliott, Derek Wesley. "Finding an Appropriate Commitment: Space Policy Development under Eisenhower and Kennedy, 1954-1963." Ph.D. diss., George Washington University, 1992. Kennedy provided a more activist leadership in space initiatives.

2705. Emme, Eugene M. "Early History of the Space Age." *Aerospace Historian* 13 (1966): 127-32. Traces rocketry from its origins through the mid-1960s.

2706. Etzioni, Amitai. *The Moon-Doggle, Domestic and International Implications of the Space Race.* Garden City, NY: Doubleday, 1964. Kennedy realized before his death that the space program was consuming more and more national resources and accentuating international tension; consequently he sought to curb it by renewing his proposal of a joint American-Russian exploration.

2707. Frutkin, Arnold W. *International Cooperation in Space.* Englewood Cliffs, NJ: Prentice Hall, 1965. Includes Kennedy's efforts to cooperate with the Soviet Union in space exploration.

2708. Frye, Alton. "The Military Danger: Our Gamble in Space." *Atlantic* 212 (August 1963): 46-50. The Republican Advisory Committee on Space and Aeronautics charged that the Kennedy administration is neglecting the needs of national security by its "niggardly" military space program, a charge Frye explores.

2709. Galloway, Jonathon F. *The Politics and Technology of Satellite Communications.* Lexington, Ma.: D. C. Heath, 1972. Covers the Kennedy administration's involvement with satellite communications.

2710. Gibney, Frank B., and George J. Feldman. *The Reluctant Space-Farers: A Study in the Politics of Discovery.* New York: New American Library, 1965. Looks at the space program on the basis of its meaning to the nation and to world society.

2711. Griffith, Alison. *The National Aeronautics and Space Act: A Study of the Development of Public Policy.* Washington: Public Affairs Press, 1962. In focusing on this significant legislation, Griffith provides the necessary background for Kennedy's space initiatives.

2712. Grossbard, Stephen Ira. "The Civilian Space Program: A Case Study of Civil-Military Relations." Ph.D. diss., University of Michigan, 1968. A case study of the relationship of NASA and the military and the problems created by the latter for never accepting the concept of peaceful exploration of outer space.

2713. Harvey, Dodd L., and Linda C. Ciccoritti. *U.S.-Soviet Cooperation in Space.* Coral Gables, Fl.: University of Miami, Center for Advanced International Studies, 1974. This study provides insights into the documentary materials that bear upon the U.S.-Soviet relationship to include the Kennedy era.

2714. Hechler, Ken. *Toward the Endless Frontier: A History of the Committee on Science and Astronautics, 1959-1979.* Washington: Government Printing Office, 1980. Two useful chapters on the Committee on Science and Astronautics during the Kennedy presidency.

2715. Hirsh, Richard, and Joseph J. Trento. *The National Aeronautics and Space Administration.* New York: Praeger, 1973. Includes the impact of Kennedy's pledge to place a man on the moon, which transformed the young agency into a federal giant.

2716. Holmes, Jay. *America on the Moon: The Enterprise of the Sixties.* Philadelphia: J. B. Lippincott, 1962. A contemporary and non-technical account of the Kennedy era's commitment to transport men to the moon.

2717. Jastrow, Robert, and Homer E. Newell. "Why Land on the Moon?": Our Gamble in Space." *Atlantic* 212 (August 1963): 41-5. The authors defend Kennedy's decision to go to the moon.

2718. Kerr, James Richard. "Congressmen as Overseers: Surveillance of the Space Program." Ph.D. diss., Stanford University, 1963. A case study of how the House Committee on Science and Astronautics coped with the complex, technical space program.

2719. Kinsley, Michael E. *Outer Space and Inner Sanctums: Government, Business, and Satellite Communication.* New York: John Wiley, 1976. Speculates that Senator Robert Kerr's communications satellite bill was a ploy that, combined with Kerr's influence over the fate of other presidential programs, obliged the White House to compromise with him.

2720. Klass, Philip J. *Secret Sentries in Space.* New York: Random House, 1971. An account of the U.S. and Soviet reconnaisance-satellite programs and their impact on world affairs.

2721. Kolcum, Edward H. "Kennedy Stresses Peaceful Theme." *Aviation Week and Space Technology* 77 (September 17, 1962): 26-7. U.S. should bolster space program primarily for peaceful purposes.

2722. Kvam, Roger A. "Comsat: The Inevitable Anomaly." In *Knowledge and Power: Essays on Science and Government.* Edited by Sanford A. Lakoff. New York: Free Press, 1966, pp. 271-92. Involves the world's communication satellite and the implementation of the Communications Satellite Act of 1962.

2723. Levine, Arthur S. *Managing NASA in the Apolla Era.* Washington: NASA, 1982. An institutional study of NASA during the 1960s with scattered references to Kennedy.

2724. Logsdon, John M. *The Decision to Go to the Moon: Project Apollo and the National Interest.* Cambridge: MIT Press, 1970. Based on personal interviews from Kennedy associates and manuscript material from the Kennedy Papers, this is the most perceptive account on the Kennedy period.

2725. McDougall, Walter A. . . .*the Heavens and the Earth: A Political History of the Space Age.* New York: Basic Books, 1985. Relying heavily on Logsdon's book, this study incorporates additional sources from the Kennedy and Johnson libraries.

2726. Murray, Charles, and Catherine Bly Cox. *Apollo: The Race to the Moon.* New York: Simon and Schuster, 1989. Long on storytelling and short on analysis.

2727. "New Frontier in Space Provides Financial Boost." *Science News Letter* 78 (April 8, 1961): 217. Kennedy asks for 11.3 percent boost in NASA budget.

2728. Nieburg, Harold L. *In the Name of Science.* Chicago: Quadrangle, 1966. Deals with federal science policy and government contracting to include the Kennedy administration and space.

2729. "Race to the Moon." *New Republic* 148 (April 13, 1963): 3-4. Critical review of what it may cost the U. S. to beat the Soviets to the moon.

2730. Ray, Thomas Wilson. "Apollo's Antecedents: The Conceptualization, Planning, Resource Build-up, and Decisions that Led to the Lunar Landing Program." Ph.D. diss., University of Colorado, 1974. Ray explains why the National Aeronautics and Space Administration (NASA) established manned lunar flights as its main objective and how it achieved that goal by modernizing its facilities, manpower, and funds.

2731. "Right Way to the Moon." *Nation* 197 (October 12, 1963): 209. Emphasizes what the U.S. and the Soviets would need to do if they are to carry out Kennedy's proposal for a joint moon flight.

2732. Rosholt, Robert Leroy. *An Administrative History of NASA, 1958-1963.* Washington: NASA, 1966. First volume in NASA's historical series, it is based on documents and interviews.

2733. _____. "Organizing the United States Civilian Space Effort: A Study of the National Aeronautics and Space Administration with Special Emphasis on Structural Change and Program Coordination." Ph.D. diss., University of Minnesota, 1965. From 1958 NASA expanded very rapidly in the next five years with its budgets doubling every year.

2734. Schauer, William H. *The Politics of Space: A Comparison of the Soviet and American Space Programs.* New York: Holmes and Meier, 1976. Kennedy, emphasizing goals other than science, tended to overlook the advice of the scientific community in his space planning.

2735. Smith, Richard Austin. "Now It's an Agonizing Reappraisal of the Moon Race." *Fortune* 68 (November 1963): 124. Two and a half years after Kennedy committed the U.S. to the moon, serious doubts about the burdens of a crash program are plaguing science, industry, and NASA.

2736. Swenson, Loyd S. Jr. "The Fertile Crescent: The South's Role in the National Space Program." *Southwestern Historical Quarterly* 71 (1967): 377-92. An examination of the impact of NASA on the South from 1957 to 1965.

2737. Swenson, Loyd S. Jr., James M. Grimwood, and Charles S. Alexander. *This New Ocean: A History of Project Mercury.* Washington: NASA, 1966. Prior to its June 1963 termination, Project Mercury, in less than three and a half years, flew two ballistic flights into space and four orbital missions.

2738. Trentom Joseph J. *Prescription for Disaster.* New York: Crown Publishers, 1987. A popular account of the space program which contains a chapter on the Kennedy years.

2739. "U.S. No. 1 in Space Now?" *U.S. News and World Report* 52 (March 5, 1962): 37-44. Report on John Glenn's orbit of the earth.

2740. Van Dyke, Vernon. *Pride and Power: The Rationale of the Space Program.* Urbana: University of Illinois, 1964. Deals mainly with the public arguments relating to various issues concerning the space program--the arguments that Congress and the voters have been asked to consider.

2741. Webb, James E. "The New Age of Discovery." *Airpower History* 11 (1964):81-7. An overview of the U.S. space program from 1954 to 1964 by Kennedy's director of NASA.

2742. _____. *Space Age Management: The Large Scale Approach.* New York: McGraw-Hill, 1969. Webb published his Columbia-McKinsey lectures on his managerial experiences.

2743. "Where the Space Billions Will Go." *U.S. News and World Report* 53 (October 1, 1962): 79-80. Breakdown of spending on NASA and the Department of Defense for the previous five years and an outline of spending for the next ten years.

2744. Wiesner, Jerome B. *Where Science and Politics Meet.* New York: McGraw-Hill, 1964. Wiesner served as Kennedy's special assistant for science and technology.

2745. Wilford, John Noble. "Riding High." *Wilson Quarterly* 4 (1980): 57-70. A review of the U.S. space program from 1955 to 1980.

2746. Wilson, George C. "Kennedy to Launch Major Space Effort." *Aviation Week and Technology* 74 (May 15, 1961): 26-7. Kennedy asks for 25 percent increase in space program.

2747. _____. "U.S. Is Formulating New Space Policy." *Aviation Week and Space Technology* 76 (June 18, 1962): 26-7. Analyzes the effect of an expanded military role in the space program.

2748. Young, Hugo, Bryan Silcock, and Peter Dunn. "Why We Went to the Moon: From the Bay of Pigs to the Sea of Tranquility." *Washington Monthly* 2 (April 1970): 28-58. The moon race was a significant--and questionable--symbol to Kennedy.

Women's Movement

2749. "The American Female: A Special Supplement." *Harper's* 225 (October 1962): 117-80. See especially "Nobody Here But Us Pompadours: A Tale of

Women, Politics, and the New Frontier."

2750. Berger, Caruthers Gholson. "Equal Pay, Equal Employment Opportunity and Equal Enforcement of the Law for Women." *Valparaiso University Law Review* 5 (1971): 326-73. Focuses on Kennedy's Equal Pay Act by a member of the Office of the Solicitor, Department of Labor.

2751. Bergquist, Laura. "What Women Really Meant to JFK." *Redbook* 141 (November 1973): 49-54. The journalist Bergquist believes that had Kennedy lived he would have learned to look at women differently.

2752. Bird, Caroline. *Born Female: The High Cost of Keeping Women Down.* rev. ed. New York: David McKay, 1974. In focusing on the 1960s, it concentrates on the social, moral, and personal costs of "keeping women down."

2753. Burns, Catherine G., and John E. Burns. "An Analysis of the Equal Pay Act." *Labor Law Journal* 24 (February 1973): 92-9. Since the enactment of the law, some employers are still computing payrolls on the basis of sex.

2754. Carter, R. "What Women Really Think of the Kennedys." *Good Housekeeping* (June 1963): 74-5, 176, 178-79, 182. The results of a national survey conducted by *Good Housekeeping.*

2755. Coover, Edwin Russell. "Status and Role Change Among Women in the United States, 1940-1970: A Quantitative Approach." Ph.D. diss., University of Minnesota, 1973. To compare status over time, a modified version of the Duncan-North-Hatt scale was used to assign scores to eleven major occupational groups.

2756. Edwards, India. *Pulling No Punches: Memoirs of a Woman in Politics.* New York: G. P. Putnam's, 1977. Contains some anecdotes about Kennedy's women appointments.

2757. "Equal Pay for Women." *Commonweal* 78 (June 7, 1963): 293-94. An endorsement of the Kennedy administration bill.

2758. "'Equal Pay' for Women: Its Effect." *U.S. News and World Report* 24 (June 15, 1964): 91-2. Many employers used the waiting period to grant pay raises to women or revised job descriptions.

2759. Evans, Sara. *Personal Politics: The Roots of Women's Liberation in the Civil Rights Movement and the New Left.* New York: Knopf, 1979. Gives brief coverage to the President's Commission on the Status of Women of 1961.

2760. Florer, John Harmon. "NOW: The Formative Years. The National Effort to Acquire Federal Action on Equal Employment Rights for Women in the 1960s." Ph.D. diss., Syracuse University, 1972. NOW's earliest efforts were directed against sex segregated job advertisements, protective labor laws, and the limited Equal Employment Opportunity Commission and Equal Pay Act.

2761. Fogel, Walter. *The Equal Pay Act*. New York: Praeger, 1984. A pedestrian work by a professor of industrial relations.

2762. Friedan, Betty. *The Feminine Mystique*. New York: W. W. Norton, 1963. An exceedingly important study that provided an impetus to the women's rights movement during the 1960s.

2763. Gould, Beatrice B. "Appointments for Women." *Ladies' Home Journal* 78 (January 1961): 64. Women's thinking and planning are needed by both political parties, by all branches and at all levels of government, in both elective and appointive posts.

2764. Harrison, Cynthia. *On Account of Sex: The Politics of Women's Issues, 1945-1968*. Berkeley: University of California Press, 1988. The most comprehensive and reliable study of women's issues during the Kennedy era.

2765. _____. "A New Frontier for Women: The Public Policy of the Kennedy Administration." *Journal of American History* 67 (December 1980): 630-46. Emphasizes the significance rather than the limitations of Kennedy's policies.

2766. Hole, Judith, and Ellen Levine. *Rebirth of Feminism*. New York: Quadrangle Books, 1971. Covers federal policy and law for the 1960s.

2767. Kanowitz, Leo. *Women and the Law: The Unfinished Revolution*. Albuquerque: University of New Mexico Press, 1969. Useful for those studying women's rights issues in the Kennedy period.

2768. Lamson, Peggy. *Few Are Chosen: American Women in Political Life Today*. Boston: Houghton Mifflin, 1968. Deals with two of President Kennedy's appointments: Esther Peterson and Eugenie Anderson.

2769. Linden-Ward, Blanche. "The ERA and Kennedy's Presidential Commission on the Status of Women." In *John F. Kennedy*. Edited by Paul Harper and Joann P. Krieg, pp. 237-49. No. **1600**. Inadvertently, the Kennedy Commission, as much as the writings of Betty Friedan or other new feminists, served as a catalyst for the rise of the women's movement.

2769a. Linden-Ward, Blanche, and Carol Hurd Green. *American Women in the 1960s: Changing the Future*. New York: Twayne, 1993. A comprehensive study that suggests that Kennedy's Commission on the Status of Women marked a watershed as an index instead of a cause of deep social and cultural change.

2770. Louchheim, Katie. *By the Political Sea*. No. **2072**. By one of Kennedy's few administrative appointments.

2771. McGlen, Nancy E., and Karen O'Connor. *Women's Rights: The Struggle for Equality in the Nineteenth and Twentieth Century*. New York: Praeger, 1983. Includes coverage of the Kennedy era.

2772. Morain, Thomas Jeffrey. "The Emergence of the Women's Movement, 1960-1970." Ph.D. diss., University of Iowa, 1974. This study posits that developments like civil rights, the New Left, and Vietnam encouraged women to emphasize the sex variables as a means of symbolically distancing themselves from discredited institutions.

2773. Murphy, Thomas E. "Female Wage Discrimination: A Study of the Equal Pay Act 1963-1970." *University of Cincinnati Law Review* 39 (Fall 1970): 615-49. The equal pay program has come of age as a result of the *Shultz v. Wheaton Glass Co.* case, which held that women who do work *substantially* equal to males must be paid equally.

2774. Ondercin, David G. "The Compleat Woman: The Equal Rights Amendment and Perceptions of Womanhood, 1920-1972." Ph.D. diss., University of Minnesota, 1973. Deals with the conflict over protective laws versus the Equal Rights Amendment, a controversy that intensified during the 1960s.

2775. Rupp, Leila, and Verta Taylor. *Survival in the Doldrums: The American Women's Rights Movement, 1945 to the 1960s*. Columbus: Ohio State University Press, 1990. Includes discussion of President Kennedy's response to women's issues.

2776. Sealander, Judith. *As Minority Becomes Majority: Federal Reaction to the Phenomenon of Women in the Workforce, 1920-1963*. Westport, Ct.: Greenwood Press, 1983. Covers the President's Commission on the Status of Women appointed by Kennedy in December 1961.

2777. _____. "John F. Kennedy's Presidential Commission on the Status of Women: 'A Dividing Line.'" In *John F. Kennedy*. Edited by Paul Harper and Joann P. Krieg, pp. 251-60. No. **1600**. Argues that the Kennedy Commission played a transitional role in terms of federal policy toward women.

2778. Simchak, Morag M. "Equal Pay Act of 1963: Its Implementation and Enforcement." *AAUW Journal* 61 (March 1968): 117-19. The principle of equal pay is being increasingly accepted by progressive employers and unions throughout the country.

2779. Stevens, Eleanor. "Some Developments in National Wage and Employment Policy for Women with Emphasis on the Years, 1962-1966." Ph.D. diss., University of Illinois, 1967. Includes an analysis of the Equal Pay Act of 1963.

2780. Tebbel, John. "JFK, the Magazines, and Peace." *Saturday Review* 46 (December 14, 1963): 56-7. Kennedy meets with the editors of seven women's magazines to answer readers' questions about world peace.

2781. Tolchin, Susan, and Martin Tolchin. *Clout: Womanpower and Politics.* New York: Coward, McCann and Geogegan, 1974. Contains an excellent anecdote regarding Kennedy and women and useful background information on the era.

2782. U.S. President's Commission on the Status of Women. *American Women: Report . . . and Other Publications of the Commission.* Edited by Margaret Mead and Francis Balgley Kaplan. New York: Charles Scribner's Sons, 1965. Chaired by Eleanor Roosevelt and assisted by Esther Peterson, this Kennedy-created commission elevated women's rights issues.

2783. "When Women Get Paid as Much as Men." *U.S. News and World Report* 54 (June 3, 1963): 97-8. Will some women lose their jobs while others are getting raises?

2784. Zelman, Patricia G. *Women, Work, and National Policy: the Kennnedy-Johnson Years.* Ann Arbor: UMI Research Press, 1982. An excellent chapter on Kennedy and women's rights.

Other Issues

2785. Allen, Marin Pearson. "The Guest-Host Archetype as Rhetorical Constraint on the Modern American Presidency." Ph.D. diss., University of Maryland, 1985. This study is a critical analysis of how the guest-host archetype put constraints on President Kennedy, with state dinners used as examples.

2786. Barber, William J., James L. Cochrane, Neil de Marchi, and Joseph A. Yager. "Energy: From John F. Kennedy to Jimmy Carter." *Wilson Quarterly* 5 (Spring 1981): 70-90. President Kennedy made few changes in the federal energy policy inherited from Eisenhower.

2787. Berthold, Carol Ann. "The Image and Character of President John F. Kennedy: A Rhetorical-Critical Approach." Ph.D. diss., Northwestern University, 1975. Examines how Kennedy used rhetoric to create and maintain a positive image.

2788. Best, James J. "Who Talked with President Kennedy: An Interaction Analysis." *Presidential Studies Quarterly* 22 (June 1992): 351-69. By analyzing the people with whom the president reacted, the medium of interaction, and the rate of interaction over time, a more focused understanding of the contemporary presidency results.

2789. Chase, Harold W. *Federal Judges: The Appointing Process*. University of Minnesota Press, 1972. The section on the Kennedy administration appointments is partially based on interviews and the author's personal observation.

2790. Curzan, Mary Hannah. "A Case Study in the Selection of Federal Judges: The 5th Circuit, 1953-1963." Ph.D. diss., Yale University, 1968. Examines federal judges and the process by which they are appointed to determine whether Eisenhower and Kennedy sought racial moderates or liberals for benches in the Deep South.

2791. Davis, James W. *The President as Party Leader*. New York: Westport, Ct.: Greenwood Press, 1992. The national party chairmen of the incumbent party have seen their organizational influence, beginning with the Kennedy administration, lessen.

2792. Fixler, Philip Eldridge, Jr. "A Content Analysis of American Presidential Rhetoric: An Exploratory Study of Misrepresentation and Descriptive Language in the Major Public Communications of Presidents Kennedy, Johnson, and Nixon." Ph.D. diss., University of Southern California, 1979. Elucidates the phenomenon of misrepresentative or deceptive language in politics by identifying the social and political conditions to which it might be related.

2793. Goldman, Sheldon. "Characteristics of Eisenhower and Kennedy Appointments to the Lower Federal Courts." *Western Political Quarterly* 18 (1965): 755-62. Offers background on, and political characteristics of, Eisenhower's and Kennedy's appointees to U.S. district courts and courts of appeal followed by the conclusion that the Eisenhower appointees tended to be of a higher socio-economic status.

2794. Greenberg, Daniel S. "Mohole--The Project That Went Away." In *Knowledge and Power: Essays on Science and Government*. Edited by Sanford A. Lakoff. New York: Free Press, 1966, pp. 87-111. Project Mohole--a design to drill the earth to unprecedented depths--stands out as an administrative fiasco--one that involved both the Eisenhower and Kennedy administrations.

2795. Lucco, Joan. "Roles of Interest Group Representatives at the White House: Consumer Units in the Modern Presidency from John F. Kennedy to Jimmy Carter." Ph.D. diss., Johns Hopkins University, 1986. Having consumer representatives on their staffs was a great help to presidents in their efforts to govern effectively and to win reelection.

2796. MacKenzie, G. Calvin. *The Politics of Presidential Appointments*. New York: Free Press, 1981. In spite of inconsistencies, the selection procedures established during the Kennedy administration were a turning point in the development of a modern and rational personnel approach in the White House Office.

2797. Marshall, Melvin Jay. "An Analysis of Values Expressed in the Presidential Speeches of John F. Kennedy." Ph.D. diss., University of Oregon, 1985. Compares the values Kennedy expressed in his speeches with those that existed in the culture, using such methods as cluster analysis.

2798. Muller, Arnold John. "Public Policy and the Presidential Election Process: A Study of Promise and Performance." Ph.D. diss., University of Missouri-Columbia, 1986. A study of the relationship between promises Kennedy made during the 1960 campaign and subsequent performance.

2799. Osborne, Leonard L. "Patterns of Arrangement in President Kennedy's Major Addresses." Ph.D. diss., University of Southern California, 1978.   Through descriptive analysis, Osborne reveals that Kennedy had favorite ways of opening and closing his talks and seemed to favor the use of certain plans of development when talking to certain audiences.

2800. _____. "Rhetorical Patterns in President Kennedy's Major Speeches: A Case Study." *Presidential Studies Quarterly* 10 (Summer 1980): 332-35.   Uses a combination of rhetorical analysis and content analysis.

2801. Rowland, C. K., Robert Carp, and Ronald A. Stidham. "Judges' Policy Choices and the Value Basis of Judicial Appointments: A Comparison of Support for Criminal Defendants among Nixon, Johnson, and Kennedy Appointees to the Federal District Courts." *Journal of Politics* 46 (August 1984): 886-902.   Least supportive of defendants have been Southern judges appointed by Kennedy.

2802. Samryk, Alexis. "The Use of the Executive Order to Implement the President's Economic Agenda: A Comparison between the Kennedy-Johnson and Reagan Administrations." Ph.D. diss., Temple University, 1991.   Concludes that the Kennedy-Johnson and Reagan administrations did not differ basically in the uses of executive orders because of ideology, party affiliation, or their respective party's control of Congress.

2803. Smith, Guy Duane. "The Pulse of Presidential Popularity: Kennedy in Crisis." Ph.D. diss., University of California at Los Angeles, 1978. Purpose is to shed light on the process of attitude change in response to political crises.

2804. "Striking the Theme." *Time* 82 (October 4, 1963): 24, 36.   Kennedy's unofficial campaigning in a conservation tour of western states.

2805. Thomison, Dennis. "Trouble in Camelot: An Early Skirmish of Kennedy's New Frontier." *Journal of Library History* 13 (Spring 1978): 148-56. An apparent attempt by newly elected President Kennedy to replace L. Quincy Mumford as Librarian of Congress in 1961.

2806. Vanocur, Sander. "Kennedy's Voyage of Discovery." *Harper's* 228 (April 1964): 41-5. A first-hand remembrance of Kennedy's western tour in the fall of 1963.

2807. "A Victory for Kennedy That May Bring Him Trouble." *U.S. News and World Report* 53 (August 27, 1962): 44-5. A Senate fight over the administration's communications bill leaves liberals disgruntled and uncooperative.

2808. Wagner, Stephen Thomas. "The Lingering Death of the National Origins Quota System: A Political History of United States Immigration Policy, 1952-1965." Ph.D. diss., Harvard University, 1986. Contains a discussion of Kennedy's views on immigration policy, especially his opposition to the national origins system.

2809. Wolanin, Thomas R. *Presidential Advisory Commissions: Truman to Nixon.* Madison: University of Wisconsin Press, 1975. Provides a systematic study of presidential advisory commissions as political institutions with a focus on the relationship between presidents and commissions and on the widely voiced criticisms of commissions.

2810. Wolfe, James Snow. "*The Kennedy Myth*: American Civil Religion in the Sixties." Ph.D. diss., Graduate Theological Union, 1975. President Kennedy was clothed in myth during his candidacy and presidency and even more so after his death.

E. FOREIGN AFFAIRS

General

2811. Ambrose, Stephen A. *Rise to Globalism: American Foreign Policy since 1938.* Baltimore: Penguin, 1971. A cold warrior most of his presidency, Kennedy showed an ability to grow, which was his most impressive asset.

2812. Aron, Raymond. *Imperial Republic: The United States and the World, 1945-1973.* Englewood Cliffs, NJ: Prentice-Hall, 1974. Critical study of postwar American foreign policy.

2813. "As Kennedy Looks at U. S. and World--His Views for '63." *U.S. News and World Report* 54 (January 14, 1963): 35-8. Kennedy reviews the past two years and looks ahead.

2814. Ball, George W. *The Past Has Another Pattern.* New York: W. W. Norton,

1982. Recollections of President Kennedy's undersecretary of state.

2815. Barnet, Richard J. *Intervention and Revolution: The United States in the Third World.* New York: World Publishing, 1968. Deals briefly with the Kennedy foreign policy.

2816. Betts, Richard K. *Soldiers, Statesmen, and Cold War Crises.* Cambridge: Harvard University Press, 1977. Focuses on the role of military advice in influencing presidential decisions.

2817. Blaufarb, Douglas S. *The Counterinsurgency Era: U.S. Doctrine and Performance 1950s to the Present.* New York: Free Press, 1977. Includes chapters on the Kennedy Doctrine and the strategic hamlet program in Vietnam.

2818. Bohlen, Charles E. *Witness to History, 1929-1969.* New York: W. W. Norton, 1973. By Kennedy's foreign policy adviser and ambassador to France.

2819. Bowles, Chester. *Promises to Keep: My Years in Public Life, 1941-1969.* New York: Harper and Row, 1971. The autobiography includes Bowles's tenure and dismissal as Kennedy's undersecretary of state.

2819a. Brands, H. W. *The Devil We Knew: Americans and the Cold War.* New York: Oxford University Press, 1993. A thoughtful account that attempts to explain why American leaders acted as they did during the cold war.

2820. Brown, Seyom. *The Faces of Power: Constancy and Change in United States Foreign Policy from Truman to Johnson.* New York: Columbia University Press, 1968. An examination of basic American policy assumptions by a RAND corporation analyst.

2821. Bundy, McGeorge. *Danger and Survival.* No. **2566.** Kennedy's national security adviser has chapters on the Berlin and Cuban missile crises.

2822. Callahan, David. *Dangerous Capabilities: Paul Nitze and the Cold War.* New York: Harper Collins, 1990. The State Department's passivity meant that the Defense Department sometimes took the lead in foreign policy with Nitze playing a part.

2823. Cleveland, Harlan. *The Obligations of Power: American Diplomacy in the Search for Peace.* New York: Harper and Row, 1966. By President Kennedy's assistant secretary of state for international affairs and later U.S. ambassador to NATO.

2824. Cohen, Warren I. *Dean Rusk.* Totowa, NJ: Cooper Square, 1980. An even-handed and perceptive assessment of Kennedy's secretary of state.

2825. Destler, I. M. *Presidents, Bureaucrats and Foreign Policy*. Princeton: Princeton University Press, 1972. A study of how government is organized to formulate policy, including an analysis of President Kennedy's efforts to reform the State Department.

2826. Destler, I. M., Leslie H. Gelb, and Anthony Lake. *Our Own Worst Enemy: The Unmaking of American Foreign Policy*. New York: Simon and Schuster, 1984. Deals with the growing politicalization of American foreign policy since World War II.

2827. Divine, Robert A. "The Education of John F. Kennedy." In *Makers of American Diplomacy from Benjamin Franklin to Henry Kissinger*. Edited by Frank Merli and Theodore A. Wilson. New York: Charles Scribner's, 1974, pp. 621-48. Argues that President Kennedy had undergone a fundamental change in outlook on foreign policy near the end of his brief presidency.

2828. FitzSimons, Louise. *The Kennedy Doctrine*. New York: Random House, 1972. To the revisionist FitzSimons, the Kennedy Doctrine represented the right to intervene politically and militarily in the internal affairs of other, less powerful, nations.

2829. Froman, Michael B. *The Development of the Idea of Détente: Coming to Terms*. New York: St. Martin's Press, 1991. The Kennedy administration saw détente as imperative despite an enduring conflict with the Soviets.

2830. Fulbright, J. William. *The Price of Empire*. New York: Pantheon, 1989. Little insight or new information on the Kennedy foreign policy.

2831. Gaddis, John Lewis. *Strategies of Containment: A Critical Appraisal of Postwar American National Security*. New York: Oxford University Press, 1982. According to Gaddis, Kennedy contended that the United States could, in principle, live comfortably in a diverse world along balance of power lines, but it could not withdraw from what were admittingly overextended positions without setting off a crisis of confidence.

2832. Galbraith, John Kenneth. *Ambassador's Journal*. No. **309**. Galbraith served as ambassador to India but offered Kennedy advice in other foreign policy areas.

2833. _____. *A Life in Our Times: Memoirs*. Boston: Houghton Mifflin, 1981. Generally critical, perceptive, and witty in his comments on the Kennedy foreign policy.

2834. George, Alexander L., and Richard Smoke. *Deterrence in American Foreign Policy: Theory and Practice*. New York: Columbia University Press, 1974. A critical examination of the deterrence theory and deterrence strategy as they have been applied in American foreign policy since the end of World War II.

2835. George, Alexander L., David K. Hall, and William Simons. *The Limits of Coercive Diplomacy: Laos, Cuba, Vietnam*. Boston: Little, Brown, 1971. Examines doctrines and strategy.

2836. Halberstam, David. *The Best and the Brightest*. New York: Random House, 1972. Remains a brilliant and indispensable study of Kennedy foreign policymakers by the *New York Times* reporter.

2837. Halle, Louis J. "The Armies of Ignorance." *New Republic* 149 (December 7, 1963): 16-17. A defense of the Kennedy foreign policy.

2838. Hartley, Anthony. "John F. Kennedy's Foreign Policy." *Foreign Policy* 4 (February 1971): 77-87. Its defect was that it overestimated American power, and it underestimated the difficulties of doing anything at all.

2839. Henry, John B., and William Espinosa. "The Tragedy of Dean Rusk." *Foreign Policy* 7 (Fall 1972): 166-89.

2840. Hilsman, Roger. *To Move a Nation: The Politics of Foreign Policy in the Administration of John F. Kennedy*. Garden City, NY: Doubleday, 1967. A generally favorable memoir by Kennedy's assistant secretary for Far Eastern Affairs.

2841. Howe, Russell W., and Sarah Hays Trott. *The Power Peddlers: How Lobbyists Mold American Foreign Policy*. Garden City, NY: Doubleday, 1977. Written by journalists with scattered references to the Kennedy presidency.

2842. Isaacson, Walter, and Evan Thomas. *The Wise Men: Six Friends and the World They Made*. New York: Simon and Schuster, 1986. Dean Acheson, Charles Bohlen, Averell Harriman, George Kennan, Robert Lovett, and John McCloy, Jr., all had Kennedy's ear.

2843. Johnson, Haynes, and Bernard M. Gwertzman. *Fulbright: The Dissenter*. Garden City, NY: Doubleday, 1968. A journalistic account of the chairman of the Senate Foreign Relations Committee who thought highly of Kennedy.

2844. Johnson, U. Alex. *The Right Hand of Power*. Englewood Cliffs, NJ: Prentice-Hall, 1984. Memoirs of President Kennedy's deputy undersecretary of state.

2845. Kamath, Padmanabh M. "National Security Policy-making: Rising Above the Formal Approach of the 1950s." *Indian Journal of American Studies* 14 (July 1984): 33-41. Kennedy disliked a formal arrangement for policymaking, particularly after the Bay of Pigs failure.

2846. Kateb, George. "Kennedy as Statesman." *Commentary* 41 (June 1966): 54-60. In reviewing Sorensen's *Kennedy* and Schlesinger's *A Thousand Days*, Kateb concludes that the break Kennedy made with the past resulted in an intensification of cold-war bellicosity, not in its lessening.

2847. Kennan, George F. *Memoirs, 1950-1963*. Boston: Little, Brown, 1972. Examines doctrines and strategy.

2848. "Kennedy Learns about Personal Diplomacy." *U.S. News and World Report* 50 (April 24, 1961): 46-7. On Kennedy's relative youth and lack of diplomatic experience compared with other world leaders.

2849. Kennedy, Robert F. *Just Friends and Brave Enemies*. New York: Harper and Row, 1962. An account of Kennedy's trip to Asia and Berlin in 1962 and his statements on foreign policy.

2850. "Kennedy Turns to a Harder Line." *U.S. News and World Report* 54 (January 7, 1963): 25-6. Kennedy takes a tougher approach on foreign affairs following the Cuban missile crisis.

2851. LaFeber, Walter. *America, Russia, and the Cold War, 1945-1992*. New York: McGraw-Hill, 1993. A thoughtful revisionist study that suggests that the Kennedy administration preferred to fight the cold war rather than risk negotiating its problems.

2852. Lane, Thomas. *Cry Peace: The Kennedy Years*. New York: Twin Circle, 1969. Compilation of Lane's newspaper columns on foreign policy from the St. Louis *Globe-Democrat, 1962-1963*.

2853. Maga, Timothy P. *John F. Kennedy and New Frontier Diplomacy, 1961-1963*. Malabar, Fl.: Krieger, 1994. This slim book sees Kennedy as a visionary who nevertheless understood the limits of power, the folly of nuclear threats, and the trauma of no-win brushfire war.

2854. Mahajani, Usha. "Kennedy and the Strategy of Aid: The Clay Report and After." *Western Political Quarterly* 18 (December 1965): 656-88. Focuses on a citizens' committee under General Lucius Clay, appointed by President Kennedy in December 1962, to investigate foreign aid questions.

2855. Martin, John Bartlow. *Adlai Stevenson and the World*. No. 1774. An impressive work that covers Stevenson's tenure as Kennedy's UN ambassador.

2856. Morgenthau, Hans. "The Trouble With Kennedy." *Commentary* 33 (January 1962): 51-5. In foreign policy matters Kennedy unwisely seeks to accomplish the task of the statesman with the tools of the politician.

2857. Nash, Philip. "Nuclear Weapons in Kennedy's Foreign Policy." *Historian* 56 (Winter 1994): 285-300. Kennedy's reliance on non-nuclear assets overshadowed his reliance on nuclear weapons.

2858. Nitze, Paul. *From Hiroshima to Glasnost: At the Center of Decisions*. New York: Weidenfeld and Nicolson, 1989.   Written by President Kennedy's assistant secretary of defense for international security affairs, who covers most of the key foreign policy matters.

2859. Packenham, Robert A. *Liberal America and the Third World: Political Development Ideas in Foreign Aid and Social Science*. Princeton: Princeton University Press, 1973.   The principal focus is on the nature and the roots of ideas about political development among policymakers and scholars in the United States to include Kennedy's Charles River group.

2860. Paterson, Thomas. "Bearing the Burden: A Critical Look at JFK's Foreign Policy." *Virginia Quarterly Review* 54 (Spring 1978): 193-212.   Kennedy bequeathed a dubious legacy in foreign policy.

2861. _____. "John F. Kennedy and the World." In *John F. Kennedy*. Edited by J. Richard Snyder, pp. 123-38. No. **1600**. Stresses the obstacles in dealing with the Kennedy foreign policy, including the ambiguity of Kennedy.

2861a. _____, ed. *Kennedy's Quest for Victory: American Foreign Policy, 1961-63*. New York: Oxford University Press, 1989.   A uniformly outstanding anthology, offering a perceptive, penetrating view of the Kennedy foreign policy.

2862. Prados, John. *Keepers of the Keys: A History of the National Security Council*. New York: William Morrow, 1991.   Prados suggests that Kennedy's goals to strengthen and simplify the National Security Council were an oxymoron.

2863. "Riding Caroline's Tricycle?" *New Republic* 145 (November 13, 1961): 2. The title comes from the remarks of the publisher of the *Dallas Morning News* who argues that the country needs "a man on horseback," not one riding his daughter's tricycle.

2864. Ruddy, T. Michael. *The Cautious Diplomat: Charles E. Bohlen and the Soviet Union, 1929-1969*. Kent, Oh.: Kent State University Press, 1986.   Ruddy faults Bohlen on his circumspection in pressing his position especially in light of doubts regarding the Bay of Pigs operation.

2865. Rusk, Dean. *As I Saw It*. New York: W. W. Norton, 1990.   Based on Richard Rusk's interviews with his secretary of state father--a first person account.

2866. _____. "Reflections on Foreign Policy." In *The Kennedy Presidency*. Edited by Kenneth W. Thompson, pp. 189-201. No. **1588**.   A useful interview.

2867. Schoenbaum, Thomas J. *Waging Peace and War: Dean Rusk in the Truman, Kennedy and Johnson Years*. New York: Simon and Schuster, 1988.   Well-grounded in primary sources, including extensive interviews with Rusk, Schoenbaum puts forth the Rusk viewpoint as Kennedy's secretary of state.

2868. Spanier, John. *American Foreign Policy since World War II*. New York: Praeger, 1973. Good at putting Kennedy's foreign policy in the context of the changing postwar containment policy.

2869. Stuart, Douglas Thomas. "The Relative Potency of Leader Beliefs as a Determinant of Foreign Policy: John F. Kennedy's Operational Code." Ph.D. diss., University of Southern California, 1979. This study employs the political scientist's "operational code" approach to evaluate Kennedy's foreign policy especially as it concerns the cold war.

2870. Thompson, Kenneth W. "Kennedy's Foreign Policy: Activism versus Pragmatism." In *John F. Kennedy*. Edited by Paul Harper and Joann P. Krieg, pp. 25-34. No. **1600.** By seeking to merge the two approaches, Kennedy got the worst of both worlds, particularly in Vietnam.

2871. "U.S. World Policy: Inside Story of Who Really Makes It." *U.S. News and World Report* 53 (September 24, 1962): 62-4. The mechanics of foreign-policy making in the Kennedy administration.

2872. Walton, Richard J. *Cold War and Counterrevolution: The Foreign Policy of John F. Kennedy*. Baltimore: Penguin Books, 1972. A trenchant revisionist account.

Economic Foreign Policy

2873. Aly, Bower, ed. *American Trade Policy: A Complete Discussion and Debate Manual*. Columbia, Mo.: Artcraft Press, 1962. Includes Kennedy's Trade Expansion Act of 1962.

2874. Baldwin, David A. *Economic Development and American Foreign Policy: 1943-1962*. Chicago: University of Chicago Press, 1966. General coverage of the Kennedy administration without making distinctions with the preceding administration.

2875. _____. "Soft Loans and American Foreign Policy, 1943-1962." Ph.D. diss., Princeton University, 1965. Focuses on the policy of soft loans to stimulate economic growth in underdeveloped countries from 1943 to 1962.

2876. Banks, Louis. "What Kennedy's Free Trade Program Means to Business." *Fortune* 65 (March 1962): 102-04. Kennedy seeks to make the United States more competitive in the world market.

2877. Block, Fred. *The Origins of International Economic Disorder: A Study of United States International Monetary Policy from World War II to the Present*.

Berkeley: University of California Press, 1977. Discusses Kennedy's tariff reduction policy, including the Dillon Round and the Kennedy Round.

2878. "Boomerang for Kennedy." *Business Week* (June 2, 1962) p. 33. European Common Market is opposing U.S. tariff increases on carpet and glass and threatening retaliation.

2879. Borden, William S. "Defending Hegemony: American Foreign Economic Policy." In *Kennedy's Quest for Victory*. Edited by Thomas Paterson, pp. 57-85. No. **2861a**. Kennedy launched an aggressive but ultimately futile defense of American economic hegemony.

2880. Brown, George Thompson, Jr. "Foreign Policy Legitimation: The Case of American Foreign Aid, 1947-1971." Ph.D. diss., University of Virginia, 1971. Focuses on the means by which foreign policy decision makers attempt to achieve domestic acceptance of their policy objectives and on the instruments for implementing their objectives.

2881. Calleo, David P. *The Imperious Economy*. Cambridge: Harvard University Press, 1982. Kennedy's foreign economic policy remained committed to Cordell Hull's venerable dream of a worldwide free market.

2882. Calleo, David P., and Benjamin M. Rowland. *America and the World Political Economy: Atlantic Dreams and National Realities*. Bloomington: Indiana University Press, 1973. A thoughtful overview of U.S. policy in the 1960s including the Kennedy Round.

2883. Coffin, Frank M. *Witness for Aid*. Boston: Houghton Mifflin, 1964. Discussion of Kennedy's Agency for International Development.

2884. Curtis, Thomas B., and John Robert Vastine, Jr. *The Kennedy Round and the Future of American Trade*. Grew out of the work of Republican Congressman Thomas B. Curtis of Missouri in his role as one of four congressional delegates for trade negotiations who was appointed in accordance with the provisions of the Trade Expansion Act of 1962.

2885. Diebold, William, Jr. "Trade Policies since World War II." *Current History* 42 (June 1962): 356-64. Overviews U.S. trade policies from 1945 to 1962 and examines the General Agreement on Tariffs and Trade and the impact of renewed European and Japanese production on tariffs and import quotas.

2886. Dobson, Alan P. "The Kennedy Administration and Economic Warfare Against Communism." *International Affairs* 64 (Autumn 1988): 599-616. Explains the Kennedy administration's views on embargo policy.

2887. Evans, John W. *The Kennedy Round in American Trade Policy: The Twilight* *of the GATT?* Cambridge: Harvard University Press, 1971. Following Kennedy's Trade Expansion Act of 1962, the trade negotiations carried out thereafter--the Kennedy Round--lasted some four years.

2888. Feis, Herbert. *Foreign Aid and Foreign Policy.* New York: St. Martin's Press, 1964. Contains a discussion of Kennedy's clashes with Congress over foreign aid.

2889. Feld, Werner. *The European Common Market and the World.* Englewood Cliffs, NJ: Prentice-Hall, 1967. Occasional references to the Kennedy Round negotiations.

2890. Frangul, Ramzi N. "The Relationship between U. S. Foreign Aid and Revolutionary Change in Governments in Developing Countries, 1953-1970." Ph.D. diss., New York University, 1973. Political ideology of a new government is the principal factor in determining the amount of foreign aid it receives from the United States.

2891. Hagan, James M., and Vernon W. Ruttan. "Development Policy under Eisenhower and Kennedy." *Journal of Developing Areas* 23 (October 1988): 1-30. In 1961 the United States joined the Organization for Economic Cooperation and Development, which emphasized the long-range economic development of recipient nations rather than short-term security concerns--a culmination of a decade of political and academic thinking.

2892. "Historic Victory for Freer Trade." *Newsweek* 60 (October 1, 1962): 17-18. Describes passage of Kennedy's Trade Expansion Act.

2893. "JFK's Trade Bill." *National Review* 13 (July 31, 1962): 52. Delineates the powers the trade bill gives the president to control tariffs and the compensation to domestic companies and workers.

2894. Johnson, Harry G. *The World Economy at the Crossroads.* New York: Oxford University Press, 1965. Contains a brief preliminary evaluation of the Kennedy Round.

2895. "Kennedy's New Trade Policy." *New Republic* 145 (December 18, 1961): 8-9. Explores the problems Kennedy's tariff bill will have with the European Common Market.

2896. Matusow, Allen J. "Kennedy, the World Economy and the Decline of America." In *John F. Kennedy.* Edited by J. Richard Snyder, pp. 111-22. No. **1600**. Perhaps for the last time the United States of the Kennedy era exercised economic leadership in a multilateral world.

2897. Metzger, Stanley D. *Trade Agreements and the Kennedy Round.* Fairfax, Va.: Coiner Publications, 1964. An attempt to analyze and appraise the significance and the prospects of The Trade Expansion Act of 1962.

2898. Morgner, Aurelius. "The American Foreign Aid Program: Costs, Accomplishments, Alternatives?" *Review of Politics* 29 (1967): 65-75. Includes the Foreign Assistance Act of 1961.

2899. Morris, William Joseph, Jr. "Direct Foreign Investment and Public Policy: A Study of the United States Postwar Experience." Ph.D. diss., American University, 1968. Analyzes the effectiveness of United States Government programs during 1946-1965 in promoting and limiting United States direct foreign investment and the appropriateness of these programs in terms of balance of payments.

2900. Palmer, John David. "Presidential Leadership and Foreign Economic Aid." Ph.D. diss., University of Texas, 1965. Examines leadership techniques employed by President Kennedy in obtaining congressional support for foreign economic aid programs.

2901. Preeg, Ernest. *Traders and Diplomats: An Analysis of the Kennedy Round of Negotiations under the General Agreement on Tariffs and Trade.* Washington: Brookings Institution, 1970. Presents a history of the negotiations, an analysis of the results, and an evaluation of the significance of the Kennedy Round for future trade policy.

2902. "Push for Free Trade." *Business Week* (December 9, 1961), pp. 25-7. In a speech before the National Association of Manufacturers, Kennedy argues for more liberal trade laws.

2903. Shaw, Harry James. "The Military Assistance Program: A Study of Interdepartmental Relations and Influences." Ph.D. diss., Syracuse University, 1967. Shaw examines the military and political purposes of the program and evaluates policymaking processes from 1960 to 1967.

2904. Stocking, Thomas Edward. "The Political Objectives of American Foreign Trade Policy, 1948-1973." Ph.D. diss., University of Minnesota, 1977. Neither trade restrictions nor increases appear to have been very successful in increasing political influence.

2905. Sullivan, Robert R. "The Politics of Altruism: An Introduction to the Food-for-Peace Partnership between the United States Government and Voluntary Relief Organizations." *Western Political Quarterly* 23 (December 1970): 762-68.

2906. _____. "Politics of Altruism: A Study of the United States Government and American Voluntary Relief Agencies for the Donation Abroad of Surplus Agricultural Commodities, 1949-1967." Ph.D. diss., University of Virginia, 1968. The partnership is based on three considerations: growing world need, deepening involvement of the United States in world politics, and troublesome agricultural surpluses.

2907. Triffin, Robert. *The World Money Maze: National Currencies in International Payments*. New Haven: Yale University Press, 1966. Discusses the Trade Expansion Act of 1962 and related topics.

2908. "Union Backs Kennedy Plan to Cut Tariffs." *Business Week* (December 2, 1961), pp. 109-11. Kennedy sends Arthur Goldberg to the International Association of Machinists to win support for trade bill.

2909. Vaughn, Sandra Yvonne Chambers. "Foreign Aid: Its Impact on Indonesian Political Development, 1950-1972." Ph.D. diss., Howard University, 1978. Foreign aid to Indonesia relates directly to the United States' need to control the country's development to serve its business interest and military policy.

2910. Viner, Jacob, George Meany, Fowler Hamilton, Otto Passman, and Paul Hoffman. "The Report of the Clay Committee on Foreign Aid: A Symposium." *Political Science Quarterly* 78 (September 1963): 321-61. The Clay Committee, headed by General Lucius Clay and appointed by Kennedy on March 20, 1963, had concern with the objectives and the administration of the current foreign aid program.

2911. Walters, Robert Stephen. "American and Soviet Aid to Less Developed Countries: A Comparative Analysis." Ph.D. diss., University of Michigan, 1967. Since World War II, similarities in American and Soviet aid are more obvious than differences, for neither nation has found its assistance to be reliable for exerting influence in the underdeveloped nations.

2912. Wilt, Daniel. "A New Strategy for Economic Aid." *Orbis* 7 (Winter 1964): 800-20. In surveying U.S. foreign aid from 1947 to 1964, Wilt views it primarily as a response to communism.

2913. Zeiler, Thomas W. *American Trade and Power in the 1960s*. New York: Columbia University Press, 1992. The United States began its economic decline as early as the Kennedy presidency primarily because of the recovery and rise of Western Europe.

2914. _____. "Free Trade Politics and Diplomacy: John F. Kennedy and Textiles." *Diplomatic History* 11 (Spring 1987): 127-42. Zeiler contends that through the Trade Expansion Act, Kennedy proved that an adept politician could conciliate opponents and still uphold America's commitment to the liberal world trading system.

2915. _____. "Kennedy, Oil Imports, and the Fair Trade Doctrine." *Business History Review* 64 (Summer 1990): 286-310. Kennedy was able to utilize a fair trade doctrine to gain enactment of legislation that would both lower trade barriers and assist domestic producers hurt by increased imports.

Central Intelligence Agency

2916. Adler, Emanuel. "Executive Command and Control in Foreign Policy." *Orbis* 23 (1979): 671-96. Adler evaluates presidential control over covert activities of the CIA between 1947 and 1969.

2917. Branch, Taylor, and George Crile III. "The Kennedy Vendetta: How the CIA Waged a Silent War Against Cuba." *Harper's* 251 (August 1975): 49-63. Following the Bay of Pigs disaster, Kennedy entrusted the CIA to a secret war against Cuba, requiring several thousand men and an expenditure of $100 million a year, a war that continued for four years.

2917a. Breckinridge, Scott D. *CIA and the Cold War: A Memoir*. Westport, Ct.: Praeger, 1993. Written by a CIA insider who served during the Kennedy years.

2918. Davis, John. *The Kennedys*. No. **1639**. Particularly good on the CIA during the Kennedy presidency.

2919. Garthoff, Raymond L. *Intelligence Assessment and Policymaking: A Decision Point in the Kennedy Administration*. Washington: Brookings Institution, 1984. Based on a declassified 1962 study, including a retrospective evaluation.

2920. Hinckle, Warren, and William W. Turner. *The Fish Is Red: The Story of the Secret War Against Castro*. New York: Harper and Row, 1981. Based on extensive personal interviews, it views the CIA not as an "invisible government" answerable to no one but as a tool of the imperial presidency.

2921. Jeffreys-Jones, Rhodri. *The CIA and American Democracy*. New Haven: Yale University Press, 1989. Includes a chapter on the presidential shake-up of the CIA following the Bay of Pigs fiasco.

2922. Kirkpatrick, Lyman B., Jr. *The Real CIA*. New York: Macmillan, 1968. A history of the CIA by the inspector general of the CIA during the Kennedy administration to include CIA reorganization following the Bay of Pigs invasion.

2923. _____. *The U.S. Intelligence Community: Foreign Policy and Domestic Activities*. New York: Hill and Wang, 1973. In focusing on the organizational makeup and operations of the intelligence community, Kirkpatrick contends that it worked well during the Cuban missile crisis and the Vietnam War.

2924. Laqueur, Walter. *A World of Secrets: The Uses and Limits of Intelligence*.

New York: Basic Books, 1985. Assesses the role of intelligence in American foreign policymaking.

2925. Marchetti, Victor, and John D. Marks. *The CIA and the Cult of Intelligence*. New York: Knopf, 1974. Written by insiders, the CIA failed to suppress its publication despite a federal court order.

2926. Powers, Thomas. "Inside the Department of Dirty Tricks." *Atlantic Monthly* 244 (August 1979): 33-50, 54, 57-60, Based on Powers's forthcoming book on the CIA, *The Man Who Kept the Secrets*.

2927. _____. *The Man Who Kept the Secrets: Richard Helms and the CIA*. New York: Knopf, 1979. A biography of the CIA's deputy director for plans during the Bay of Pigs and other CIA activities during the Kennedy presidency.

2928. Ranelagh, John. *The Agency: The Rise and Decline of the CIA*. New York: Simon and Schuster, 1986. A well-researched work arguing that the CIA has almost invariably acted on the orders of the president or his appointed supervisors.

2929. Smist, Frank John. "Congress Oversees the United States Intelligence Community, 1947-1984." Ph.D. diss., University of Oklahoma, 1988. Deals with the interaction of the legislative and executive branches in American intelligence policy following World War II.

2930. Smith, Joseph B. *Portrait of a Cold Warrior*. New York: G. P. Putnam's Sons, 1976. A covert action specialist in the clandestine services of the CIA during the Kennedy presidency.

2931. Usowski, Peter Stanley. "John F. Kennedy and the Central Intelligence Agency: Policy and Intelligence." Ph.D. diss., George Washington University, 1987. Examines the impact the CIA had on foreign policy decisions during the Kennedy administration especially in Cuba and Vietnam.

2932. Walters, Vernon A. *Silent Missions*. Garden City, NY: Doubleday, 1978. The memoirs of a former deputy director of the CIA who served several presidents, including Kennedy.

2933. "Why John McCone?" *New Republic* 145 (October 23, 1961): 7-8. Questions McCone's qualifications to be acting head of the CIA.

2934. Wise, David. *The American Police State: The Government Against the People*. New York: Random House, 1976. Deals with the Rockefeller Commission and the Senate intelligence committee revelations of CIA activities during the Kennedy presidency.

2935. Wise, David, and Thomas B. Ross. *The Invisible Government*. New York:

Random House, 1964. A very critical assessment of the CIA and the intelligence community in general in the Eisenhower-Kennedy years.

Peace Corps

2936. Amin, Julius Atemkeng. *The Peace Corps in Cameroon.* Kent, Oh.: Kent State University Press, 1992. The volunteers made important strides in education and friendships but were unable to do much in community development.

2937. Ashabranner, Brent A. *A Moment in History: The First Ten Years of the Peace Corps.* Garden City, NY: Doubleday, 1971. The author served in the Peace Corps in Nigeria during the Kennedy administration.

2938. Bush, Gerald W. "The Peace Corps as a Value-oriented Movement." Ph.D. diss., Northern Illinois University, 1968. From its inception the Peace Corps did not fit the characteristics of a modern bureaucracy.

2939. Carey, Robert G. *The Peace Corps.* New York: Praeger, 1970. An early readable account that was done without the use of the Peace Corps files.

2940. Dobyns, Henry, Paul L. Doughty, and Alan R. Holmberg. *Peace Corps Program Impact in the Peruvian Andes.* Ithaca, NY: Department of Anthopology, Cornell University, 1964. Based on a Cornell University study that began late in 1962.

2941. Ellickson, Jean. "Librarian in the Peace Corps." *Wilson Library Bulletin* 36 (June 1962): 833-34. Describes training and library service work in East Pakistan.

2942. Fairfield, Roy P. "The Peace Corps and the University: Promises and Problems for Higher Education." *Journal of Higher Education* 35 (April 1964): 189-201. The Peace Corps programs threaten to strain regular instructional programs at participating universities.

2943. Hapgood, David, and Meridan Bennett. *Agents of Change: A Close Look at the Peace Corps.* Boston: Little, Brown, 1968. Former Peace Corps evaluators utilize their reports on the overseas programs to write about the work and experiences of the volunteers.

2944. Harris, Louis, and Associates. *A Survey of Returned Peace Corps Volunteers.* New York: Louis Harris and Associates, 1969. A useful and detailed study of returned volunteers to determine the extent to which the experience has changed them.

2945. Havenstock, Nathan A. "Profile of a Peace Corpsman." *Saturday Evening Post* 235 (September 8, 1962): 77-81. Profile of a worker in Colombia.

2946. Hayes, Samuel P. *An International Peace Corps: The Promise and Problems.* Washington: Public Affairs Institute, 1961. An extension of a memorandum prepared by Hayes at the request of President Kennedy's campaign staff.

2947. Hoopes, Roy. *The Complete Peace Corps Guide.* New York: Dial Press, 1961. Contains a brief account of its background, outlines its objectives, and provides information to prospective volunteers.

2948. _____, ed. *The Peace Corps Experience.* New York: Clarkson N. Potter, 1968. Written by Peace Corps volunteers, these popular and personal accounts are accompanied by many photographs.

2949. Jones, Charles Clyde. "The Peace Corps: An Analysis of the Development, Problems, Preliminary Evaluation and Future." Ph.D. diss., West Virginia University, 1967. The Peace Corps expanded rapidly in the beginning without adequate evaluation, which created some problems and shortcomings.

2950. Landrum, Roger L. *The Role of the Peace Corps In Education in Developing Countries: A Sector Study.* Washington: U.S. Peace Corps, 1981. Puts the Kennedy years into a twenty-year context.

2951. Liston, Robert A. *Sargent Shriver: A Candid Portrait.* New York: Farrar Straus, 1964. A nonscholarly biography of the first Peace Corps director that is anything but candid.

2952. Lowther, Kevin, and C. Payne Lucas. *Keeping Kennedy's Promise: The Peace Corps: Unmet Hope of the New Frontier.* Boulder, Co.: Westview Press, 1978. Written by former Peace Corps participants, this is a critical study that concludes that the Peace Corps has not lived up to its promise, but that it can.

2953. McCarthy, Colman. "Shriver: The Lightweight Label." *Washington Monthly* 8 (June 1976): 4-10. An assessment of Shriver and his Kennedy connection at the time he was the Democratic vice-presidential nominee.

2954. May, Gary. "Passing the Torch and Lighting Fires: The Peace Corps." In *Kennedy's Quest for Victory.* Edited by Thomas G. Paterson, pp. 284-316. No. **2861a.** Based on extensive interviews, it provides a sober view of the Peace Corps experience in Ethiopia.

2955. Meisler, Stanley. "Peace Corps Teaching in Africa." *Africa Report* 11 (December 1966): 16-20. One quarter of all Peace Corps Volunteers are teachers in Africa.

2956. Mothner, Ira. "JFK's Legacy: The Peace Corps." *Look* 30 (June 14, 1966): 34-7. A tribute to JFK that includes paintings by Norman Rockwell.

2957. Parmer, J. Norman. "The Peace Corps." *Annals of The American Academy of Political and Social Science* 365 (May 1966): 1-146. A special edition of thirteen articles devoted to the Peace Corps.

2958. "The Peace Corps." *New Republic* 144 (March 13, 1961): 3-4. Editorial analyzing the motives behind the Peace Corps.

2959. "Peace Corps: Negroes Play Vital Role in U.S. Quest for Friends Abroad." *Ebony* 17 (November 1961): 38-40. Kennedy seeks to staff Corps with a cross-section of American youth.

2960. "The Peace Corps at Home." *New Republic* 144 (March 20, 1961): 9. Discusses Eleanor Roosevelt's suggestion that a Peace Corps be established in the United States in slums and distressed areas.

2961. "Peace Corps Is Born." *New Republic* 144 (June 12, 1961): 4-5. Outlines the actual Peace Corps legislation.

2962. "Peace Corps Training at Howard." *Ebony* 18 (November 1962): 69-70. Known for its African studies program, Howard's training groups are interracial.

2963. "A Question of Black or White." *New Republic* 145 (November 6, 1961): 8-9. Focuses on controversy in Nigeria over lack of black workers in Peace Corps.

2964. Redmon, Coates. *Come as You Are: The Peace Corps Story.* San Diego: Harcourt Brace Jovanovich, 1986. A readable anecdotal look at the Kennedy years based on extensive interviewing.

2965. Rice, Gerard T. *The Bold Experiment: JFK's Peace Corps.* Notre Dame: University of Notre Dame Press, 1986. The best book on the Peace Corps: gracefully written, well researched, and balanced in interpretation.

2966. _____. *Twenty Years of Peace Corps.* Washington: U.S. Peace Corps, 1981. Contains a historical and an accomplishments overview.

2967. Schwarz, Karen. *What You Can Do for Your Country: An Oral History of the Peace Corps.* New York: William Morrow, 1991. Contains a chapter on the Kennedy years.

2968. "She Had No Idea." *Time* 78 (October 27, 1961): 24. Peace Corps volunteer Margery Jane Michelmore's infamous postcard found by a Nigerian.

2969. Sheffield, Glenn Francis. "Peru and the Peace Corps, 1962-1968." Ph.D. diss., University of Connecticut, 1991. Peru hosted one of the largest Peace Corps contingents in the world, which served as a model in its rural and urban community development programs.

2970. Shriver, Sargent. *Point of the Lance*. New York: Harper and Row, 1964. A selection of the Peace Corps director's speeches and writings of the origins and early days of the Peace Corps.

2971. Shute, Nancy. "After a Turbulent Youth, the Peace Corps Comes of Age." *Smithsonian* 16 (February 1986): 80-9. Discusses the Peace Corps' first twenty-five years and its prospects for the future.

2972. Stein, Morris L. *Volunteers for Peace: The First Group of Peace Corps Volunteers in a Rural Community Development Program in Colombia, South America*. New York: John Wiley, 1966. A favorable view of the impact of the program upon the Colombians, the volunteers, and the United States.

2973. Sullivan, George. *The Story of the Peace Corps*. New York: Fleet Publishing, 1964. A short narrative of the first three years.

2974. Textor, Robert B., ed. *Cultural Frontiers of the Peace Corps*. Cambridge: M.I.T. Press, 1966. The thrust is upon the overseas programs in selected host countries with each analysis written by an authority on that particular country.

2975. Vaughn, Jack, ed. *The Peace Corps Reader*. Washington: U.S. Peace Corps, 1968. An anthology that includes an essay by Sargent Shriver on "Five Years with the Peace Corps."

2976. Viorst, Milton, ed. *Making a Difference: The Peace Corps at Twenty-five*. New York: Weidenfeld and Nicolson, 1986. A retrospective that contains essays from several Kennedy era participants including Sargent Shriver, Harris Wofford, and Bill Moyers.

2977. Windmiller, Marshall. *The Peace Corps and Pax Americana*. Washington: Public Affairs Press, 1970. A former participant writes favorably of the program in dealing primarily with its development under Kenendy and its continuation under Johnson.

2978. Wingenbach, Charles E. *The Peace Corps--Who, How, and Where*. New York: John Day, 1961. A brief, not very useful, source book for the general public.

2979. Wofford, Harris. *Of Kennedys and Kings*. No. **1972**. The Kennedy administrative assistant and Peace Corps director for Ethiopia recalls his involvement with the Peace Corps.

2980. Zalba, Serapio R. "The Peace Corps--Its Historical Antecedents and Its Meaning for Social Work." *Duquesne Review* 11 (Fall 1966): 125-37. The Peace Corps is an extension of traditional American institutions for social betterment.

2981. Zimmerman, Robert F. "Peace Corps/Philippines: Image or Performance?"

Ph.D. diss., American University, 1968. In terms of meeting specific needs of the host country, Peace Corps volunteers sent to the Philippines failed during the first three years of activity there, but they were much more successful as young American image builders.

2982. Zuniga, Ricardo Burmester. "The Peace Corps as a Value-oriented Movement." Ph.D. diss., Harvard University, 1968. The more anxiety the public feels about Vietnam or the Middle East, the more impenetrable the Peace Corps fantasy becomes.

Alliance for Progress and Latin America

2983. Alba, Victor. *Alliance without Allies: The Mythology of Progress in Latin America*. New York: Praeger, 1965. From the very beginning the United States has failed to reach out to ordinary Latin Americans.

2984. Black, Jan Knippers. *United States Penetration of Brazil*. Philadelphia: University of Pennsylvania Press, 1977. Deals briefly with the deterioration of U.S.-Brazilian relations during the Kennedy presidency.

2985. Blazier, Cole. *The Hovering Giant: U.S. Responses to Revolutionary Changes in Latin America*. Pittsburgh: University of Pittsburgh Press, 1976. President Kennedy adopted a carrot and stick approach to social change in Latin America.

2986. "Brim Full of Bienvenido." *Life* 53 (July 13, 1962): 22-7. President and Mrs. Kennedy's trip to Mexico.

2987. Cayer, Napoleon Joseph. "Political Development: The Case of Latin America." Ph.D. diss., University of Massachusetts, 1972. Latin American political development has been studied from the perspective of models developed in the United States and Northern Europe, creating a cultural bias to much of the literature on Latin American development.

2988. Dosal, Paul J. "Accelerating Dependent Development and Revolution: Nicaragua and the Alliance for Progress." *Inter-American Economic Affairs* 38 (4 1985): 75-96. Suggests that President Kennedy's Alliance for Progress actually accelerated underdevelopment and dependency in Nicargua by providing investments that only benefited the political elite especially the Somoza family.

2989. Draper, Thomas J. "The Alliance for Progress: Failures and Opportunities." *Yale Review* 55 (December 1965): 182-90. The Alliance for Progress must be revised, for what is needed is not more money but more thought.

2990. Dreier, John C., ed. *The Alliance for Progress: Problems and Perspectives*. Baltimore: Johns Hopkins Press, 1962. A series of lectures including contributions by Milton S. Eisenhower, Teodoro Moscoso, and Dean Rusk.

2991. Gonzalez, Heliodoro (pen name). "The Failure of the Alliance for Progress in Colombia." *Inter-American Economic Affairs* 23 (Summer 1969): 87-96. Based on various government reports including one from the Agency for International Development.

2992. "Good Neighbor." *Newsweek* 58 (December 25, 1961): 16-17. President and Mrs. Kennedy's good-will trip to Venezuela and Colombia.

2993. Gordon, Lincoln. *A New Deal for Latin America: The Alliance for Progress.* Cambridge: Harvard University Press, 1963. Gordon was the U.S. ambassador to Brazil from October 1961 to August 1962.

2994. Hanson, Simon G. *Dollar Diplomacy Modern Style: Chapters in the Failure of the Alliance for Progress.* Washington: Inter-American Affairs Press, 1970. Concludes that the Kennedy program soon dissolved into a new form of dollar diplomacy.

2995. _____. *Five Years of the Alliance for Progress: An Appraisal.* Washington: Inter-American Affairs Press, 1967. In the Alliance's first five years, Latin America lost ground politically, economically, and socially in responding to the challenges of the time.

2996. Krause, Walter. "La Alianza Para El Progreso." *Journal of Inter-American Studies* 5 (1 1963): 67-82. The Alliance for Progress was a reaction to the emergence of a Communist regime in Cuba.

2997. LaFeber, Walter. *Inevitable Revolutions: The United States in Central America.* New York: W. W. Norton, 1983. The Kennedy administration viewed the Alliance for Progress as a weapon to fight revolution in Latin America.

2998. Langley, Lester D. *Mexico and the United States.* Boston: Twayne, 1991. Deals briefly with Kennedy and Mexico.

2999. _____. "Military Commitments in Latin America, 1960-1968." *Current History* 56 (June 1969): 346-51, 367. The Alliance for Progress hoped to foster progressive social change as an alternative to revolution; at the same time, through a military assistance program, the Latin American military received special training in counterinsurgency and civic action.

3000. Leacock, Ruth. "JFK, Business and Brazil." *Hispanic American Historical Review* 59 (4 1979): 636-73. The Kennedy administration became more business-oriented in its dealings with Brazil following the coming to power of a leftist government.

3001. _____. *Requiem for Revolution: The United States and Brazil, 1961-1969*. Kent, Oh.: Kent State University, 1990. Kennedy's idealistic reformism was soon compromised by the overriding goal of stopping the expansion of Soviet influence.

3002. Lehman, Kenneth Duane. "U.S. Foreign Aid and Revolutionary Nationalism in Bolivia, 1952-1964: The Pragmatics of a Patron-Client Relationship." Ph.D. diss., University of Texas, 1992. The interference that accompanied American aid undermined the moderates whom State Department officials purportedly hoped to strengthen.

3003. Levinson, Jerome, and Juan de Onis. *The Alliance That Lost Its Way: A Critical Report on the Alliance for Progress*. Chicago: Quadrangle, 1970. A decade of the Alliance has yielded more shattered hopes than solid accomplishments, more discord than harmony, more disillusionment than satisfaction.

3004. Lieuwen, Edwin. *Generals vs. Presidents: Neomilitarism in Latin America*. New York: Praeger, 1964. The high hopes of a democratic social revolution, in conjunction with the Alliance for Progress, has eroded since 1961 with the advent of seven military coups which has deposed constitutional regimes.

3005. Lowenthal, Abraham F. "United States Policy toward Latin America: 'Liberal,' 'Radical,' and 'Bureaucratic' Perspectives." *Latin American Research Review* 8 (Fall 1973): 3-25. Analyzes the "dwindling" literature on the Alliance for Progress in order to illuminate the state of scholarship on United States-Latin American relations.

3006. Martin, Edwin M. "Haiti: A Case Study in Futility." *SAIS Review* 2 (Summer 1981): 61-70. The Alliance for Progress and the cold war with Cuba aroused President Kennedy's interest in Haiti.

3006a. _____. *Kennedy and Latin America*. Lanham, Ma.: University Press of America, 1994. Written by the Assistant Secretary of State for Inter-American Affairs under Kennedy, he concludes that progress in Latin America was inevitably postponed by growing U.S. involvement in Vietnam and because of Fidel Castro.

3007. Martin, John Bartlow. *Overtaken by Events: The Dominican Crisis from the Fall of Trujillo to the Civil War*. Garden City, NY: Doubleday, 1966. An intriguing, riveting account by Kennedy's ambassador to the Dominican Republic.

3008. Mason, Edward S. *Foreign Aid and Foreign Policy*. New York: Harper and Row, 1964. Chapter on the Alliance for Progress focusing on trade policy.

3009. May, Herbert K. *Problems and Prospects of the Alliance for Progress: A Critical Examination*. New York: Praeger, 1968. Emphasizes the limitations of the Alliance, including the widespread disenchantment throughout Latin America.

3010. Montalva, Eduardo Frei. "The Alliance That Lost Its Way." *Foreign Affairs* 45 (April 1967): 437-48. After early success, what soon governed were the renewed attacks against democracy, the loss of markets for Latin American primary commodities, the decline of foreign investment, the consolidation in power of unjust regimes and the acceptance of alternative, evolutionary processes which only retarded revolutionary changes that so many of these countries needed.

3011. Morrison, DeLesseps. *Latin American Mission: An Adventure in Hemisphere Democracy.* New York: Simon and Schuster, 1965. Written by the former U.S. Ambassador to the Organization of American States about the OAS during the period of 1961-63.

3012. Parker, Phyllis. *Brazil and the Quiet Intervention, 1964.* Austin, Tx.: University of Texas Press, 1979. Deals with President Kennedy's relations with Brazilian President Joao Goulart.

3013. Perloff, Harvey S. *Alliance for Progress: A Social Invention in the Making.* Baltimore: Johns Hopkins Press, 1969. The basic concepts of the Alliance are sound and imaginative but a major restructuring is in order.

3014. Rabe, Stephen G. "Controlling Revolutions: Latin America, the Alliance for Progress and Cold War Anti-Communism." In *Kennedy's Quest for Victory.* Edited by Thomas Paterson, pp. 105-22. No.**2861a**. The Alliance for Progress was a cold war policy that all too often bolstered regimes and groups that were undemocratic, conservative, and frequently repressive.

3015. _____. *The Road to OPEC: United States Relations with Venezuela, 1919-1976.* Austin, Tx: University of Texas Press, 1982. Covers the Kennedy administration's relations with the Betancourt government.

3016. Rockefeller, David. "What Private Enterprise Means to Latin America." *Foreign Affairs* 44 (April 1966): 403-16. The ultimate success or failure of the Alliance for Progress will be determined primarily by the attitudes and actions of the business community in both the United States and Latin America.

3017. Roett, Riordan. *The Politics of Foreign Aid in the Brazilian Northeast.* Nashville: Vanderbilt University Press, 1972. The Kennedy administration saw Brazil's Northeast as an ideal location in which to demonstrate the United States' new foreign aid policy.

3018. Scheman, L. Ronald, ed. *The Alliance for Progress: A Retrospective.* New York: Praeger, 1988. Collection of essays by Kennedy administration officials and others delivered at a conference held in Washington in March 1988.

3019. Schlesinger, Arthur, Jr. "The Alliance for Progress: A Retrospective." In *Latin America: The Search for a New International Role.* Edited by Ronald G. Hellman and H. Jan Rosenbaum. New York: John Wiley, 1975, pp. 57-92. Blamed the Johnson administration for transforming the Alliance from a reform and democratization emphasis to one of only economic aid.

3020. _____. *Thousand Days*. No. **1624.** An adviser to JFK on Latin America, Schlesinger views the Alliance as a major accomplishment in channeling the energies of both public and private agencies as never before.

3021. Schoultz, Lars. *Human Rights and United States Policy toward Latin America*. Princeton: Princeton University Press, 1981. Scattered references to Kennedy in a study that more focuses on the 1970s.

3022. Slater, Jerome. "Democracy Versus Stability: The Recent Latin American Policy of the United States." *Yale Review* 55 (December 1965): 169-81. The Kennedy administration was considerably less obsessed with the subversion danger than the Johnson administration and therefore more considerably sophisticated in its anti-communism.

3023. _____. *The OAS and the United States Foreign Policy*. Columbus: Ohio State University Press, 1967. Very little on the Kennedy administration and the Organization of American States.

3024. _____. "The United States, the Organization of American States, and the Dominican Republic, 1961-63." *International Organization* 18 (Spring 1964): 268-91. Whether through collective or unilateral action, intervention against the right such as in the Dominican Republic involves far fewer problems than intervention against the left such as in Cuba.

3025. Smetherman, Robert M., and Bobbie B. Smetherman. "The Alliance for Progress Unfulfilled." *American Journal of Economics and Sociology* 31 (January 1972): 79-85. Evaluates the Alliance for Progress as only a mixed success due to the complexities of the problems and the resistance to change.

3026. Smith, Joseph Burkholder. *Portrait of a Cold Warrior*. New York: G. P. Putnam's, 1976. The memoirs of a covert action specialist in the Clandestine Services of the CIA who was much involved with Latin America.

3027. Townsend, Joyce Carol. "Retrieving Lost Ideals: United States Foreign Policy toward Brazil, 1960-1968." Ph.D. diss., University of Oklahoma, 1980. Explores the duplicity involved in Kennedy's foreign policy regarding Brazil and the Alliance for Progress.

3028. Van Cleve, Jonathan V. "The Latin American Policy of President Kennedy: A Reexamination Case: Peru." *Inter-American Economic Affairs* 30 (Spring 1977): 29-44. The Kennedy policy was pragmatic rather than idealistic, hardly a break from previous foreign policy, and geared to obtain favorable publicity.

Cuba

3029. "Another Cuban Fiasco?" *U.S. News and World Report* 54 (April 29, 1963): 33-6. The Kennedy administration backs down on support of anti-Castro activities by Cuban exiles.

3030. Bayard, James. *The Real Story on Cuba*. Derby, Ct.: Monarch Books, 1963. On the Cuban underground opposing Fidel Castro.

3031. Bonsal, Philip W. *Cuba, Castro, and the United States*. Pittsburgh: University of Pittsburgh Press, 1971. Written by the former American ambassador to Cuba.

3032. Carbonell, Nestor T. *And the Russians Stayed: The Sovietization of Cuba*. New York: William Morrow, 1989. Focuses on the author's experiences in the Cuban underground and the Cuban exile community and contains chapters on the Bay of Pigs and the missile crisis.

3033. Goodwin, Richard. "Annals of Politics: A Footnote." *New Yorker* 44 (May 25, 1968): 93-4, 96, 98, 101-02, 104, 107-08, 110, 113-14. Kennedy official Richard Goodwin, Ernesto (Ché) Guevara, and Cuba.

3034. Gosse, Van E. *Where the Boys Are: Cuba, Cold War America and the Making of a New Left*. New York: Verso Books, 1993. Examines the popularity of Fidel Castro's revolution with liberals, African-Americans, and youth in the late 1950s and early 1960s in spawning the Fair Play for Cuba Committee.

3035. Halper, Thomas. *Foreign Policy Crises: Appearance and Reality in Decision Making*. Columbus, Oh.: Merrill, 1971. Includes Bay of Pigs invasion and missile crisis.

3036. Halperin, Maurice. *The Rise and Decline of Fidel Castro: An Essay in Contemporary History*. Berkeley: University of California Press, 1972. Written by a scholar who spent six years in Cuba during the 1960s; see especially the chapter on the Kennedy-Castro "dialogue."

3037. Langley, Lester D. *The United States, Cuba, and the Cold War: American Failure or Communist Conspiracy?* Lexington, Ma.: D. C. Heath, 1970. An anthology dealing with conflicting interpretations regarding the U. S. responses to Castro's Cuba.

3038. Lazo, Mario. *Dagger in the Heart: American Policy Failures in Cuba*. New York: Funk and Wagnalls, 1968. Narrative of American policy toward Cuba concentrating on the postwar period.

3039. Losman, Donald. "The Embargo of Cuba: An Economic Appraisal."

Caribbean Studies 14 (October 1974): 95-120. Cuba's ability to survive despite sanctions indicates the limits of American economic power for coercive purposes.

3040. Mankiewicz, Frank, and Kirby Jones. *With Fidel: A Portrait of Castro and Cuba*. Chicago: Playboy Press, 1975. See especially the Castro interview on John Kennedy.

3041. Matthews, Herbert L. *Revolution in Cuba: An Essay in Understanding*. New York: Scribner's 1975. See the chapter on the "Pigs and Missiles."

3042. Morgenthau, Hans J. "Cuba: The Wake of Isolation." *Commentary* 34 (November 1962): 427-30. The United States must take whatever steps are necessary to isolate Cuba physically from the rest of the hemisphere.

3043. Morley, Morris. *Imperial State and Revolution: The United States and Cuba, 1952-1987*. New York: Cambridge University Press, 1987. Written by a sociologist, this well-researched study includes the Kennedy-Johnson policy of seeking to terminate the island's relations with the capitalist world.

3044. Neustadt, Richard E., and Ernest R. May. *Thinking in Time: The Uses of History for Decision-makers*. New York: Free Press, 1986. Includes decisionmaking for the Bay of Pigs invasion and the missile crisis.

3045. Nixon, Richard M. "Cuba, Castro and John F. Kennedy." *Reader's Digest* 85 (November 1964): 281-92, 295-300. Nixon explains where he differed with Kennedy on Cuban policy.

3046. Orman, John Michael. "Secrecy, Deception, and Presidential Power: John F. Kennedy to Gerald R. Ford." Ph.D. diss., Indiana University, 1979. Explores how secrecy, deception, and presidential power were used in the Kennedy administration to eliminate the Castro regime.

3047. Paterson, Thomas G. *Contesting Castro: The United States and the Triumph of the Cuban Revolution*. New York: Oxford University Press, 1994. In explaining the origins of the U. S. collision with revolutionary Cuba and the reasons for the U.S. failure to block Castro, it touches on activity in the Kennedy period.

3048. _____. "Fixation with Cuba: The Bay of Pigs, Missile Crisis, and Covert War Against Castro." In *Kennedy's Quest for Victory*. Edited by Thomas G. Paterson, pp. 123-55. No. **2861a**. Kennedy's style, the cold war, and American politics influenced the failed administration's Cuba policy.

3049. Plank, John, ed. *Cuba and the United States: Long-Range Perspectives*. Washington: Brookings Institution, 1967. Ten essays written between 1963 and 1965.

3050. Scheer, Robert, and Maurice Zeitlin. *Cuba: An American Tragedy*. Mitcham, Victoria (Australia): Penguin, 1964. Cuba epitomizes the failure and dangers of United States foreign policy.

3051. Schreiber, Anna P. "Economic Coercion as an Instrument of Foreign Policy: U. S. Economic Measures Against Cuba and the Dominican Republic." *World Politics* 25 (April 1973): 387-413. Some of the effects of the economic coercion policy against Cuba have been detrimental to U.S. interests.

3052. Smith, Wayne S. *The Closest of Enemies: A Personal and Diplomatic Account of U.S.-Cuban Relations since 1957*. New York: W. W. Norton, 1987. Written by a political officer on the Cuban desk.

3053. Sobel, Lester, ed. *Cuba, the U.S. and Russia, 1960-63*. New York: Facts on File, 1964. A synopsis of events in Cuba and of Cuban relations with the U.S. and the Soviet Union.

3054. Szulc, Tad. *Fidel: A Critical Portrait*. New York: William Morrow, 1986. By a *New York Times* correspondent who knew Castro well.

3055. Tetlow, Edwin. *Eye on Cuba*. New York: Harcourt, Brace and World, 1966. Analyzes the Cuban revolution on the basis of the author's fourteen visits there from 1959 to 1965.

3056. Thomas, Hugh. *Cuba: The Pursuit of Freedom*. New York: Harper and Row, 1971. A mammoth book that includes Kennedy's responses to the Cuban revolution.

3057. Tierney, Kevin Beirne. "American-Cuban Relations: 1957-1963." Ph.D. diss., Syracuse University, 1979. Explores the disastrous relationship of Cuba and the United States.

3058. Welch, Richard E., Jr. "Lippmann, Berle, and the U.S. Response to the Cuban Revolution." *Diplomatic History* 6 (Spring 1982): 125-43. These two members of the foreign policy public elite had contrasting views on Fidel Castro, the Bay of Pigs invasion, and the Cuban missile crisis.

3059. _____. *Response to Revolution: The United States and the Cuban Revolution, 1959-1961*. Chapel Hill: University of North Carolina Press, 1985. U.S. response to the Cuban revolution serves as a mirror of the beliefs and discontents of the American public, its conviction of national righteousness, and its periodic sense of national frustration.

Bay of Pigs

3060. Alsop, Stewart. "The Lessons of the Cuban Disaster." *Saturday Evening Post* 234 (June 24, 1961): 27-8, 68-70. Raises questions about the Bay of Pigs operation.

3061. Bernstein, Barton, Jr. "Kennedy and the Bay of Pigs Revisited--Twenty Four Years Later." *Foreign Service Journal* 62 (March 1985): 28-33. For Kennedy both domestic pressures and personal inclinations made the project attractive; it promised to rid the hemisphere of Castro, establish democracy in Cuba, and warn other left-wing movements of possible U.S. intervention.

3062. Bissell, Richard, Jr. "Response to Lucien S. Vandenbroucke, the 'Confessions' of Allen Dulles: New Evidence on the Bay of Pigs." *Diplomatic History* 8 (Fall 1984): 377-80. Bissell of the CIA questions that intelligence advisers lobbied for the invasion with the deliberate intent of drawing the president into a situation where he would be forced to abandon his policy restrictions.

3063. Higgins, Trumbull. *The Perfect Failure: Kennedy, Eisenhower, and the CIA at the Bay of Pigs*. New York: W. W. Norton, 1987. A balanced and well researched work although sometimes poorly written.

3064. "How President Kennedy Upset Cuban Invasion of April, 1961." *U.S. News and World Report* 54 (February 4, 1963): 29-30, 32-3. On Kennedy's decision that determined the fate of the Bay of Pigs invasion.

3065. Janis, Irving. *Victims of Groupthink: A Psychological Study of Foreign-policy Decisions and Fiascoes*. Boston: Houghton Mifflin, 1972. Contains an excellent chapter on how group-think or the herd instinct stifled independent thought among Kennedy advisers at key meetings involving the approval of the Bay of Pigs operation.

3066. Johnson, Haynes. *The Bay of Pigs: The Leaders' Story of Brigade 2506*. New York: Dell, 1964. A journalist provides a vivid account from the perspective of the exile leaders.

3067. "Kennedy's Fateful Decision: The Night the Reds Clinched Cuba." *U.S. News and World Report* 53 (September 17, 1962): 41-2. Critical of the way Kennedy handled the Bay of Pigs operation.

3068. Kirkpatrick, Lyman B. "Paramilitary Case Study: The Bay of Pigs." *Naval War College Review* 2 (November-December 1972): 32-42. Inaccurate intelligence was the basis for the Bay of Pigs disaster.

3069. Madden, John Patrick. "Operation Bumpy Road: The Role of Admiral Arleigh Burke and the U. S. Navy in the Bay of Pigs Invasion." M.A. thesis, Old Dominion University, 1988.

3070. Matthews, Herbert L. "The Bay of Pigs." In *The Cuba Reader: the Making of a Revolutionary Society*. Edited by Philip Brenner, William M. LeoGrande, Donna Rich, and Daniel Siegel. New York: Grove Press, 1989, pp. 331-36. From Matthews's *Revolution in Cuba*.

3071. Meyer, Karl E., and Tad Szulc. *The Cuban Invasion: The Chronicle of a Disaster*. New York: Praeger, 1962. An early account of the Bay of Pigs invasion.

3072. Murphy, Charles J. V. "Cuba: The Record Set Straight." *Fortune* 64 (September 1961): 92-7, 223-24, 227-28, 230, 233, 236. Murphy wonders after the Bay of Pigs whether Kennedy has yet mastered the government machinery, whether he is effectively served by some of his close advisers, and whether they understand the use of power in world politics.

3073. *Operation Zapata: The "Ultrasensitive" Report and Testimony of the Board of Inquiry on the Bay of Pigs*. Frederick, Md.: University Publications of America, 1981. Contains the Taylor Report (that part that has been declassified) and minutes of the meetings that led to it.

3074. Persons, Albert C. *Bay of Pigs: A Firsthand Account of the Mission by a U.S. Pilot in Support of the Cuban Invasion Force in 1961*. Jefferson, NC: McFarland, 1990. The invasion failed because of unanticipated, last-minute, nonmilitary restrictions.

3075. Sandman, Joshua H. "Analyzing Foreign Policy Crisis Situations: The Bay of Pigs." *Presidential Studies Quarterly* 16 (Spring 1986): 310-16. From the failure of the Bay of Pigs invasion, Kennedy learned the need for effective communications, consultation with allies, consideration of an action's moral and legal implications, and crisis preparedness, according to this heavily Sorensen-influenced piece.

3076. Szulc, Tad. "Cuba: Anatomy of a Failure." *Look* 25 (July 18, 1961): 76-82. Analysis of Kennedy's and the CIA's failure to carry out the Bay of Pigs invasion.

3077. Vandenbroucke, Lucien S. "Anatomy of a Failure: The Decision to Land at the Bay of Pigs." *Political Science Quarterly* 99 (Fall 1984): 471-91. Applies Graham Allison's concepts as expressed in the *Essence of Decision* to the Bay of Pigs.

3078. _____. "The 'Confessions' of Allen Dulles--New Evidence on the Bay of Pigs." *Diplomatic History* 8 (Fall 1984): 365-75. In his unpublished notes Dulles acknowledges that he and other senior planners ignored some of Kennedy's misconceptions of the operation; in the end they gambled that the president would commit U.S. forces to prevent a disaster.

3079. "What System Please? The Disaster Button, and History Will Not Absolve

Him." *Nation* 192 (May 6, 1961): 381-83. A condemnation of Kennedy's involvement in the invasion.

3080. Wyden, Peter. *Bay of Pigs: The Untold Story.* New York: Simon and Schuster, 1979. A well written study by a journalist based on interviews with planners and participants that claims that Kennedy was weak and indecisive and that his cancelled air strikes might have made a difference.

Missile Crisis

3081. Abel, Elie. *The Missile Crisis.* Philadelphia: J. B. Lippincott, 1966. A day-to-day account of the thirteen-day crisis.

3082. Acheson, Dean. "Dean Acheson's Version of Robert Kennedy's Version of the Cuban Missile Affair." *Esquire* 71 (February 1969): 76-7, 44, 46. Acheson responds to Robert Kennedy's posthumous memoir of the crisis by criticizing the decision making process.

3083. Allison, Graham T. "Conceptual Models and the Cuban Crisis." *American Political Science Review* 63 (September 1969): 689-718. The purpose of this essay is to explore the fundamental assumptions and categories employed by analysts in thinking about problems of governmental behavior as it relates to the missile crisis.

3084. _____. "Cuban Missiles and Kennedy Macho: New Evidence to Dispel the Myth." *Washington Monthly* 4 (October 1972): 14-19. In view of new evidence showing JFK to be more accommodating than previously thought, the machismo story must be radically revised.

3085. _____. *Essence of Decision: Explaining the Cuban Missile Crisis.* Boston: Little, Brown, 1971. A significant work that views the missile crisis in terms of bureaucratic politics and concludes that its resolution had much to do with the struggle of personalities and bureaucratic interests within the ExComm than it did with any decision Kennedy made.

3086. Allyn, Bruce J. "Essence of Revision: Moscow, Havana, and the Cuban Missile Crisis." *International Security* 14 (Winter 1989/90): 136-72. Based on dramatic new oral testimony from the Soviets and Cubans without corroboration from Soviet and Cuban documentation.

3087. Allyn, Bruce J., James G. Blight, and David A. Welch. *Back to the Brink: Proceedings of the Moscow Conference on the Cuban Missile Crisis, January 27-28, 1989.* Lanham, Md.: University Press of America, 1992. Based on the testimony of American, Soviet, and Cuban missile crisis participants and scholars in the third of five extraordinary conferences on the missile crisis.

3088. Alsop, Stewart, and Charles Bartlett. "In Time of Crisis." *Saturday Evening Post* 235 (December 8, 1962): 15-20. A personal account of the personalities, discussions, and decisions surrounding the crisis with Adlai Stevenson unfairly exposed as seeking a Munich-like settlement.

3089. Anderson, George W., Jr. "The Cuban Blockade: An Admiral's Memoir." *Washington Quarterly* 5 (Autumn 1982): 83-7. The missile crisis legitimized the first successful violation of the Monroe Doctrine.

3090. Armstrong, Scott, and Philip Brenner. "Putting Cuba Back in the Cuban Missile Crisis." In *The Cuba Reader*. Edited by Philip Brenner, William M. LeoGrande, Donna Rich, and Daniel Siegel, pp. 336-39. No. **3070**. The missile crisis teaches us to be more cautious with countries about which we know too little.

3091. Ascoli, Max. "Escalation from the Bay of Pigs." *Reporter* 27 (November 8, 1962): 24-5. A defense of Kennedy's actions during the missile crisis.

3092. "Back from the Brink: Cuban Missile Crisis Correspondence between John F. Kennedy and Nikita S. Khrushchev." *Problems of Communism* 41 (Special Issue-Spring 1992): 1-120. Covers twenty-five texts from October 22 through December 14, 1962.

3093. Beggs, Robert. *The Cuban Missile Crisis*. London: Longman, 1971. For classroom use, it includes a short commentary and a number of documents.

3094. Belkin, Aaron, and James G. Blight. "Triangular Mutual Security: Why the Missile Crisis Matters in a World beyond the Cold War." *Political Psychology* 12 (December 1991): 727-45. The missile crisis matters because in 1962, tiny Cuba, the repository of Soviet weapons of mass destruction, had acquired the capacity to raise the odds of their use.

3095. Bernstein, Barton J. "Bombers, Inspections, and the No Invasion Pledge." *Foreign Service Journal* 56 (July 1979): 8-12. Kennedy's final negotiations with the Soviets in the aftermath of the missile crisis led to the Soviet withdrawal of bombers and some Soviet troops from Cuba in return for a vague pledge that America had no intent to launch a military invasion of Cuba.

3096. _____. "Commentary: Reconsidering Khrushchev's Gambit--Defending the Soviet Union and Cuba." *Diplomatic History* 14 (Spring 1990): 231-39. Even after the passing of twenty-five years and the recent testimony of second-echelon Soviet figures of the missile crisis, many of the basic issues remain in dispute.

3097. _____. "Courage and Commitment: The Missiles of October." *Foreign Service Journal* 52 (12 1975): 9-11, 24-7. Discusses the missile crisis and the pattern of negotiation conducted by President Kennedy and Soviet Premier Nikita Khrushchev in averting nuclear war.

3098. _____. "The Cuban Missile Crisis." In *Reflections on the Cold War: A Quarter of Century of American Foreign Policy*. Edited by Lynn H. Miller and Ronald Preussen. Philadelphia: Temple University Press, 1974, pp. 108-42. Bernstein questions President Kennedy's misleading statement of October 22, 1962 that Soviet missiles threatened to upset the nuclear balance of power.

3099. _____. "The Cuban Missile Crisis: Trading the Jupiters in Turkey?" *Political Science Quarterly* 95 (Spring 1980): 97-125. New evidence confirms that Kennedy privately offered a hedged promise to Khrushchev on October 27, 1962 to withdraw the Jupiter missiles from Turkey at a future time.

3100. _____. "The Week We Almost Went to War." *Bulletin of the Atomic Scientists* 32 (February 1976): 12-21. Questions whether the threat of nuclear war was as great as it was thought to be during the missile crisis.

3101. Bernstein, Barton J., and Roger Hagan. "Military Value of Missiles in Cuba." *Bulletin of Atomic Scientists* 19 (February 1963): 8-13. Soviet missiles may have been placed in Cuba in order to decentralize Moscow's nuclear power.

3102. Beschloss, Michael R. *The Crisis Years: Kennedy and Khrushchev, 1960-1963*. New York: HarperCollins, 1991. In his well-researched study, Beschloss devotes four chapters to the missile crisis.

3103. Blight, James G. *The Shattered Crystal Ball: Fear and Learning in the Cuban Missile Crisis*. Savage, Md.: Rowman and Littlefield, 1990. An appreciation of the role of fear is an absolutely essential prerequisite to an accurate understanding of why the missile crisis was resolved peacefully.

3104. _____. "Toward a Policy-relevant Psychology of Avoiding Nuclear War: Lessons for Psychologists from the Missile Crisis." *American Psychologist* 42 (January 1987): 12-29. A policy-relevant psychology of avoiding nuclear war must begin by focusing on salient psychological aspects of the prevention and management of nuclear crises.

3105. Blight, James G., Bruce J. Allyn, and David A. Welch. *Cuba on the Brink: Castro, the Missile Crisis, and the Soviet Collapse*. New York: Pantheon Books, 1993. Based largely on the testimony of missile crisis participants and scholars at the Havana Conference of January 1992, the editors argue the importance of Cuba in that crisis and assert that Castro was rational throughout the crisis; moreover, for the first time, it was revealed that Soviets had tactical weapons in Cuba, which would have been used against a U.S. invasion.

3106. _____. "Kramer vs. Kramer: Or, How Can You Have Revisionism in the Absence of Orthodoxy?" *Cold War International History Project Bulletin* 3 (Fall 1993): 41, 47. The authors find Mark Kramer's evidence (see **3151**), which disputes that the Soviet commander was authorized to use tactical nuclear weapons in Cuba, weak.

3107. Blight, James G., Joseph S. Nye, Jr., and David Welch. "The Cuban Missile Crisis Revisited." *Foreign Affairs* 66 (Fall 1987): 170-88. Focuses on the recent disagreement among scholars and former ExComm members regarding the lessons the crisis holds for Americans in 1987.

3108. Blight, James G., and David A. Welch. *On the Brink: Americans and Soviets Reexamine the Cuban Missile Crisis.* New York: Hill and Wang, 1989. An indispensable source book based in part on the dialogue of American and Soviet scholars and participants at the Hawk's Cay and Cambridge conferences of 1987.

3108a. Bostdorff, Denise M. *The Presidency and the Rhetoric of Foreign Crisis.* Columbia: University of South Carolina Press, 1994. Includes a chapter on Kennedy and the missile crisis, which focuses on the way that crisis contributed to structural and legal changes that paved the way for later crisis promotion and management.

3109. Brenner, Philip. "Cuba and the Missile Crisis." *Journal of Latin American Studies* 22 (February 1990): 115-42. The historian's ability to learn from the crisis is fundamentally impaired without a full appreciation of the way Cuba affected the history of this unprecedented confrontation.

3110. _____. "Thirteen Months: Cuba's Perspective on the Missile Crisis." In *The Cuban Missile Crisis Revisited.* Edited by James A. Nathan. New York: St. Martin's Press, 1992, pp. 187-217. Virtually the same article Brenner wrote in 1990.

3111. Brugioni, Dino A. *Eyeball to Eyeball: The Inside Story of the Cuban Missile Crisis.* New York: Random House, 1991. Although not adding to the knowledge of the diplomacy of the crisis, it provides scholars with more information on the intelligence and military side of it.

3112. Brune, Lester H. "The First Day of the Missile Crisis, October 16, 1962." In *John F. Kennedy.* Edited by Paul Harper and Joann P. Krieg, pp. 71-80. No. **1600.** Based on Excomm's transcribed tapes.

3113. _____. *The Missile Crisis of October 1962: A Review of Issues and References.* Claremont, Ca.: Regina Books, 1985. Examination of scholarly studies of the crisis.

3114. Bundy, McGeorge. *Danger and Survival.* No. **2567.** Contains a chapter on the missile crisis from the viewpoint of a participant.

3115. Caldwell, Dan. "The Cuban Missile Affair and the American Style of Crisis

Management." *Parameters* 19 (March 1989): 49-60. Kennedy's handling of the 1962 Cuban missile crisis is a casebook example of the American style of crisis management, which supposedly contains seven elements.

3116. Chang, Laurence, and Peter Kornbluh eds. *The Cuban Missile Crisis, 1962: A National Security Archive Documents Reader.* New York: New Press, 1992. A collection of documents bearing on the missile crisis from the State Department and the Kennedy Library, many of the former obtained through a Freedom of Information Act lawsuit.

3117. Chayes, Abram. *The Cuban Missile Crisis: International Crises and the Role of Law.* New York: Oxford University Press, 1974. Legal adviser to the State Department during the missile crisis reveals how international law shaped the United States response.

3118. _____. "Law and the Quarantine of Cuba." *Foreign Affairs* 41 (April 1963): 550-57. In adopting the quarantine approach against the Soviet Union as approved by the Organization of American States, the United States followed the provisions of the Rio Treaty of 1947 which sanctioned such collective action.

3119. Cline, Ray. "A CIA Reminiscence." *Washington Quarterly* 5 (Autumn 1982): 88-92. The CIA's deputy director for intelligence recalls the discovery of missiles in Cuba.

3120. _____. "Commentary: The Cuban Missile Crisis." *Foreign Affairs* 68 (Fall 1989): 190-96. Cline, CIA deputy director of intelligence from 1962-66, argues that Mikhail Gorbachev's official intellectuals are engaged in selective historical revisionism to serve the Soviet interests--a conclusion drawn from the U.S.-Soviet-Cuban symposium held in Moscow in January 1989.

3121. Crosby, Ralph D., Jr. "The Cuban Missile Crisis: Soviet View." *Military Review* 56 (September 1976): 58-70. Discusses the Soviets' desire to gain a strategic balance of power with the United States in placing nuclear missiles in Cuba in 1962.

3122. Daniel, James, and John G. Hubbell. *Strike in the West: The Complete Story of the Missile Crisis.* New York: Holt, Rinehart, and Winston, 1963. Journalists recount the missile crisis.

3123. Detzer, David. *The Brink: Cuban Missile Crisis, 1962.* New York: Thomas Y. Crowell, 1979. Written in a journalistic style, this work portrays the tension of the missile crisis, as Detzer includes the day-to-day life in the United States, Cuba, and the Soviet Union during that period.

3124. Dinnerstein, Herbert S. *The Making of a Missile Crisis: October 1962.* Baltimore: Johns Hopkins University Press, 1976. Much of the study is based on the contemporary press (*New York Times*, *Pravada*, and *Noticias de Hoy*) of the three major participants.

3125. Divine, Robert A. "Alive and Well: The Continuing Cuban Missile Crisis Controversy." *Diplomatic History* 18 (Fall 1994): 551-60. An excellent review essay that raises questions about the recent testimony of Russian officials and also concludes that as our knowledge of the crisis expands, our perception of the behavior of Kennedy and Khrushchev also changes as well.

3126. _____ , ed. *The Cuban Missile Crisis: The Continuing Debate*. Rev. ed. New York: Markus Wiener Publishers, 1988. A collection of writings by journalists, political analysts, and government officials.

3127. Fulbright, J. William. "Fulbright's Role in the Cuban Missile Crisis." *Inter-American Economic Affairs* 27 (Spring 1974): 86-94. Challenges Dean Rusk's 1973 comment that Senator Fulbright favored all out bombing of Cuba.

3128. Garthoff, Raymond L. "Commentary: Evaluating and Using Historical Hearsay." *Diplomatic History* 14 (Spring 1990): 223-29. In the absence of Soviet documentary records, accounts by Soviet participants are valuable, but they must be treated with appropriate reservations.

3129. _____. "Cuban Missile Crisis: The Soviet Story." *Foreign Policy* 72 (Fall 1988): 61-80. Discloses new information from the Soviet Union, which sometimes significantly changes the previous U.S. understanding of Soviet decisions during the missile crisis.

3130. _____. "The Havana Conference on the Cuban Missile Crisis." *Cold War International History Project Bulletin* (Spring 1992), pp. 1, 3. The Havana Conference of 1992 represented for Castro not only an opportunity to present his views on the 1962 crisis, but also the chance to engage in dialogue with the United States on current issues.

3131. _____. "The Meaning of the Missiles." *Washington Quarterly* 5 (Autumn 1982): 76-82. Based on Garthoff's memoranda of October 27, which emphasized the military dangers and the offensive nature of the missiles in Cuba.

3132. _____. *Reflections on the Cuban Missile Crisis*. Rev. ed. Washington: Brookings Institution, 1989. An adviser on Russian affairs in the State Department during the missile crisis, Garthoff provides, in this comparatively brief account, a well-written study that is based on recently declassified documents and on an emphasis of Soviet motivations.

3133. George, Alexander L. "The Impact of Crisis-Induced Stress on Decision Making." In *Medical Implications of Nuclear War*. Edited by Frederic Solomon and Robert Q. Marston. Washington: National Academic Press, 1986, pp. 529-52.

Important in its application to the missile crisis.

3134. _____. *Presidential Control of Force: The Cuban Missile Crisis*. Santa Monica, Ca.: RAND Corporation, 1967. Force in the missile crisis was used as a refined instrument of coercion and persuasion.

3135. Ghent, Jocelyn Maynard. "Canada, the United States, and the Cuban Missile Crisis." *Pacific History Review* 48 (May 1979): 159-84. The missile crisis heightened differences between the United States and Canadian governments.

3136. Greiner, Bernd. "The Cuban Missile Crisis Reconsidered: The Soviet View: An Interview with Sergo Mikoyan." *Diplomatic History* 14 (Spring 1990): 205-22. Mikoyan--the son of Anastas Mikoyan, Khrushchev's first deputy foreign minister-- was political secretary to his father and a firsthand witness to the missile crisis.

3137. Gribkov, Anatoli I., and William Y. Smith. *Operation Anadyr: U. S. and Soviet Generals Recount the Cuban Missile Crisis*. Chicago: edition q., 1994. An account primarily by General Gribkov who oversaw the deployment of Soviet forces in Cuba in 1962 while William Smith served as an assistant to General Maxwell Taylor at the Joint Chiefs of Staff and in the White House.

3138. Hafner, Donald L. "Bureaucratic Politics and 'Those Frigging Missiles': JFK, Cuba, and U.S. Missiles in Turkey." *Orbis* 21 (Summer 1977): 307-34. Dispels two myths that President Kennedy did not know that U. S. Jupiter missiles were still in Turkey when the Soviets suggested they be removed in a trade-off for their missiles in Cuba and that Kennedy was a prisoner of bureaucratic politics.

3139. Hammarskjold Forum. *The Inter-American Security System and the Cuban Crisis*. Dobbs Ferry, NY: Oceana Publications, 1964. Background papers and proceedings of the Third Hammarskjold Forum, November 1962.

3140. Hampson, Fen Osler. "The Divided Decision-maker: American Domestic Politics and the Cuban Crisis." *International Security* 9 (Winter 1984/85): 130-65. For largely domestic reasons, some sort of military action was deemed essential as a way of handling the missile crisis--the blockade was the most sensible way since it left other military options open.

3141. Herandez, Rafael. "The October 1962 Crisis: Lesson and Legend." *Latinskaya amerika* (January 1988): 58-67. In the context of a confrontation between imperialism and the Third World, the crisis contained the danger of a regional conflict as well as a threat to the entire world. In Russian.

3142. Hershberg, James G. "Before the Missiles of October: Did Kennedy Plan a Missile Strike Against Cuba?" *Diplomatic History* 14 (Spring 1990): 163-98. Recently declassified materials indicate that the United States was making preparations to launch a military invasion against Cuba in late September or early October 1962.

3143. Hilsman, Roger. "The Cuban Crisis: How Close We Were to War." *Look* 28 (August 25, 1964): 17-21. Kennedy's former assistant secretary of state focuses on the startling events of the missile crisis.

3144. Holsti, Ole R. *Crisis, Escalation, War.* Toronto, Ontario: McGill-Queens University Press, 1972. A study of policy making in "high-stress" situations, using the weeks preceding World War I and the Cuban missile crisis as instances of intense international crises.

3145. Horelick, Arnold L. "The Cuban Missile Crisis: An Analysis of Soviet Calculations and Behavior." *World Politics* 16 (April 1964): 363-89. A thoughtful early effort to discern Soviet motivations, suggesting that missiles were deployed to overcome strategic shortcomings.

3146. Johns, Forrest R. "The Naval Quarantine of Cuba, 1962." M.A. thesis, University of California, San Diego, 1984. Proposes to disprove the popular opinion that the crisis could have escalated into a nuclear war and seeks to show that the Kennedy administration knew a great deal more about the deployment of Soviet strategic missiles before October 14, 1962.

3147. Keating, Kenneth. "My Advance View of the Cuban Crisis." *Look* 28 (November 3, 1964): 96, 99-100, 102, 104, 106. Without revealing his source, Keating writes about his warning that Soviet intermediate missiles were in Cuba before October 1962.

3148. Kennedy, Robert. *Thirteen Days: A Memoir of the Cuban Missile Crises*. New York: W. W. Norton, 1969. Based on Robert Kennedy's Journal and published posthumously, this brief account was edited, if not written, by Theodore Sorensen.

3149. Knebel, Fletcher. "In Crisis: 154 Hours on the Brink." *Look* 26 (December 18, 1962): 42-4, 49-50, 52, 54. A leading journalist recounts the day-to-day crisis.

3150. Knox, William E. "Close-up of Khrushchev during a Crisis." *New York Times Magazine* (November 18, 1962), pp. 32, 128-29. Knox, president of Westinghouse Electric, writes about his extraordinary conversation with Khrushchev during the missile crisis.

3151. Kramer, Mark. "Tactical Nuclear Weapons, Soviet Command Authority, and the Cuban Missile Crisis." *Cold War International History Project Bulletin* 3 (Fall 1993): 40, 42-6. Kramer refutes the notion that the commander of Soviet troops had full authority during the missile crisis to launch tactical nuclear strikes against attacking U.S. forces.

3152. Kramer, Mark, Bruce J. Allyn, James G. Blight, and David Welch. "Remembering the Cuban Missile Crisis: Should We Swallow Oral History?" *International Security* 15 (Summer 1990): 212-18. Focuses on the possible pitfalls of relying on the oral testimony of former missile crisis participants.

3153. Larson, David L., ed. *The "Cuban Crisis" of 1962: Selected Documents, Chronology and Bibliography.* Lanham, Md.: University Press of America, 1986. A compilation of important materials on the missile crisis.

3154. Layson, Walter Wells. "The Political and Strategic Aspects of the 1962 Cuban Crisis." Ph.D. diss., University of Virginia, 1969. Examines the interrelationship between the crisis' political and strategic aspects.

3155. Lebow, Richard Ned. "The Cuban Missile Crisis: Reading the Lessons Correctly." *Political Science Quarterly* 98 (Fall 1983): 431-58. The various interpretations of the missile crisis tells us as much about the scholars as it does about Kennedy and Khrushchev.

3156. _____. "Domestic Politics and the Cuban Missile Crisis: The Traditional and Revisionist interpretations Reevaluated." *Diplomatic History* 14 (Fall 1990): 471-92. A close analysis of the crisis--considering American domestic and foreign policy issues, motives on both sides, as well as personalities of both President Kennedy and Nikita Khrushchev--reveals truths and errors in traditional and revisionist interpretations.

3157. _____. "Provocative Deterrence: A New Look at the Cuban Missile Crisis." *Arms Control Today* (July-August 1988), pp. 15-16. Deterrence, as praticed by both superpowers, was provocative instead of preventive.

3158. _____. "Was Khrushchev Bluffing in Cuba?" *Bulletin of the Atomic Scientists* 44 (April 1988): 38-42. Suggests that Khrushchev never intended to send warheads to Cuba.

3159. Leighton, Richard M. *The Cuban Missile Crisis of 1962: A Case in National Security Crisis Management.* Washington: National Defense University, 1978. A case study developed during the 1960s for use by the Industrial College of the Armed Forces.

3160. Lukacs, J. Anthony. "Class Reunion: Kennedy's Men Relive the Cuban Missile Crisis." *New York Times Magazine* (August 30, 1987), pp. 22-7, 51, 58, 61. Coverage of the Hawk's Cay Conference of March 1987, the first of five symposia involving participants and scholars of the missile crisis.

3161. McAuliffe, Mary S., ed. *CIA Documents on the Cuban Missile Crisis.* Washington: Central Intelligence Agency History Staff, 1992. Based on recently declassified documents, which are duplicated for this study.

3162. _____. "Return to the Brink: Intelligence Perspectives on the Cuban Missile Crisis." *SHAFR Newsletter* 24 (June 1993): 4-18. Recent evidence suggests that the missile crisis was more complex and far more dangerous than anyone at the time could appreciate.

3163. Medland, William James. "The American-Soviet Nuclear Confrontation of 1962: An Historiographical Account of the Cuban Missile Crisis." Ph.D. diss., Ball State University, 1980. Examines the works written from the traditionalist's, right-wing revisionist's, left-wing revisionist's, and the Sovietologist's points of view.

3164. _____. *The Cuban Missile Crisis of 1962: Needless or Necessary?* New York: Praeger, 1988. Historiographical examination of the crisis.

3165. Nash, Philip. "Nuisance of Decision: Jupiter Missiles and the Cuban Missile Crisis." *Journal of Strategic Studies* 14 (March 1991): 1-26. Politics played an influential or dominant role in the decisions to send Jupiters to Turkey, to keep them there, and to pull them out.

3166. Nathan, James A., ed. *The Cuban Missile Crisis Revisited.* New York: St. Martin's Press, 1992. Based largely on the resources of the National Security Archive and recently released documents, this anthology includes original essays by Barton Bernstein, Philip Brenner, Raymond Garthoff, and others.

3167. _____. "The Missile Crisis: His Finest Hour Now." *World Politics* 27 (January 1975): 256-81. The "lessons" of the Cuban missile crisis contributed to President Johnson's decision to use airpower against North Vietnam in 1965.

3168. Pachter, Henry M. *Collision Course: The Cuban Missile Crisis and Coexistence.* New York: Praeger, 1963. Study of American-Cuban-Soviet relations during the crisis.

3169. Paper, Lewis J. "The Moral Implications of the Cuban Missile Crisis." *American Scholar* 41 (Spring 1979): 276-83. President Kennedy assumed an awesome and dangerous burden initially designed by the American political system to be shared by Congress and the citzenry.

3170. Paterson, Thomas G. "Commentary: The Defense-of-Cuba Theme and the Missile Crisis." *Diplomatic History* 14 (Spring 1990): 249-56. Khrushchev would never have had the opportunity to install missiles in Cuba if the United States had not been attempting to overthrow the Cuban government.

3171. _____. "The Historian as Detective: Senator Kenneth Keating, The Missiles in Cuba, and His Mysterious Sources." *Diplomatic History* 11 (Winter 1987): 67-9. Keating probably received his information about the Soviet buildup in Cuba from the Cuban exile community and American government officers.

3172. _____. "John F. Kennedy and the Cuban Missile Missile Crisis." *The David A. Sayre History Symposium: Collected Lectures, 1985-1989*. Edited by F. Kevin Simon. Lexington, Ky.: Sayre School, 1991, pp. 217-228. Adapted from Paterson's "Fixation with Cuba" essay in his *Kennedy's Quest for Victory*.

3173. Paterson, Thomas G., and William J. Brophy. "October Missiles and November Elections: The Cuban Missile Crisis and American Politics, 1962." *Journal of American History* 73 (June 1986): 87-119. Dispels the myth that President Kennedy used the missile crisis for political purposes in the congressional elections of November 1962.

3174. Piper, Don C. "The Cuban Missile Crisis and International Law: Precipitous Decline of Unilateral Development." *World Affairs* 128 (Summer 1975): 26-31. One of the by-products of the missile crisis may be the growth and development of the international legal order, not its precipitous decline as other scholars would have it.

3175. Pohlmann, Marcus D. "Constraining Presidents at the Brink: The Cuban Missile Crisis." *Presidential Studies Quarterly* 19 (Spring 1989): 337-46. Examines the role played by the general public in the course of such a crisis and also looks at how that role could be strengthened, given the public's tremendous stake in those decisions.

3176. Pollard, Robert A. "The Cuban Missile Crisis: Legacies and Lessons." *Wilson Quarterly* 5 (Autumn 1982): 148-58. Over the long term no one "won" very much from the missile crisis.

3177. Pomerance, Josephine W. "The Cuban Crisis and the Test Ban Negotiations." *Journal of Conflict Resolution* 7 (September 1963): 553-59. The missile crisis increased the possibility of greater East-West accommodation regarding a nuclear test ban agreement.

3178. Pope, Ronald R., ed. *Soviet Views on the Cuban Missile Crisis: Myth and Reality in Foreign Policy Analysis*. Washington: University Press of America, 1992. A careful reading of Soviet sources suggests some interesting differences among former Soviet participants over past action and motivation.

3179. Riccards, Michael P. "The Dangerous Legacy: John F. Kennedy and the Cuban Missile Crisis." In *John F. Kennedy*. Edited by Paul Harper and Joann P. Krieg, pp. 81-104. No. **1600**. Based largely on secondary sources, it contends that the missile crisis is neither a textbook case of managerial skill nor a good example of how to deal with the Russians.

3180. Rimkus, Raymond Alston. "The Cuban Missile Crisis: A Decision-making Analysis of the Quarantine Policy with Special Emphasis upon the Implications for Decision-making Theory." Ph.D. diss., University of Oklahoma, 1971. Based upon the decision-making approach put forth by Richard C. Snyder, H. W. Bruck, and Burton Sapin.

3181. Ross, Bernard H. "American Government in Crisis: An Analysis of the Executive Branch of Government during the Cuban Missile Crisis." Ph.D. diss., New York University, 1971. Evaluates how the national security machinery in the executive branch had been revamped because of international security demands and how this reorganized structure funtioned during the missile crisis.

3182. Sandman, Joshua Harry. "The Cuban Missile Crisis: Developing a Prescriptive Model for Handling Nuclear Age Crisis." Ph.D. diss., New York University, 1979. There are two distinct aspects to the prescriptive model: One involves developing a general strategy for dealing with nuclear age crises and the other establishes the required decision-making patterns needed to manage nuclear age crises.

3183. Scali, John. "I Was the Secret Go-Between in the Cuban Missile Crisis." *Family Weekly* (October 25, 1964), pp. 4-5, 12-14. The journalist Scali played a key role in the resolution of the missile crisis.

3184. *The Secret Cuban Missile Crisis Documents: Central Intelligence Agency.* Washington: Brassey's (US), 1994. Recently declassified U.S. documents.

3185. Skillern, William Gustaf. "An Analysis of the Decision-making Process in the Cuban Missile Crisis." Ph.D. diss., University of Idaho, 1971. Examines the decision-making process in terms of a theoretical framework adapted from Richard C. Snyder and Glen Page.

3186. Statsenko, Igor D. "On Some Military-Political Aspects of the Caribbean Crisis." *Latinskaya amerika* (November-December 1977): 108-17. The causes of the crisis resulted from the Bay of Pigs invasion and U.S. preparations for invading Cuba again. In Russian.

3187. Steele, John L. "The Adlai Stevenson Affair." *Life* 53 (December 14, 1962): 44-6. Stevenson's defense of the charge, published in a November *Saturday Evening Post* essay by Stewart Alsop and Charles Bartlett, that he wanted a Munich-like settlement of the missile crisis.

3188. Thompson, Robert Smith. *The Missiles of October: The Declassified Story of John F. Kennedy and the Cuban Missile Crisis.* New York: Simon and Schuster, 1992. A clearly written study that is too anti-Kennedy to provide a balanced account; it also ignores the issues and events that followed the crisis.

3189. Trachtenberg, Marc. "Commentary: New Light on the Cuban Missile Crisis?" *Diplomatic History* 14 (Spring 1990): 241-47. Despite the testimony of former Soviet participants, Soviet sources have not provided much hard evidence.

3190. _____. "The Influence of Nuclear Weapons in the Cuban Missile Crisis." *International Security* 10 (Summer 1985): 137-63. Examines three schools of thought on the role that nuclear weapons played in the missile crisis.

3191. _____. "White House Tapes and Minutes of the Cuban Missile Crisis: Introduction to Documents." *International Security* 10 (Summer 1985): 164-203. Contains a transcript of ExComm meetings of October 16, 1962.

3192. Utz, Curtis A. *Cordon of Steel: The U.S. Navy and the Missile Crisis.* Washington: Naval Historical Center, 1993. Shows how the Navy played a pivitol role in the crisis.

3193. Weintal, Edward, and Charles Bartlett. *Facing the Brink: An Intimate Study of Crisis Diplomacy.* New York: Charles Scribner's Sons, 1967. The missile crisis is one of five crises examined.

3194. Welch, David A., and James G. Blight. "The Eleventh Hour of the Cuban Missile Crisis: An Introduction to the ExComm Transcripts." *International Security* 12 (Winter 1987/88): 5-92. Focuses on the McGeorge Bundy's recent transcription of the October 27, 1962 ExComm meeting.

3195. "White House Tapes and Minutes of the Cuban Missile Crisis: ExComm Meetings, October 1962." *International Security* 10 (Summer 1985): 164-203.

3196. White, Mark Jonathan. *The Cuban Missile Crisis.* Houndmills, Basingstoke, United Kingdom: Macmillan, 1995. Critical of JFK's performance before and during the early stages of the missile crisis but argues that Kennedy became more adroit as the crisis went on.

3197. _____. "Belligerent Beginnings: John F. Kennedy on the Opening Day of the Cuban Missile Crisis." *Journal of Strategic Studies* 15 (March 1992): 30-49. At first Kennedy was rash and impulsively hawkish and looked to a military response.

3198. _____. "Dean Rusk's Revelation: New British Evidence on the Cordier Ploy." *Society for Historians of American Foreign Relations Newsletter.* 25 (September 1994): 1-9. British documentation suggests that the Cordier ploy was not as Rusk described it.

3199. _____. "Hamlet in New York: Adlai Stevenson during the First Week of the Cuban Missile Crisis." *Illinois Historical Journal* 86 (Summer 1993): 71-84. A rehabilitation of Stevenson and a clarification of his ideas.

3200. "Who Really Gained in the Cuban Showdown?" *U.S. News and World Report* 53 (November 12, 1962): 42-4, 46. An analysis of the Cuban crisis, including world reaction.

3201. Wilson, Larman C. "International Law and the United States Cuban Quarantine of 1962." *Journal of Inter-American Studies* 7 (October 1965): 485-92. The quarantine was consistent with contemporary realities and the evolving nature of international law and advanced the law's positive transition in that decade.

3202. Wohlstetter, Albert, and Roberta Wohlstetter. *Controlling the Risks in Cuba.* London: Institute for Strategic Studies, 1965. The real problem was that each side tended to project its own psychology and stereotypes about the behavior of the other side.

3203. Wohlstetter, Roberta. "Cuba and Pearl Harbor: Hindsight and Foresight." *Foreign Affairs* 43 (July 1965): 691-707. A comparison of the failure at Pearl Harbor and the Cuban success reveals a good deal about the basic uncertainties affecting the success and failure of intelligence.

Canada

3204. "Canada: Defensive Gap." *Time* 80 (November 9, 1962): 41. Prime Minister Diefenbaker opposes placing nuclear weapons on Canadian soil.

3205. Clark, Gerald. *Canada: The Uneasy Neighbor.* Toronto: David McKay, 1965. Two dominant themes: English Canada vis-à-vis French Canada and Canada as a whole vis-à-vis the United States.

3206. Davis, Jerome D. "To the NATO Review: Constancy and Change in Canadian NATO Policy, 1949-1969." Ph.D. diss., Johns Hopkins University, 1973. An analysis of the change in Canadian attitudes and policy toward NATO from initial enthusiasm to skepticism.

3207. Diefenbaker, John G. *One Canada: Memoirs of the Right Honourable John G. Diefenbaker: The Years of Achievement, 1957-1962.* Toronto: Macmillan of Canada, 1976. Some interesting anecdotes amid Diefenbaker's castigation of Kennedy for insensitivity toward Canada.

3208. _____. *One Canada: Memoirs of the Right Honourable John G. Diefenbaker: The Tumultuous Years, 1962-1967.* Toronto: Macmillan of Canada, 1977. The continuation of the deteriorating relationship with President Kennedy.

3209. "Diefenbaker Falls: Did He Jump or Was He Pushed?" *Newsweek* 61 (February 18, 1963): 33-6. Explores the economic and political relationship between U. S. and Canada and how Diefenbaker's ouster affected that association.

3210. Ghent, Jocelyn Maynard. "Canada, the United States, and the Cuban Missile Crisis." No. **3135.** Provides fresh insight into the dynamics of the United States-Canadian relationship.

3211. _____. "Canadian-American Relations and the Nuclear Weapons Controversy." Ph.D. diss., University of Illinois, 1976. The controversy, provoking a domestic crisis and a grievous dispute with the United States, centered around the question of whether the Diefenbaker government should accept a nuclear role within the American alliance system.

3212. _____. "Did He Fall or Was He Pushed? The Kennedy Administration and the Fall of the Diefenbaker Government." *International History Review* 1 (April 1979): 246-70. The U.S., by the interaction of the Canadian-American military and through the initiative of the ambassador in Ottawa, helped to bring the collapse of the Diefenbaker government.

3213. Granatstein, J. L. *Canada, 1957-1967: The Years of Uncertainty and Innovation.* Toronto: McClelland and Stewart, 1986. Excellent on Kennedy-Diefenbaker differences.

3214. _____. *A Man of Influence: Norman A. Robertson and Canadian Statecraft, 1929-68.* Ottawa: Deneau Publishers, 1981. A biography of the undersecretary of state for external affairs during the Diefenbaker years, which includes a crisis over nuclear arms.

3215. _____. "When Push Came to Shove: Canada and the United States." In *Kennedy's Quest for Victory.* Edited by Thomas Paterson, pp. 86-104. No. **2861a.** Kennedy was the first president in the postwar era to use American muscle with Canada to achieve his ends.

3216. Holmes, John W. "Canada and the United States in World Politics." *Foreign Affairs* 40 (October 1961): 105-17. Explores the changing political relationship between the U. S. and Canada.

3217. Lentner, Howard H. "Foreign Policy Decision Making: The Case of Canada and Nuclear Weapons." *World Politics* 29 (October 1976): 29-66. The decision to accept nuclear weapons from the United States was unusual because it was made by the leader of the opposition, not by the prime minister and his cabinet.

3218. Lyon, Peyton V. *Canada in World Affairs, 1961-1963.* Toronto: Oxford University Press, 1968. Extensive coverage of the Kennedy presidency.

3219. McLin, Jon B. *Canada's Changing Defense Policy, 1957-1963: The Problems of a Middle Power in Alliance.* Baltimore: Johns Hopkins University Press, 1967. Only brief coverage of Kennedy.

3220. Martin, Harold H. "Are the Canadians Still Our Friends?" *Saturday Evening Post* 234 (June 17, 1961): 13-15, 52-3. Explores Canadian nationalism and resentment of American dominance.

3221. Martin, Lawrence. *The Presidents and the Prime Ministers: Washington and Ottawa Face to Face: The Myth of Bilateral Bliss, 1867-1982.* New York: Doubleday, 1982. See the chapter on "The Diefenbaker-Kennedy Schism."

3222. Milsten, Donald Ellis. "Canadian Peace Keeping Policy--A Meaningful Role for a Middle Power." Ph.D. diss., University of Michigan, 1968. Includes Canada's disappointment with its decision-making role in NATO and the UN from the 1940s through the 1960s.

3223. Nash, Knowlton. *Kennedy and Diefenbaker: Fear and Loathing Across the Undefended Border.* Toronto: McClelland and Stewart, 1990. Written by a journalist who knew Kennedy and Diefenbaker personally, this well researched and well written book emphasizes their mutual hostility.

3224. Newman, Peter C. *Renegade in Power: The Diefenbaker Years.* Toronto: McClelland and Stewart, 1963. Written by a journalist who outlines Diefenbaker's stormy relationship with Kennedy.

3225. Pearson, Lester B. *Mike: The Memoirs of the Right Honorable Lester B. Pearson.* Vol. 3. New York: Quadrangle Books, 1975. Briefly covers the warm relationship between Prime Minister Pearson and Kennedy.

3226. Rawlyk, George A. "A Question of 'Self or No Self'": Some Reflexions on the English-Canadian Identity within the Context of Canadian-U. S. Relations." *Humanities Association Review* 30 (4 1979): 281-301. To Canadians, in manner and style the sophisticated Kennedy symbolized the "New Politics," while their leaders were tired, old men who mouthed meaningless platitudes.

3227. Redford, Robert W. *Canada and Three Crises.* Lindsay, Ontario: The Canadian Institute of International Affairs, 1968. Cuba, one of the three covered crises, represented a classic example of the traditional dilemma of Canada's relations with the United States.

3228. Swanson, Roger Frank. "An Analytical Study of the U. S./Canadian Defense Relationship as a Structure, Response and Process: Problems and Potentialities." Ph.D. diss., American University, 1969. Analyzes the American-Canadian defense relationship for three decades since its inception in 1940 to include accumulative Canadian frustration and American irritation.

Europe--General

3229. "The Alliance: Whose Grand Design?" *Newsweek* 61 (February 11, 1963): 17-19. Discusses Kennedy's efforts with Britain, France, Italy, West Germany, and Belgium.

3230. Alsop, Stewart. "The Collapse of Kennedy's Grand Design." *Saturday Evening Post* 236 (April 6, 1963): 78-81. Kennedy's plans are blocked by Charles de Gaulle of France.

3231. Calleo, David P. *Beyond American Hegemony: The Future of the Western Alliance.* New York: Basic Books, 1987. Because of supposed U.S. nuclear vulnerability, the Kennedy administration vigorously reasserted itself with NATO.

3232. Costigliola, Frank. "The Pursuit of Atlantic Community: Nuclear Arms, Dollars, and Berlin." In *Kennedy's Quest for Victory.* Edited by Thomas G. Paterson, pp. 24-56. No. **2861a**. The Kennedy administration talked community but practiced hegemony.

3233. Hartley, Livingston. "Atlantic Partnership--How?" *Atlantic Community Quarterly* 2 (2 1964): 174-85. Since January 1963 the actions of Charles de Gaulle have momentarily destroyed the basis for an Atlantic partnership.

3234. Kaplan, Lawrence S. *NATO and the United States: The Enduring Alliance.* Boston: Twayne, 1988. Covers Kennedy presidency in the context of NATO.

3235. Kissinger, Henry A. *The Troubled Partnership: A Re-appraisal of the Atlantic Alliance.* New York: McGraw Hill, 1965. Sharp disagreements among European allies has undercut Kennedy's Grand Design, a partnership between the United States and a united Europe.

3236. Kleiman, Robert. *Atlantic Crisis: American Diplomacy Confronts A Resurgent Europe.* New York: W. W. Norton, 1964. No setbacks in office, except perhaps the Bay of Pigs, was more disturbing to Kennedy than President de Gaulle's veto of the Amerian design for the Atlantic future.

3237. Kraft, Joseph. *The Grand Design: From Common Market to Atlantic Partnership.* New York: Harper and Brothers, 1962. Reflecting the views of the Kennedy administration, Kraft explains the Grand Design as creative harmony between the United States and Europe for economic, military, and political purposes.

3238. Loeb, Larry M. "Jupiter Missiles in Europe: A Measure of Presidential Power." *World Affairs* 139 (Summer 1976): 27-39. President Eisenhower implemented the Jupiter missile policy and Kennedy terminated it.

3239. Powaski, Ronald E. *The Entangling Alliance: The United States and European Security, 1950-1993.* Westport, Ct.: Greenwood Press, 1994. Includes a chapter on Kennedy, Johnson, and the Grand Design.

3240. Taber, George M. *John F. Kennedy and a Uniting Europe: The Politics of Partnership.* Bruges, Belgium: College of Europe, 1969. Kennedy stamped his own personal mark on a U. S. policy of European integration, proposing a partnership of two separate but equal powers.

3241. "U.S. Failing in Europe?" *U.S. News and World Report* 54 (March 25, 1963): 48-52. A review of U.S. policy failures in Europe.

3242. Von Borch, Herbert. "Amerika und der Europaische Status Quo." ["America and the European Status Quo."] *Aussenpolitik* 15 (2 1964): 81-91. Under President Kennedy U.S. policies took a much more sophisticated and promising turn in favoring "liberalism," not "liberation" of East Europe as a policy goal. In German.

3243. Winand, Pascaline. *Eisenhower, Kennedy, and the United States of Europe.* New York: St. Martin's, 1993. The proponents of European integration, which included George Ball and McGeorge Bundy, helped shape the European policies of the Eisenhower and Kennedy administrations and provided critical support to visionary Europeans like Jean Monnet.

3244. "With the Big Two--Meetings in Europe." *U.S. News and World Report* 50 (June 12,1961): 41-3. Consultations with Macmillan of England and Adenauer of West Germany in Washington and de Gaulle of France in Paris.

Great Britain

3245. "Anger. . .Dismay. . . Suspicion." *U.S. News and World Report* 54 (January 7, 1963): 28. Discusses the negative reactions in London and Paris concerning the agreement between Kennedy and Prime Minister Harold Macmillan to substitute Polaris for Skybolt missiles in Britain.

3246. "Beyond Skybolt." *Time* 80 (December 28, 1962): 13-14. Kennedy's scrapping of the Skybolt project and Prime Minister Macmillan's reaction to it.

3247. Boyd, Laslo Victor. "The Anglo-American Special Relationship and British-European Integration, 1958-1970." Ph.D. diss., University of Pennsylvania, 1971. Examines Britain's relations with the United States and with the European Community in the context of the former's search for a role.

3248. Horne, Alistair. *Harold Macmillan.* Vol. 2. *1957-1986.* New York: Viking, 1989. A full account of Kennedy's special relationship with the British prime minister.

3249. "Jack and Mac." *Time* 77 (April 14, 1961): 26. Focuses on the issues that Kennedy and Macmillan discussed in Washington: NATO, economics, China, Southeast Asia, and atomic testing.

3250. Just, Ward S. "The Scrapping of Skybolt." *Reporter* 28 (April 11, 1963): 19-

21. An analysis of the Skybolt project and the decision not to sell the missiles to Great Britain.

3251. Macmillan, Harold. *At the End of the Day: 1961-1963*. New York: Harper and Row, 1973. Prime Minister Macmillan's account of American-British relations during the last two years of the Kennedy presidency.

3252. _____. *Pointing the Way: 1959-1961*. New York: Harper and Row, 1972. Covers the first year of American-British relations during the Kennedy presidency.

3253. Neustadt, Richard E. *Alliance Politics*. New York: Columbia University Press, 1970. Discussion of U.S.-British relations during the Kennedy administration, including the cancellation of the Skybolt agreement.

3254. Nunnerly, David. *President Kennedy and Britain*. New York: St. Martin's Press, 1972. Anglo-American relations during the Kennedy-Macmillan era.

3255. "Tension Builds Up as Talks Go on." *Business Week* (December 22, 1962), pp. 17-18. Discusses the Kennedy-Macmillan talks in Nassau concerning Britain's and France's desire to possess their own nuclear defense.

France

3256. "Advice De Gaulle Gives Kennedy on Dealing with Khrushchev." *U.S. News and World Report* 50 (June 5, 1961): 39-41. De Gaulle advises Kennedy to concentrate on Berlin and suggests four ways to deal with Khrushchev.

3257. Aron, Raymond. "De Gaulle and Kennedy: The Nuclear Debate." *Atlantic* 210 (August 1962): 33-8. Criticizes Kennedy for wanting better relations with de Gaulle while not giving an inch on French autonomy regarding NATO.

3258. Artaud, Denise. "Le Grand Dessein de J. F. Kennedy: Proposition Mythique du Occasion Manquee?" ["J. F. Kennedy's Grand Design: Myth or Missed Opportunity?"] *Review d' Historie Moderne et Contemporaine* 29 (April-June 1982): 235-66. President Kennedy's design for a new Atlantic partnership was not a myth but a project to reestablish American world leadership and to prevent Western Europe from diverging politically and militarily from the U.S. In French.

3259. Ascoli, Max. "A Meeting of Two Minds." *Reporter* 28 (February 25, 1963): 22-3. An editorial analyzing the relationship between France and the United States.

3260. Costigliola, Frank. "The Failed Design: Kennedy, De Gaulle, and the Struggle for Europe." *Diplomatic History* 8 (Summer 1984): 227-51. Describes the unsuccessful political maneuvering by the Kennedy administration to implement its plan for shaping European developments while redressing a relative decline in U.S. power.

3261. _____. *France and the United States: The Cold Alliance since World War II*. New York: Twayne Publishers, 1992. Costigliola deals critically of Kennedy--and other American leaders--in arguing that while the U.S. sought a loyal follower, France desired to adopt an independent track.

3262. Daniel, Jean. "Kennedy and De Gaulle." *New Republic* 144 (May 29, 1961): 8-9. Discusses the differences between the two leaders.

3263. Gavin, James M. "On Dealing with De Gaulle." *Atlantic Monthly* 215 (June 1965): 49-54. General Gavin discusses his experiences as ambassador to France during the Kennedy administration.

3264. Harrison, Michael M. *The Reluctant Ally: France and Atlantic Security*. Baltimore: Johns Hopkins University Press, 1981. From the French perspective, Harrison deals with the irreconcilable differences between de Gaulle's belief in an independent European defense system and Kennedy's Grand Design.

3265. Laurendeau, Jennifer. "Webs of Influence: Policy Development and Decision Making during the Presidential Transition, 1952 and 1960." Ph.D. diss., Harvard University, 1986. Despite the title, this includes a case study of the Kennedy administration's policy concerning de Gaulle's France, which was subtly guided by long-held negative attitudes.

3266. Luce, Clare Boothe. "Cuba Crisis and Nuclear Arms--Why De Gaulle Goes His Own Way." *U.S. News and World Report* 54 (February 18, 1963): 64-5. Luce analyzes de Gaulle's strategy following the Cuban crisis.

3267. "Measuring Mission." *Time* 71 (June 9, 1961): 9-13. On President and Mrs. Kennedy's trip to Paris and Vienna.

3268. Morris, Richard B. "Our Friendly Quarrel with France." *New York Times Magazine* (April 29, 1962), pp. 12, 97-9. Points out many similarities between France and the U.S. in the face of France's resentment over U.S. domination of NATO.

3269. "New Frontier . . . to the Old World." *Newsweek* 57 (June 5, 1961): 36-8, 41-2, 44. Focuses on President Kennedy's trip to Paris.

3270. Newhouse, John. *De Gaulle and the Anglo-Saxons*. New York: Viking Press, 1970. Kennedy's deteriorating relations with de Gaulle caused him to say that the latter required a certain amount of tension in his association with Washington.

3271. "Why a U.S. Ally Insists on Its Own Nuclear Forces." *U.S. News and World*

Report 53 (September 24, 1962): 70-3. France's mistrust of having NATO nuclear forces in the hands of one commander-in chief.

West Germany and the Berlin Crisis

3272. Barker, Elisabeth. "The Berlin Crisis, 1958-1962." *International Affairs* 39 (1963): 59-73. Instead of pursuing serious negotiations, Khrushchev prefers to use the Berlin problem as a future bargaining chip with the United States on wider issues.

3272a. Brandt, Willy. *My Life in Politics*. London, England: Hamish Hamilton, 1992. The mayor of West Berlin includes his differences with JFK over the Berlin Wall.

3273. Cate, Curtis. *The Ides of August: The Berlin Wall Crisis, 1961*. New York: M. Evans, 1978. An excellent detailed account based on eyewitness interviews and German and other newspapers.

3274. Catudal, Honoré Marc. *Kennedy and the Berlin Wall Crisis: A Case Study in U.S. Decision-making*. Berlin: Berlin-Verlag, 1980. Kennedy's decision not to challenge Khrushchev in his own sphere of influence by intervening in East Berlin represents an example of an American chief executive rising above bureaucratic inertia to play an rational, active, and crucial role in decision-making.

3275. Clay, Lucius. "Berlin." *Foreign Affairs* 41 (October 1962): 47-58. General Clay argues that the United States must remain firm in West Berlin.

3276. Dean, Kevin W. "'We Seek Peace--But We Shall Not Surrender': JFK's Use of Juxtaposition for Rhetorical Success in the Berlin Crisis." *Presidential Studies Quarterly* 21 (Summer 1991): 531-44. Kennedy preserved the peace by constructing a rhetorical wall which the Soviets dared not cross.

3277. Dulles, Eleanor Lansing. *The Berlin Wall: A Crisis in Three Stages*. Columbia, University of South Carolina Press, 1972. Written in the form of a play, Dulles chides the Kennedy administration for relinquishing East Berlin to the Communists in August 1961.

3278. _____. *One Germany or Two: The Struggle at the Heart of Europe*. Stanford, Ca.: Hoover Institution Press, 1970. Deals briefly with the Kennedy administration.

3279. Gelb, Norman. *The Berlin Wall: Kennedy, Khrushchev and a Showdown in the Heart of Europe*. New York: Times Books, 1986. Written by the chief European correspondent for the Mutual Broadcasting Network who was in Berlin at the time.

3280. Hoagland, Steven William. "Operational Codes and International Crises: The Berlin Wall and the Cuban Missile Cases." Ph.D. diss., Arizona State University, 1978. In featuring Kennedy and Khrushchev, Hoagland looks at the significance of a national leader's operational code in determining his actions in an international crisis.

3281. Hyman, Sidney. "The Testing of Kennedy." *New Republic* 145 (October 2, 1961): 11-14. Hyman believes that Kennedy will be able to meet the Berlin challenge.

3282. Keller, John Wendell. *Germany, the Wall and Berlin: International Politics during an International Crisis.* New York: Vantage, 1964. A detailed account from the West German perspective.

3283. McGhee, George. *At the Creation of A New Germany: From Adenauer to Brandt: An Ambassador's Account.* New Haven: Yale University Press, 1989. Recollections of President Kennedy's and President Johnson's ambassador to West Germany.

3284. Mander, John. *Berlin, Hostage for the West.* Westport, Ct.: Greenwood Press, 1962. A brief summation of the Berlin crisis through 1962.

3285. "Meeting the Berlin Threat." *Business Week* (July 29, 1961), pp. 15-19. Kennedy regards Berlin as a global matter.

3286. Morris, Eric. *Blockade: Berlin and the Cold War.* New York: Stein and Day, 1973. Contains a chapter on the Berlin Wall.

3287. Schick, Jack M. *The Berlin Crisis, 1958-1962.* Philadelphia: University of Pennsylvania Press, 1971. Kennedy unintentionally misled Khrushchev, and he in turn miscaluated badly.

3288. Slusser, Robert M. "The Berlin Crisis of 1958 and 1961." In *Force without War: U.S. Armed Forces as a Political Instrument.* Edited by Barry M. Blechman and Stephen S. Kaplan. Washington: Brookings Institution, 1977, pp. 343-439. The United States failure to use force early in the crisis may have encouraged the Soviets to press ahead with its efforts to push the West out of Berlin.

3289. _____. *The Berlin Crisis of 1961: Soviet Relations and the Struggle for Power in the Kremlin, June-November 1961.* Baltimore: Johns Hopkins University Press, 1973. Refutes the allegation that Kennedy was a cold warrior and contends that the Soviet leadership was so badly split over fundamental policy that it was subject to no single unifying force.

3290. Smith, Jean Edward. "Berlin: The Erosion of a Principle." *Reporter* 29

(November 21, 1963): 32-7. Continued problems over Berlin with the Soviets detaining American convoys.

3291. _____. *The Defense of Berlin*. Baltimore: Johns Hopkins Press, 1963. A personal friend of Mayor Willy Brandt of Berlin, Smith believes that the West should have reacted more quickly and more strongly to the building of the Wall.

3292. Stützle, Walther. *Kennedy und Adenauer in der Berlin-Krise, 1961-1962*. Bonn-Bad Godesberg: Forschungsinstitut der Friedrich-Ebert-Stiftung, 1973. The Berlin crisis imposed a strain on the Kennedy-Adenauer relationship, an association troubled by differences in personality and policy. In German.

3293. Wiegele, Thomas C. *Leaders under Stress: A Psychophysiological Analysis of International Crises*. Durham: Duke University Press, 1985. Devotes a chapter to Kennedy and the 1961 Berlin crisis.

3294. Williams, Joan Mildred. "The Use of Berlin as a Rhetorical Symbol in the Presidential Rhetoric of John F. Kennedy, 1961-1963." Ph.D. diss., University of Pittsburgh, 1981.

3295. Windsor, Philip. *City on Leave: A History of Berlin, 1945-1962*. New York: Praeger, 1963. An early history on the Berlin crisis by a British scholar.

3296. Wright, Quincy. "Some Legal Aspects of the Berlin Crisis." *American Journal of International Law* 55 (October 1961): 959-65. From the viewpoint of international law, the West cannot object to Soviet recognition of East Germany, but it should enjoy continuous access, at least civilian, to West Berlin, which would not become legally a part of East Germany.

3297. Wyden, Peter. *Wall: The Inside Story of Divided Berlin*. New York: Simon and Schuster, 1989. A detailed narrative based on extensive interviews with Americans and Germans emphasizing Kennedy's preoccupation with the unprecedented nuclear dangers of the Berlin crisis.

3298. Zolling, Hermann, and Uwe Bahnsen. *Kalter Winter im August: Die Berlin-Krise, 1961-63: Ihre Hintergründe und Folgen*. Oldenburg und Hamburg: Gerhard Stalling Verlag, 1967. See chapter on "Kennedy und die Deutschen." In German.

Other European Nations

3299. Hadian, Ronald Franklin. "United States Foreign Policy toward Spain, 1953-1970." Ph.D. diss., University of California at Santa Barbara, 1976. Among the significant issues explored is the impact of Spanish-Cuban trade relations on the U.S. during the 1960s.

3300. Harrington, Joseph F. "American-Romanian Relations in the 1960s." *New England Social Studies Bulletin* 43 (1985-86): 18-56. The Kennedy-Johnson administrations contrasted sharply with the Eisenhower period as the U. S. began to reach out to Eastern Europe, particularly to Romania.

3301. _____. "Romanian-American Relations during the Kennedy Administration." *East European Quarterly* 18 (June 1984): 215-36. Outlines the events that made it possible for President Kennedy to move toward closer relations with Romania, leading to a trade pact in June 1964.

3302. Kaplan, Stephen S. "United States Aid to Poland, 1957-1964: Concerns, Ojectives, and Obstacles." *Western Political Quarterly* 28 (March 1975): 147-66. As in other areas of foreign policy, the Kennedy administration continued a policy initiated by the Eisenhower administration.

3303. Kennan, George. *Memoirs, 1950-1963*. No. **2847**. Kennan served as Kennedy's ambassador to Yugoslavia.

3304. Korbonski, Andrzej. "East Europe and the United States." *Current History* 56 (April 1969): 201-05, 242-43. Presidents Kennedy and Johnson initiated a new East European policy of bridge building, emphasizing limited aid to Poland and Yugoslavia, relaxation of trade barriers, and educational and cultural exchanges.

3305. Kubricht, A. Paul. "Politics and Foreign Policy: A Brief Look at the Kennedy Administration's Eastern European Diplomacy." *Diplomatic History* 11 (Winter 1987): 55-65. Seeing Eastern Europe as the Achilles' heel of the Soviet Empire, President Kennedy hoped to use economic aid and cultural exchanges as a weapon.

3306. _____. "United States-Czechoslovak Relations during the Kennedy Administration." *East European Quarterly* 23 (September 1989): 355-64. The Kennedy administration policy toward Czechoslovakia suffered the same fate as its policy toward Eastern Europe; initial hopes of an improved relationship collapsed as a result of the cold war escalation in Cuba, Berlin, and Southeast Asia.

3307. Larson, David L. *United States Foreign Policy toward Yugoslavia, 1943-1963*. Washington: University Press of America, 1979. Chronicles the deterioration of U.S. policy following the Belgrade Conference of Non-Aligned Nations of September 1961.

3308. Radvanyi, Janos. "The Problem of Hungary at the United Nations: A Case Study in U.S.-Soviet-Hungarian Relations, 1956-1963." Ph.D. diss., Stanford University, 1971. Analyzes the Hungary question from the revolution in 1956 to the formal recognition of the government by the Kennedy administration.

3309. Roubatis, Yiannis P. "The United States Involvement in the Army and Politics of Greece, 1946-1967." Ph.D. diss., Johns Hopkins University Press, 1981. In the first two decades after World War II, American policy makers were guided by one primary consideration: that a certain stability be brought to Greece that would assist American national interests in that part of the world.

3310. Sturner, William Francis. "Aid to Yugoslavia: A Case Study of the Influence of Congress on Foreign Policy Implementation." Ph.D. diss., Fordham University, 1966. U.S. aid to Yugoslavia from 1950 to 1962 fluctuated with changes in Yugoslav-Soviet relations.

3311. Weeks, Stanley B. "United States Defense Policy toward Spain, 1950-1976." Ph.D. diss., American University, 1977. American policy of ostracism of Fascist Spain shifted dramatically in 1951 when the decision was made to establish U.S. military bases there; by the early 1960s the original purpose of such bases had changed.

Soviet Union

3312. Barnet, Richard. *The Giants: Russia and America*. New York: Simon and Schuster, 1977. The U.S. nuclear superiority could not be harnessed successfully to political goals; it instead became a spur for the Soviets to catch up.

3313. Bartoli, Yvonne Marie. "U.S. Responses to Soviet Violations: Too Little, Too Late?" Ph.D. diss., University of Southern California, 1987. Soviet violations of understandings were dismissed by a Western legalistic approach that excused Soviet behavior and favored accommodation.

3313a. Beschloss, Michael R. *The Crisis Years*. No. **3102**. Written by a free-lance writer, this detailed and important work is particularly good in analyzing the people around Kennedy and Khrushchev.

3314. "Did Khrushchev Win at Vienna?" *U.S. News and World Report* 50 (June 19, 1961): 37-9. On the Kennedy and Khrushchev summit.

3315. Eckhardt, William, and Ralph K. White. "A Test of Mirror-Image Hypothesis: Kennedy and Khrushchev." *Journal of Conflict Resolution* 11 (September 1967): 325-32. Kennedy and Khrushchev were nearly equally aggressive in defining their own nation's sovereignty and equally denunciatory of each other's aggression, dominance, and immorality, according to a value analysis of their public speeches.

3316. Firestone, Bernard J. *The Quest for Nuclear Stability: John F. Kennedy and the Soviet Union*. Westport, Ct.: Greenwood Press, 1982. Concentrating on President Kennedy's last year, this study views Kennedy's détente as both an extension of his predecessors' cold war legacy and as a transition to a more systematic treatment of the inherent ambivalences in U.S.-Soviet relations.

3317. Folts, David William. "The Role of the President and Congress in the Formation of United States Economic Policy towards the Soviet Union, 1947-1968." Ph.D. diss., University of Notre Dame, 1971. Examines the impact of the separation of powers on the development of American economic policy toward the Soviet Union from 1947 to 1968.

3318. Goure, Daniel. "Capabilities and Intentions: Soviet Perceptions of U. S. Strategic Policy, 1945-1980." Ph.D. diss., Johns Hopkins University, 1987. Soviet perceptions of U.S. strategic policy were conditioned by a surprisingly realistic assessment of the constraints within which Washington formulated its course.

3319. Griffith, William E. *The Sino-Soviet Rift*. Cambridge: M.I.T. Press, 1964. The rift was an important phenomenon of the Kennedy era.

3320. Gromyko, Anatolii A. *Through Russian Eyes: President Kennedy's 1036 Days*. Washington: International Library, 1973. Authored by the son of Soviet Foreign Minister Andrei Gromyko.

3321. Gromyko, Andrei. *Memoirs*. New York: Doubleday, 1989. The Soviet foreign minister recalls his various meetings with Kennedy.

3322. Horelick, Arnold L., and Myron Rush. *Strategic Power and Soviet Foreign Policy*. Chicago: University of Chicago Press, 1966. Amply covers the Kennedy presidency.

3323. "Is a U.S. Deal with Russia Near?" *U.S. News and World Report* 55 (July 22, 1963): 27-9. A U.S.-Soviet treaty, covering a range of topics, is in the formative stages.

3324. Kohler, Foy O. *Understanding the Russians: A Citizen's Primer*. New York: Harper and Row, 1970. Written by Kennedy's ambassador to the Soviet Union.

3325. Kress, John Horace. "N. S. Khrushchev's Political Style." Ph.D. diss., University of Washington, 1973. Focuses on the Soviet leader's political style between 1953 and 1964 as the best available means for evaluating his leadership.

3326. Lockwood, Jonathon Samuel. "The Evolution of the Soviet View of U.S. Strategic Doctrine (1954-1976): Its Implications for Future U. S. Strategic Policy Decision-making." Ph.D. diss., University of Miami, 1980. Contends that Soviet analysts consistently projected their own strategic concepts of nuclear warfare and victory onto U.S. strategic doctrine.

3327. McSherry, James E. *Khrushchev and Kennedy in Retrospect*. Palo Alto: Open Door Press, 1971. A dated and uninsightful account of the Khrushchev-Kennedy years.

3328. Morris, Charles R. *Iron Destinies, Lost Opportunities: The Arms Race between the U.S.A. and the U.S.S.R., 1945-1987.* New York: Harper and Row, 1988. Entertainingly written but based only on published sources.

3329. Sidey, Hugh. "What the Ks Really Told Each Other." *Life* 50 (June 16, 1961): 48-9. Snatches of dialogue between Kennedy and Khrushchev.

3330. "What Vienna Revealed." *Business Week* 126 (June 10, 1961): 25-6. Some details on the Kennedy-Khrushchev Vienna meeting.

3331. "When Kennedy Faces Khrushchev. . ." *U.S. News and World Report* 50 (May 29, 1961): 39-40. Background on the upcoming Vienna summit.

3332. "When One Man Sizes Up Another." *Newsweek* 60 (December 3, 1962): 23-4. On the general state of U.S.-Soviet affairs.

Nuclear Test Ban Treaty

3333. Briggs, Philip J. "Kennedy and the Congress: The Nuclear Test Ban Treaty." In *John F. Kennedy.* Edited by Paul Harper and Joann P. Krieg, pp. 35-55. No. **1600**. Kennedy actively and successfully pursued bipartisan senatorial support.

3334. Carroll, George Thompson. "American Presidential Level Public Diplomacy: A Study in Timing and Receptivity." Ph.D. diss., Tufts University, 1989. A study of how Kennedy used public diplomacy at American University to pass the Test Ban Treaty of 1963

3335. Cousins, Norman. *The Improbable Triumvirate: John F. Kennedy--Pope John Paul--Nikita Khrushchev.* New York: W. W. Norton, 1972. An account of the author's role as an intermediary in promoting a rapprochement between the Vatican and the Kremlin and furthering test ban treaty negotiations.

3336. Dean, Arthur H. *Test Ban and Disarmament: The Path of Negotiation.* New York: Harper and Row, 1966. Brief study by President Kennedy's chief negotiator at Geneva and published for the Council on Foreign Relations.

3337. Divine, Robert A. *Blowing in the Wind: The Nuclear Test Ban Debate, 1954-1960.* New York: Oxford University Press, 1978. See epilogue, which covers the Kennedy presidency.

3338. Lepper, Mary Milling. *Foreign Policy Formulation: A Case Study of the Nuclear Test Ban Treaty of 1963.* Columbus, Oh.: Charles E. Merrill, 1971. Analyzes the role of public opinion and interest groups as well as the executive and legislative branches of government in foreign policy formulation.

3339. McBride, James Hubert. *The Test Ban Treaty: Military, Technological, and Political Implications*. Chicago: Henry Regnery, 1967. Analysis of the impact of the treaty on the future security of the United States.

3340. Meyer, Frank S. "Khrushchev-Kennedy Treaty." *National Review* 15 (August 13, 1963): 107. A conservative criticizes the test-ban treaty.

3341. Seaborg, Glenn T. *Kennedy, Khrushchev, and the Nuclear Test Ban*. Berkeley: University of California Press, 1981. Written by the chairman of the U.S. Atomic Energy Commission, Seaborg argues that the achievement of the treaty can be traced in large part to the deep commitment and skilled leadership of President Kennedy.

3342. Terchek, Ronald J. *The Making of the Test Ban Treaty*. The Hague: Martinus Nijhoff, 1970. A study of the roles of the president, Congress, the media, and the public.

Africa

3343. Agyeman-Duah, Baffour. "United States Military Assistance Relationship with Ethiopia, 1953-1977: Historical and Theoretical Analysis." Ph.D. diss., University of Denver, 1984. The military assistance program in Ethiopia stimulated an arms race by that country with Somalia and diverted Ehiopian energies from economic development.

3344. Chaesbulan, F. Usgboaja. "Containment in Africa: From Truman to Reagan." *TransAfrica Forum* 6 (Fall 1988): 7-33.

3345. Chester, Edward W. *Clash of Titans: Africa and U.S. Foreign Policy*. Maryknoll, NY: Orbis Books, 1974. Brief coverage of the Kennedy presidency.

3346. Chilcote, Ronald H. "Angola or the Azores?" *New Republic* 147 (July 30, 1962): 21-2. Discusses the dilemma faced by the U.S. over whether to support independence for Angola and antagonize NATO ally Portugal or stand by Portuagal and anger African nationalists.

3347. Cotman, John W. "South African Strategic Minerals and U. S. Foreign Policy, 1961-1968." *Review of Black Political Economy* 8 (Spring 1978): 277-300. Regardless of the Kennedy administration's verbal attacks on apartheid, South Africa was granted favored nation status during the period despite a U.S. arms embargo.

3348. Davis, John. "Black Americans and United States Policy toward Africa." *Journal of International Affairs* 23 (2 1969): 236-49. Since 1963 it has become more difficult for American blacks to relate to Africa because of the emergence of militant black nationalism in the U. S. and the spread of dictatorships in Africa.

3349. Dickson, David A. "U.S. Foreign Policy toward Southern and Central Africa: The Kennedy and Johnson Years." *Presidential Studies Quarterly* 23 (Spring 1993): 301-16. The author charges that during the Kennedy and Johnson administration certain misperceptions regarding southern and central Africa emerged which had an adverse impact on U.S. policy for the next quarter of a century.

3350. El-Khawas, Mohamed A., and Francis A. Kornegay, Jr. *American-Southern African Relations: Bibliographical Essays.* Westport, Ct.: Greenwood Press, 1975. Scattered references to the Kennedy administration.

3351. Emerson, Rupert. *Africa and the United States Policy.* Englewood Cliffs, NJ: Prentice-Hall, 1967. Summarizes American policy toward Africa from presidents Truman to Johnson.

3352. Gullion, Edmund A. "Crisis Management: Lessons from the Congo." *Crises and Concepts in International Affairs* (April 1965): 49-63. Written by Kennedy's ambassador to the Congo for the sixth annual meeting of the International Studies Association.

3353. Gurtov, Melvin. *The United States Against the Third World: Antinationalism and Intervention.* New York: Praeger, 1974. Contains a chapter on Kennedy and Africa.

3354. Hamburger, Robert Lee. "Franco-American Relations, 1940-1962: The Role of United States Anticolonialism and Anticommunism in the Formulation of United States Policy on the Algerian Question." Ph.D. diss., University of Notre Dame, 1971. Anticommunism was more influential than the evils of colonialism in developing an American policy for Algeria.

3355. Holder, Calvin B. "Racism toward Black African Diplomats during the Kennedy Administration." *Journal of Black Studies* 14 (1 1983): 31-48. Kennedy worked to stop discrimination against black African diplomats along Route 40 in Maryland and throughout the South.

3356. Howe, Russell Warren. *The African Revolution.* New York: Barnes and Noble, 1969. Written by a *Washington Post* journalist who covered the African revolution and treated Kennedy's policies even handedly.

3357. _____. *Along the Afric Shore: An Historic Review of Two Centuries of U.S.-African Relations.* New York: Barnes and Noble, 1975. Good summation of U.S. relations with African countries during the Kennedy period.

3358. Isaacman, Allen, and Jennifer Davis. "United States Policy toward Mozambique since 1945." *Africa Today* 25 (January-March 1978): 29-55. Despite an initial anticipation of change, Kennedy's presidency brought only a slight and temporary shift in U.S. policy since the U.S. did not wish to alienate Portugal, a NATO ally.

3359. Jackson, Henry F. *From the Congo to Soweto: U.S. Foreign Policy toward Africa since 1960*. New York: William Morrow, 1982. Takes a favorable view of Kennedy's African foreign policy, emphasizing the departures from previous policies.

3360. James, Elizabeth Mathis. "State Department Adaptation to Independent Africa, 1952-1962: A Study in Thought and Practice." Ph.D. diss., George Washington University, 1968. Partly based on interviews with fifty-two foreign affairs practitioners who were active in African affairs during the period from 1952 through 1962.

3361. Kalb, Madeleine. *The Congo Cables: The Cold War in Africa from Eisenhower to Kennedy*. New York: Macmillan, 1982. A well researched and fair minded work that reveals the problems of a chaotic country, U.S. hostility to the left, and Kennedy's openness to the Third World.

3362. McKay, Vernon. *Africa in World Politics*. Westport, Ct.: Greenwood Press, 1963. Includes a brief account of U.S. policy toward Africa during the Kennedy years.

3363. Mahoney, Richard D. *JFK: Ordeal in Africa*. New York: Oxford University Press, 1983. Based heavily on the manuscript materials at the Kennedy library, well researched, and judiciously argued, this is probably the best book on Kennedy and Africa.

3364. Metzmeier, Kurt Xavier. "John F. Kennedy, Ghana and the Volta River Project: A Study in American Foreign Policy towards Neutralist Africa." M.A. thesis, University of Louisville, 1989. An example of Kennedy seeking to win over neutralist Africa.

3365. Nielsen, Waldemar A. *The Great Powers and Africa*. New York: Praeger, 1969. The Kennedy administration altered basic U.S. policy toward Africa far less than is commonly supposed.

3366. Noer, Thomas. *Cold War and Black Liberation: The United States and White Rule in Africa, 1948-1968*. Columbia: University of Missouri Press, 1985. One chapter title summarizes Noer's conclusions about Kennedy's African policies: "New Frontiers and Old Priorities."

3367. _____. "The New Frontier and African Neutralism: Kennedy, Nkrumah, and the Volta River Project." *Diplomatic History* 8 (Winter 1984): 61-80. Kennedy's decision to fund the Volta project was made reluctantly and only after

Nkrumah was forced to accept, at least verbally, certain principles in economics, politics, and international relations.

3368. _____. "New Frontiers and Old Priorities in Africa." In *Kennedy's Quest for Victory*. Edited by Thomas G. Paterson, pp. 253-83. No. **2861a**. Kennedy's sustained interest in Africa and his effective personal diplomacy altered dramatically the style of United States relations with the continent, even though the substance was largely unchanged.

3369. Ohaesbulam, F. Usgboaja. "Containment in Africa: From Truman to Reagan." *TransAfrica Forum* 6 (Fall 1988): 7-33. Kennedy's rapprochement with Africa was short-lived as U. S. security requirements received their traditional, political, and strategic considerations.

3370. Orwa, D. Katete. "Responses of the United Nations and the United States to the Congo Crisis: Events and Issues." Ph.D. diss., University of Akron, 1979. In covering the period from July 1960 to January 1962, this study concludes that factionalism within the administration and opposition in Congress led to the Kennedy administration's ambivalence and caution to the Congo crisis.

3371. Seikman, Philip. "Edgar Kaiser's Gamble in Africa." *Fortune* 64 (November 1961): 128-31, 199-206. Describes the efforts of Edgar Kaiser of Kaiser Industries to aid, with the help of two American presidents, the State Department, the World Bank, and U.S. taxpayers, the president of Ghana's hydroelectric project on the Volta River.

3372. Struelens, Michael. "ONUC and International Politics." Ph.D. diss., American University, 1968. Examines the role of the United Nations in the Congo crisis of 1960 which continued into the Kennedy presidency.

3373. Volman, Daniel Henry. "United States Foreign Policy and the Decolonization of British Central Africa, 1945-1965." Ph.D. diss., University of California at Los Angeles, 1991. Includes an examination of Kennedy's policies concerning the decolonization of British Central Africa.

3374. Walters, Ronald William. "The Formulation of United States Foreign Policy toward Africa, 1958-1963." Ph.D. diss., American University, 1971. A case study of Katanga and the Congo crisis, the U.S. arms embargo against South Africa, the U.S. role in settling the Franco-Algerian War, and U.S. relations with Guinea, along with an analysis regarding the variations in approaches between the Eisenhower and Kennedy administrations.

3375. Weissman, Stephen R. *American Policy in the Congo, 1960-1964*. Ithaca: Cornell University Press, 1974. Account of American response to the Katanga secession crisis.

3376. Williams, G. Mennen. *Africa for the Africans*. Grand Rapids, Mi.: William B. Eerdmans, 1969. A personal narrative by President Kennedy's assistant secretary of state for Africa, which emphasizes the African independence movement and America's role.

3377. Williams, Michael Wayne. "America and the First Congo Crisis, 1960-1963." Ph.D. diss., University of California at Irvine, 1991. Whereas Eisenhower believed that the Afro-Asian bloc was an obstacle, which had to be overcome in bringing about a successful revolution to the Congo crisis, Kennedy thought that courting the Afro-Asians would result in continuing support for the UN's Congo operation.

Middle East

3378. Ashur, George Arthur. "The Kennedy-Nasir Correspondence: A Policy of Accommodation." Ph.D. diss., Harvard University, 1991. Examines the personal and public correspondence of Kennedy and Nasser and its impact on public policy concerning Egypt.

3379. Badeau, John S. *The American Approach to the Arab World*. New York: Harper and Row, 1968. Written by Kennedy's ambassador to Egypt, it touches on Kennedy administration policies throughout the Arab world.

3380. _____. *The Middle East Remembered*. Washington: Middle East Institute, 1983. Covers his ambassadorship to Egypt, including some interesting anecdotes about Kennedy.

3381. Ball, George W. "The Coming Crisis in Israeli-American Relations." *Foreign Affairs* 58 (Winter 1979-80): 231-56. Kennedy's undersecretary of state traces U.S.-Israeli relations from the 1950s.

3382. Barbarash, Ernest, comp. *John F. Kennedy on Israel*. No. **15**. A compilation of statements that Kennedy made on Israel and Jews from the 1950s into 1963.

3383. Bickerton, Ian J. "John F. Kennedy, the Jewish Community and Israel: Some Preliminary Observations." *Australasian Journal of American Studies* 2 (December 1983): 32-43. Kennedy, although bringing a distinct style to the White House, did not attempt to alter significantly the direction of United States policy toward Israel.

3384. Bill, James A. *The Eagle and the Lion: The Tragedy of American-Iranian Relations*. New Haven: Yale University Press, 1988. Kennedy's reform policy entangled Americans more deeply in Iran's affairs, leading to the shah's repression that soon followed.

3385. Burns, William J. *Economic Aid and American Policy toward Egypt, 1955-1981*. Albany: State University of New York Press, 1985. Despite expanded U.S.

food-aid shipments, President Kennedy failed to sustain improved relations with Egypt as the result of Nasser's intervention in Yemen and the Egyptian military buildup.

3386. Bustami, Zaha. "The Kennedy/Johnson Administrations and the Palestinians." *Arab Studies Quarterly* 12 (Winter/Spring 1990): 101-20. Despite the sincerity of Kennedy's effort to resolve the refugee problem, his initiative remained secondary to other American interests in the region.

3387. Farzanegan, Bahram. "United States Response and Reaction to the Emergence of Arab and African States in International Politics." Ph.D. diss., American University, 1966. The United States has assumed a bewildering array of responsibilities and has made extensive commitments to these new nations.

3388. Fishburne, Charles Carroll. "United States Policy toward Iran, 1959-1963." Ph.D. diss., Florida State University, 1964. Kennedy's policy differed in emphasis from Eisenhower's.

3389. Fuchs, Lawrence. "JFK and the Jews." *Moment* 9 (June 1983): 22-8. Kennedy was unequivocally pro-Israel; consequently, it is likely that had he run against Goldwater in 1964 he would have matched the more than 90 percent of the Jewish vote that Roosevelt had won some twenty years earlier.

3390. Gazit, Mordechai. *President Kennedy's Policy toward the Arab States and Israel.* Tel Aviv: Shiloah Center for Middle Eastern and African Studies, 1983. By a former attaché at the Israeli embassy in Washington during the Kennedy administration.

3391. Ghassemi, Ali. "U.S.-Iranian Relationships, 1953-1978: A Case Study of Patron-Client State Relationships." Ph.D. diss., University of Oklahoma, 1988. After the coup in 1953, Iran became an American client-state and joined the cold war alliance system.

3392. Goode, James. "Reforming Iran during the Kennedy Years." *Diplomatic History* 15 (Winter 1991): 13-29. Kennedy administration policy toward Iran set in motion a chain of events that ultimately brought about the Iranian revolution of 1978.

3393. Kenen, Isaiah L. *Israel's Defense Line: Her Friends and Foes in Washington.* Buffalo: Prometheus Books, 1981. Written by the founder of the American Israel Public affairs Committee.

3394. Kerr, Malcom. "'Coming to Terms with Nasser': Attempts and Failures." *International Affairs* 43 (1967): 65-84. An analysis of the causes of breakdown in relations between Egypt and the United States and Great Britain from 1952 to 1966 with Kerr exhibiting no understanding of Kennedy's relationship with Nasser.

3395. Little, Douglas. "From Even-Handed to Empty-Handed: Seeking Order in the Middle East." In *Kennedy's Quest for Victory*. Edited by Thomas G. Paterson, pp. 156-77. No. **2861a**. Kennedy's even-handed solution to the Mideast proved difficult to sustain because he was unable to enlist the support of several key players.

3396. _____. "The New Frontier on the Nile: JFK, Nasser, and Arab Nationalism." *Journal of American History* 75 (September 1988): 501-27. Despite Kennedy's acceptance of Egyptian neutrality and his largely successful personal diplomacy, Kennedy was unable to keep Egypt out of the larger struggles of the Arab world and thus lost Nasser in the end.

3397. McMullen, Christopher J. *Resolution of the Yemen Crisis, 1963*. Washington: Institute for the Study of Diplomacy, 1980. Excellent on President Kennedy's emissary, Ellsworth Bunker, who mediated the resolution of the Yemen crisis involving Nasser and Faisal.

3398. Peretz, Don. "The United States, the Arabs, and Israel: Peace Efforts of Kennedy, Johnson, and Nixon." *Annals of the American Academy of Political and Social Science* 401 (1972): 116-25. Not since the Kennedy presidency have both sides had confidence in the United States, but Kennedy's efforts to break the impasse also failed.

3399. Perry, Glenn Earl. "United States Relations with Egypt, 1951-1963: Egyptian Neutralism and the American Alignment Policy." Ph.D. diss., University of Virginia, 1964. Perry explains that Americans dislike of neutralism was the major reason for the deterioration of U.S.-Egyptian relations during the period.

3400. Rubin, Barry. *Paved with Good Intentions: The American Experience and Iran*. New York: Oxford University Press, 1980. Deals with Kennedy's efforts to shift the shah's preoccupation from military security to economic progress.

3401. Schmidt, Dana. *Yemen: The Unknown War*. New York: Holt, Rinehart and Winston, 1968. Includes Kennedy's involvement in the Yemen controversy.

3402. Spiegel, Steven. *The Other Arab-Israel Conflict: Making America's Middle East Policy, from Truman to Reagan*. Chicago: University of Chicago Press, 1985. By Kennedy's death, the fear of falling Arab dominoes and Nasser's own limitations had undermined Kennedy's Egypt-first strategy.

3403. Stivers, William. *America's Confrontation with Revolutionary Change in the Middle East, 1948-83*. New York: St. Martin's Press, 1986. While Kennedy felt far stronger sympathies for Third World nationalism than Eisenhower, he was even more strongly committed to preserving the Western position through military force.

3404. Stookey, Robert W. *America and the Arab States: An Uneasy Encounter*. New

York: John Wiley, 1975. The Kennedy administration pursued much the same aims in the Arab states as its predecessor.

3405. Tivnan, Edward. *The Lobby: Jewish Political Power and American Foreign Policy.* New York: Simon and Schuster, 1987. Although American Jews supported Kennedy, they were not always pleased with his Middle East policy.

China

3406. Bachrack, Stanley. *The Committee of One Million: "China Lobby" Politics, 1953-1971.* New York: Columbia University Press, 1976. Covers the activities of the Committee, including its opposition of Communist China to the United Nations, during the Kennedy presidency.

3407. Chang, Gordon H. "JFK, China, and the Bomb." *Journal of American History* 74 (March 1988): 1287-1310. Kennedy actively pursued the possibility of taking military action with the Soviet Union against China's nuclear installations.

3408. Chen, Chin-yuen. "American Economic Policy toward Communist China, 1950-1970." Ph.D. diss., Columbia University, 1972. Examines the efficacy of the American trade embargo against China from 1950-1970.

3409. Clubb, Oliver E., Jr. *The United States and the Sino-Soviet Bloc in Southeast Asia.* Washington: Brookings Institution, 1963. An account of power-bloc competition in Southeast Asia.

3410. Cohen, Warren I. *America's Response to China: An Interpretative History of Sino-American Relations.* New York: John Wiley, 1980. Brief coverage of the Kennedy presidency.

3411. _____. "The United States and China since 1945." In *New Frontiers in American-East Asia Relations: Essays Presented to Dorothy Borg.* Edited by Warren I. Cohen. New York: Columbia University Press, 1983, pp. 129-67. Little on Kennedy's policies to suggest that he was interested in seeking accommodation with Communist China.

3412. Colombo, Claudius Michael. "Chinese Communist Perceptions of the Foreign Policy of John F. Kennedy." Ph.D. diss., New York University, 1982. Examines the adversarial foreign policy of the Kennedy administration toward the People's Republic of China and how China used hostility toward the U.S. to divert attention from economic difficulties.

3413. Dulles, Foster Rhea. *American Policy toward Communist China, 1949-1969.* New York: Thomas Y. Crowell, 1972. Late in his presidency Kennedy wanted to break new ground in the United States approach to Communist China.

3414. Fetzer, James. "Clinging to Containment: China Policy." In *Kennedy's Quest for Victory*. Edited by Thomas G. Paterson, pp. 178-97. No. **2861a.** Kennedy believed that China was in a "Stalinist" phase of development, comparable to Soviet aggressiveness in the 1940s.

3415. Gordon, Leonard H. D. "United States Opposition to the Use of Force in the Taiwan Strait, 1954-1962." *Journal of American History* 72 (December 1985): 637-60. Kennedy did not alter Eisenhower's policy regarding the Taiwan Strait.

3416. Lampton, David M. "The U.S. Image of Peking in Three International Crises." *Western Political Quarterly* 26 (March 1973): 28-50. A study of three crises to include Laos (1961-62) to determine the images of the Chinese held by U.S. policymakers.

3417. MacFarquhar, Roderick, ed. *Sino-American Relations, 1949-1971*. New York: Praeger, 1972. Good especially on China's comments on Kennedy policy.

3418. "Meeting No. 103: A Civil Tongue." *Newsweek* 57 (March 20, 1961): 50. Kennedy testing the waters for improved Sino-U.S. relations, while declaring a firm stance.

3419. Sigal, Leon V. "The 'Rational Policy' Model and the Formosa Straits Crisis." *International Studies Quarterly* 14 (1970): 121-56. In including the Formosa crisis of 1962, the author attempts to explain Chinese actions through criticism of the "rational policy" model of events.

3420. Thomson, James C. Jr. "On the Making of U.S. China Policy, 1961-1969: A Study of Bureaucratic Politics." *China Quarterly* 50 (April/June 1972): 220-43. Following the missile crisis, efforts to undertake small unilateral initiatives toward China--most notably relating to the travel ban--were regularly rejected on the ground that they might jeopardize the process of Soviet-American rapprochement.

3421. Vinson, J. Chal. "The United States and China." *Current History* 43 (November 1962): 290-94. Kennedy was faced with containing Communist China while finding a more flexible approach to open relations with that country.

3422. Young, Kenneth T. "American Dealings with Peking." *Foreign Affairs* 45 (1966): 77-87. An evaluation of ambassadorial talks held at Geneva and Warsaw from 1955 to 1966 between China and the United States.

3423. _____. *Negotiating with the Chinese Communists: The United States Experience, 1953-1967*. New York: McGraw-Hill, 1968. John Kennedy remained disturbed and baffled by Peking's instant and constant antagonism toward him and his administration.

South Asia

3424. Ahmad, Bashir. "The Politics of the Major Powers toward the Kashmir Dispute, 1947-1965." Ph.D. diss., University of Nebraska, 1972. Provides a comprehensive analysis of the politics of the United States, the USSR, the United Kingdom, France, and the People's Republic of China toward the Kashmir dispute.

3425. Alam, Mohammed Badrul. "Between Conflict and Rapproachment: Indo-American Relations, 1961-1963, an Examination of Selected Events." Ph.D. diss., Cornell University, 1990. A study of U.S.-Indian relations during the Kennedy presidency.

3426. Barnds, William J. *India, Pakistan, and the Great Powers.* New York: Praeger, 1972. In retrospect, the Kennedy administration placed too much credence on the arguments of neutralist leaders that their anti-Western attitudes were a reaction to specific Western policies and actions.

3427. Brecher, Michael. "Non-Alignment under Stress: The West and the India-China Border War." *Pacific Affairs* 52 (Winter 1979-80): 612-30. Kennedy moved cautiously regarding India's request for military assistance during the border war.

3428. Chakravarti, P. C. "Indian Non-alignment and United States Policy." *Current History* 44 (March 1963): 129-34, 179. Despite U.S. disapproval of India's nonalignment policy, the period from 1956 to 1963 saw a strengthening of ties between the two nations.

3429. Chary, Srinivas M. "Kennedy and Nonalignment: An Analysis of Indo-American Relations." In *John F. Kennedy.* Edited by Paul Harper and Joann P. Krieg, pp. 119-30. No. **1600**. Kennedy's India policy represented a considerable break from the Eisenhower presidency.

3430. Choudhury, G. W. *India, Pakistan, Bangladesh, and the Major Powers: Politics of a Divided Subcontinent.* New York: Free Press, 1975. While Kennedy moved closer to India, he antagonized Pakistan, which improved relations with China.

3431. Gopal, Sarvepalli. *Jawaharlal Nehru: A Biography, III: 1956-1964.* Cambridge: Harvard University Press, 1984. Good on Nehru-Kennedy relationship.

3432. Harrison, Selig S. "South Asia and U.S. Policy." *New Republic* 145 (December 11, 1961): 11-16. The Indo-Chinese conflict offered a momentous opportunity for the consolidation of closer U.S. ties with India; yet it also heightened Indian solicitude for the Soviet Union as a natural ally.

3433. Irshad Khan, Shaheen. *Rejection Alliance? A Case Study of U.S. Pakistan Relations (1947-1967).* Lahore: Ferozsons, 1972. Written by a Pakistani political scientist, it describes the deterioration of U.S.-Pakistani relations during the Kennedy presidency.

3434. Jain, B. J. "The Kennedy Administration's Policy towards Colonialism: A Case Study of Goa, 1961 in the Indian Context." *Indian Journal of American Studies* 14 (July 1984): 145-54. Kennedy opposed reprisals against India after the seizure of Goa.

3435. Khan, Mohammed Ayub. "The Pakistan-American Alliance: Stesses and Strains." *Foreign Affairs* 42 (January 1964): 195-209. Reasons why Pakistan objects to the U.S.'s military and increased economic assistance to India.

3436. Loomba, Joanne F. "U.S. Aid to India, 1951-1967: A Study in Decisionmaking." *India Quarterly* 28 (October-December 1972): 304-31. A study of American foreign aid to India, which indicates that American policymakers gave little attention to the idea of demanding either domestic political changes or modifications in foreign policy on India's part as prerequisites to receiving U. S. assistance.

3437. McMahon, Robert J. "Choosing Sides in South Asia." In *Kennedy's Quest for Victory*. Edited by Thomas G. Paterson, pp. 198-222. No. **2861a**. Kennedy failed to achieve his policy objectives because his actions rested on a number of dubious assumptions, foremost of which was the belief that the United States could have friendly relations with both India and Pakistan.

3437a. _____. *The Cold War on the Periphery: The United States, India, and Pakistan*. New York: Columbia University Press, 1994. Contains a chapter on the Kennedy foreign policy, which was based on McMahon's earlier work.

3438. Maga, Timothy P. "The New Frontier v. Guided Democracy: JFK, Sukarno, and Indonesia, 1961-1963." *Presidential Studies Quarterly* 20 (Winter 1990): 91-102. Although Kennedy saw Sukarno as vain, intellectually limited, and troublesome, he continued a diplomatic dialogue to prevent a Communist threat should Sukarno fall.

3439. Merrill, Dennis. *Bread and the Ballot: The United States and India's Economic Development, 1947-1963*. Chapel Hill: University of North Carolina Press, 1990. The first historical analysis of Indo-American relations based largely on recently declassified United States government documents, it amply covers the Kennedy period.

3440. Raziq, Abdur. "China as an Irritant in Pak-U.S. Relations, 1962-68." *Pakistan Journal of American Studies* 9 (Spring-Fall 1991): 89-105. Pakistan was forced to seek close ties with China after the Kennedy administration began to arm India.

3441. Ripley, Randall B. "Interagency Committees and Incrementalism: The Case of Aid to India." *Midwest Journal of Political Science* 8 (May 1964), pp. 143-65. A study of the interagency committees in the U. S. government regarding economic aid to India from 1951 through 1962.

3442. Singh, Mahendra. *Indo-U.S. Relations, 1961-64.* Shahdara, Delhi: Sidhu Ram, 1982. The early promise of the Kennedy presidency did not result in a major change in U. S.-Indo relations.

3443. "Visitor with a Question." *Newsweek* 58 (July 17, 1961): 38. The Pakistani president was upset at Kennedy's closer relations with India.

3444. Weaver, David Roll. "Public Law 480, India, and the Objectives of United States Foreign Aid, 1954-1966." Ph.D. diss., University of Cincinnati, 1971. Despite U. S. foreign aid to India from 1954 to 1966, America's ability to influence Indian behavior was limited.

Laos

3445. "Another 'Korea' in Laos?" *U. S. News and World Report* 50 (April 3, 1961): 42-7. Assesses the positions of Khrushchev and Kennedy in Laos.

3445a. Castle, Timothy N. *At War in the Shadow of Vietnam: Military Aid to the Royal Lao Government, 1955-1975.* New York: Columbia University Press, 1993. Briefly surveys the Kennedy era and the 1962 Geneva agreements.

3445b. Dommen, Arthur J. *Conflict in Laos: The Politics of Neutralization.* New York: Praeger, 1964. The Kennedy administration skillfully restored the "bridge of confidence" with neutralist leader Souvanna Phouma.

3446. Goldstein, Martin E. *American Policy toward Laos.* Cranbury, NJ: Associated University Presses, 1973. Covers the Kennedy presidency in some detail.

3447. Greenstein, Fred I., and Richard H. Immerman. "What Did Eisenhower Tell Kennedy about Indochina? The Politics of Misperception." *Journal of American History* 79 (September 1992): 568-87. Contradictory summations of what was said between Eisenhower and Kennedy at the January 19, 1961 meeting provides vivid evidence of misperception and miscommunication, even among experienced, sophisticated leaders.

3448. Hannah, Norman B. *The Key to Failure: Laos and the Vietnam War.* Lanham, Md.: Madison Books, 1987. Study of the Geneva Accords regarding Laos as a "critical limiting factor" on America's ability to fight the war in Vietnam.

3449. Hill, Kenneth L. "President Kennedy and the Neutralization of Laos." *Review of Politics* 31 (July 1969): 353-69. After questioning the wisdom of Eisenhower's commitments, Kennedy decided to neutralize Laos; by increasing military assistance to South Vietnam, he doomed the 1962 Laotian agreement to failure.

3450. Karnow, Stanley. "Laos: The Settlement That Settled Nothing." *Reporter* 28 (April 25, 1963): 34-7. An analysis of the political forces at work that will prevent the neutrality settlement from working.

3451. Kerby, Robert L. "American Military Airlift during the Laotian Civil War, 1958-1963." *Aerospace History* 24 (March 1977): 1-10. The Laotian operation suggests that Kennedy's appreciation of the uses of conventional forces was more subtle and sophisticated than some historians admit.

3452. Mahajani, Usha. "President Kennedy and United States Policy in Laos, 1961-63." *Journal of Southeast Asian Studies* 2 (September 1971): 87-99. It was to Kennedy's credit that his pragmatism restrained him from making Laos a battleground, but he negated his achievement by continuing after July 1962 the same policies Eisenhower followed after the Geneva Agreement of 1954.

3453. Mirsky, Jonathan, and Stephen E. Stonefield. "The United States in Laos, 1945-1962." In *America's Asia: Dissenting Essays on Asian-American Relations.* Edited by Edward Friedman and Mark Selden. New York: Pantheon Books, 1971, pp. 253-323. American anti-communism in Laos has for years subordinated Lao nationalism to Washington's "interests."

3454. Patrick, Richard. "Presidential Leadership in Foreign Affairs Reexamined: Kennedy and Laos without Radical Revisionism." *World Affairs* 140 (Winter 1978): 245-58. Despite what revisionists have written, Kennedy's response to the Laotian crisis was calm, restrained, and realistic instead of militant and strident.

3455. Pelz, Stephen. "'When Do I Have Time to Think?' John F. Kennedy, Roger Hilsman, and the Laotian Crisis of 1962." *Diplomatic History* 3 (Spring 1979): 215-29. Based on an interesting memo of May 1962 by Roger Hilsman recounting the decision-making process whereby Kennedy sent the Seventh Fleet to the Gulf of Siam and troops to Thailand, contributing to the warring Laotian parties reaching a compromise position.

3456. Stevenson, Charles A. *The End of Nowhere: American Policy toward Laos since 1954.* Boston: Beacon Press, 1972. Probably the most reliable summary of the Kennedy administration approach.

Vietnam

3457. Ball, Moya Ann. "A Case Study of the Kennedy Administration's Decision-making Concerning the Diem Coup of November 1963." *Western Journal of Speech Communication* 54 (Fall 1990): 557-74. Decision-making by the American government on whether to support the insurgent generals in their coup was characterized by conflict, confusion, and vacillation.

3458. _____. "A Descriptive and Interpretive Analysis of the Small Group Communication of Presidents Kennedy, Johnson and Their Key Advisers Concerning the Decisions from January 1965 to Expand the Vietnam War." Ph.D. diss., University of Minnesota, 1988. Analyzes the written and spoken words of Kennedy to understand his decision to escalate the war.

3459. Baritz, Loren. *Backfire: A History of How American Culture Led Us into the Vietnam War and Made Us Fight the Way We Did.* New York: William Morrow, 1985. The New Frontier, for all its recoil from the overheated, moralistic rhetoric of Secretary of State John Foster Dulles, shared a worldview similar to the one it ridiculed.

3460. Bassett, Lawrence J., and Stephen E. Pelz. "The Failed Search for Victory: Vietnam and the Politics of War." In *Kennedy's Quest for Victory.* Edited by Thomas G. Paterson, 223-52. No. **2861a**. Kennedy had bequeathed to President Johnson a failing counterinsurgency program and a deepened commitment to the war in South Vietnam.

3461. Beck, Kent M. "The Kennedy Image: Politics, Camelot, and Vietnam." *Wisconsin Magazine of History* 58 (December 1974): 45-55. As Vietnam escalated, revisionists began to see Kennedy's foreign policy as one of the most strikingly negative aspects of this administration.

3461a. Berman, Larry. *Planning a Tragedy: The Americanization of the War in Vietnam.* New York: W. W. Norton, 1982. Kennedy's decisions made Vietnam an extraordinarily more difficult problem for his successor.

3462. Berry, Fred, Jr. "Counterinsurgency: Kennedy's War in Vietnam, 1961-1963." M.A. thesis, University of Houston, 1990. A study of Kennedy's policy of promoting counterinsurgency during the Vietnam war.

3463. Bouscaren, Anthony Trawick. *The Last of the Mandarins: Diem of Vietnam.* Pittsburgh: Duquesne University Press, 1965. A highly favorable account of the South Vietnamese president.

3464. Bundy, William P. "Kennedy and Vietnam." In *The Kennedy Presidency.* Edited by Kenneth W. Thompson, pp. 241-70. No. **1588**. A valuable interview with Kennedy's deputy assistant secretary of defense whose detailed unpublished manuscript on Vietnam decision-making is housed at the Kennedy Library.

3465. Buttinger, Joseph. *Vietnam: A Dragon Embattled.* Vol. 2. *Vietnam at War.* New York: Frederick A. Praeger, 1967. Little focus on Kennedy and much on Diem and his regime.

3466. _____. *Vietnam: A Political History*. New York: Praeger, 1968. Based on Buttinger's earlier books, it contains, in a final chapter on the Americanization of the war, fresh material.

3467. Cable, Larry E. *Conflict of Myths: The Development of American Counterinsurgency Doctrine and the Vietnam War*. New York: New York University Press, 1966. Critical evaluation of America's ability to fight a guerrilla war in Southeast Asia.

3468. Cockerham, William C. "Green Berets and the Symbolic Meaning of Heroism." *Urban Life* 8 (April 1979): 94-113. Although the Vietnam war produced negative portrayals of the American armed forces, the Green Berets received considerable publicity in the mass media.

3469. Colby, William. *Lost Victory: A Firsthand Account of America's Sixteen-Year Involvement in Vietnam*. Chicago: Contemporary Books, 1989. Had Kennedy lived he would have been more sensitive to a political approach and would have prevented the war from becoming a U.S.-dominated massive military affair, according to the former director of the CIA.

3470. Cooper, Chester. *The Lost Crusade: America in Vietnam*. New York: Dodd Mead, 1970. Written by an aide to McGeorge Bundy.

3471. Currey, Cecil B. *Edward Lansdale: The Unquiet American*. Boston: Houghton Mifflin, 1988. A favorable biography of the maverick CIA operative who helped shape the unsuccessful counterinsurgency program in Vietnam.

3472. Davidson, Phillip B. *Vietnam at War, the History: 1946-1975*. Novato, Ca.: Presidio Press, 1988. Includes a brief descriptive account of Kennedy and Vietnam.

3473. Edwards, Theodore. "Kennedy's War in Vietnam." *International Socialist Review* 24 (Summer 1963): 84-7. The Kennedy administration was fighting an imperialistic and brutal war in South Vietnam without the authorization of the American people.

3474. Ellsberg, Daniel. *Papers on the War*. New York: Simon and Schuster, 1972. See the chapter on "The Quagmire Myth and the Stalemate Machine," which is especially pertinent to the Kennedy period.

3474a. Fall, Bernard B. *The Two Viet-Nams: A Political and Military Analysis*. New York: Praeger, 1967. Scattered references to JFK in a classic work by a journalist who wrote so extensively--and critically--about the Vietnam War.

3475. Fitzgerald, Frances. *Fire in the Lake: The Vietnamese and the Americans in Vietnam*. Boston: Little, Brown, 1972. A readable and important book offering multi-dimensional insights into the Vietnamese social and intellectual landscape and the tortuous relationships between Americans and Vietnamese.

3476. Galloway, John, ed. *The Kennedys and Vietnam*. New York: Facts on File, 1971. A compilation of statements by John, Robert, and Edward Kennedy on the U.S. and Vietnam.

3477. Gelb, Leslie H., with Richard K. Betts. *The Irony of Vietnam: The System Worked*. Washington: Brookings Institution, 1979. An analysis of how the U.S. decision-making system worked while policy failed.

3478. Gibbons, William Conrad. *The U.S. Government and the Vietnam War: Executive and Legislative Roles and Relationships, Part II: 1961-1964*. Princeton: Princeton University Press, 1986. Detailed factual account characterized by lengthy quotations from participants and observers.

3479. Greenstein, Fred I. "Taking Account of Individuals in International Political Psychology: Eisenhower, Kennedy, and Indochina." *Political Psychology* 15 (March 1994): 61-74. Purpose is to make a general case for linking individual-level analysis of the sort that concerned Alexander George in his earlier work to the system-level concerns of his later work.

3480. Halberstam, David. *The Best and the Brightest*. No. **2836**. Excellent analysis of how the U.S. became more involved in Vietnam during the Kennedy presidency.

3481. _____. *The Making of a Quagmire: America and Vietnam during the Kennedy Era*. New York: Random House, 1965. *New York Times* correspondent Halberstam, in his damning indictment of American involvement, contends that the U. S. made its Vietnam quagmire.

3482. Hallin, Daniel C. *The "Uncensored" War: The Media and Vietnam*. New York: Oxford University Press, 1986. The media as an establishment institution represents, rather than determines, public opinion.

3483. Hammer, Ellen J. *A Death in November: America in Vietnam, 1963*. New York: E. P. Dutton, 1987. A pro-Diem account emphasizing that the Saigon leader sought to lessen American influence in South Vietnam.

3484. Hatcher, Patrick Lloyd. *The Suicide of an Elite: American Internationalists and Vietnam*. Stanford: Stanford University Press, 1990. Kennedy saw himself losing in South Vietnam; rather than cutting his losses, he tried to increase the odds in his favor, in the end entrapping himself.

3485. Hellmann, John. *American Myth and the Legacy of Vietnam*. New York: Columbia University Press, 1986. With John Kennedy as their youthful yet sophisticated image, Americans dreamed in the early 1960s of carrying forth their revolutionary heritage into the frontier of the emerging nations.

3486. Herring, George C. "America and Vietnam: The Debate Continues." *American Historical Review* 92 (April 1987): 350-62. Much more than the review of three recent books on the Vietnam war.

3487. _____. *America's Longest War: The United States and Vietnam, 1950-1975*. Second edition. New York: Alfred Knopf, 1986. Kennedy's cautious middle course significantly enlarged the American role and commitment in Vietnam as the United States assumed direct responsibility for the South Vietnam government following the coup.

3488. _____. "Sources for Understanding the Vietnam Conflict." *Society for Historians of American Foreign Relations Newsletter* 16 (March 1985): 8-30. For manuscript and archival material available as of August 1984.

3489. Hess, Gary R. "Commitment in the Age of Counter-Insurgency: Kennedy and Vietnam." In *Shadow on the White House: Presidents and the Vietnam War*. Edited by David L. Anderson. Lawrence: University Press of Kansas, 1993, pp. 63-86. Kennedy's greatest fault was the tendency to approach Vietnam as a series of problems, without fully considering the reasons for the commitment to South Vietnam or the ramifications of the steps being taken.

3490. Hilsman, Roger. *To Move a Nation: The Politics of Foreign Policy in the Administration of John F. Kennedy*. No. **2840**. In the Kennedy period, Hilsman played a key role in counterinsurgency policy in Vietnam.

3491. Hurley, Robert Michael. "President John F. Kennedy and Vietnam, 1961-1963." Ph.D. diss., University of Hawaii, 1970. Conclusions had to be qualified because of the scarcity of available reliable sources on Kennedy and Vietnam.

3492. Jeffries, Jean. "Why Vietnam is Kennedy's War." *National Review* 20 (April 23, 1968): 396-97, 411. Even though the focus is on Robert Kennedy and 1968, the article surveys the Kennedy administration's position on Vietnam.

3493. Kahin, George McT. *Intervention: How America Became Involved in Vietnam*. New York: Alfred A. Knopf, 1986. Exhaustively researched, Kahin emphasizes the indigenous roots of the war and attacks U.S. intervention on moral and strategic grounds.

3494. _____. "The Pentagon Papers: A Critical Evaluation." *American Political Science Review* 69 (June 1975): 675-84. On the value and deficiencies of the various Pentagon Papers editions as historical sources.

3495. Kahin, George McT., and John W. Lewis. *The United States in Vietnam*. New York: Dial Press, 1967. Kennedy had tried to draw a line of distinction between tactful assistance and direct American military and political intervention that would ultimately prove self-defeating.

3496. Karnow, Stanley. *Vietnam: A History*. New York: Viking Press, 1983. The well-written journalistic account largely relies on personal recollections and interviews and the *Pentagon Papers*.

3497. Kattenburg, Paul M. *The Vietnam Trauma in American Foreign Policy, 1945-75*. New Brunswick, NJ: Transaction Books, 1980. Because of its adoption of the Taylor-Rostow proposals, leading it to break the armistice provisions of the 1954 Geneva accords, the Kennedy administration bears the principal responsibility for involving the U.S. militarily in Vietnam.

3497a. Kinnard, Douglas. *The Certain Trumpet: Maxwell Taylor and the Ameican Experience in Vietnam*. Washington: Brassey's, 1991. Written by a junior officer who knew Taylor well and based on extensive primary sources, it focuses on Taylor's association with the Kennedy administration.

3498. Koger, Daniel Allan. "The Liberal Opinion Press and the Kennedy Years in Vietnam: A Study of Four Journals." Ph.D. diss., Michigan State University, 1983. Traces the changes of opinion on U.S. involvement in Vietnam in the *New Leader*, the *Reporter*, the *New Republic*, and the *Nation*.

3499. Kolko, Gabriel. *Anatomy of a War: Vietnam, the United States, and the Modern Historical Experience*. New York: Pantheon Books, 1985. A neo-Marxist, Kolko argues that U.S. intervention was counterrevolutionary and destructive and concludes that the U.S. defeat was the result of the failure to create a viable alternative to the National Liberation Front.

3500. Komer, Robert W. *Bureaucracy at War: U.S. Performance in the Vietnam Conflict*. Boulder, Co.: Westview Press, 1986. Examines why, despite their enormous superiority, the U.S. and the South Vietnamese performed so poorly in the Vietnam War.

3501. Krepinevich, Andrew F. *The Army and Vietnam*. Baltimore: Johns Hopkins University Press, 1986. Covers the deficiencies of Kennedy's counterinsurgency program.

3502. McCarthy, Joseph E. "The Concept and Evolution of American Foreign Policy toward Viet-Nam, 1954-1963." Ph.D. diss., University of Maryland, 1965. American officials did not always appreciate the difficulties that were inherent in occidental-oriental cooperative efforts, a factor contributing to the deterioration of the American-sponsored Diem regime.

3503. Martin, Robert P. "New Tactics--or Endless War?" *U.S. News and World Report* 53 (July 30, 1962): 62-3. A correspondent returning from Vietnam concludes that the war cannot be won without a change in tactics.

3504. _____. "What Happens Next to the War in Vietnam." *U.S. News and*

World Report 55 (November 18, 1963): 47-9. A report from Saigon following the death of Diem relating to the future prospects of the war.

3505. Mecklin, John. *Mission in Torment: An Intimate Account of the U.S. Role in Vietnam.* Garden City, NY: Doubleday, 1965. An inside report on the causes of American errors in Vietnam policy estimates by a former senior U.S. diplomat in Saigon.

3506. Newman, John M. *JFK and Vietnam: Deception, Intrigue, and the Struggle for Power.* New York: Warner Books, 1992. Newman speculates that Kennedy would have continued to mislead Americans until after his 1964 election victory when he would have begun the process of American military withdrawal.

3507. "No Win in Vietnam." *New Republic* 146 (April 9, 1962): 1, 3-5. Critical of American policies in Vietnam especially the administration's new "operation sunrise," which forced rural villagers into stockades.

3508. Nolting, Frederick. "Kennedy, NATO and Southeast Asia." In *The Kennedy Presidency.* Edited by Kenneth W. Thompson, pp. 225-40. No. **1588**. A useful interview.

3509. _____. *From Trust to Tragedy: The Political Memoirs of Frederick Nolting, Kennedy's Ambassador to Diem's Vietnam.* New York: Praeger, 1988. Nolting argues that America's cause in Vietnam was lost as a result of the overthrow of the Diem government of South Vietnam.

3510. Olson, James S., and Randy Roberts. *Where the Domino Fell: America and Vietnam, 1945 to 1990.* New York: St. Martin's Press, 1991. Kennedy's policy is judiciously covered in the chapter on "The New Frontier in Vietnam, 1961-1963."

3511. Palmer, David Richard. *Summons of the Trumpet: U.S.-Vietnam in Perspective.* San Rafael, Ca.: Presidio Press, 1978. Covers the military activities in Vietnam during the Kennedy years.

3512. Park, Jong-Chul. "The China Factor in United States Decision-making toward Vietnam, 1945-1965." Ph.D. diss., University of Connecticut, 1990. Examines the influence of the China factor on five decisions, including the 1961 deployment of American advisers and special forces.

3513. Pelz, Stephen. "John F. Kennedy's 1961 Vietnam War Decisions." *Journal of Strategic Studies* 4 (December 1981): 356-85. During his first year, President Kennedy expanded the U.S. commitment in South Vietnam in a variety of ways.

3514. *The Pentagon Papers: The Defense Department History of United States Decisionmaking on Vietnam.* Senator Gravel edition, 5 vols. Boston: Beacon Press,

1971. The most orderly and usable of the larger editions, volume 2 covers the Kennedy era.

3515. Podhoretz, Norman. *Why We Were in Vietnam*. New York: Simon and Schuster, 1982. The only way the United States could have avoided defeat in Vietnam was by staying out of the war altogether.

3516. Poole, Peter A. *The United States and Indochina from FDR to Nixon*. Hinsdale, Il.: Dryden Press, 1973. The Kennedy administration adopted the art of walking a political tightrope between direct involvement in the Vietnam war and disengagement.

3517. Post, Ken. *Revolution, Socialism and Nationalism in Vietnam*. Vol. 4. *The Failure of Counter-insurgency in the South*. Aldershot, England: Darthmouth, 1990. Written from a Marxist revolution/counter-revolution framework.

3518. "The Report the President Wanted Published." *Saturday Evening Post* 234 (May 20, 1961): 31, 69-70. A report by an unidentified air force officer on the efforts of a small village in Vietnam to ward off Communist guerrillas.

3519. Rust, William J. *Kennedy in Vietnam*. New York: Da Capo, 1985. An excellent study that argues that the lack of clear direction to Kennedy's Vietnam policy precludes a confident answer as to future policy had he lived.

3520. Schlesinger, Arthur, Jr. *The Bitter Heritage: Vietnam and American Diplomacy, 1941-1966*. New York: Fawcett Crest, 1967. President Johnson escalated Kennedy's counterinsurgency operation into a full-scale war involving extensive American ground forces and the bombing of North Vietnam, something Kennedy would never have done.

3520a. Schwab, Orrin. "Defending the Free World: John F. Kennedy, Lyndon Johnson and the Vietnam War, 1961-1965." Ph.D. diss., University of Chicago, 1993.

3521. Shafer, D. Michael. *Deadly Paradigms: The Failure of U.S. Counter-insurgency Policy*. Princeton: Princeton University Press, 1988. Analyzes the failure of counterinsurgency in Vietnam.

3521a. Shaplen, Robert. *The Lost Revolution: The Story of Twenty Years of Neglected Opportunities in Vietnam and of America's Failure to Foster Democracy There*. New York: Harper and Row, 1965. Critical of the U.S. government for its part in the "lost revolution."

3522. Sheehan, Neil. *A Bright Shining Lie: John Paul Vann and America in Vietnam*. New York: Random House, 1988. By a war correspondent for United

Press International who reported first hand the limitations of the American effort in Vietnam during the Kennedy years.

3523. Smith, R. B. *An International History of the Vietnam War*. Vol. II. *The Kennedy Strategy*. New York: St. Martin's Press, 1985. Argues that the Vietnam war was the product of a global conflict that must be analyzed in global terms, and Smith defends U.S. escalation.

3524. _____. *An International History of the Vietnam War*. Vol. I. *Revolution Versus Containment, 1955-61*. New York: St. Martin's Press, 1983. Covers the beginning of the Kennedy involvement in 1961.

3525. Spark, Alasdair. "The Soldier at the Heart of the War: The Myth of the Green Beret in the Popular Culture of the Vietnam Era." *Journal of American Studies* 18 (April 1984): 29-48. Despite the failure of the American effort in Vietnam and the great unpopularity of the armed forces with elements of the public, the Green Berets receives attention in the popular culture.

3526. Thomson, James C. "How Could Vietnam Happen? An Autopsy." *Atlantic Monthly* 221 (April 1968): 47-53. Thomson, an East Asia specialist at Harvard, wrote a thoughtful essay covering the 1961-1968 years.

3527. "U.S. Imperialism and Vietnam." *Political Affairs* 42 (November 1963): 1-7. Calls for America's complete withdrawal from Vietnam.

3528. Warner, Geoffrey. "The United States and the Fall of Diem, Part I: The Coup That Never Was." *Australian Outlook* 29 (December 1974): 245-58. Focuses on the abortive coup plot of August 1963.

3529. _____. "The United States and the Fall of Diem, Part II: The Death of Diem." *Australian Outlook* 29 (March 1975): 3-17. From the viewpoint of *Realpolitik*, American policy toward Diem in 1963 was a failure; from the viewpoint of international morality, it was unsavory in the extreme.

3530. Whitlow, Robert H. *U.S. Marines in Vietnam: The Advisory and Combat Assistance Era, 1954-1964*. Washington: Government Printing Office, 1976. See especially chapter 4, "An Expanding War, 1962."

Rest of Asia

3531. Eilenberg, Matthew. "American Policy in Micronesia." *Journal of Pacific History* 17 (April 1982): 62-4. National Security Action Memoranda 145 (1962) and 243 (1963) marked Kennedy's decision to hasten the development and decolonization process in Micronesian Trust territories.

3532. Jackson, William C. "The Effects of American Military and Economic Aid to the Republic of Korea, 1953-1968." *Towson State Journal of International Affairs* 4 (1969): 25-43. With mixed results, American aid to South Korea from 1953 to 1968 was designed to create stability in that country.

3533. Maga, Timothy P. *John F. Kennedy and the New Pacific Community, 1961-1963*. New York: St. Martin's Press, 1990. Focuses on the ignored larger vision of Kennedy's New Frontier for the Asian/Pacific region to include Australia, the Philippines, Japan, and Guam.

3534. _____. "The Promise Fulfilled: John F. Kennedy and the 'New Frontier' in Guam and the Trust Territory of the Pacific Islands, 1961-1963." In *John F. Kennedy*. Edited by Paul Harper and Joann P. Krieg, pp. 105-18. No. **1600**. Kennedy combined the promise of change with a record of achievement in Guam and the Trust Territory of the Pacific Islands.

3535. Reischauer, Edwin O. *My Life between Japan and America*. New York: Harper and Row, 1986. Discusses his ambassadorship to Japan during the Kennedy administration.

Other Issues

3536. Chai, Jai Hyung. "Presidential Control of the Foreign Policy Bureaucracy: The Kennedy Case." *Presidential Studies Quarterly* 8 (Fall 1978): 391-403. The Kennedy foreign policy moved from institutionalized decision making in the State Department to personalized-centralized control from the White House.

3537. Chester, Edward. *United States Oil Policy and Diplomacy: A Twentieth-Century Overview*. Westport, Ct.: Greenwood Press, 1983. Although more liberal and less favorably disposed toward big business, Kennedy did not significantly modify the Eisenhower administration's foreign policy on oil.

3538. Cochran, Charles Leo. "The Recognition of States and Governments by President John F. Kennedy: An Analysis." Ph.D. diss., Tufts University, 1969. Examines the criteria and politics used by the Kennedy administration in the recognition of governments.

3539. Dion, Susan Frances. "Challenges to Cold War Orthodoxy: Women and Peace, 1945-1963." Ph.D. diss., Marquette University, 1991. Women activists supported a strong United Nations, a nuclear test ban, expansion of international human rights, the renewed American civil rights movement, and the abolition of HUAC.

3540. Drischler, Alvin Paul. "The Sources of the American Hegemonic Strategy: A Comparison of Foreign Policies under Presidents Nixon and Kennedy." Ph.D. diss.,

Princeton University, 1973.   Seeks to determine why American policymakers followed an imperial strategy in Vietnam and elsewhere.

3541. Garthoff, Raymond L. "Banning the Bomb in Outer Space." *International Security* 5 (Winter 1980-81): 25-40. In 1963 the U.N. General Assembly passed Resolution 1884 banning nuclear arms in outer space, a resolution which President Kennedy believed would gain more widespread American support than a treaty or executive agreement.

3542. Minter, William Maynard. "The Council on Foreign Relations: A Case Study in the Societal Bases of Foreign Policy Formation." Ph.D. diss., University of Wisconsin, 1974. The council plays an important unofficial role in the formation of foreign policy.

3543. Reichart, John Frederick. "National Security Advice to the President: A Comparative Case Study Analysis of the Structural Variable in Decision-making." Ph.D. diss., Ohio State University, 1979. Explores the relationship between the structure of the advisory system that a president relies upon for national security advice and the quality of advice he receives.

3544. Sicinski, Andrzej. "Dallas and Warsaw: The Impact of a Major National Political Event on Public Opinion Abroad." *Public Opinion Quarterly* 33 (Summer, 1969): 190-96. Two surveys of adults in Warsaw, Poland, showed that many opinions about international affairs remained unchanged by the Kennedy assassination.

3545. Smith, Bromley K. *Organizational History of the National Security Council during the Kennedy and Johnson Administrations.* Washington: National Security Council, 1988. Smith was executive secretary of the National Security Council during the Kennedy and Johnson administrations.

3546. Smith, Gaddis. "Two Worlds of Samuel Flagg Bemis." *Diplomatic History* 9 (Fall 1985): 295-302. Bemis, a diplomatic historian at Yale University during the 1930s through the 1960s, corresponded with John Kennedy on historical matters.

3547. Sorensen, Thomas C. *The Word War: The Story of American Propaganda.* New York: Harper and Row, 1968. An account of the activities of the USIA under the directorship of Edward R. Murrow by the deputy director and brother of Theodore Sorensen, President Kennedy's special counsel.

9

Administration Personnel

A. THE VICE PRESIDENT

3548. Baker, Bobby. *Wheeling and Dealing.* No. **2084**. Includes some revealing anecdotes by an insider.

3549. Baker, Leonard. *The Johnson Eclipse: A President's Vice-Presidency.* No. **2697**. A journalistic, sympathetic, and the most extensive account of Johnson's vice presidency.

3550. Conkin, Paul K. *Big Daddy from the Pedernales: Lyndon Baines Johnson.* Boston: Twayne, 1986. In this excellent study, Conkin argues that Kennedy brought out Johnson's deepest insecurities.

3551. Evans, Rowland, and Robert Novak. *Lyndon B. Johnson: The Exercise of Power, A Political Biography.* New York: New American Library, 1966. Full of excellent anecdotes, the authors conclude that Vice President Johnson kept his temper, his dignity, and his reputation during three trying years.

3552. Henggeler, Paul R. *In His Steps: Lyndon Johnson and the Kennedy Mystique.* Chicago: Ivan R. Dee, 1991. Henggeler characterizes Vice President Johnson as a troubled figure about whom Kennedy was ambivalent.

3553. Johnson, Lyndon Baines. *The Vantage Point: Perspectives of the Presidency, 1963-1969.* New York: Holt, Rinehart and Winston, 1971. Johnson said little regarding his vice presidency except that he and President Kennedy had a cordial and productive relationship.

3554. Kearns, Doris. *Lyndon Johnson and the American Dream.* New York: Harper and Row, 1976. Contains a perceptive short chapter on Johnson as vice president.

3555. Lincoln, Evelyn. *Kennedy and Johnson.* New York: Holt, Rinehart, and Winston, 1968. President Kennedy's personal secretary writes an unflattering assessment of Johnson's relationship with Kennedy.

3556. Miller, Merle. *Lyndon: An Oral History.* New York: G. P. Putnam's Sons, 1980. A chapter of interesting interviews on Johnson as vice president.

3557. Reedy, George. *Lyndon B. Johnson, A Memoir.* New York: Andrews and McMeel, 1982. Concludes that President Kennedy was generous to Vice President Johnson.

3558. Rulon, Philip Reed. *The Compassionate Samaritan: The Life of Lyndon Baines Johnson.* Chicago: Nelson-Hall, 1981. Education was the deepest bond between Kennedy and Johnson.

3559. Steinberg, Alfred. *Sam Johnson's Boy: A Close-up of the President from Texas.* New York: Macmillan, 1968. Extensive, interesting, but undocumented coverage of Vice President Johnson.

3560. Valenti, Jack. *A Very Human President.* New York: W. W. Norton, 1975. Deals briefly with Kennedy-Johnson relationship.

3561. "What Happened to LBJ." *Time* 81 (April 5, 1963): 27-8. Johnson professes to be happy as vice president.

3562. White, William S. *The Professional: Lyndon B. Johnson.* Boston: Houghton Mifflin, 1964. White focuses on Vice President Johnson's missions abroad.

3563. Wicker, Tom. "Lyndon Johnson vs. the Ghost of Jack Kennedy." *Esquire* 64 (November 1965): 87, 145, 148, 150, 152, 154, 158, 160. Includes Vice President Johnson's cordial relationship with Kennedy.

B. THE CABINET

Collective Accounts

3564. Coughlan, Robert. "Kennedy's 'Best Men' Move into Power." *Life* 50 (February 17, 1961): 100-02, 104, 106, 109-10, 112, 114, 116, 121. Kennedy compiles a bright, brisk, tough cabinet that he will use in a new way.

3565. Fenno, Richard F., Jr. "Balance in the Cabinet." *New Republic* 144 (January 9, 1961): 19-21. Concern for the cabinet members as representative symbols will give way to concern for them as policymakers in particular areas of national interest.

3566. _____. "The Cabinet: Index to the Kennedy Way." *New York Times Magazine* (April 22, 1962), pp. 13, 62-4. More openly than any other modern president, Kennedy has minimized the importance of cabinet meetings in the decision-making process; instead, individual members informally meet with him.

3567. Heller, Deane, and David Heller. *The Kennedy Cabinet: America's Men of Destiny.* Freeport, NY: Books for Libraries, 1961. Biographies of President Kennedy's cabinet and subcabinet appointees.

3568. "Kennedy Cabinet Moves into Position." *Business Week* 92 (December 24, 1960): 15-16. It is a cabinet designed to reassure both U.S. business and foreign diplomatic communities.

3569. "Kennedy's Cabinet." *U.S. News and World Report* 49 (December 26, 1960): 32-6. For the most part cabinet members are young, full of enthusiasm and energy, and middle of the road liberals.

3570. "Kennedy's Men." *New Republic* 143 (December 26, 1960): 3-7. A detailed mixed review of Kennedy's cabinet appointees.

3571. Lewis, Ted. "Kennedy's Cabinet." *Nation* 192 (January 14, 1961): 23-5. Although composed of men on their way up, on careful analysis, it is no better than most.

3572. Martin, Janet Marie. "Cabinet Secretaries from Truman to Johnson: An Examination of Theoretical Frameworks for Cabinet Studies." Ph.D. diss., Ohio State University, 1985. The emphasis is on cabinet secretaries rather than on the cabinet collectively; background characteristics and recruitment of cabinet secretaries are discussed.

3573. Opotowsky, Stan. *The Kennedy Government.* New York: E. P. Dutton, 1961. Includes a chapter on each cabinet appointee.

3574. "Predictable and Unpredictable." *Commonweal* 73 (December 30, 1960): 352-53. Kennedy's cabinet choices represent marked departures from the cabinets of the recent past in terms of youth, intellectual or academic successes, and religion, with the selection of two Jews.

3575. "The President and His Cabinet." *Commonweal* 73 (December 23, 1960): 328-29. While Kennedy's cabinet appointees are of undeniable talent, they do not give evidence of being distinguished collectively.

3576. "President's Big Ten." *Christian Century* 78 (January 4, 1961): 3-4. Kennedy's cabinet, containing two Jews, two Methodists, two Presbyterians, an Episcopalian, a Mormon, a Lutheran, and a Roman Catholic, was not selected on the basis of religious considerations--or for the purpose of paying political debts or to promote liberalism.

3577. "Report Card on the Cabinet." *Life* 51 (July 28, 1961): 33. Secretary of Defense McNamara ranked highest, Secretary of Agriculture Freeman, lowest.

3578. Schlesinger, Arthur M., Jr. *Thousand Days*. No. **1624**. Offers the fullest coverage of the Kennedy cabinet of the general works on Kennedy.

3579. "Six for the Kennedy Cabinet." *Time* 76 (December 26, 1960): 12-14. Biographies of the following appointees: Robert McNamara, Douglas Dillon, Arthur Goldberg, Orville Freeman, Robert Kennedy, and J. Edward Day.

3580. Tanzer, Lester, ed. *The Kennedy Circle*. No. **1966**. Biographical sketches of nineteen top officials in the Kennedy administration, including cabinet members.

3581. "Under Kennedy a Different Kind of Cabinet." *U.S. News and World Report* 50 (February 27, 1961): 49-51. President Kennedy is downgrading his cabinet as a decision-making group and upgrading its members as individuals, putting them more on their own to get things done.

3582. *Washington Star. The New Frontiersmen: Profiles of the Men Around Kennedy*. Washington: Public Affairs Press, 1961. Includes essays on members of Kennedy's cabinet and their subordinates.

3583. White, William S. "Twelve at the Table." *Harper's Magazine* 223 (September 1961): 92-5. This presidential cabinet, for the first time in history, is dominated intellectually by the have-not classes--economically and socially.

3584. Yarmolinsky, Adam. "The Kennedy Talent Hunt." *Reporter* 24 (June 8, 1961): 22-5. Yarmolinsky discusses the considerations that went into the selection process for cabinet officers.

J. Edward Day

3585. Day, J. Edward. "Mr. Day Goes to Washington." *New York Times Magazine* (April 2, 1961), pp. 14, 25. A first-person account by the postmaster general on his experiences as an "outsider" in the world of Washington politics.

3586. _____. *My Appointed Round: 929 Days as Postmaster General*. New York: Holt, Rinehart and Winston, 1965. Day saw little of President Kennedy.

3587. _____. "Post Office Gives Its Side of a Controversy over the Mails." *U.S. News and World Report* 52 (April 9, 1962): 82-4. Day explains why higher postal rates will be charged on magazines.

C. Douglas Dillon

3588. "Dillon vs. Hodges: Two Views on Tax Cuts." *U.S. News and World Report* 52 (June 11, 1962): 20. Treasury Secretary Dillon's opposition to tax cuts to bolster the economy and Commerce Secretary Hodges's support of such measures.

3589. "Eisenhower's Reaction to Dillon's Appointment." *U.S. News and World Report* 50 (January 2, 1961): 79. President Eisenhower's disappointment that the Republican Dillon accepted a cabinet post in the Kennedy administration.

3590. "Everybody's Man." *Newsweek* 56 (December 26, 1960): 16, 19. A biographical sketch of Dillon.

3591. Kraft, Joseph. "Treasury Dillon: The Conservative Power Center in Washington." *Harper's Magazine* 226 (June 1963): 51-6. Kraft assesses Dillon as a strong and competent secretary.

3592. "Man with the Purse." *Time* 78 (August 18, 1961): 13-17. Includes a biography of Dillon and addresses his policies as treasury secretary.

3593. "Republican in the Cabinet and His Task." *Newsweek* 57 (January 30, 1961): 27-9. An overview of Dillon's view of the economy and his impact on the policies of a Democratic administration.

Orville L. Freeman

3594. "The Dismemberment of Orville Freeman." *Time* 78 (July 7, 1961): 13. The congressional defeat of Secretary of Agriculture Freeman's omnibus farm bill.

3595. Freeman, Orville. "A Cabinet Perspective." In *The Kennedy Presidency*. Edited by Kenneth W. Thompson, pp. 161-74. No. **1588**. Freeman's recollections of John Kennedy.

3596. _____. "Freeman Weighs the Farm Surpluses." *New York Times Magazine* (September 24, 1961), pp. 36-7. Troublesome oversupplies exist in wheat and feed grains.

3597. _____. "Secretary Freeman Fires Back at Critics of His Farm Program." *U.S. News and World Report* 51 (December 4, 1961): 101-02. Freeman defends the emergency feed-grain program.

3598. Giglio, James N. "New Frontier Agricultural Policy: The Commodity Side, 1961-1963." No. **2130**. Includes Freeman's farm policies.

3599. "A Hard Row to Hoe." *Time* 81 (April 5, 1963): 21-5. Cover story on Freeman's difficult task.

3600. "Inside of the Farm Problem." *U. S. News and World Report* 51 (July 31, 1961): 50-4. An interview with Freeman.

Arthur J. Goldberg

3601. "Arthur Goldberg: Whirlwind at Work." *Newsweek* 57 (March 6, 1961): 35-6, 39-40. Covers the early challenges Secretary of Labor Goldberg faced.

3602. "Changes Coming in Labor Policies." *U.S. News and World Report* 50 (February 27, 1961): 60-5. An interview with Goldberg on the major problems between management and labor.

3603. Goldberg, Arthur. "Suggestions for a New Labor Policy." *Reporter* 23 (September 15, 1960): 27-30. Goldberg proposes ways in which to promote cooperation between labor and management and the government.

3604. _____. "What Can Be Done about Unemployment?" *Saturday Evening Post* 234 (April 29, 1961): 15, 73-5. Discusses unemployment problems facing the U.S. and the possible solutions.

3605. Goldberg, Dorothy. *A Private View of a Public Life*. New York: Charterhouse, 1975. In a chatty vein, Goldberg's wife covers his stint as secretary of labor.

3606. "Gray Haired Wonder." *Fortune* 65 (April 1962): 229-30, 234. Deals with the strengths of Goldberg and his successes as labor secretary.

3607. "Labor's Plenipotentiary." *Fortune* 61 (March 1960): 216, 218, 220, 224. On Goldberg's career as a labor lawyer and his abilities as an attorney and liaison between labor and government.

3608. Lasky, Victor. *Arthur J. Goldberg, The Old and the New*. New Rochelle, NY: Arlington House, 1970. A negative and brief biography by a conservative reporter.

3609. Raskin, A. H. "Trouble Shooter on the New Frontier." *New York Times Magazine* (February 12, 1961), pp. 10, 17. Concentrates on the talent and effectiveness of Goldberg.

John Austin Gronouski

3610. "Hyphenated General." *Newsweek* 62 (September 23, 1963): 29-30. On the new postmaster general following Day's resignation.

Luther H. Hodges

3611. Hodges, Luther. *The Business Conscience*. No. **2163**. Insights into Secretary of Commerce Hodges's attitude on the ethical and social responsibilities of businessmen.

3612. _____. "We're Flunking Our Economic ABC's" *Saturday Evening Post* 235 (March 10, 1962): 8, 10. Centers on the American people's ignorance of economics and why they fail to understand.

3613. Ivey, Alfred G. *Luther Hodges, Practical Idealist*. Minneapolis: T. S. Denison, 1968. A favorable popular biography written for young people.

3614. "Luther Hodges Wants to Be Friends." *Fortune* 64 (August 1961): 106-09, 206-12. Hodges's ceaseless energy, devotion to his task, and his moderate stand on issues.

3615. Piehl, Charles K. "Luther Hartwell Hodges." In *Dictionary of American Biography*. Supplement 9, 1971-1975. Edited by Kenneth T. Jackson. New York: Charles Scribner's Sons, 1994, pp. 391-93. Kennedy's secretary of commerce found himself often out of sync with the administration.

Robert F. Kennedy

3616. Bickel, Alexander M. "Robert F. Kennedy: The Case Against Him for Attorney General." *New Republic* 144 (January 9, 1961): 15-19. Argues that Robert Kennedy is unfit to be attorney general based on his actions as chief counsel for the Senate McClellan committee.

3617. "'Bobby' Kennedy: Is He the 'Assistant President'"? *U.S. News and World Report* 52 (February 19, 1962): 48-52. Examines the close relationship of John and Robert Kennedy and the power Robert wields in White House decisions.

3618. Childs, Marquis. "Bobby and the President." *Good Housekeeping* 154 (May 1962): 80-3, 162-64, 167-69. This chatty article discusses the close and personal relationship between Robert Kennedy and the president.

3619. Coffin, Tristram. "The Department of Justice." *Holiday* 33 (March 1963): 134-41. An analysis of the attorney general's office and how it is changing under Kennedy's leadership.

3620. Guthman, Edwin O. *We Band of Brothers*. No. **2217**. Written by Attorney General Kennedy's chief press officer and close friend.

3621. Guthman, Edwin O., and C. Richard Allen, eds. *RFK: Collected Speeches*. New York: Viking, 1993. Includes sixteen speeches as attorney general.

3622. Guthman, Edwin O., and Jeffrey Shulman, eds. *Robert Kennedy in His Own Words*. No. **1644**. The most invaluable printed primary source on Kennedy as attorney general.

3623. Kennedy, Robert F. "Attorney General's Opinion on Wiretaps." *New York Times Magazine* (June 3, 1962), pp. 21, 80-1. Kennedy discusses his beliefs that the laws regarding wiretapping need to be extended to allow law enforcement officials to catch criminals without endangering the right to privacy.

3624. _____. "Robert Kennedy Defends the Menace." *New York Times Magazine* (October 13, 1963), pp. 15, 105-08. Discusses the extent of organized crime and racketeering in the U.S.

3625. Knebel, Fletcher. "Bobby Kennedy: He Hates to Be Second." *Look* 27 (May 21, 1963): 91-102. A popular portrait of the attorney general at work and at play, including quotes from friends and foes.

3626. Lewis, Anthony. "What Drives Bobby Kennedy?" *New York Times Magazine* (April 7, 1963), pp. 52-60. An examination of the qualities of Robert Kennedy.

3627. Lowi, Theodore J., ed. *Robert F. Kennedy: The Pursuit of Justice*. New York: Harper and Row, 1964. Twelve essays by Attorney General Kennedy on his position relating to domestic and foreign matters.

3628. Manning, Robert. "Someone the President Can Talk To." *New York Times Magazine* (May 28, 1961), pp. 22-9. Discusses Robert Kennedy's personality, work habits, and the absolute confidence and reliance the president places in him.

3629. Navasky, Victor S. *Kennedy Justice*. No. **2258**. A probing analysis of Kennedy's Justice Department.

3630. Ross, Douglas, ed. *Robert F. Kennedy: Apostle of Change*. New York: Trident Press, 1968. The most complete collection of Robert Kennedy's public utterances.

3631. Schlesinger, Arthur M., Jr. "Robert Francis Kennedy." In *Dictionary of American Biography*. Supplement 8, 1966-1970. Edited by John A. Garraty and Mark C. Carnes. New York: Charles Scribner's Sons, 1988, pp. 321-24. Robert Kennedy's relationship to President Kennedy carried his duties considerably beyond the Justice Department.

3632. _____. *Robert Kennedy and His Times*. No. **1659**. From largely the Kennedy point of view, the most thorough coverage of Kennedy's attorney generalship.

3633. Stein, Jean, and George Plimpton, eds. *American Journey*. No. **2281**. Several interviews on Robert Kennedy as attorney general.

Robert S. McNamara

3634. McNamara, Robert S. *The Essence of Security: Reflections in Office*. New York: Harper and Row, 1968. A brief overview by the secretary of defense.

3635. Shapley, Deborah. *Promise and Power*. No. **2614**. The most definitive account on Secretary of Defense Robert McNamara.

3636. Trewhitt, Henry. *McNamara: His Ordeal at the Pentagon*. New York: Harper and Row, 1968. Written by the diplomatic correspondent of *Newsweek*, Trewhitt focuses on McNamara's unprecedented influence.

Abraham Ribicoff

3637. "Man on a Cabinet Hot Spot." *Newsweek* 56 (February 20, 1961): 26-30. Covers the abilities, philosophy, and early problems of the secretary of housing, education, and welfare.

3638. White, William S. "Mr. Ribicoff of Welfare Street." *Harper's Magazine* 224 (January 1962): 88-90. Covers Ribicoff's politics and his stand on public aid and federal programs.

Dean Rusk

3639. Cohen, Warren I. *Dean Rusk*. No. **2824**. A thoughtful and balanced assessment.

3640. Kenworthy, E. W. "Evolution of Our No. 1 Diplomat." *New York Times Magazine* (March 18, 1962), pp. 31, 136-37, 139. Through his candor and tough-mindedness, Secretary of State Rusk has become Kennedy's principal agent in foreign affairs.

3641. "The New Team at State." *New Republic* 143 (December 19, 1960): 3-5. An analysis of the past activities and style of the newly appointed members of the State Department: Rusk, Chester Bowles, Adlai Stevenson, and Walt Rostow.

3642. Rusk, Dean. "America's Brightest Opportunities." *Nation's Business* 51 (June 1963): 76-83. Rusk outlines the great changes taking place in the world such as the emergence of new nations, unity in Western Europe, and the spread of communism in explaining the role of the American government and private business.

3643. _____. *As I Saw It*. No. **2865**. Secretary of State Rusk provides a brief and discreet account of the Kennedy years.

3644. _____. "The Winds of Freedom." *Saturday Evening Post* 235 (June 30, 1962): 68-70. Discusses how this country's historical principles still remain a strong force for change throughout the world.

3645. Schoenbaum, Thomas J. *Waging Peace and War*. No. **2867**. Using a variety of primary sources, Schoenbaum writes favorably of Secretary of State Rusk.

3646. "Secretary Rusk: Close-up of Washington's Busiest Man." *U.S. News and World Report* 51 (September 11, 1961): 53-5. A candid and confidential appraisal of Rusk by insiders.

3647. Shannon, William V. "Dean Rusk and the President." *Commonweal* 78 (March 29, 1963): 5-6. Deals with Rusk's ambiguous relations with President Kennedy.

3648. Smith, Beverly, Jr. "Quarterback of the Cabinet." *Saturday Evening Post* 234 (July 22, 1961): 26-7, 72-4. Deals with the relationship between Rusk and Kennedy.

3649. "Where U.S. Is Headed in Today's World." *U.S. News and World Report*. 52 (January 29, 1962): 52-62. An extensive interview with Rusk in which he explains the official position of the administration on a wide array of world events.

3650. "Why Rusk Was Picked for State." *Business Week* (December 17, 1960), pp. 23-4. An analysis of the qualities possessed by Rusk.

Adlai E. Stevenson

3651. "Ambassador Stevenson." *New Yorker* 36 (January 28, 1961): 24-6. A personal interview with the new ambassador to the United Nations in which he discusses his hopes for the U.N.

3652. Biggs, James W. "A Rhetorical Analysis of the Speechmaking of Adlai Stevenson Inside and Outside the United Nations on Major Issues during the 17th, 18th, and 19th Sessions of the General Assembly." Ph.D. diss., Southern Illinois University, 1970. Stevenson remained firm in his conviction that democracy could become the accepted form of government for all nations because it offers man his greatest opportunity for self-fulfillment.

3653. Broadwater, Jeff. *Adlai Stevenson and American Politics: The Odyssey of a Cold War Liberal*. New York: Twayne, 1994. A balanced viewpoint of one of America's most engaging and influential public figures.

3654. Brown, Stuart Gerry. *Conscience in Politics: Adlai Stevenson in the 1960s.* Syracuse: Syracuse University Press, 1961. On the politics of national leadership by a statesman out of power.

3655. Cochran, Bert. *Adlai Stevenson.* New York: Funk and Wagnalls, 1969. Cochran contends that America is ruled by an upper class of which Stevenson was a part.

3656. Davis, Kenneth S. *The Politics of Honor: A Biography of Adlai E. Stevenson.* New York: G. P. Putnam's, 1967. A laudatory biography.

3657. Gervis, Stephanie. "Stevenson at the UN." *Commonweal* 77 (March 1, 1963): 591-93. A favorable assessment of Ambassador Stevenson.

3658. Graham, Robert A. "America's Apostle of Peace." *America* 107 (June 2, 1962): 344-46. A positive assessment of Stevenson's work at the U.N.

3659. Harrison, Gilbert A. "Why Stevenson?" *New Republic* 147 (December 15, 1962): 7-10. Discusses criticisms of Ambassador Stevenson as too soft on communism especially during the Cuban missile crisis.

3660. Lyon, Peter. "Mr. Ambassador." *Holiday* 33 (June 1963): 35-9, 136-37, 139, 143, 147. A detailed explanation of the United States involvement in the U.N under Stevenson's leadership.

3661. Martin, John Bartlow. *Adlai Stevenson of Illinois.* Garden City, NY: Doubleday, 1976. First volume of Stevenson's life from birth through the election of 1952.

3662. _____. *Adlai Stevenson and the World.* No. 1744. Based on Stevenson's papers and interviews, it covers his life from 1952 to 1965, including his years as U.S. ambassador to the United Nations during the Kennedy period for which he had cabinet status.

3663. Roberts, John W. "Cold War Observer: Adlai Stevenson on American Foreign Relations." *Journal of the Illinois State Historical Society* 76 (1983): 49-60. Stevenson believed that American interests were global, the Soviets promoted an alien philosophy, and collective action would ensure security.

3664. Sievers, Rodney M. "Adlai E. Stevenson: An Intellectual Portrait." Ph.D. diss., University of Virginia, 1971. The metamorphosis of American society during Stevenson's lifetime--Progressivism, New Deal, World War Two, Cold War--colored his image of the past, his understanding of the present, his expectations for the future.

3665. _____. "Adlai Stevenson and the Crisis of Liberalism." *Midwestern*

Quarterly 14 (1973): 135-49. The flames in Vietnam and the urban ghettoes have led to a reaction against modern liberalism, and Stevenson's image has suffered as a result.

3666. Stevenson, Adlai E. "New Men in New Worlds." *Saturday Review* 45 (July 21, 1962): 17. The U.N ambassador explains how the U.N should be involved in a changing world of nations.

3667. _____. "Red Shadows over Latin America." *New York Times Magazine* (August 6, 1961), pp. 11, 60-1. Consists of excerpts of a report made by Stevenson after an extensive tour of Latin America.

Stewart L. Udall

3668. Manning, Robert. "Secretary of Things in General." *Saturday Evening Post* 234 (May 20, 1961): 38-9, 79-81. Discusses Udall's background and his controversial manner on Capitol Hill.

3669. Prokop, John. "Well Done, Mr. Secretary." *American Forests* 69 (March 1963): 8-9, 41-4. Praising Secretary of Interior Udall for his increasing of the grazing fee on public lands.

3670. Udall, Stewart L. *The Quiet Crisis*. New York: Holt, Rinehart and Winston, 1964. On the plundering of America's natural resources.

3671. "Udall's Job as Big as All Outdoors." *Business Week* (July 28, 1962), pp. 76-7, 80, 82. Discusses Udall's ambitious plans for more conservation, expansion of state recreation facilities, and larger tracts of undisturbed national parks.

3672. "Who Needs Enemies?" *Newsweek* 57 (May 15, 1961): 30-1. Covers some of the controversies created by Udall.

W. Willard Wirtz

3673. "New Secretary Has First Crisis." *Business Week* (September 8, 1962), pp. 132-34. Discusses the problems facing Wirtz as he takes over the Department of Labor especially the disputes in the aerospace industry.

3674. Raskin, A. H. "As Wirtz Sees His Basic Job." *New York Times Magazine* (November 11, 1962), pp. 30, 140. Covers the style of Wirtz in dealing with labor disputes and how that style differed from his predecessor.

3675. "Where New Labor Secretary Stands." *U.S. News and World Report* 53 (October 8, 1962): 101. Covers Wirtz's position on such issues as a shorter work week, compulsory arbitration in the railroad industry, and strike insurance.

C. MEMBERS OF CONGRESS

3676. Anderson, Clinton P. *Outsider in the Senate: Senator Clinton Anderson's Memoirs*. New York: World, 1970. Regarding Kennedy, the senator from New Mexico focuses on the 1960 race and the Medicare fight in the Senate.

3677. Anson, Robert Sam. *McGovern: A Biography*. New York: Holt, Rinehart and Winston, 1972. Covers McGovern's directorship of Food for Peace and his service in the U.S. Senate during the Kennedy period.

3678. Ashby, LeRoy, and Rod Gramer. *Fighting the Odds: The Life of Senator Frank Church*. Pullman: Washington State University Press, 1994. A well composed and detailed biography of the Democratic Idaho Senator who strongly identified with the crisis-oriented, activist approach of the Kennedy presidency.

3679. Baldwin, Louis. *Hon. Politician: Mike Mansfield of Montana*. Missoula, Mt.: Montain Press, 1979. Mostly a compilation of Senator Mansfield's speeches.

3680. Banks, James G. "Strom Thurmond and the Revolt Against Modernity." Ph.D. diss., Kent State University, 1970. Senator Thurmond of South Carolina has been an outspoken critic of civil rights legislation and Democratic liberalism.

3681. Berman, William C. *William Fulbright and the Vietnam War: The Dissent of a Political Realist*. Kent Oh.: Kent State University Press, 1988. Based on the cooperation of Senator Fulbright and grounded in extensive manuscript sources, Berman's book gives short shrift to the Kennedy period.

3682. Bolling, Richard. *Power in the House: A History of the Leadership of the House of Representatives*. New York: E. P. Dutton, 1968. A Missouri congressman and influential Kennedy supporter discusses Kennedy's relationship with the House leadership.

3683. Brown, Eugene. *J. William Fulbright: Advice and Dissent*. Iowa City: University of Iowa Press, 1985. Focusing on Senator Fulbright's foreign policy views, Brown contends, that of all the postwar presidents Fulbright worked with, Kennedy was his favorite.

3684. "Byrd vs. Kennedy." *New Republic* 47 (July 9, 1962): 2. Senator Byrd of Virginia remains a major obstacle regarding Kennedy's domestic legislation.

3685. Champagne, Anthony. *Sam Rayburn: A Bio-Bibliography*. Westport Ct.: Greenwood Press, 1988. A biographical sketch and a compilation of works and sources relating to the House speaker from Texas.

3686. Coffin, Tristram. *Senator Fulbright*. No. **1709**. The Democratic senator from Arkansas from 1945 to 1975 who chaired the Senate Foreign Relations Committee during the Kennedy era.

3687. Cohodas, Nadine. *Strom Thurmond and the Politics of Southern Change*. New York: Simon and Schuster, 1993. The Republican senator from South Carolina was at odds with the Kennedy administration over civil rights.

3688. Collins, Frederick. "Senator Russell in the Last Ditch." *New York Times Magazine* No. **2200**. On Senator Russell's stance on civil rights legislation.

3689. Curtis, Carl T., and Regis Courtemanche. *Forty Years Against the Tide: Congress and the Welfare State*. Lake Bluff, Il.: Regnery Gateway, 1986. The memoirs of a conservative Nebraska senator who lambasts the Kennedy presidency and who played a leading part in the investigation of Billy Sol Estes, implicated in an administration scandal.

3690. Dierenfield, Bruce J. *Keeper of the Rules: Congressman Howard W. Smith of Virginia*. Charlottesville: University of Virginia Press, 1987. A competent biography of the powerful chairman of the House Rules Committee who obstructed Kennedy's legislative program.

3691. Dirksen, Louella. *The Honorable Mr. Marigold: My Life with Everett Dirksen*. Garden City, NY: Doubleday, 1972. Mrs. Dirksen writes of a father-son relationship between her husband and John Kennedy.

3692. Douglas, Paul H. *In the Fullnes of Time*. No. **1714**. Indispensable regarding the legislative issues during the Kennedy presidency.

3693. Fite, Gilbert C. *Richard B. Russell, Jr.: Senator from Georgia*. Chapel Hill: University of North Carolina Press, 1991. This old fashioned biography of the powerful Georgia senator devotes a chapter to Kennedy and the New Frontier.

3694. Fontenay, Charles L. *Estes Kefauver*. No. **1718**. Written by a journalist, this biography focuses on Senator Kefauver's personal and political life, including his involvement with the Kefauver-Harris Drug Control Act of 1962.

3695. Garrettson, Charles Lloyd III. *Hubert H. Humphrey: The Politics of Joy*. New Brunswick: Transaction Publishers, 1993. A favorable biography based on personal interviews and the Humphrey papers of the senate majority whip during the Kennedy presidency.

3696. Goldwater, Barry M. *Goldwater*. New York: Doubleday, 1988. The conservative Arizona senator mentions his affection for Jack Kennedy.

3697. _____. *With No Apologies: The Personal and Political Memoirs of*

United States Senator Barry M. Goldwater. New York: Morrow, 1979. Much on the Kennedy presidency.

3698. Gore, Albert. *Let the Glory Out: My South and Its Politics*. New York: Viking Press, 1972. Senator Albert Gore of Tennessee, close to President Kennedy, reveals some interesting stories.

3699. Gorman, Joseph B. *Kefauver: A Political Biography*. No. **1720**. Covers the activity of Senator Kefauver of Tennessee on the Antitrust and Monopoly Subcommittee during the Kennedy years.

3700. Griffith, Winthrop. *Humphrey: A Candid Biography*. New York: Morrow, 1965. Written by an assistant to Senator Humphrey during the early 1960s, it concentrates on the Kennedy era.

3701. Gruening, Ernest. *Many Battles: The Autobiography of Ernest Gruening*. New York: Liveright, 1973. The senator from Alaska expresses his disappointment with the Kennedy presidency.

3702. Hardeman, D. B., and Donald C. Bacon. *Rayburn*. No. **1724**. The best biography on Rayburn, it is based on previously unpublished material and Hardeman's long association with Rayburn.

3703. Harrison, Gilbert A. "Carry Me Back." *New Republic* 144 (March 27, 1961): 13-19. Discusses the personality and politics of Senator Barry Goldwater.

3704. Hartke, Vance, and John M. Redding. *Inside the New Frontier*. New York: McFadden-Bartell, 1962. By the Democratic senator from Indiana who praises President Kennedy.

3705. Humphrey, Hubert H. *The Education of a Public Man: My Life and Politics*. Garden City, NY: Doubleday, 1976. Some revealing insights into the Kennedy presidency by the senator from Minnesota.

3706. Javits, Jacob. *Javits: An Autobiography of a Public Man*. Boston: Houghton Mifflin, 1981. The liberal senator from New York mostly deals with Kennedy in the context of national health insurance.

3707. Johnson, Haynes, and Bernard M. Gwertzman. *Fulbright the Dissenter*. Garden City, NY: Doubleday, 1968. A very readable biography written by a journalist and based on the senator's papers and on extensive interviews with him.

3708. Little, Dwayne Lee. "The Political Leadership of Speaker Sam Rayburn, 1940-1961." Ph.D. diss., University of Cincinnati, 1970. Views Rayburn as a power broker instead of a politician with his own ideological agenda.

3709. McFayden, Richard E. "Estes Kefauver and the Tradition of Southern Progressivism." *Tennessee Historical Quarterly* 37 (Winter 1978): 430-43. Details the intricacies of the senate struggle, which ultimately led in 1962 to the Kefauver-Harris amendments to the Food, Drug and Cosmetic Act, largely over the opposition of President Kennedy who was allied with the pharmaceutical giants.

3710. McNeil, Neil. *Dirksen, Portrait of a Public Man.* New York: World Publishing, 1970. Written by an intimate of Dirksen and with his cooperation, it extensively covers the Senator Dirksen-Kennedy relationship.

3711. Miller, William. *Fishbait: The Memoirs of the Congressional Doorkeeper.* Englewood Cliffs, NJ: Prentice-Hall, 1977. Scattered anecodotes involving John Kennedy.

3712. Morgan, Anne Hodges. *Robert S. Kerr: The Senate Years.* Norman: University of Oklahoma Press, 1977. Until his death on New Year's Day, 1963, this Democratic senator from Oklahoma played a major legislative role during the Kennedy presidency.

3713. Olson, Gregory Allen. "Mike Mansfield's Ethos in the Evolution of United States Policy in Indo China." Ph.D. diss., University of Minnesota, 1988. The senate majority leader's increasing criticism of the Vietnam war and his friendship with Kennedy are explored.

3714. O'Neill, Thomas P. *Man of the House: The Life and Political Memoirs of Speaker Tip O'Neil.* New York: Random House, 1987. The House speaker from Boston, who held John Kennedy's former congressional district seat, frankly recalls his association with Kennedy.

3715. Phillips, William G. *Yarborough of Texas.* Washington: Acropolis, 1969. A brief uncritical biography of the Democratic senator from Texas who was present at Kennedy's assassination.

3716. Pickett, William B. *Homer E. Capehart: A Senator's Life, 1897-1979.* Indianapolis: Indiana Historical Society, 1990. The Republican Indiana senator found it difficult to adjust to the more liberal early 1960s, losing reelection to Birch E. Bayh, Jr., in November 1962.

3717. Potenziani, David Daniel. "Look to the Past: Richard B. Russell and the Defense of Southern White Supremacy." Ph.D. diss., University of Georgia, 1981. Portrays a white southerner defending his native culture.

3718. Powell, Lee Riley. *J. William Fulbright and America's Lost Cause: Fulbright's Opposition to the Vietnam War.* Little Rock: Rose Publishing Co., 1984. An expansion of Riley's master's thesis at the Unversity of Virginia, this study actually covers more than Fulbright's opposition to the Vietnam war.

3719. Prochnau, William W., and Richard W. Larsen. *A Certain Democrat: Senator Henry M. Jackson*. Englewood Cliffs, NJ: Prentice-Hall, 1972. This undocumented biography reveals that even though Senator Jackson of Washington was a Democrat he was often at odds with Kennedy on matters of foreign policy.

3720. Rayburn, Sam. "The Speaker Speaks of Presidents." *New York Times Magazine* (June 4, 1961), pp. 32, 34, 37, 39, 42, 44. House Speaker Rayburn discusses the presidents with whom he has served.

3721. Schapsmeier, Edward L., and Frederick H. Schapsmeier. *Dirksen of Illinois: Senatorial Statesman*. Urbana: University of Illinois Press, 1985. Excellent on the Kennedy-Dirksen relationship.

3722. Scheele, Henry Z. *Charlie Halleck: A Political Biography*. New York: Exposition Press, 1966. A sympathetic biography of House Minority Leader Halleck who was a major thorn to Kennedy's legislative program.

3723. Seib, Charles B. "Steering Wheel of the House." *New York Times Magazine* (March 18, 1962), pp. 30, 140-41, 146. House Ways and Means Committee chair Mills and his handling of administration programs.

3724. Sherrill, Robert, and Harry W. Ernst. *The Drugstore Liberal: Hubert H. Humphrey in Politics*. New York: Grossman, 1968. Viewing Humphrey as a political opportunist, this unscholarly biography deals with Kennedy in the context of the 1960 campaign.

3725. Smith, A. Robert. *The Tiger in the Senate: The Biography of Wayne Morse*. Garden City, NY: Doubleday, 1962. The last chapter on the Oregon senator covers his relationship with John Kennedy.

3726. Solberg, Carl. *Hubert Humphrey*. No. **1765**. Includes a short chapter on Humphrey's tenure as the senate's majority whip during the Kennedy presidency.

3727. Steinberg, Alfred. *Sam Rayburn*. No. **1767**. Highly descriptive work offering little analysis or insight.

3728. Sykes, Jay C. *Proxmire*. Washington: Robert B. Luce, 1972. A biography of the maverick Republican senator from Wisconsin who was a major obstacle to Kennedy's legislative initiatives.

3729. Taylor, John Raymond. "Homer E. Capehart: United States Senator, 1944-1962." Ph.D. diss., Ball State University, 1977. The conservative Indiana senator and cold warrior was a political foe of Kennedy, particularly during the missile crisis.

3730. Tower, John G. *Consequences: A Personal and Political Memoir*. Boston:

Little, Brown, 1991. A freshman senator from Texas during the missile crisis, Tower was vice chairman of the Church committee in 1975, which was involved in the investigation of past intelligence activities leading to the unearthing of the President Kennedy-Judith Campbell relationship.

3731. Unruh, Gail Quentin. "Eternal Liberal Wayne L. Morse and the Politics of Liberalism." Ph.D. diss., University of Oregon, 1987. Explores the background and reasons for Morse's liberalism and his place as a liberal spokesman.

3732. Walker, Donald Edwin. "The Congressional Career of Clare E. Hoffman, 1935-1963." Ph.D. diss., Michigan State University, 1982. Hoffman was a conservative isolationist congressman from Michigan.

3733. Wilkins, Lee. *Wayne Morse: A Bio-Bibliography*. Westport, Ct.: Greenwood Press, 1985. A sketchy biography with a bibliography of works by and about the Oregon senator.

3734. Wilkins, Lillian Claire. "Wayne Morse: An Exploratory Biography." Ph.D. diss., University of Oregon, 1982. Employs psychoanalytical theory to analyze the motivating forces in Morse's career in the senate from 1944 to 1968.

3735. Wilkinson, J. Harvie III. *Harry Byrd and the Changing Face of Virginia Politics, 1945-1966*. Charlottesville: University of Virginia Press, 1968. Byrd was a powerful senate leader and member of the conservative coalition.

3736. Womack, Steven Douglas. "Charles A. Halleck and the New Frontier: Political Opposition through the Madisonian Model." Ph.D. diss., Ball State University, 1980. Focuses on the performance of Halleck as House Republican minority leader during the Kennedy administration and his opposition to most New Frontier programs.

D. DIPLOMATS AND STATE DEPARTMENT OFFICIALS

3737. Abramson, Rudy. *Spanning the Century: The Life of W. Averell Harriman, 1891-1986*. New York: William Morrow, 1992. Based on Harriman's personal papers, Abramson covers Harriman's diplomatic activities during the "days of the crocodile."

3738. Ball, George. *The Past Has Another Pattern*. No. **2814**. As Kennedy's undersecretary of state, Ball sought to play a moderating role on the major issues of foreign policy.

3739. Bergquist, Laura. "JFK's No. 1 Russian Expert." *Look* 27 (February 12, 1963): 21-5. Llewellyn Thompson, former ambassador to the Soviet Union and Kennedy's chief adviser on Soviet affairs, is well-respected by the Soviet leadership.

3740. Bohlen, Charles. *Witness to History*. No. **2818**. Kennedy's ambassador to France and adviser to Kennedy on Soviet policy.

3741. Bowles, Chester. *Promises to Keep*. No. **2819**. Includes Bowles's dismissal from the State Department, his service as roving ambassador for the Third World, and his ambassadorship to India in 1963.

3742. Brinkley, Douglas. *Dean Acheson: The Cold War Years, 1953-71*. New Haven: Yale University Press, 1992. A critical but fair appraisal of a sometimes inflexible and acerbic personality who helped mold Kennedy's thinking on European matters.

3743. Burke, Lee H. "The Ambassador at Large: A Study in Diplomatic Method." Ph.D. diss., University of Maryland, 1971. Since it was institutionalized in 1949, three of eight ambassadors at large--W. Averell Harriman, Chester Bowles, and Llewellyn Thompson--were appointed during the Kennedy presidency.

3744. Denman, Dorothy I. "The Riddle of Containment: As Reflected in the Advice and Dissent of George F. Kennan." Ph.D. diss., University of Miami, 1975. Contains a chapter on Kennan's ambassadorship to Yugoslavia during the Kennedy administration.

3745. DiLeo, David L. *George Ball, Vietnam, and the Rethinking of Containment*. Chapel Hill: University of North Carolina Press, 1991. As Kennedy's undersecretary of state, Ball opposed the escalation of the American role in Vietnam.

3746. Galbraith, John Kenneth. *Ambassador's Journal*. No. **309**. Galbraith provides a chatty and insightful account from his private journal while serving as U. S. ambassador to India until July 1963.

3747. _____. *A Life in Our Times*. No. **2833**. Excellent on Galbraith's ambassadorship to India.

3748. Heintz, Stephen. "Frustration at Foggy Bottom: Chester Bowles as Undersecretary of State, January-November 1961." Senior thesis, Yale University, 1974. An excellent essay on Bowles's problems with the Department of State.

3749. Hixon, Walter L. *George F. Kennan: Cold War Iconoclast*. New York: Columbia University Press, 1989. A reinterpretation of Kennan's approach to containment and covering Kennan's frustrating ambassadorship to Yugoslavia during the Kennedy years.

3750. Hoffman, Ralph N. "Latin American Diplomacy: The Role of the Assistant Secretary of State, 1957-1969." Ph.D. diss., Syracuse University, 1969. Seeks to determine the role of the assistant secretary of state for Inter-Latin American Affairs.

3751. Issacson, Walter, and Evan Thomas. *The Wise Men.* No. **2842.** Penetrating essays on Dean Acheson, Charles Bohlen, Averell Harriman, George Kennan, Robert Lovett, and John McCloy, all of whom had impact on Kennedy.

3752. Hilsman, Roger. *To Move a Nation.* No. **2840.** Hilsman served as director of the Bureau of Intelligence and Research at the State Department and assistant secretary of state for Far Eastern Affairs.

3753. Johnson, U. Alexis. *The Right Hand of Power.* No. **2844.** Memoirs of President Kennedy's deputy undersecretary of state.

3754. Layton, Teresa L. "Llewellyn E. Thompson." In *Dictionary of American Biography.* Supplement 9, 1971-1975. Edited by Kenneth T. Jackson, pp. 798-800. Thompson was a career diplomat and adviser to Kennedy on Soviet affairs especially during the Cuban missile crisis.

3755. Lodge, Henry Cabot. *The Storm Has Many Eyes: A Personal Narrative.* New York: W. W. Norton, 1973. Povides only brief coverage of his ambassadorship to South Vietnam.

3756. McLellan, David S., and David C. Acheson, eds. *Among Friends.* No. **310.** Includes Acheson's memoranda and letters relating to Kennedy whom Truman's former secretary of state advised.

3757. Mayers, David. *George Kennan and the Dilemmas of U.S. Foreign Policy.* New York: Oxford University Press, 1988. A political and intellectual biography.

3758. Miller, William J. *Henry Cabot Lodge.* No. **1746.** Undocumented and unrevealing coverage of Lodge's ambassadorship to Saigon in 1963.

3759. Richardson, George Granberry. "George Ball's Grand Design, 1961-1966." Ph.D diss., University of South Carolina, 1992. As one of the most influential "Europeanists" in the Kennedy administration, Ball worked tirelessly to implement the Grand Design, a new Atlantic partnership between the United States and Western Europe.

3760. Rostow, Walt W. *The Diffusion of Power.* No. **2610.** From December 1961 to April 1966, Rostow chaired the Policy Planning Council at the Department of State.

3761. Ruddy, Thomas Michael. *The Cautious Diplomat.* No. **2864.** Charles Bohlen, the former ambassador to the Soviet Union, was an adviser to Kennedy on Soviet relations and became ambassador to France in October 1962.

3762. Schaffer, Howard B. *Chester Bowles: New Dealer in the Cold War.* Cambridge: Harvard University Press, 1993. Sympathetically written by one who had worked with Bowles in the embassy in India and in the State Department.

3763. Schwarz, Jordan A. *Liberal: Adolf A. Berle and the Vision of an American Era.* New York: Free Press, 1987. In 1961 the former New Dealer Berle controversially served in the State Department as chairman of an interdepartmental task force on Latin America.

3764. Shoup, Lawrence H., and William Minter. *The Imperial Brain Trust: The Council on Foreign Relations and United States Foreign Policy.* New York: Monthly Review Press, 1977. Fifty-one percent of Kennedy's top foreign policy officials were members of the Council on Foreign Relations.

3765. Wieck, Randolph. *Ignorance Abroad: American Educational and Cultural Foreign Policy and the Office of the Assistant Secretary of State.* Westport, Ct.: Praeger, 1992. A public biography of Philip Coombs, the first assistant secretary of state for educational and cultural affairs, who served during the Kennedy presidency.

3766. Wofford, Harris. "You're Right, Chet, You're Right. And You're Fired." *Washington Monthly* 12 (July/August 1980): 46-54, 56. Undersecretary Bowles's consistent correctness was largely ignored because of his attention to principle and morality on matters of foreign policy.

E. SUPREME COURT JUSTICES AND RELATED COURT MATTERS

3767. Becker, Robert Myron. "Chief Justice Earl Warren and Civil Liberties." Ph.D. diss., New School for Social Research, 1974. Analyzes Warren's opinions in civil rights and civil liberties cases.

3768. Beth, Loren P. "Mr. Justice Black and the First Amendment: Comments on the Dilemma of Constitutional Interpretation." *Journal of Politics* 41 (November 1979): 1105-24. Black believed that substantive due process of law should be defined within the limits of the first eight amendments to prevent judges from following their own preferences.

3769. Birkby, Robert H. "Supreme Court Libertarians and the First Amendment: An Analysis of Voting and Opinion Agreement, 1956-1964." *Southwestern Social Science Quarterly* 48 (March 1968): 586-94. Analyzes the votes and opinions of Chief Justice Earl Warren and Associate Justices Hugo Black, William O. Douglas, Arthur Goldberg, and William Brennan in fifty-nine cases involving freedom of speech, press, or assembly.

3770. Dorin, Dennis A. "Mr. Justice Clark and State Criminal Justice, 1949-1967."

Ph.D. diss., University of Virginia, 1974. Examines Clark's conceptualization of his role on the Supreme Court in formulating policies for state criminal justice.

3771. Dorsen, Norman. "John M. Harlan." In Leon Friedman and Fred L. Israel, eds. *The Justices of the United States Supreme Court 1789-1969: Their Lives and Major Opinions.* New York: Chelsea House, 1969. 5 volumes. 4: 2803-46. Harlan believed that a balance must be achieved between individual rights and governmental power in a free society.

3772. Douglas, William O. *The Court Years, 1939-1975: The Autobiography of William O. Douglas.* New York: Random House, 1980. Memoirs of Justice Douglas who writes about his association with the Kennedys.

3773. Dunne, Gerald T. *Hugo Black and the Judicial Revolution.* New York: Simon and Schuster, 1977. Black sought to overturn the restrictions on Communists and was a critic of loyalty oaths.

3774. Fortas, Abe. "Chief Justice Warren: The Enigma of Leadership." *Yale Law Journal* 84 (January 1975): 405-12. Fortas, a justice who served with Warren, believes that he ranks with John Marshall and Charles Evans Hughes.

3775. Frank, John P. "Hugo Black." In Leon Friedman and Fred L. Israel, eds. *The Justices of the United States Supreme Court*, 3: 2321-70. No. **3771**. Black usually joined Justice Douglas in defending individual liberties.

3776. _____. "William O. Douglas." In Leon Friedman and Fred L. Israel, eds. *The Justices of the United States Supreme Court*, 4: 2447-90. No. **3771**. Douglas consistently was the Court's foremost exponent of individual liberty and freedom of speech and press.

3777. Friedman, Stephen J. "William Brennan." In Leon Friedman and Fred L. Israel, eds. *The Justices of the United States Supreme Court*, 4: 2849-89. No. **3771**. An Eisenhower appointee, Brennan was part of the moderate-to-liberal group in decisions affecting individual liberties.

3778. _____. "Arthur J. Goldberg." In Leon Friedman and Fred L. Israel, eds. *The Justices of the United States Supreme Court*, 4: 2977-89. No. **3771**. Serving on the Court from October 1962 through June 1965, Goldberg soon became a leading activist regarding civil liberties cases.

3779. Grogan, Susan Edra. "The Result-orientation of William O. Douglas: Political Activities on and off the Bench." Ph.D. diss., Cornell University, 1988. Examines Douglas's judicial and extra-judicial behavior to determine how he sought to shape American politics and law.

3780. Heck, Edward Victor. "Justice Brennan and the Changing Supreme Court."

Ph.D. diss., Johns Hopkins University, 1978. Reveals and explains shifts in Brennan's positions in which he became, between 1962 and 1969, increasingly the central figure on a Court committed to the libertarian viewpoint.

3781. Israel, Fred L. "Byron R. White." In Leon Friedman and Fred L. Israel, eds. *The Justices of the United States Supreme Court,* 4: 2951-61. No. **3771.** Kennedy's first appointment to the Court, White surprisingly sided with the conservative wing.

3782. Israel, Jerold H. "Potter Stewart." In Leon Friedman and Fred L. Israel, eds. *The Justices of the United States Supreme Court,* 4: 2921-47. No. **3771.** Stewart was often the "swing man" on the Court and usually voted to sustain governmental power versus the rights of the individual.

3783. Kennedy, Harry L. "Justice William O. Douglas on Freedom of the Press." Ph.D. diss., Ohio University, 1980. Traces Douglas's attitudes toward freedom of the press in his Court opinions from 1939 to 1975.

3784. Kirkendall, Richard. "Tom C. Clark." In Leon Friedman and Fred L. Israel, eds. *The Justices of the United States Supreme Court,* 4: 2665-77. No. **3771.** Clark voted consistently to support national security over individual rights during the McCarthy period and thereafter remained a conservative on such matters.

3785. Lewis, Anthony. "Earl Warren." In Leon Friedman and Fred L. Israel, eds. *The Justices of the United States Supreme Court,* 4: 2721-2800. No. **3771.** Under Warren's leadership, the Court became the nation's conscience on civil rights, yet critics maintain that the Court intruded into legislative matters and became a permanent constitutional convention.

3786. Lytle, Clifford Merle, Jr. "The Warren Court and Its Political Critics." Ph.D. diss., University of Pittsburgh, 1963. Examines examples of criticism of the Warren Court to ascertain their basis and assesses the attacks.

3787. Magee, James J. *Mr. Justice Black: Absolutist on the Court.* Charlottesville: University Press of Virginia, 1980. The focus is on Justice Black's well-known, but frequently misconstrued, absolutist interpretation of the First Amendment.

3788. Mauney, Connie Pat. "Mr. Justice Black and First Amendment Freedoms: A Study in Constitutional Interpretation." Ph.D. diss., University of Tennessee, 1975. In cases dealing with obscenity, libel, subversive activities, and contempt of court, Black was remarkably consistent in voting to protect the individual.

3789. Pollack, Jack Harrison. *Earl Warren: The Judge Who Changed America.* Englewood Cliffs, NJ: Prentice-Hall, 1979. Popular biography that was influenced by Warren's critique of part of the manuscript just prior to his death.

3790. Pollock, Paul K. "Judicial Libertarianism and Judicial Responsibilities: The

Case of Justice William O. Douglas." Ph.D. diss., Cornell University, 1968. Finds Douglas to be deficient in his judicial philosophy because it denied personal, democratic, and institutional responsibility.

3791. Rodell, Fred. "It Is the Warren Court." *New York Times Magazine* (March 13, 1966), pp. 30, 93-4, 96, 98-100. Surveys the decisions of the Court during the Kennedy years.

3792. Rubin, Eva R. "The Judiciary Apprenticeship of Arthur J. Goldberg, 1962-1965." Ph.D. diss., Johns Hopkins University, 1967. While Goldberg played an activist role relating to civil liberties cases, Rubin argues that on labor cases and on other types of economic policy-making, Goldberg believed that the Court should defer to Congress.

3793. Schwartz, Bernard. *Super Chief: Earl Warren and His Supreme Court--A Judicial Biography.* New York: New York University Press, 1983. Little on Warren's life and much on the Court, but this readable work does include information on the Warren-Kennedy relationship.

3794. Schwartz, Bernard, and Stephan Lesher. *Inside the Warren Court.* Garden City, NY: Doubleday, 1983. Brief account of the personalities and inner workings of the Court under Warren.

3795. Sowell, Randy Lee. "Judicial Vigor: The Warren Court and the Kennedy Administration." 2 vols. Ph.D. diss., University of Kansas, 1992. Explores the close relationship and interest in liberal activism of the Kennedy administration and the Warren Court.

3796. Thompson, Dennis L. "The Kennedy Court: Left and Right of Center." *Western Political Quarterly* 26 (June 1973): 263-79. Analyzes the judicial impact of Kennedy's appointments of Byron White and Arthur Goldberg to the Supreme Court.

3797. Warnock, Alvin Timothy. "Associate Justice Tom C. Clark: Advocate of Judicial Reform." Ph.D. diss., University of Georgia, 1972. Clark was an excellent judge of character, a leader of men, and a master politician.

3798. Warren, Earl. *The Memoirs of Earl Warren.* Garden City, NY: Doubleday, 1977. Includes the Supreme Court years and the Warren Commission investigation of the Kennedy assassination.

3799. Weaver, John D. *Warren: The Man, The Court, The Era.* Boston: Little, Brown, 1967. This biography lacks detachment and analysis.

3800. White, G. Edward. *Earl Warren: A Public Life.* New York: Oxford University Press, 1982. White argues that Warren's judicial decisions were based on ethical imperatives in which he put himself into the shoes of those harrassed or injured; White is much more critical of Warren's role in President Kennedy's assassination investigation.

3801. Wilkerson, J. Harvie, Jr. "Justice John M. Harlan and the Values of Federalism." *Virginia Law Review* 57 (October 1971): 1185-1221. Harlan advocated judicial restraint in tampering with state obscenity laws, law enforcement, and legislative reapportionment.

F. OTHER ADMINISTRATION OFFICIALS

3802. Alsop, Stewart. "The White House Insiders." *Saturday Evening Post* 234 (June 10, 1961): 19-21, 91, 94, 95, 98. The White House staff who surround the president include the "Irish Mafia" and the "Eggheads."

3803. Anderson, Patrick. *The Presidents' Men: White House Assistants of Franklin Roosevelt, Harry S. Truman, Dwight D. Eisenhower, John F. Kennedy and Lyndon B. Johnson.* Garden City, NY: Doubleday, 1968. The coverage of Kennedy staffers, eg., McGeorge Bundy, Richard Goodwin, Pierre Salinger, Arthur Schlesinger, Jr., and Theodore Sorensen is signficant because it is based on personal interviews.

3804. Barnhill, John Hershel. "Politician, Social Reformer, and Religious Leader: The Public Career of Brooks Hays." Ph.D. diss., Oklahoma State University, 1981. Examines Hays's public career as a southern progressive congressman from Arkansas and as an administrative assistant in the Kennedy administration.

3805. Bird, Kai. *The Chairman: John McCloy, The Making of the Ameican Establishment.* New York: Simon and Schuster, 1992. McCloy was Kennedy's special assistant on disarmament.

3805a. Burke, Mary Kathleen. "Liege Man at Camelot: The Role of David F. Powers in the Career of John F. Kennedy." Ph.D. diss., Providence College, 1987. JFK's close friend since the 1946 campaign, Powers virtually lived in the White House.

3806. Connally, John. *In History's Shadow: An American Odyssey.* New York: Hyperion, 1993. By Kennedy's first secretary of the navy, who admired JFK's judgment and sense of distance; mostly focuses on events leading to Kennedy's tragic trip to Dallas.

3807. Depoe, Stephen P. *Arthur M. Schlesinger, Jr., and the Ideological History of American Liberalism.* Tuscaloosa: University of Alabama Press, 1994. A communications professor, Depoe analyzes Kennedy's intellectual adviser's tides concept from a rhetorical perspective.

3808. Flannelly, Margaret Ellen. "An Analysis of the Role of the White House Staff in the Administration of President Dwight D. Eisenhower and President John F. Kennedy." Ph.D. diss., University of Notre Dame, 1969. Explores the structure and operation of the White House staff.

3809. Goldman, Barry M. "Evelyn Speaks: An Interview with Evelyn Lincoln." *Manuscripts* 43 (Winter 1991): 5-22. President Kennedy's personal secretary claims that his authentic signature can be found on pale green personal stationery, not on white stationery with blue imprinting.

3810. Hyman, Sydney. "Inside the Kennedy 'Kitchen Cabinet.'" *New York Times Magazine* (March 5, 1961), pp. 27, 86, 88-9. Speculation on the role of the White House staff.

3811. Johnson, Richard T. *Managing the White House: An Intimate Study of Three Presidents*. New York: Harper and Row, 1974. Study of presidential use of White House assistants; with Kennedy the emphasis was upon teamwork and collegiality.

3812. Kendrick, Alexander. *Prime Time: The Life of Edward R. Murrow*. Boston: Little, Brown, 1969. The journalist Murrow served as the Kennedy administration's director of the United States Information Agency.

3813. Kinnard, Douglas. "A Soldier in Camelot: Maxwell Taylor in the Kennedy White House." *Parameters* 18 (4 1988): 13-24. Taylor served as Kennedy's White House military adviser and as chairman of the joint chiefs of staff by July 1962.

3814. Knebel, Fletcher. "Kennedy and His Pals." *Look* 25 (April 25, 1961): 117-18, 120, 123-24, 126. A discussion of eight of Kennedy's old friends, some of whom served in the administration.

3815. Medved, Michael. *The Shadow Presidents: The Secret History of the Chief Executives and Their Top Aides*. New York: Times Books, 1979. Contains a chapter on Kennedy aide Theodore Sorensen, entitled "Kennedy's co-author."

3816. Reston, James, Jr. *The Lone Star: The Life of John Connally*. New York: Harper and Row, 1989. Kennedy's secretary of the navy who became governor of Texas in January 1963; later that year he and Kennedy were shot in Dallas.

3817. Ritchie, Donald Arthur. "James M. Landis: New Deal, Fair Deal, and New Frontier Administrator." Ph.D. diss., University of Maryland, 1975. A former associate of Joseph Kennedy and an honorary uncle to the Kennedy children, Landis joined the Kennedy administration as special assistant to the president for regulatory policy, resigning in September 1961.

3818. _____. "Reforming the Regulatory Process: Why James Landis Changed His Mind." *Business History Review* 54 (Autumn 1980): 283-302.

Landis's 1960 report to President-elect Kennedy on regulatory performance focused on administrative deficiencies and stimulated New Frontier reform proposals.

3819. "Shift at the Pentagon." *U.S. News and World Report* 51 (December 25, 1961): 13. Deals with the selection of Fred Korth to replace John Connally as secretary of the navy.

3820. Solliday, Michael Archer. "The Special Assistant to the President for National Security Affairs and the National Security Council: A Comparative Study in Presidential Decision-making." Ph.D. diss., Southern Illinois University, 1975. Based largely on published sources, Solliday concludes that the special assistant, McGeorge Bundy, supervised the NSC staff and the NSC agenda, but President Kennedy ran the meetings of the Council and informal groups.

3821. Talbott, Strobe. *The Master of the Game: Paul Nitze and the Nuclear Peace.* New York: Alfred A. Knopf, 1988. Focuses on Nitze's role regarding arms control; Nitze served as assistant secretary for international security affairs, housed in the Department of Defense.

3822. Taylor, John M. *General Maxwell Taylor: The Sword and the Pen.* New York: Doubleday, 1989. The eldest son and a historian writes a scholarly biography of his father who served as Kennedy's chief of staff.

3823. Taylor, Maxwell. *Swords and Plowshares.* No. **2619**. Taylor writes about his involvement in the major issues of foreign policy.

3824. "With Uncommon Speed." *Newsweek* 62 (October 28, 1963): 22. Covers the controversial resignation of Kennedy's Secretary of the Navy Fred Korth.

G. JOURNALISTS

3825. Abell, Tyler, ed. *Drew Pearson Diaries: 1949-1959.* New York: Holt, Rinehart and Winston, 1974. The Washington columnist, frequently a thorn to Kennedy, provides information on Kennedy's *Profiles in Courage* and his other writings.

3826. Alsop, Joseph. *"I've Seen the Best of It": Memoirs.* New York: W. W. Norton, 1992. The influential journalist and friend of John Kennedy includes a number of anecdotes on the Kennedy family.

3827. Baughman, James L. *Henry R. Luce and the Rise of the American News Media.* Boston: Twayne, 1987. Excellent account of the Kennedy-Luce relationship and an evaluation of how Luce's publications--*Life* and *Time*--treated President Kennedy.

3828. Bradlee, Benjamin C. *Conversations With Kennedy*. No. **1903**. Excellent on Kennedy's press relations by the chief of the Washington bureau of *Newsweek*.

3829. Broder, David S. *The Party's Over: The Failure of Politics in America*. New York: Harper and Row, 1971. A reporter, in the early 1960s for the Washington *Evening Star* and the *New York Times*, divides Kennedy's time on the national stage into three phases.

3830. Cater, Douglass. *Power in Washington: A Critical Look at Today's Struggle to Govern in the Nation's Capital*. New York: Random House, 1964. Written by the national affairs editor of the *Reporter*, Cater comments on the news managers of the Kennedy administration.

3831. Chesire, Maxine. *Maxine Chesire, Reporter*. Boston: Houghton Mifflin, 1978. A syndicated columnist for the *Washington Post* who covered the Kennedy White House.

3832. Childs, Marquis. *Witness to Power*. New York: McGraw-Hill, 1975. The chief of the St. Louis *Post-Dispatch* Washington bureau refers to Kennedy's influential press friends.

3833. "Columnists JFK Reads Every Morning." *Newsweek* 58 (December 18, 1961): 65-70. Includes Walter Lippmann, Joseph Alsop, James Reston.

3834. Dickerson, Nancy. *Among Those Present: A Reporter's View of Twenty-Five Years in Washington*. New York: Random House, 1976. The first woman to report national news on television, Dickerson had a close relationship with Kennedy.

3835. Donovan, Hedley. *Roosevelt to Reagan: A Reporter's Encounters with Nine Presidents*. New York: Harper and Row, 1985. Written by Henry Luce's key deputy, Donovan had something to do with the evenhanded reporting of Kennedy in *Time*.

3836. Halberstam, David. *The Powers That Be*. New York: Knopf, 1979. Halberstam of the *New York Times* provides insights into Kennedy's relationship with Benjamin Bradlee of *Newsweek*, Hugh Sidey of *Time* magazine, and the media in general.

3837. Judis, John B. *William F. Buckley, Jr.: Patron Saint of the Conservatives*. New York: Simon and Schuster, 1988. Buckley, the founder of the conservative *National Review*, broke with the Kennedy administration in the spring of 1961 over policy toward the Third World.

3838. King, Larry. *Tell It to the King*. Thorndike, Me.: Thorndike Press, 1988. King provides some revealing stories about President Kennedy's personal life.

3839. Klurfeld, Herman. *Winchell: His Life and Times*. New York: Praeger, 1976. The syndicated columnist Winchell lashed out against the Kennedy administration.

3840. Kraft, Joseph. *Profiles in Power: A Washington Insight*. New York: New American Library, 1966. The Washington correspondent of *Harper's Magazine*, Kraft provides portraits of Kennedy and other administration officials.

3841. Krock, Arthur. *In the Nation, 1932-1966*. New York: McGraw-Hill, 1966. A compilation of Krock's columns including those from the Kennedy period.

3842. _____. *Memoirs*. No. **2512**. A *New York Times* columnist and a close friend of the Kennedy family, Krock writes about the severing relationship by 1963.

3843. _____. "Mr. Kennedy's Management of the News." *Fortune* 67 (March 1963): 82, 199, 201-02. Krock wrote that President Kennedy's news management policy has been enforced more cynically and boldly than by any previous administration in peacetime.

3844. Lawrence, Bill. *Six Presidents, Too Many Wars*. New York: Saturday Review Press, 1972. Lawrence, a *New York Times* reporter who covered Kennedy's 1960 campaign and was a personal friend of Kennedy, joined ABC News in 1961.

3845. Lippmann, Walter. *Conversations with Walter Lippmann*. Boston: Atlantic Monthly, 1965. Seven conversations Lippmann had with Howard K. Smith and other television commentators during the 1960s.

3846. Martin, Harold H. *Ralph McGill, Reporter*. Boston: Little, Brown, 1973. McGill, a nationally known liberal journalist for the *Atlanta Constitution*, was appointed by Kennedy to the President's Committee on Labor and Management Policy.

3847. Pierpoint, Robert. *At the White House: Assignment to Six Presidents*. New York: G. P. Putnam's Sons, 1981. Emphasizes Kennedy's personal charm in several revealing anecdotes.

3848. Pilat, Oliver. *Drew Pearson: An Unauthorized Biography*. New York: Harper's Magazine Press, 1973. President Kennedy avoided this unfriendly journalist.

3849. Reston, James. *Deadline: A Memoir*. New York: Random House, 1991. This *New York Times* journalist comments on Kennedy's press relations.

3850. Roberts, Chalmers M. *First Rough Draft: A Journalist's Journal of Our Times*. New York: Praeger, 1973. The *Washington Star* journalist contains a chapter on John Kennedy.

3851. Roberts, Charles. "JFK and the Press." In *Ten Presidents and the Press.* Edited by Kenneth W. Thompson. Lanham, Md.: University Press of America, 1983, pp. 63-87. Personal account by the White House correspondent for *Newsweek.*

3852. _____."Kennedy and the Press: Image and Reality." In *The Kennedy Presidency.* Edited by Kenneth W. Thompson, pp. 175-87. No. **1588.** Interview that argues that the press made Kennedy and destroyed Lyndon Johnson.

3853. Rovere, Richard. *Arrivals and Departures: A Journalist's Memoirs.* New York: Macmillan, 1976. The Washington correspondent for the *New Yorker* writes about his conversations with Kennedy.

3854. _____. *Final Reports.* New York: Doubleday, 1984. In his final work, Rovere provides some thoughtful comment on John Kennedy.

3855. Rowan, Carl T. *Breaking Barriers.* No. **2269.** Anecdotes on Kennedy and his press conferences.

3856. Salisbury, Harrison. *A Time of Change: A Reporter's Tale of Our Time.* New York: Harper and Row, 1988. Argues that Kennedy actually despised the press.

3857. _____. *Without Fear or Favor: The New York Times and Its Times.* New York: Time Books, 1980. Much on President Kennedy and the press.

3858. Schapsmeier, Edward L., and Frederick H. Schapsmeier. *Walter Lippmann: Philosopher-Journalist.* Washington: Public Affairs Press, 1969. Kennedy, who always read Lippmann's column, respected Lippmann because the latter took a position and defended his views with courage.

3859. Schorr, Daniel. *Clearing the Air.* Boston: Houghton Mifflin, 1977. A CBS News correspondent occasionally refers to his coverage of Kennedy.

3860. Sidey, Hugh. *John F. Kennedy, President.* New York: Atheneum, 1963. Sidey of *Time* magazine comments on Kennedy's press relations.

3861. Smith, Timothy G., ed. *Merriman Smith's Book of Presidents: A White House Memoir.* New York: W. W. Norton, 1972. Press-related stories regarding the White House correspondent of the United Press International.

3862. Steel, Ronald. *Walter Lippmann and the American Century.* Boston: Little, Brown, 1980. The *Washington Post* columnist Lippmann's relationship with Press Secretary Pierre Salinger.

3863. Strout, Richard L. *TRB: Views and Perspectives on the Presidency.* New York: Macmillan, 1979. A compilation of Strout's *New Republic* columns, including those covering the Kennedy years.

3864. Sulzberger, C. L. *An Age of Mediocrity: Memoirs and Diaries, 1963-1972.* New York: Macmillan, 1973. Full of scattered recollections on President Kennedy.

3865. _____. *The Last of the Giants.* New York: Macmillan, 1970. Cyrus Sulzberger, the publisher of the *New York Times*, contains a number of references to Kennedy in his journal.

3866. Swanberg, W. A. *Luce and His Empire.* New York: Scribner's Sons, 1972. On *Time*'s supposed unfairness toward Kennedy.

3867. Thomas, Helen. *Dateline: White House.* New York: Macmillan, 1975. United Press Internatinal White House correspondent devotes a chapter to Kennedy.

3868. Tohan, Walter. *Political Animals: Memoirs of a Sentimental Cynic.* Garden City, NY: Doubleday, 1975. A journalist for the Chicago *Tribune* shares his personal observations on the Kennedys since the 1930s.

3869. White, Theodore H. *In Search of History--A Personal Expedition.* New York: Harper and Row, 1978. Contains two moving and perceptive chapters on Kennedy whom White, the author of *The Making of the President, 1960*, compares to a gatekeeper.

3870. Wicker, Tom. *Kennedy without Tears: The Man Behind the Myth.* New York: William Morrow, 1964. Based on Wicker's essay in *Esquire*, it contains a foreword by Arthur Krock.

3871. _____. *On Press.* New York: Viking Press, 1978. *New York Times* White House correspondent during the Kennedy years.

3872. Winchell, Walter. *Winchell Exclusive.* Englewood Cliffs, NJ: Prentice-Hall, 1975. No Kennedy admirer, Winchell, the syndicated columnist, shares an interesting anecdote on Kennedy from 1960.

3873. Wreszin, Michael. *A Rebel in Defense of Tradition: The Life and Politics of Dwight Macdonald.* New York: Basic Books, 1994. Macdonald, the radical intellectual journalist from New York, found himself in opposition to the Kennedy foreign policy.

10

Elections of 1962

Despite a president's party often losing substantial numbers of seats in Congress in midterm elections, the Democrats in 1962 increased their margin in the Senate by four and lost only four seats in the House of Representatives. Moreover, the House losses were by southern Democrats. Some observers claim that Democratic successes were related to Kennedy's vigorous campaigning and his personal popularity following the Cuban missile crisis. All indications are that local issues and incumbency were the determining considerations.

3874. Alsop, Stewart. "What Made Teddy Run?" *Saturday Evening Post* 235 (October 27, 1962): 15-21. Ted Kennedy is seeking the U.S. Senate seat from Massachusetts because of a desire to prove that he is a Kennedy among Kennedys.

3875. Anderson, Totton J., and Eugene C. Lee. "The 1962 Election in California." *Western Political Quarterly* 16 (June 1963): 396-420. According to this study--a part of a symposium on the 1962 elections in the West to include congressional and gubernatorial contests--the electorate in California preferred the status quo.

3876. Ascoli, Max. "Elections." *Reporter* 27 (November 22, 1962): 20. The president's gamble, of fighting as leader of his party during the congressional campaigns, paid off, enabling him to claim a personal victory out of party victory.

3877. "Bad News for Kennedy in '62? Congressional Elections." *U.S. News and World Report* 51 (November 27, 1961): 70-1. Redistricting and traditional off-year losses for the party in power suggests a mid-term election defeat for President Kennedy in 1962.

3878. Balmer, Donald G. "The 1962 Election in Oregon." *Western Political Quarterly* 16 (June 1963): 453-59. All incumbents won as voters split their ballots; the biggest Democratic win was the reelection of Senator Wayne Morse of Oregon for whom Kennedy had high regard.

3879. "Barry Goldwater Predicts: A Conservative Sweep in 1962." *Look* 26 (July

3, 1962): 69-70, 72. The Arizona senator predicts sizable gains for the Republican party in 1962 congressional and senatorial elections because of a conservative shift nationally.

3880. Beall, Charles. "The 1962 Election in Wyoming." *Western Political Quarterly* 16 (June 1963): 477-82. The outcome was a Republican sweep of all five state elective offices in addition to the congressional and senatorial seats.

3881. "Big Switch of '62." *Business Week* (November 10, 1962), pp. 29-31. Despite the Democratic election success, no easy victories await the New Frontier programs the next year.

3882. "Bipartisanship on November 6." *Nation* 195 (October 27, 1962): 250. The *Nation* advised voters to support moderate Republicans such as Rockefeller and Javits in New York State whenever Democrats have failed to present acceptable candidates.

3883. Bone, Hugh A. "The 1962 Election in Washington." *Western Political Quarterly* 16 (June 1963): 467-76. Washington voters generally supported the status quo as they voted a split ticket to elect incumbents, the majority of whom were Republicans who opposed Kennedy's major liberal domestic initiatives.

3884. "Both Ike and JFK Hit the 1962 Campaign Trail." *Newsweek* 60 (October 22, 1962): 26-7. A comparison of their effectiveness.

3885. Campbell, Angus. "Prospects for November: Why We Can Expect More of the Same." *New Republic* 147 (October 8, 1962): 13-15. Campbell suggests that the public mood is generally favorable toward Democratic party congressional candidates because of Kennedy's personal popularity, the public's perception of economic conditions, and its approval of the administration's management of foreign affairs.

3886. Campbell, James E. "Explaining Presidential Losses in Midterm Congressional Elections." *Journal of Politics* 47 (4 1985): 1140-57. Losses traditionally have resulted from the lack of a coattail effect, but the state of economy has also been a factor.

3887. Cater, Douglass. "How Teddy Beat Eddie." *Reporter* 27 (July 5, 1962): 15-18. An explanation of Edward Kennedy's victory over Edward J. McCormack, Jr., for the party's senatorial endorsement at the Massachusetts Democratic convention.

3888. Folliard, Edward. "President's Reason for Hustling." *America* 107 (October 27, 1962): 947. Kennedy's real aim is to hold down Democratic losses in the House of Representatives.

3889. Grant, Philip, Jr. "Kennedy and the Congressional Elections of 1962." In *John*

F. Kennedy. Edited by J. Richard Snyder, pp. 85-95. No. **2077.** No conclusive evidence exists to suggest that Kennedy's endorsement was a pivotal factor in the outcome of any race, but he probably helped candidates in several states by dramatizing key issues and arousing voter interest.

3890. Grow, Stewart L. "The 1962 Election in Utah." *Western Political Quarterly* 16 (June 1963): 460-66. Republicans retained their senate seat, swept both congressional seats, and won control of both houses of the state legislature; the Republican senator, Wallace Bennett, was aided by his decisive support of Kennedy's blockade of Cuba.

3891. "The 'In' Party's Dramatic Triumph." *Newsweek* 60 (November 19, 1962): 31-2. Election results were a victory for the Kennedy administration that ranks with the victories of 1902 and 1934--the only two previous years in which an "in" party had improved its standing.

3892. Irion, Frederick C. "The 1962 Election in New Mexico." *Western Political Quarterly* 16 (June 1963): 448-52. Democrats won all national and state offices with little attention being given to national issues.

3893. "Issues for '62 Elections as Republicans See Them." *U.S. News and World Report* 52 (June 18, 1962): 88. The Republican members of Congress adopted "A Declaration of Republican Principle and Policy" that amounted to a party platform for the approaching congressional elections.

3894. "JFK vs. 'Rocky' in 1964?" *U. S. News and World Report* 53 (November 19, 1962): 50-2. Because of Rockefeller's sweeping victory in the New York gubernatorial race, the prediction of party leaders is that he will be the Republican nominee in 1964.

3895. Jaffe, Erwin A., and Stanley A. Pearl. "The 1962 Election in Nevada." *Western Political Quarterly* 16 (June 1963): 426-31. Democratic incumbents won reelection, including Congressman Walter Baring who publicly diassociated himself from almost every policy of the Kennedy administration.

3896. Jonas, Frank H. "The 1962 Elections in the West." *Western Political Quarterly* 16 (June 1963): 375-85. The Republicans fared better in the West than they did in the nation.

3897. Joyner, Conrad. "The 1962 Election in Arizona." *Western Political Quarterly* 16 (June 1963): 390-95. Democrats and Republicans split the six major races, one indication that the once dominant Democratic party is losing ground.

3898. Lewis, William O. "The 1962 Election in Idaho." *Western Political Quarterly* 16 (June 1963): 432-38. There is no substantial indication that the Cuban crisis had a major effect on the outcome of any race as a Republican governor easily won reelection as did Democratic Senator Frank Church.

3899. McCarthy, Joe. "One Election JFK Can't Win." *Look* 26 (November 6, 1962): 23-7. Addresses the question of why President Kennedy permitted his younger brother, Edward, to run for the U.S. Senate from Massachusetts.

3900. McConachie, Michael Paul. "Presidential Campaigning for Congressional Candidates in Midterm Elections, 1962-1982." Ph.D. diss., University of Missouri, 1985. Describes, analyzes, and evaluates the president's role as campaigner in midterm congressional elections.

3901. Martin, Curtis. "The 1962 Election in Colorado." *Western Political Quarterly* 16 (June 1963): 421-25. The Republicans overthrew an incumbent Democratic governor and U.S. senator, captured most of the statewide offices, and split the four congressional seats.

3902. Meyer, Frank S. "The 1962 Elections: The Turning of the Tide." *National Review* 13 (December 4, 1962): 434, 440. Meyer sees a quiet, but massive, turning of the tide toward conservatism in the 1962 election results.

3903. "New Faces in the Senate." *U.S. News and World Report* 53 (November 19, 1962): 20. Ten new senators will take their seats in January including Edward Kennedy, the president's youngest brother.

3904. Paterson, Thomas G., and William J. Brophy, "October Missiles and November Elections: The Cuban Missile Crisis and American Politics," pp. 87-119. No. **3173**. The effects of the missile crisis helped some Democrats and hurt some Democrats; it buoyed some Republicans and weakened some Republicans and in some instances Cuba was not even a major campaign issue.

3905. Payne, Thomas. "The 1962 Election in Montana." *Western Political Quarterly* 16 (June 1963): 439-42. Election results produced a checkerboard pattern as voters chose one Democrat and one Republican for the two congressional seats; no national issue was more important than Kennedy's farm program.

3906. "Political Fallout: Who Gains? Effect of President's Blockade of Cuba." *Newsweek* 60 (November 5, 1962): 35-6. The recent resolution of the Cuban crisis will help incumbents especially those identified with President Kennedy, but in gubernatorial races that matter is marginal at best.

3907. "Politics of Personality: Symposium." *Nation* 195 (October 27, 1962): 252-62. Concentrates on those contests which are of more than local interest because of the personalities and issues involved or because the outcome is likely to affect national policy either immediately or in 1964.

3908. "Republicans, The House, the States, the Unsolid South, the Senate, the Governors." *Time* 80 (November 16, 1962): 22-8. Detailed coverage of the various national and state races.

3909. Roper, Elmo. "Who Really Won the Elections of '62?" *Saturday Review* 45 (December 15, 1962): 13. Large number of voters left political loyalties behind to vote for whichever candidate seemed the best; nevertheless, the Democratic congressional vote dropped to 51.9 percent.

3910. "Some Election Results You May Have Missed." *U.S. News and World Report* 53 (November 26, 1962): 54, 56. As witness the rebellious mood of voters, governors were turned out of office on a wholesale basis; congressional candidates who challenged Washington won wide favor; black voters were crucial in some southern states; and farmers often supported opponents of Kennedy's farm programs.

3911. "Three Great Big Grins to Jolt the Ins." *Life* 53 (November 16, 1962): 38-45. Three Republicans in major states--William Scranton (Pennsylvania), George Romney (Michigan), and Nelson Rockefeller (New York)--won gubernatorial races and thus are possible challengers to JFK in 1964.

3912. "Trends That Are Making the Democrats Unhappy." *U.S. News and World Report* 53 (November 26, 1962): 50-2. Kennedy can no longer count on a solid South, and the right Republican ticket could give that party a sweep.

3913. Tuttle, Daniel, Jr. "The 1962 Election in Hawaii." *Western Political Quarterly* 16 (June 1963): 426-31. A sweep for Democrats, including victories in all national congressional races, but the Cuban crisis played only an incidental role.

3914. "Who Really Won the '62 Election?" *U.S. News and World Report* 53 (November 19, 1962): 40-2. Experts have called the 1962 election a narrow victory for President Kennedy, which means a continued difficult time for his legislative program.

3915. "Whose Victory Was It?" *New Republic* 147 (November 17, 1962): 3-6. In surveying the various congressional, gubernatorial, and state legislative races, the lead article contends that neither foreign nor national issues, except possibly medicare and "big government," seem to have much to do with the victories.

3916. "Why I Won; Why I Lost: Candidates' Own Analysis." *U.S. News and World Report* 53 (November 19, 1962): 64-6, 69-72. A state-by-state analysis of U.S. Senate and House of Representative results in which support of President Kennedy was the decisive factor, according to many winning Democrats.

3917. Wicker, Tom. "Kennedy, Too, Hits the Election Trail." *New York Times*

Magazine (October 14, 1962), pp. 24-5, 121-22. The reasons for Kennedy's involvement is discussed.

3918. "Widening Crack in the Solid South." *U.S. News and World Report* 53 (November 9, 1962): 60. Republicans are making significant inroads because of southern discontent with President Kennedy's "liberal" policies.

11

The Kennedy Assassination

The literature on the Kennedy assassination is voluminous, comprising a virtual cottage industry of assassination scholars, most of whom are freelance writers or lawyers. Several have devoted their lives to the study of the assassination. From the very beginning, most assassination scholars have rejected the findings of the President's Commission on the Assassination of President Kennedy (Warren Commission) and have concluded that Lee Harvey Oswald did not alone assassinate President Kennedy and that Jack Ruby did not kill Oswald out of grief for the Kennedy family. The conspiracy, these scholars have insisted, involved organized crime, the Castro government, and/or anti-Castro Cubans. Even the CIA became a conspirator in some studies. The best works nevertheless hesitate to define the specific nature of the conspiracy since the necessary facts are missing to substantiate any particular scenario. Oliver Stone's 1991 film, *JFK*, has done much to popularize the conspiratorial point of view and to focus public attention on the controversial aspects of the "crime of the century." More recently Gerald Posner's much publicized *Case Closed* has intensified the controversy by calling into question all conspiratorial assumptions. Because of the constraints of space, only the more significant works can be treated below. Otherwise the assassination would consume this entire volume.

3919. Adelson, Alan. *The Ruby-Oswald Affair*. Seattle: Romar Books, 1988. Based partly on Ruby family material, this study seeks to refute the charges that Ruby was a Mafia hit man or part of any other conspiracy.

3920. Adler, Bill, ed. *The Weight of the Evidence: The Warren Report and Its Critics*. New York: Meredith, 1968. Summarizes the Warren Report and presents its principal critics and defenders.

3921. Alvarez, Luis W. "A Physicist Examines the Kennedy Assassination Film." *American Journal of Physics* 44 (September 1976): 813-27. The author uses the tools of the physicist to draw some conclusions that escaped the notice of the Warren Commission.

3922. Ansbacher, Heinz, Rowena R. Ansbacher, David Shiverick, and Kathleen Shiverick. "Lee Harvey Oswald: An Adlerian Interpretation." *Psychoanalytic Review* 53 (Fall 1966): 55-68. Oswald's problems are attributed to his relationship with his mother.

3923. Anson, Robert Sam. *"They've Killed the President!": The Search for the Murderers of John F. Kennedy.* New York: Bantam, 1975. A correspondent for *New Times* magazine reviews possible motives of conspirators and calls for a major congressional investigation.

3924. Artwohl, Robert R. "JFK's Assassination: Conspiracy, Forensic Science, and Common Sense." *JAMA* 269 (March 24-31, 1993): 1540-43. Artwohl maintains that autopsy findings and all photographic and available assassination films support the fact that two shots from the rear of the motorcade hit the president.

3925. Associated Press. *The Torch Is Passed: The Associated Press Story of the Death of a President.* New York: Associated Press, 1963. A memorial of the assassination and funeral that sold more than 4 million copies.

3926. Baker, Dean C. *The Assassination of President Kennedy: A Study of the Press Coverage.* Ann Arbor: University of Michigan Department of Journalism, 1965. Case studies conducted by department of journalism students.

3927. Belin, David W. *Final Disclosure: The Full Truth about the Assassination of President John F. Kennedy.* New York: Scribner's, 1987. Written by the Warren Commission counsel, Belin intends to show how the American public has been misled by a relatively small combination of assassination sensationalists and cultists.

3928. _____. *November 22, 1963: You Are the Jury.* New York: Quadrangle, 1973. Belin goes over the evidence and the conspiracy theories before concluding that the Warren Commission report is irrefutable.

3929. Belli, Melvin M., and M. C. Carroll. *Dallas Justice: The Real Story of Jack Ruby and His Trial.* New York: David McKay, 1964. The chronicle of Ruby's defense attorney.

3930. Bishop, James A. *The Day Kennedy Was Shot.* New York: Funk and Wagnalls, 1968. A best seller, this work is also one of the more error-filled and factually distorted books on the assassination.

3931. Blakey, G. Robert, and Richard N. Billings. *Fatal Hour: The Assassination of President Kennedy by Organized Crime.* New York: Berkley, 1992. Reprint, with updated introduction, of *The Plot to Kill the President.*

3932. _____. *The Plot to Kill the President.* New York: Times Books, 1981. Blakely, general counsel of the 1978 Select House of Representatives Committee on Assassinations, believes that elements of organized crime were involved in the assassination of Kennedy.

3933. Bloomgarden, Henry S. *The Gun: A "Biography" of the Gun That Killed John F. Kennedy*. New York: Grossman, 1975. A history of the Italian-made Mannlicher-Carcano, Oswald's rifle.

3934. Bonner, Judy W. *Investigation of a Homicide: The Murder of John F. Kennedy*. Anderson, SC: Droke House, 1969. Report of the assassination and its investigation from the Dallas police department viewpoint.

3935. Breo, Dennis L. "JFK's Death, Part II. Dallas MDs Recall Their Memories." *JAMA* 267 (May 27, 1992): 2804-07. Four Parkland Memorial Hospital physicians, all present at the time of Kennedy's death, say that the autopsy photos of the throat wound are very compatible with what they saw in Parkland Trauma Room 1.

3936. _____. "JFK's Death, Part III. Dr. Finck Speaks Out: Two Bullets from the Rear." *JAMA* 268 (October 7, 1992): 1748-54). Pathologist Pierre Finck was in attendance with Humes and Boswell at the Kennedy autopsy in Bethesda, Md.; he agrees with Humes and Boswell that Kennedy was struck by two bullets from the rear.

3937. _____. "JFK's Death: The Plain Truth from the MDs Who Did the Autopsy." *JAMA* 267 (May 27, 1992): 2794-803. Centers on the two Navy pathologists, Humes and Boswell, who did the autopsy of John Kennedy on the night of November 22; they both contend that Kennedy was struck by two bullets that came from above and behind him.

3938. Brogan, Dennis W. "Death in Dallas: Myths After Kennedy." *Encounter* 23 (December 1964): 20-6. The reasons for myths of conspiracy.

3939. Brown, Walt. *People vs. Lee Harvey Oswald: History on Trial*. New York: Carroll and Graf, 1992. This book gives Oswald the belated defense he never had.

3940. Buchanan, Thomas G. *Who Killed Kennedy?* New York: G. P. Putnam's Sons, 1964. A journalist briefly criticizes the Warren Commission.

3941. Canfield, Michael, and Alan J. Weberman. *Coup d'etat in America: The CIA and the Assassination of John F. Kennedy*. New York: Third Press, 1975. Alleges that JFK was murdered by the CIA.

3942. Conant, Jennet. "The Man Who Shot 'JFK.'" *GQ* (January 1992): 137-39. A thoughtful analysis of Oliver Stone's film, *JFK*.

3943. Costigliola, Frank C. "'Like Children in the Darkness': European Reaction to the Assassination of John F. Kennedy." *Journal of Popular Culture* 20 (Winter

1986): 115-24. The intensity of European reaction to the assassination of President Kennedy was a direct reflection of American power and influence.

3944. Crenshaw, Charles, and J. Gary Shaw. *JFK: Conspiracy of Silence.* New York: Penguin, 1992. Crenshaw, one of the surgeons at Parkland Hospital, claims that the president was shot twice from the front.

3945. Curry, Jesse E. *JFK Assassination File.* Dallas: American Poster, 1969. By the Dallas police chief, it contains a slightly altered police log report for November 22, 1963.

3946. Cushman, Robert F. "Why the Warren Commission?" *New York University Law Review* 40 (May 1965): 477-503. Explores the purposes and validity of the Warren Commission from a constitutional perspective.

3947. Cutler, Robert B. *Crossfire: Evidence of Conspiracy.* Danvers, Ma.: Bett's and Mirror Press, 1975. One of several efforts by Cutler who questioned the lone-assassin theory.

3948. Davis, John H. *The Kennedy Contract.* New York: Harper Paperbacks, 1993. In February 1963 mob lawyer Frank Ragano supposedly carried a message from Teamster head Jimmy Hoffa to mobsters Santos Trafficante, Jr., and Carlos Marcello to kill the president, the result of which was a contract that led to the assassination.

3949. _____. *Mafia Kingfish: Carlos Marcello and the Assassination of John F. Kennedy.* New York: McGraw-Hill, 1989. Because of Attorney General Robert Kennedy's crusade against Marcello--the Louisiana Mafia chieftain--and organized crime in general, Marcello engineered the assassination of President Kennedy.

3950. Davison, Jean. *Oswald's Game.* New York: W. W. Norton, 1983. A neglected but credible anti-conspiracy account that views Kennedy's assassination as the result of Oswald's character and background interacting with circumstance.

3951. DiEugenio, James. *Justice Betrayed: The Kennedy Assassination and the Garrison Trial.* New York: Sheridan Square, 1992. Argues on the basis of Jim Garrison's contentions: that members of the U.S. intelligence community were behind the conspiracy, that the assassination was designed to change government policy, and that the truth was covered up by an invisible government.

3952. Duffy, James. *Conspiracy: Who Killed JFK?* New York: Shapolsky, 1989. Oswald was not the loner he has been made out to be, and he was associated with people connected with American intelligence.

3953. Duffy, James, and Vincent Ricci. *The Assassination of John F. Kennedy: A Complete Book of Facts.* New York: Thunder's Mouth, 1992. A useful compilation of accurate information of people, places, events, facts, objects, and theories associated with President Kennedy's death.

3954. Dunning, John L. "The Kennedy Assassination as Viewed by Communist Media." *Journalism Quarterly* 41 (Spring 1964): 163-69. The Communist radio consistently treated the story of Kennedy's death in a dignified manner and paid qualified tribute to him.

3955. Eddowes, Michael. *The Oswald File.* New York: Clarkson N. Potter, 1977. Without credible evidence, this English lawyer believes that Oswald was actually a Soviet assassin assigned by Premier Khrushchev to kill Kennedy.

3956. Epstein, Edward Jay. *The Assassination Chronicles: Inquest, Counterplot, and Legend.* New York: Carroll and Graf, 1992. The reproduction of Epstein's earlier works along with three new essays, including an afterward summarizing the state of the evidence in 1992.

3957. _____. *Counterplot.* New York: Viking Press, 1969. Examines the credibility of the investigation conducted by New Orleans District Attorney Jim Garrison.

3958. _____. *Inquest: The Warren Commission and the Establishment of Truth.* New York: Viking, 1966. The Warren Commission was not interested in truth but in the settling of doubts and suspicions.

3959. _____. *Legend: The Secret World of Lee Harvey Oswald.* New York: Reader's Digest, 1978. Epstein expands our knowledge of Oswald's past and, in a narrative devoid of analysis, he implicates him in Kennedy's assassination.

3960. _____."Who's Afraid of the Warren Report?" *Esquire* 60 (December 1966): 204, 330-32, 334. Concentrates on the growing number of Americans conducting investigations on the Warren Commission findings and on the assassination itself.

3961. Evica, George Michael. *And We Are All Mortal: New Evidence and Analysis in the Assassination of John F. Kennedy.* West Hartford, Ct.: University of Hartford, 1978. Concludes that the material evidence suggests that no convincing case can be made against Oswald, that the most important hard evidence is at least tainted, and that all of the reliable physical evidence proves that multiple weapons were fired at the president.

3962. Fensterwald, Bernard, Jr., ed. *Coincidence or Conspiracy?* New York: Zebra Books, 1977. One of many conspiracy books coming out of the 1970s as the result of the CIA-Mafia revelations of that time.

3963. Fonzi, Gaeton. *The Last Investigation.* New York: Thunder's Mouth Press,

1993. Written by a staff investigator of the House Select Committee on Assassinations who accepts the conspiracy viewpoint, Fonzi contends that the U.S. government has deceived Americans.

3964. Ford, Gerald R., and John M. Stiles. *Portrait of an Assassin.* New York: Simon and Schuster, 1965. Ford, a member of the Warren Commission and a persistent defender of its report, and Stiles base their narrative on the Commission's findings.

3965. Fox, Sylvan. *The Unanswered Questions about President Kennedy's Assassination.* New York: Award Books, 1965. A reporter gives an informed and brief critical statement in a widely distributed paperback that spurred other journalistic efforts.

3966. Freese, Paul L. "The Warren Commission and the Fourth Shot: A Reflection on the Fundamentals of Forensic Fact Finding." *New York University Law Review* 40 (May 1965): 424-65. An early critique of the operations of the Warren Commission.

3967. Furiati, Claudia. *ZR Rifle: The Plot to Kill Kennedy and Castro.* Melbourne, Victoria, Australia: Ocean Press, 1994. Using some recently released documents from the Cuban government, Furiati, a Brazilian journalist and film-maker, accuses Richard Helms of the CIA of masterminding the assassination.

3968. Garrison, Jim. *A Heritage of Stone.* New York: G. P. Putnam's Sons, 1970. The New Orleans district attorney institutes an extensive investigation concentrating on military-business efforts to silence Kennedy, a supposed critic of the cold war expansion into Southeast Asia.

3969. _____. *On the Trail of the Assassins: My Investigation and Prosecution of the Murder of President Kennedy.* New York: Sheridan Square Press, 1988. Garrison's last book on his investigation of the Kennedy assassination, it influenced Oliver Stone's film, *JFK.*

3970. Gertz, Elmer. *Moments of Madness: The People v. Jack Ruby.* Chicago: Follett, 1968. Contends that Ruby acted on his own in killing Oswald.

3971. Giglio, James N. "Oliver Stone's *JFK* in Historical Perspective." *Perspectives* (American Historical Association Newsletter) 30 (April 1992): 18-19. Stone's film builds on a twenty-five year tradition of conspiratorial viewpoints regarding the Kennedy assassination.

3972. Goodhart, Arthur L. "The Mysteries of the Kennedy Assassination and the English Press." *Law Quarterly Review* 83 (January 1967): 23-63. The greatest mystery is that the English press has always assumed that there must be a mystery attached to the assassination.

3973. _____. "The Warren Commission from a Procedural Standpoint." *New York University Law Review* 40 (May 1965): 404-23. The commission was outstandingly successful in setting up its own machinery and procedures.

3974. Greenberg, Bradley S., and Edwin B. Parker, eds. *The Kennedy Assassination and the American Public: Social Communication in Crisis.* Stanford: Stanford University Press, 1965. An effort to portray the responses of the mass media and the American public.

3975. Griffin, Leland M. "When Dreams Collide: Rhetorical Trajectories in the Assassination of President Kennedy." *Quarterly Journal of Speech* 70 (May 1984): 111-31. Although Oswald acted alone, he was not a loner, for he saw himself as the leader of a movement, imaginary though it was.

3976. Groden, Robert J. *The Killing of a President: The Complete Photographic Record of the JFK Assassination, The Conspiracy and the Cover-up.* New York: Viking Studio Books, 1993. In depicting Kennedy's assassination as a conspiracy, Groden, in a well crafted book, introduces many unpleasant and sensitive photographs that have not been previously published.

3977. Groden, Robert J., and Harrison Edward Livingstone. *High Treason: The Assassination of President John F. Kennedy and the New Evidence of Conspiracy.* New York: Berkley Books, 1990. Presents a massive conspiracy involving, among others, the FBI, CIA, and various commission investigators with Oswald being the "fall guy" in the assassination.

3978. Hamilton, James W. "Some Observations on the Motivation of Lee Harvey Oswald." *Journal of Psychology* 14 (Summer 1986): 43-54. Oswald's psychological disturbances led to his assassination of Kennedy.

3979. Hanson, William H. *The Shooting of John F. Kennedy: One Assassin, Three Shots, Three Hits, No Misses.* San Antonio: Naylor, 1969. Asserts that Kennedy was struck by all three bullets and confirms the Warren Commission's conclusion that a single assassin, acting alone, fired those three bullets.

3980. Hartogs, Renatus. *The Two Assassins.* New York: Crowell, 1965. A psychiatric comparison of Oswald and Ruby.

3981. Henderson, Bruce, and Sam Summerlin. *1:33.* New York: Cowles, 1968. An account of the reaction of people around the world to the news of Kennedy's death at 1:33 p.m.

3982. Hock, Paul, Peter Dale Scott, and Russell Stetler, eds. *The Assassination: Dallas and Beyond: A Guide to Cover-ups and Investigations.* New York: Vintage, 1976. Largely an anthology of critical writings on the Warren Commission findings.

3983. Holland, Max. "After Thirty Years: Making Sense of the Assassination." *Reviews in American History* 22 (June 1994): 191-209.   In disputing various conspiracy theories, Holland suggests that the JFK assassination literature is the contemporary strain of the resilient paranoid style in American politics.

3984. House of Representatives. Select Committee on Assassinations. *Investigation of the Assassination of President John F. Kennedy: Appendix to Hearings Before the Select Committee on Assassinations of the U.S. House of Representatives.* 7 vols. 95 Cong., 2nd Session. Washington: Government Printing Office, 1979.   The cumulative testimony and documentation are in twelve volumes of the House hearings.

3985. _____. Select Committee on Assassinations. *Investigation of the Assassination of President John F. Kennedy: Hearings Before the Select Committee on Assassinations of the U.S. House of Representatives.* 5 vols. 95th Cong., 2nd Session. Washington: Government Printing Office, 1978-79.   See above.

3986. _____. Select Committee on Assassinations. *Report of the Select Committee on Assassinations.* 94th Cong., 2nd Session. Washington: Government Printing Office, 1979.   Like the Warren Report, this report concludes that the president was struck by two rifle shots fired from behind him, but based on the acoustical evidence, since refuted, it also contends that an additional shot came from the front and that, however unlikely organized crime as a group was involved, individual mobsters had the motive, opportunity, and means to assassinate the president.

3987. Hurt, Henry. *Reasonable Doubt: An Investigation into the Assassination of John F. Kennedy.* New York: Holt, Rinehart and Winston, 1987.   In a generally well researched study, Hurt provides a thoughtful analysis in his pro-conspiracy account that leans toward the anti-Castro Cuban element; its weakness is its dependance on the testimony of Robert Easterling, a questionable source.

3988. *Investigation of the Assassination of President John F. Kennedy: Hearings Before the President's Commission on the Assassination of President Kennedy.* 26 volumes. Washington: Government Printing Office, 1964.   Still a signficant primary source.

3989. James, Rosemary, and Jack Wardlaw. *Plot or Politics? The Garrison Case and Its Cast.* New Orleans: Pelican, 1967.   Two newspaper reporters provide an account of the Garrison investigation.

3990. Joesten, Joachim. *Oswald: Assassin or Fall Guy?* New York: Morzani and Munsell, 1964.   Assumes the existence of a right wing plot.

3991. Jones, Penn J. *Forgive My Grief.* Midlothian, Tx.: Midlothian Mirror, 1966-

1969. 3 vols. Three slim volumes of essays and analysis of Warren Commission witness testimony drawn from intensive research.

3992. Jovich, John B. *Reflections on JFK's Assassination: 250 Famous Americans Remember November 22, 1963*. Kensington, Md.: Woodbine House, 1988. Mostly the reproduction of letters from prominent Americans regarding their reactions to President Kennedy's death.

3993. Kantor, Seth. *Who Was Jack Ruby?* New York: Everest House, 1978. Both Ruby and Oswald had been manipulated by the mob.

3994. Kaplan, John. "Controversy: The Assassins." *American Scholar* 36 (Spring 1967): 271-308. After a very thoughtful critique of the assassination literature and the Warren Commission findings, Kaplan concludes that the full truth about the assassination will never be known.

3995. Kaplan, John, and Jon R. Waltz. *The Trial of Jack Ruby*. New York: Macmillan, 1965. Ruby, the assassin of Oswald, was stripped of both his self-respect and his illusions at his trial, which explains his subsequent mental deterioration.

3996. Kurtz, Michael L. "The Assassination of John F. Kennedy: A Historical Perspective." *Historian* 45 (November 1982): 1-19. Overviews the salient features of Kennedy's assassination and concludes that, beyond a reasonable doubt, more than one assassin fired at the president.

3997. _____. *Crime of the Century: The Kennedy Assassination from a Historian's Perspective*. Second edition. Knoxville: University of Tennessee Press, 1993. The only academic historian to write a book on the Kennedy assassination, Kurtz devotes a lengthy introduction to refute Gerald Posner's 1993 findings and concludes that a conspiracy involved a minimum of three gunmen and that the assassination was ordered by Fidel Castro in retaliation for the assassination attempts against his own life by the CIA.

3998. _____. "Lee Harvey Oswald in New Orleans: A Reappraisal." *Louisiana History* 21 (Winter 1980): 7-22. Because the Warren Commission failed to investigate Oswald's anti-Castro activities in New Orleans, it mistakenly concluded that his actions in that city fit the lone assassin, no conspiracy thesis.

3999. Lane, Mark. *A Citizen's Dissent: Mark Lane Replies*. New York: Holt, Rinehart and Winston, 1968. The attorney Lane writes about those who criticized his *Rush to Judgment*.

4000. _____. *Plausible Denial: Was the CIA Involved in the Assassination of JFK?* New York: Thunder's Mouth, 1991. The CIA conspiracy to assassinate Kennedy implicated E. Howard Hunt, who was involved in the Bay of Pigs fiasco and later in the Watergate break-in, but Lane provides no convincing evidence that the CIA was involved.

4001. _____. *Rush to Judgment: A Critique of the Warren Commission's Inquiry into the Murders of President John F. Kennedy, Officer J. D. Tippit and Lee Harvey Oswald.* New York: Holt, Rinehart and Winston, 1966. Besides rejecting the Warren Commission report, without evidence Lane made Chief Justice Warren responsible for the inquiry's failure.

4002. Lattimer, John L. "Additional Data on the Shooting of President Kennedy." *JAMA* 269 (March 24-31, 1993): 1544-47. Lattimer, a urologist, concludes from the data that bullet 399 was deformed, not pristine; that it went through Kennedy and Connally; that the backward recoil from Kennedy's head resulted from a bullet from the rear; that the small size of the exit wound on the front of the neck was due to the buttressing of the skin by his shirt collar.

4003. _____. "Factors in the Death of President Kennedy." *JAMA* 198 (October 24, 1966): 327-33. Lattimer explains the significance of Kennedy's back brace contributing to the fatal bullet wound to the back side of the head.

4004. _____. "Observations Based on A Review of the Autopsy Photographs, X-Rays, and Related Materials of the Late President John F. Kennedy." *Resident and Staff Physician* 34 (May 1972): 34-64. Lattimer, the first non-government person to study the restricted Kennedy material, is in basic agreement with the Warren Commission Report.

4005. Lattimer, John K., Gary Lattimer, and John Lattimer. "Could Oswald Have Shot President Kennedy? Further Ballistic Studies." *Bulletin of the New York Academy of Medicine.* 48 (April 1972): 513-24. The authors, employing in tests a Carcano rifle like Oswald's, argue that the rifle was accurate, dependable, and adaptable enough to have killed President Kennedy.

4006. _____. "An Experimental Study of the Backward Movement of President Kennedy's Head." *Surgery, Gynecology and Obstetrics* 142 (February 1976): 246-54. The backward and sideways lurch of President Kennedy's head does not mean he was hit by a bullet from the front or right front.

4007. _____. "The Kennedy-Connally One Bullet Theory: Further Circumstantial and Experimental Evidence." *Medical Times* 102 (November 1974): 33-56. This study coincides with the Warren Commission's thesis that a single bullet (Exhibit 399) struck both President Kennedy and Governor Connally.

4008. Lewis, Richard Warren. *The Scavengers and Critics of the Warren Report.* New York: Delacorte Press, 1967. Superficially scrutinizes the theories and methods of the Commission's major critics.

4009. Lifton, David S. *Best Evidence: Disguise and Deception in the Assassination of John F. Kennedy.* Rev. ed. New York: Carroll and Graf, 1988. This best seller claims that the president's body was altered before the official autopsy was performed.

4010. Livingstone, Harrison Edward. *High Treason 2: The Great Cover-up, the Assassination of President John F. Kennedy.* New York: Carroll and Graf, 1992. Concludes that the conspiracy included the forgery of the autopsy evidence and the planting of considerable evidence to implicate Oswald.

4011. _____. *Killing the Truth: Deceit and Deception in the JFK Case.* New York: Carroll and Graf, 1993. A sloppily researched effort that argues that JFK's autopsy photos were faked.

4012. Love, Ruth L. "Television and the Death of a President: Network Decisions in Covering Collective Events." Ph D. diss., Columbia University, 1969. Based on interviews of executives from ABC, NBC, two wire services, and local television and radio stations in Dallas.

4013. Lundberg, George D. "Closing the Case in *JAMA* on the John F. Kennedy Autopsy." *JAMA* 268 (October 7, 1992): 1736-38. The autopsy of Kennedy indicates that he suffered from Addison's disease, probably idiopathic, but not of tuberculous in origin.

4014. McDonald, Hugh C. *Appointment in Dallas: The Final Solution to the Assassination of JFK.* New York: Hugh McDonald, 1975. A veteran law enforcement officer traces and interviews the "real" assassin.

4015. MacDonald, Neil. "Confidential and Secret Documents of the Warren Commission Deposited in U.S. Archives." *Computers and Automation* 19 (November 1970): 44-7. A list of over 200 documents of the Warren Commission in the National Archives, which have been classified as confidential, secret, or top secret.

4016. McKinney, Bruce Converse. "Decision Making in the President's Commission on the Assassination of President Kennedy: A Descriptive Analysis Employing Irving Janis' Groupthink Hypothesis." Ph.D. diss., Pennsylvania State University, 1985. Questions the decisions made by the Warren Commission, contending that members were victims of the group think syndrome.

4017. McMillan, Priscilla Johnson. *Marina and Lee.* New York: Harper and Row, 1977. A former Russian-language translator who wrote about her personal encounters with Kennedy in the 1950s in the prologue, McMillan also interviewed Oswald in 1959 and won the trust of his wife out of which came this book.

4018. Manchester, William. *The Death of a President: November 20-November 25,*

1963. New York: Harper and Row, 1967. The official commissioned version of the Kennedy family, this work has inspired much controversy and, despite its wealth of primary material--mostly interviews--is considered dated.

4019. Marcus, Raymond. *The Bastard Bullet: A Search for Legitimacy for Commission Exhibit 399*. Los Angeles: Rendell Publications, 1966. A brief scholarly study of one aspect of the investigation of the Warren Commission.

4020. Marina, William. "Shooting Down the Conspiracy Theory." *Reason* 11 (May 1979): 18-24. While admitting that the Warren Commission made errors of judgment, Marina concludes that alternative theories--especially those suggesting conspiracy--are implausible and that the Warren Commission's conclusions are basically correct.

4021. Marrs, Jim. *Crossfire: The Plot That Killed Kennedy*. New York: Carroll and Graf, 1989. The journalist Marrs's wide-ranging conspiratorial scenario even implicates Vice President Lyndon Johnson.

4022. Matthews, Jim. *Four Dark Days in History, November 22, 23, 24, 25, 1963*. Los Angeles: Special Publications, 1963. A photo-history of the assassination.

4023. Mayo, John B. *Bulletin from Dallas: The President Is Dead*. New York: Exposition Press, 1967. The story of the assassination as covered by radio and television.

4024. Meagher, Sylvia. *Accessories After the Fact: The Warren Commission, the Authorities, and the Report*. Indianapolis: Bobbs-Merrill, 1967. After an exhaustive study of the Warren Commission evidence, Meagher, a research librarian for the United Nations, concludes that the Commission failed to prove that Oswald killed Kennedy.

4025. _____. *Subject Index to the Warren Report and Hearings and Exhibits*. New York: Scarecrow, 1966. The objective is to provide guidance to all information in the twenty-six volumes of Hearings and Exhibits and in the Report itself.

4026. _____. "Wheels Within Deals: How the Kennedy Investigation Was Organized." *Minority of One* 10 (July/August 1968): 23-7. Political considerations and self-interest dominated.

4027. Menninger, Bonar. *Mortal Error: The Shot That Killed JFK*. New York: St. Martin's, 1992. Menninger summarizes the research findings of ballistics expert Howard Donahue whose startling conclusion is that the fatal headshot was accidently fired by special agent George Hickey who was in the car behind Kennedy.

4028. Meunier, Robert. *Shadows of Doubt: The Warren Commission Cover-up*. New York: Exposition Press, 1976. Produces evidence in calling for a new investigation.

4029. Micozzi, Marc S. "Lincoln, Kennedy and the Autopsy." *JAMA* 267 (May 27, 1992): 2791. Accepts the originial autopsy results and the Warren Commission report.

4030. Moore, Jim. *Conspiracy of One: The Definitive Book on the Kennedy Assassination*. Fort Worth: Summit Group, 1990. Beginning as a critic, Moore has come to believe in much of the official version of the assassination.

4031. Morrow, Robert D. *Betrayal*. Chicago: H. Regnery, 1976. Asserts that Cuban exiles plotted with the CIA in the murder of President Kennedy.

4032. _____. *First Hand Knowledge: How I Participated in the CIA-Mafia Murder of President Kennedy*. New York: Shapolksy, 1992. A former CIA agent claims to have participated in the Kennedy assassination on the direct orders of CIA covert operations.

4033. Moss, Armand. *Disinformation, Misinformation, and the 'Conspiracy' to Kill JFK Exposed*. Hamden, Ct.: Archon Books, 1987. Argues that not a line has to be changed in the Warren Report regarding the facts except for Oswald's motivation.

4034. Newman, Albert H. *The Assassination of John F. Kennedy: The Reasons Why*. New York: Clarkson N. Potter, 1970. A strong supporter of the Warren Commission findings.

4035. North, Mark. *Act of Treason: J. Edgar Hoover and the Assassination of President Kennedy*. New York: Carroll and Graf, 1991. In September 1962, FBI Director J. Edgar Hoover supposedly learned that the Mafia boss Carlos Marcello of New Orleans had a contract out on the life of John Kennedy but nevertheless suppressed this information.

4036. Oglesby, Carl. *The JFK Assassination: The Facts and the Theories*. New York: Signet, 1992. Oglesby, the founder and director of the Assassination Information Bureau and a long-time critic of the Warren Commission findings, includes some of his earlier writings as well as new pieces on the assassination.

4037. Olson, Don, and Ralph Turner. "Photographic Evidence and the Assassination of President John F. Kennedy." *Journal of Forensic Sciences* 16 (October 1971): 399-419. Suggests that Kennedy was first shot during the frames 186-190 in the Zapruder film--earlier than reported by the Warren Commission.

4038. Oren, Karen, and Paul Peterson. "The Kennedy Assassination: A Case Study in the Dynamics of Political Socialization." *Journal of Politics* 29 (May 1967): 388-404. Interviewers of the National Opinion Research Center asked parents with children (ages four to twelve) whether and how they explained the Kennedy assassination to their children.

4039. Oswald, Robert L. *Lee: A Portrait of Lee Harvey Oswald by His Brother.* New York: Coward-McCann, 1967. A product of a thousand rejections, Lee Oswald was on a dangerous course by the age of thirteen.

4040. O'Toole, George. *The Assassination Tapes: An Electronic Probe into the Murder of John F. Kennedy and the Dallas Coverup.* New York: Penthouse Press, 1975. O'Toole uses the psychological stress evaluator on a tape recording of Oswald's press conference and concludes that Oswald was telling the truth when he denied shooting the president.

4041. Oxford, Edward. "Destiny In Dallas." *American History Illustrated* 23 (November 1988): 12-27, 46-7. A descriptive account, based on the testimony of eyewitnesses, of the events relating to President Kennedy's assassination.

4042. _____. "Lights and Shadows." *American History Illustrated* 23 (January 1989): 42-8. Good summary of the contributions and ambiguities of the Kennedy assassination.

4043. Payne, Darwin. *The Press Corps and the Kennedy Assassination.* Lexington, Ky.: Association for Education in Journalism, 1969. A former Dallas newsman summarizes the coverage.

4044. Petty, Charles S. "JFK--An Allonge." *JAMA* 269 (March 24-31, 1993): 1552-53. The autopsy at Bethesda was done under less than ideal circumstances.

4045. Popkin, Richard H. *The Second Oswald.* New York, Avon, 1966. Argues that a fake Oswald probably existed to divert investigators.

4046. Posner, Gerald. *Case Closed: Lee Harvey Oswald and the Assassination of JFK.* New York: Random House, 1993. The best of the anticonspiracy works, the attorney Posner uses computer enhancements of the Zapruder film and other evidence to uphold the Warren Commission findings that Oswald fired three shots at the president, one of which also struck Governor Connelly of Texas.

4047. Raskin, Marcus. "*JFK* and the Culture of Violence." *American Historical Review* 97 (April 1992): 487-99. On the complex question of the Kennedy assassination, according to Raskin, the Oliver Stone film, *JFK*, holds its own against the Warren Commission.

4048. *Report of the President's Commission on the Assassination of President John F. Kennedy.* Washington: Government Printing Office, 1964.

4049. Roberts, Charles. *The Truth About the Assassination.* New York: Grosset and

Dunlap, 1967. An effort by a White House correspondent to uphold the findings of the Warren Commission by attacking those who wrote against it.

4050. Roffman, Howard. *Presumed Guilty: Lee Harvey Oswald in the Assassination of President Kennedy*. Cranbury, NJ: Associated University Press, 1975. Contends that the Warren Commission engaged in a cover-up of the truth and issued a report that misrepresented or distorted every relevant fact about the crime.

4051. Rogin, Michael. "*JFK*: The Movie." *American Historical Review* 97 (April 1992): 500-05. Sexual conotations dominate Stone's paranoid film style.

4052. Rosenstone, Robert A. "*JFK*: Historical Fact/Historical Fiction." *American Historical Review* 97 (April 1992): 506-11. Focuses on the distinctions between written history and historical film.

4053. Sauvage, Léo. *The Oswald Affair: An Examination of the Contradictions and Omissions of the Warren Report*. Cleveland: World Publishing, 1965. First published in Paris by this French journalist, it critiques the Warren Commission report and doubts Oswald's guilt.

4054. Scheim, David E. *Contract on America: The Mafia Murder of President John F. Kennedy*. New York: Shapolsky, 1988. Following nearly ten years of investigation, Scheim, a computer systems analyst, concludes that the Mafia played a preponderant role in both the assassination of Kennedy and the murder of his accused assassin.

4055. Schonfeld, Maurice W. "The Shadow of a Gunman: An Account of a Twelve-year Investigation of a Kennedy Assassination Film." *Columbia Journalism Review* 14 (July/August 1975): 46-50. Orville Nix's film scanned the grassy knoll area and revealed what appeared to be a man with a gun aimed at President Kennedy.

4056. Schuyler, Michael. "The Bitter Harvest: Lyndon B. Johnson and the Assassination of John F. Kennedy." *Journal of American Culture* 8 (Fall 1985): 101-09. Continuing concerns about the Kennedy assassination robbed Johnson of a sense of legitimacy, limited his options, obscured his own achievements, and exaggerated his natural desire for acceptance and recognition.

4057. _____. "Ghosts in the White House: LBJ, RFK, and the Assassination of JFK." *Presidential Studies Quarterly* 17 (Summer 1987): 503-18. For Johnson one of the most important consequences of the assassination was the instant martyrdom of President Kennedy.

4058. Scobey, Alfredda. "A Lawyer's Notes on the Warren Commission Report." *American Bar Association Journal* 51 (January 1965): 39-43. Written by a member of the Warren Commission staff.

4059. Scott, Peter Dale. *Crime and Cover-up: The CIA, the Mafia, and the Dallas-Watergate Connection.* Berkeley: Westworks, 1977. Sees the Watergate Committee approach as a model in investigating the Kennedy assassination.

4060. _____. *Deep Politics and the Death of JFK.* Berkeley: University of California Press, 1993. Focuses on the structural defects in governance and society that allowed the assassination to be so badly investigated.

4061. Senate Select Committee to Study Governmental Operations With Respect to Intelligence Activities. *The Investigation of the Assassination of President John F. Kennedy: The Performance of the Intelligence Agencies.* Book 5, *Final Report of the Select Committee to Study Government Operations With Respect to Intelligence Activities.* 94th Cong., 2nd Session. Senate Report 94-755. Washington: Government Printing Office, 1976. Brings out the CIA and FBI relationship with the Warren Commission.

4062. Shaw, J. Gary, and Larry R. Harris. *Cover-up: The Governmental Conspiracy to Conceal the Facts About the Public Execution of John Kennedy.* Cleburne, Tx.: J. Gary Shaw, 1976. Claims that governmental officials are guilty of altering, suppressing, and destroying various forms of evidence in the Kennedy assassination.

4063. Sheatsley, Paul B., and Jacob J. Feldman. "The Assassination of President Kennedy: A Preliminary Report on Public Reactions and Behavior." *Public Opinion Quarterly* 28 (Summer 1964): 189-215. Among its many findings, this study reveals that 72 percent of the respondents were convinced that Oswald was the assassin.

4064. Simon, Arthur. "The Site of Crisis: Representation and the Assassination of JFK." Ph.D. diss., New York University, 1993. An analysis of the Kennedy assassination as seen through the visual arts.

4065. Sloan, Bill. *JFK: The Last Dissenting Witness.* Gretna, La.: Pelican, 1992. Focuses on the testimony of eyewitness Jean Hill, the "lady in red" in the Zapruder film.

4066. Smith, Matthew. *JFK: The Second Plot.* Edinburgh, United Kingdom: Mainstream Publishing, 1992. The second plot involved the concealment of renegade CIA agents who had employed the marksmen and had laid the blame at the door of Castro.

4067. Sparrow, John Hanbury Anges. *After the Assassination: A Positive Appraisal of the Warren Report.* New York: Chilmark Press, 1967. In a seventy-five page book, Sparrow attacks critics of the Warren Report such as Mark Lane, Harold Weisberg, and Sylvia Meagher.

4068. Sprague, Richard E. "The Assassination of President John F. Kennedy: The

Application of Computers to the Photographic Evidence." *Computers and Automation* 19 (May 1970): 29-60. A computer specialist lists and assigns numbers to all 510 known photographs of the murder scene and immediate events taken by seventy-five photographers.

4069. Stone, Nancy-Stephanie. "A Conflict of Interest: The Warren Commission, the FBI and the CIA." Ph.D. diss., Boston College, 1987. Conflicts of interest were a hindrance to a complete and accurate investigation and report.

4070. Summers, Anthony. *Conspiracy*. Updated and expanded edition. New York: Paragon House, 1989. An investigative reporter for the BBC links U.S. intelligence with the assassination.

4071. Thompson, Josiah. *Six Seconds in Dallas: A Micro-Study of the Kennedy Assassination.* New York: Bernard Geis, 1967. Purpose is to synthesize the evidence and concludes that three gunmen fired four shots at President Kennedy.

4072. Toplin, Robert Brent, ed. "Forum: Oliver Stone's *JFK.*" *Journal of American History* 79 (December 1992): 1262-68. Includes commentary by Toplin, Thomas C. Reeves, and William W. Phillips.

4073. Trask, Richard B. "The Day Kennedy Was Shot." *American Heritage* 39 (November 1988): 142-49. Cecil W. Stoughton, official photographer for John Kennedy, photographed the events of November 22.

4074. United Press International and *American Heritage Magazine. Four Days: The Historical Record of the Death of President Kennedy.* New York: American Heritage, 1964. Mostly photographs, it includes the journalist Merriman Smith's account of the assassination.

4075. Vogt, Allen R. "The Kennedy Assassination and the History Teacher." *History Teacher* 20 (November 1986): 7-26. Kennedy's assassination was one of the most traumatic events of recent American history, but history teachers largely ignore it in the classroom.

4076. Wecht, Cyril H. "A Critique of the Medical Aspects of the Investigation into the Assassination of President Kennedy." *Journal of Forensic Sciences* 11 (July 1966): 300-17. Notes that the autopsy report is incomplete and concludes that the Warren Commission should have called upon the American Academy of Forensic Sciences in a consultant capacity.

4077. _____. "JFK Assassination: 'A Prolonged and Willful Cover-up.'" *Modern Medicine* 42 (October 28, 1974): 40x-40ff. New spectrographic evidence reaffirms Wecht's belief in a government cover-up.

4078. _____. "Pathologist's View of JFK Autopsy: An Unsolved Case."

Modern Medicine 70 (November 27, 1972): 28-32.   The director of Forensic Sciences, Duquesne School of Law, concludes that the forensic evidence fails to uphold the Warren Commission conclusions.

4079. Wecht, Cyril H., and Robert P. Smith. "The Medical Evidence in the Assassination of President John F. Kennedy." *Forensic Science* 3 (April 1974): 105-28.   Concludes that the Warren Commission's single-bullet and single-assassin theories are untenable.

4080. Weisberg, Harold. *Case Open: Unanswered JFK Assassination Questions.* New York: Carroll and Graf, 1994.   Since the mid-1960s Weisberg has been a major critic of the establishment's explanation of the Kennedy assassination and remains a leading assassination researcher; this latest effort is an intemperate rebuttal of Posner's *Case Closed.*

4081. _____. *Oswald in New Orleans: Case of Conspiracy With the CIA.* New York: Canyon Books, 1967.   An exhaustive treatment of Jim Garrison's New Orleans investigation.

4082. _____. *Post-Mortem: JFK Assassination Cover-Up Smashed.* Frederick, Md.: H. Weisberg, 1975.   Probably Weisberg's best work because it contains documents that had been unavailable to researchers.

4083. _____. *Whitewash.* 4 vols. Hyattstown-Frederick, Md.: H. Weisberg, 1965-75.   Weisberg's first volume was the first book to establish a factual basis for rejecting the conclusions of the Warren Commission; other volumes focus on the unprofessional way the federal investigative agencies treated the evidence to promote the conclusion of a lone assassin.

4084. Wickey, John, and Eli Saltz. "Resolutions of the Liberal Dilemma in the Assassination of President Kennedy." *Journal of Personality* 33 (December 1965): 636-48.   Concerned with the factors which might influence the attitudes and beliefs of political liberals concerning Oswald and the assassination of Kennedy.

4085. Wilber, Charles G. "The Assassination of the Late President John F. Kennedy: An Academician's Thoughts." *American Journal of Forensic Medicine and Pathology* 7 (March 1986): 52-8.   A follow-up of Wilber's 1978 book and an endorsement of David Lifton's conclusions.

4086. _____. *Medicolegal Investigation of the Assassination of President John F. Kennedy Murder.* Springfield, Il.: Charles C Thomas, 1978.   A forensic biologist writes of governmental collusion in suppressing information.

4087. Wills, Gary B., and Ovid Demaris. *Jack Ruby.* New York: New American Library, 1968.   Seeks to prove that Ruby's murder of Oswald was not part of a sinister conspiratorial plot.

4088. Wise, Dan, and Marietta Maxfield. *The Day Kennedy Died*. San Antonio: Naylor, 1964. A recreation of the events of November 22 based on interviews with witnesses and police officers.

4089. Zelizer, Barbie. *Covering the Body: The Kennedy Assassination, the Media, and the Shaping of Collective Memory*. Chicago: University of Chicago Press, 1992. Zelizer writes how journalists established themselves as the preferred interpretors of Kennedy's death and how, in the process, they redefined journalism itself.

12
The Personal Life of John F. Kennedy

A. PERSONAL GLIMPSES

4090. Anson, Robert S. "Jack, Judy, Sam, and Johnny . . . and Frank, Fidel, Edgar . . . ." *New Times Magazine* (January 23, 1976): 20-3, 27-30, 32-3. Judith Campbell Exner's testimony before Senator Frank Church's Select Committee on Intelligence about her friendship with John Kennedy inspired this article.

4091. Bergquist, Laura. "Fiddle and Faddle." *Look* 26 (January 2, 1962): 30-3, 35. Bergquist's contemporary account of two young White House secretaries who became close to President Kennedy tells only part of the story.

4092. Bishop, Jim. *A Day in the Life of President Kennedy*. New York: Random House, 1964. The journalist Bishop spent four days at the White House in 1963 to fashion one representative day.

4093. "The Blauvelt Campaign." *Newsweek* 60 (September 24, 1962): 86-7. On Kennedy's supposed first marriage.

4094. Brown, Peter Harry, and Patte B. Barham. *Marilyn: The Last Take*. New York: Dutton, 1992. Details Monroe's tragic last year which involved Jack and Robert Kennedy.

4095. Bryan, C. D. B. "Say Goodbye to Camelot: Marilyn Monroe and the Kennedys." *Rolling Stone* (December 5, 1985): 36, 39, 41, 74-6, 80. Based on Anthony Summers's *Goddess*, the cancelled ABC television *20/20* segment, and the BBC documentary *Marilyn: Say Goodbye to the President*.

4096. Bryant, Traphes. *Dog Days at the White House: The Outrageous Memoirs of the Presidential Kennel Keeper*. New York: Macmillan, 1975. Bryant was an observer of Kennedy's escapades at the White House pool.

4097. Cassini, Igor. *I'd Do It All Over Again*. New York: G. P. Putnam's Sons, 1977. The Hearst gossip columnist was a long-time observer of JFK's personal life.

4098. Cheshire, Maxine. *Maxine Cheshire, Reporter*. No. **3825**. A journalist writes about the sexual escapades of the Kennedy White House.

4099. Childs, Marquis. "Bobby and the President." *Good Housekeeping* 154 (May 1962): 80-1, 162. On the close bond between the president and his younger brother.

4100. Collins, Herbert Ridgeway. *Presidents on Wheels*. New York: Bonanza Books, 1971. Incomplete since it only covers President Kennedy's official car.

4101. Dallas, Rita, and Jeanira Ratcliff. *The Kennedy Case*. New York: G. P. Putnam's Sons, 1973. Written by Joseph Kennedy's private nurse, it provides personal glimpses of President Kennedy and the Kennedy family especially at Hyannis Port.

4102. "A Day with John F. Kennedy." *New York Times Magazine* (February 19, 1961), pp. 10-13. A photographic chronology.

4103. Exner, Judith (Campbell). *My Story*. No.**2638**.

4104. Hirshey, Gerri. "The Last Act of Judith Exner." *Vanity Fair* 53 (April 1990): 162-67, 221-22, 224-25. A rehash of her association with John Kennedy.

4105. "How Kennedy Works: An Exclusive Story of the President in Action." *U.S. News and World Report* 50 (March 6, 1961): 40-9. Three staff members of *U.S. News and World Report* spend a day with Kennedy.

4106. "J.F.K. and the Mobsters' Moll." *Time* 106 (December 29, 1975): 10-11. An allegation that Judith Campbell Exner was the mobsters' moll at the White House.

4107. "Jack Kennedy's Other Women." *Time* (December 29, 1975): 11-12. Even after entering the White House Kennedy never stopped pursuing attractive women.

4108. Kelley, Kitty. "The Dark Side of Camelot." No. **2641**. Judith Campbell Exner admitted for the first time that she acted as Kennedy's courier to the mob.

4109. _____. *His Way: The Unauthorized Biography of Frank Sinatra*. No. **2642**. Covers Sinatra's friendship with Kennedy, including the involvement of mobsters and women.

4110. Knebel, Fletcher. "What You Don't Know about Kennedy." *Look* 25 (January 17, 1961): 81-5. His personal habits, likes, and dislikes.

4111. Lawford, Patricia Seaton. *The Peter Lawford Story: Life with the Kennedys,*

Monroe and the Rat Pack. New York: Carroll and Graf Publishers, 1988. Actor Peter Lawford's last wife provides Lawford's undocumented startling recollections of the so-called Camelot years.

4112. Lincoln, Evelyn. *My Twelve Years with John F. Kennedy*. No. **1740**. By Kennedy's personal White House secretary.

4113. Manchester, William. *Portrait of a President: John F. Kennedy in Profile*. Boston: Little, Brown, 1962. Covers roughly President Kennedy's first year, much of which is based on a sanitized view of Kennedy's personal life.

4114. Martin, Ralph G. *A Hero for Our Times*. No. **1613**. Based on a large number of personal interviews by a journalist, it is especially excellent on President Kennedy's private life.

4115. Mellon, Rachel Lambert. "President Kennedy's Rose Garden." *White House History* (1983): 5-11. President Kennedy provided the inspiration and guidance for the renovation of the White House rose garden.

4116. "Money Talk." *Time* 80 (November 23, 1962): 12. A wealthy Kennedy, ever since serving in Congress, has donated his government salary to charity.

4117. "The Monogram on This Man's Shirt Is J. F. K." *Esquire* 57 (January 1962): 35-40. On a fashion-setting president.

4118. "More Pillow Talk." *Newsweek* 87 (March 1, 1976): 32. Based on the story of the Kennedy-Mary Meyer relationship published in the *National Enquirer* in March 1976.

4119. Nobile, Phillip, and Ron Rosenbaum. "The Curious Aftermath of JFK's Best and Brightest Affair." *New Times* 7 (July 9, 1976): 22-33. Deals with President Kennedy's affair with Mary Meyer from 1962 through 1963 and her mysterious death in 1964.

4120. "The President Who Loved Sport." *Sports Illustrated* 19 (December 2, 1963): 20-1. On Kennedy's lifelong interest in sports.

4121. "Richest President--How Much He Has, How Much He Gets." *U.S. News and World Report* 52 (June 18, 1962): 82-4. John Kennedy, the richest man ever to live in the White House, could not afford the annual operational costs of the White House.

4122. "A Shadow over Camelot." *Newsweek* 86 (December 29, 1975): 14-16. Covers the Senate committee testimony of Judith Campbell Exner, a close friend of John Kennedy and mobsters Sam Giancana and John Rosselli.

4123. Sidey, Hugh. "The President's Voracious Reading Habits." *Life* 50 (March 17, 1961): 55-64. Includes titles of Kennedy's ten favorite books.

4124. _____. "Upstairs at the White House." *Time* 129 (May 18, 1987): 20. The *New York Times* journalist reports various stories regarding Kennedy and attractive female companions, including those escorted to the upstairs White House when his family was on Cape Cod.

4125. Sullivan, Michael John. *Presidential Passions: The Love Affairs of America's Presidents--From Washington and Jefferson to Kennedy and Johnson.* New York: Shapolsky Publishers, 1991. A detailed undocumented summary of Kennedy's compulsive womanizing.

4126. Summers, Anthony. *Goddess: The Secret Lives of Marilyn Monroe.* New York: New American Library, 1986. In a convincing, disturbing fashion Summers details the relationship of Marilyn Monroe with John and Robert Kennedy.

4127. Summers, Anthony, and Stephen Dorril. *Honeytrap: The Secret Worlds of Stephen Ward.* London: Weidenfeld and Nickolson, 1987. Kennedy's supposed tangential ties to the Profumo affair in England was reported in the anti-Kennedy *New York Journal-American*, which asserted that he had affairs with two young women from London.

4128. Ward, Bernie, and Granville Toogood. "JFK's 2-Year White House Romance. *National Enquirer* 50 (March 2, 1976): 4. Based on the notes of James Truitt, a former *Washington Post* executive, it focuses on Kennedy's two-year affair with Mary Meyer, later confirmed by the White House gate logs.

4129. "Well Suited for the White House." *Life* 51 (October 13, 1961): 29, 31. The style of a clothes-conscious president.

4130. "When the President Gives Away His Pay Check." *U.S. News and World Report* 53 (November 26, 1962): 59. Kennedy's net cost of donating his $100,000 salary to charity is $9,524.

4131. "White House: Man at Work." *Newsweek* 57 (February 27, 1961): 23-4. A day in the life of the president.

B. HEALTH OF JOHN F. KENNEDY

4132. "Backache." *Life* 50 (June 23, 1961): 51-3. President Kennedy's back problems.

4133. Blair, and Blair. *The Search for JFK*. No.**1593**. Much of what we know of Kennedy's medical history comes from the Blairs.

4134. Bumgarner, John R. *The Health of the Presidents: The 41 United States Presidents through 1993 from a Physician's Point of View.* Jefferson, NC: McFarland, 1994. In a brief chapter, Bumgarner stresses how little scholars know about Kennedy's health problems because of the family's refusal to open the medical records.

4135. Crispell, Kenneth R., and Carlos F. Gomez. *Hidden Illness in the White House.* Durham: Duke University Press, 1988. Excellent on its coverage of Kennedy's Addison's disease.

4136. Ferrell, Robert H. *Ill-Advised: Presidential Health and Public Trust.* Columbia: University of Missouri Press, 1992. Using secondary sources, Ferrell deals with Kennedy's back problems and the Addison's disease coverup.

4137. Gilbert, Robert E. *The Mortal Presidency: Illness and Anguish in the White House.* New York: Basic Books, 1992. An excellent chapter on Kennedy's assorted ailments and an evaluation of the impact of illness and medication on his presidency.

4138. "Kennedy's Back Injury: Another Flare-up." *U.S. News and World Report* 55 (September 9, 1963): 22. The president was limping again and stopped playing golf.

4139. "Kennedy's Backache--How Bad It Really Is." *U.S. News and World Report* 50 (June 19, 1961): 40-1. On the severe aggravation of Kennedy's back problems at an Ottawa tree planting ceremony.

4140. L'Etang, Hugh. *Fit to Lead?* London: William Heinemann Medical Books, 1980. Kennedy's voracious appetite was a possible sign of steroid overdose.

4141. MacMahon, Edward B., and Leonard Curry. *Medical Cover-ups in the White House.* Boston: Farragut, 1987. Focus is on Kennedy's Addison's disease.

4142. "Minor Ailment." *Time* 77 (June 23, 1961): 9-10. President Kennedy's back problems and the treatment he receives.

4143. Nichols, John. "President Kennedy's Adrenals." *JAMA* 201 (July 10, 1967): 129-30. Argues rightly that the 1955 essay--James A. Nicholas, et al. "Management of Adrenocortical Insufficiency During Surgery." *Archives of Surgery* 71 (November 1955): 737-42--was on John Kennedy, the thirty-seven-year-old man who recovered from back surgery despite having Addison's disease.

4144. Park, Bert. *Ill-Fated History: Ailing, Aging and Addicted Leaders.* Knoxville: University Press of Tennessee, 1993. Park articulates the most potentially serious aspect of Kennedy's medical problems: he was consuming amphetamines and steroids--the latter from two separate sources.

4145. "President's Health." *U.S. News and World Report* 50 (June 26, 1961): 44-7. An incomplete history of Kennedy's ailments since 1935.

4146. "The State of the President's Health." *U.S. News and World Report* 50 (January 30, 1961): 21. After enumerating JFK's former physical problems, the article declares him in top physical condition.

4147. Travell, Janet. *Office Hours, Day and Night: The Autobiography of Janet Travell, M. D.* New York: World Publications, 1968. A less than candid effort by President Kennedy's physician who was relieved of her authority to treat the president by the fall of 1961.

4148. "Up and Down." *Time* 77 (June 30, 1961): 10-11. Kennedy's personal physician holds a press conference to explain his recent health problems.

C. JACQUELINE KENNEDY ONASSIS

4149. Anthony, Carl Sferrazza. *First Ladies.* Vol. 2. *The Saga of the Presidents' Wives and Their Power.* New York: William Morrow, 1991. Provides an idyllic view of the Kennedys in the White House and emphasizes Mrs. Kennedy's substance over style.

4150. _____. "Love, Jackie." *American Heritage* 45 (September 1994): 90-6, 98, 100. The correspondence between Mrs. Kennedy and the Lyndon Johnsons reflected a suprisingly warm relationship particularly after President Kennedy's assassination.

4151. Baldrige, Letita. *Of Diamonds and Diplomats.* Boston: Houghton Mifflin, 1968. The account of Mrs. Kennedy's social secretary regarding White House social activities.

4152. Birmingham, Stephen. *Jacqueline Bouvier Kennedy Onassis.* New York: Grosset and Dunlap, 1978. An attractive, undocumented popular biography with numerous photographs.

4153. Boller, Paul, Jr. *Presidential Wives: An Anecdotal History.* New York: Oxford University Press, 1988. A chapter on Mrs. Kennedy.

4154. Caroli, Betty Boyd. *First Ladies.* New York: Oxford University Press, 1987. Thoughtfully emphasizes the contradictions of Mrs. Kennedy as First Lady.

4155. Carpozi, George, Jr. *The Hidden Side of Jacqueline Kennedy.* New York: Pyramid, 1967. A popular biography that treats Mrs. Kennedy in ambivalent fashion.

4156. Curtis, Charlotte. *First Lady*. New York: Pyramid, 1962. A brief popular biography on her first year and a half in the White House.

4157. David, Lester. *Jacqueline Kennedy Onassis: A Portrait of Her Private Years*. Secaucus, NJ: Carol Publishing Group, 1994. Published shortly after Mrs. Kennedy's death, David's brief biography claims that despite some problems, Jackie and John Kennedy remained close to the end and that she had a deep interest in the political process.

4158. Davis, John H. *The Bouviers: Portrait of an American Family*. New York: Farrar, Strauss and Giroux, 1969. Mrs. Kennedy's first cousin provides the fullest account of her family background and her youth.

4159. _____. *The Kennedys*. No.**1639**. Davis writes thoughtfully about Mrs. Kennedy and her relationship with John Kennedy.

4160. Gallagher, Mary Barelli. *My Life with Jacqueline Kennedy*. New York: David McKay, 1969. A less than flattering appraisal by Mrs. Kennedy's personal secretary.

4161. Gould, Lewis L. "Modern First Ladies in Historical Perspective." *Presidential Studies Quarterly* 15 (Summer 1985): 532-40. Jacqueline Kennedy made the White House a center of fashion, culture, and historical restoration.

4162. Gutin, Myra G. *The President's Partner: The First Lady in the Twentieth Century*. New York: Greenwood Press, 1989. Even though a reluctant First Lady who spent much time avoiding communication, Mrs. Kennedy had projects that she advanced.

4163. Hall, Gordon Langley, and Ann Pinchot. *Jacqueline Kennedy: A Biography*. New York: Frederick Fell, 1964. A popular sympathetic biography written right after JFK's assassination.

4164. Heymann, C. David. *A Woman Named Jackie*. New York: Lyle Stuart and Carol Communications, 1989. The fullest account on Mrs. Kennedy, based on extensive interviews; it also contains extensive personal information on the president, but it should be used carefully because of its occasional unreliability.

4165. Kelley, Kitty. *Jackie Oh!* New York: Ballantine Books, 1978. This popular biography lacks a scholarly apparatus and contains unconfirmed rumors, but it brings in new information gained through personal interviews.

4166. Mailer, Norman. "An Evening with Jackie Kennedy: Being an Essay in Three Acts." *Esquire* 58 (July 1962): 57-61. A panning of Mrs. Kennedy's national television tour of the White House restoration.

4167. Means, Marianne. *The Woman in the White House: The Lives, Times and Influences of Twelve Notable First Ladies*. New York: Random House, 1963. Written by a White House correspondent.

4168. "Mrs. Kennedy's Cabinet." *New Yorker* 36 (January 14, 1961): 77-8, 80. Amusingly underlines the parallels in appointments made by John and Jacqueline Kennedy.

4169. Pioneer Books. *A Proposal to Jacqueline Kennedy*. New York: Pioneer Books, 1966. A maudlin account pleading that Mrs. Kennedy seek the presidency.

4170. Pollard, Eve. *Jackie*. London: Macdonald, 1969. An undocumented popular biography.

4171. Rhea, Mini. *I Was Jacqueline Kennedy's Dressmaker*. New York: Fleet Publishing Corporation, 1962. For anyone interested in the Jackie look.

4172. Shulman, Irving. *"Jackie!": The Exploitation of a First Lady*. New York: Trident, 1970. A study of the exploitation of Mrs. Kennedy especially by fan magazines.

4173. Thayer, Mary Von Rensselaer. *Jacqueline Kennedy: The White House Years*. Boston: Little, Brown, 1967. Written by a newspaper correspondent and columnist, this biography was written with the full cooperation of Mrs. Kennedy and her friends and associates.

4174. Watney, Hedda Lyons. *Jackie*. New York: Tudor Publishing, 1990. One of many brief popular biographies.

4175. Watson, Mary Ann. "An Enduring Fascination: The Papers of Jacqueline Kennedy." *Prologue: Journal of the National Archives* 19 (Summer 1987): 117-25. Little textual documents exist on Jacqueline Kennedy because of the lack of access to her personal papers and the slow process of opening the White House social files.

4176. "A Week in the Life of JFK's Wife." *Life* 51 (November 24, 1961): 32-40. Includes son's first birthday, a fox hunt, and a concert at the White House featuring Pablo Casals.

4177. West, J. B. *Upstairs at the White House: My Life with the First Ladies*. New York: Coward, McCann and Geoghegan, 1973. In a perceptive work the White House head usher thought Mrs. Kennedy had the most complex personality of all the first ladies he had served.

4178. Wolff, Perry S. *A Tour of the White House with Mrs. John F. Kennedy*. Garden City, NY: Doubleday, 1962. A photographic account with television text and annotations on the television tour of the White House.

D. THE KENNEDYS IN THE WHITE HOUSE AND ELSEWHERE

4179. Avedon, Richard. "An Informal Visit with Our New First Family." *Look* 25 (February 28, 1961): 100-06. Accompanied by pictures of Mrs. Kennedy with the children.

4180. Bergquist, Laura. "Caroline." *Look* 25 (September 26, 1961): 76-86. On the Kennedys' young daughter.

4181. _____. "The President and the Son." *Look* 27 (December 3, 1963): 26-31, 36. A human interest piece--mostly photographs--of two-year-old John Kennedy, Jr. in the Oval Office during working hours.

4182. Bradlee, Benjamin. *Conversations with Kennedy*. No. **1903**. The Washington bureau chief of *Newsweek* magazine and his wife Toni socialized extensively with the Kennedys in the White House.

4183. "Bright Day, Blue Day." *Newsweek* 58 (October 9, 1961): 23-4. A short account of the Kennedy family's vacation to Newport, Rhode Island.

4184. Caroli, Betty Boyd. *Inside the White House: America's Most Famous Home, The First 200 Years*. New York: Canopy Books, 1992. Covers Jacqueline Kennedy's White House restoration project.

4185. Cassini, Igor. "How the Kennedy Marriage Has Fared." *Good Housekeeping* 155 (September 1962): 68-9, 183-84, 187-88, 192, 195, 198. Despite some stormy years, Cassini writes of a marriage that is strong and full of mutual respect.

4186. Cassini, Oleg. *In My Own Fashion: An Autobiography*. New York: Simon and Schuster, 1987. A close family friend and Jacqueline's key fashion designer.

4187. "Family Thanksgiving." *Time* 78 (December 1, 1961): 12. The Kennedy family's Thanksgiving at Hyannisport and a children's birthday party at the White House.

4188. Gelb, Arthur, and Barbara Gelb. "Culture Makes a Hit at the White House." *New York Times Magazine* (January 28, 1962), pp. 9, 64, 66. The emphasis on the arts sets the Kennedy White House apart from other administrations.

4189. "A Glimpse at Life in Today's White House." *U.S. News and World Report* 50 (April 3, 1961): 63-6. Discusses the changes in the White House such as the serving of hard liquor and the emphasis on informal gatherings.

4190. "The Hollywood Set and the Kennedy Family." *U.S. News and World Report*

51 (October 16, 1961): 60. Critical article on the Kennedys's choice of friends such as Frank Sinatra.

4191. Jensen, Amy La Follette. *The White House and Its Thirty-five Families.* New York: McGraw-Hill, 1970. Contains a chapter of pictures and narrative on the White House during the Kennedy years.

4192. "Kennedys on Vacation." *Ladies Home Journal* 78 (August 1961): 32-7. At the summer home at Hyannis Port.

4193. "New Folks at Home." *Time* 80 (February 10, 1961): 14-15. The Kennedy family's adjustment in the White House.

4194. "On the High Board." *Newsweek* 57 (April 10, 1961): 23-4. On the first family's first Easter which was spent in Palm Beach.

4195. Shaw, Maud. *White House Nannie: My Years with Caroline and John Kennedy, Jr.* New York: New American Library, 1965. Insights into Kennedy family life.

4196. "Simply Everywhere." *Time* 19 (February 23, 1962): 24-5. The popularity of the Kennedys and their influence on fashion and on other social matters.

4197. "Vacation Time." *Time* 80 (August 3, 1962): 10. Vacation habits of the first family.

4198. "Ways a New President is Changing the White House." *U.S. News and World Report* 50 (February 20, 1961): 35-7. On the changes both Kennedys are making in the White House.

13

Historiographical Materials

A. PRESIDENTIAL RATINGS

4199. Bailey, Thomas A. *Presidential Greatness: The Image and the Man from George Washington to the Present*. New York: Appleton Century Crofts, 1966. Perspective is too short, the term was too short, the shock of death was too great, and the growth of the legend too rapid to permit a satisfying evaluation of President Kennedy.

4200. Barber, James David. *The Presidential Character: Predicting Performance in the White House*. Englewood Cliffs, NJ: Prentice-Hall, 1985. Categorizes Kennedy as an active-positive president.

4201. Kynerd, Tom. "An Analysis of Presidential Greatness and 'Presidential Rating.'" *Southern Quarterly* 9 (April 1971): 309-29. Rating presidents has no systematic, objective, or scientific basis.

4202. Maranell, Gary M. "The Evaluation of Presidents: An Extension of the Schlesinger Polls." *Journal of American History* 57 (June 1970): 104-13. The essay enlarges upon and updates the Schlesinger polls (Kennedy is also included) and introduces methodological changes such as the use of social-psychological scaling methods.

4203. Maranell, Gary M., and Richard Doddler. "Political Orientation and the Evaluation of Presidential Prestige: A Study of American Historians." *Social Science Quarterly* 51 (September 1970): 415-21. A random sample of members of the Organization of American Historians who rated the presidents on the basis of seven attributes, placing Kennedy in the top ten.

4204. Murray, Robert K., and Tim H. Blessing. *Greatness in the White House: Rating the Presidents, Washington through Carter*. Updated edition. University Park: Pennsylvania State University Press, 1994. The nearly 1,000 American historians holding Ph.D.s who responded ranked Kennedy 13th (above average) among the 36 presidents evaluated.

4205. Neal, Steve. "Our Best and Worst Presidents." *Chicago Tribune Magazine* (January 10, 1982), pp. 8-11, 12-13, 15, 18. A survey of 49 leading historians and political scholars rated Kennedy 14th from the top, tied with John Adams.

4206. Pederson, William D., and Ann M. McLaurin, eds. *The Rating Game in American Politics: An Interdisciplinary Approach.* New York: Irvington Publishers, 1987. Contains the results of the David Porter poll, which involved 85 noted historians who ranked Kennedy as average (13th out of 36 presidents).

4207. Sokolsky, Eric. *Our Seven Greatest Presidents.* New York: Exposition Press, 1964. With little research and analysis, it includes Kennedy as one of the seven.

B. APPRAISALS OF KENNEDY

4208. Alden, John R. "Overrated and Underrated Americans." *American Heritage* 39 (July/August 1988): 48-54, 56, 58-9, 62-3. Historians and other scholars, asked to select the most overrated and underrated public figures in American history, discuss why they selected John Kennedy as most overrated.

4209. Attwood, William. "Twenty Years after Dallas." *Virginia Quarterly Review* 59 (Autumn 1983): 557-63. Discusses why Kennedy's death profoundly affected so many people.

4210. Berendt, John. "Ten Years Later: A Look at the Record. What the School Books Are Teaching Our Kids about JFK." *Esquire* 80 (November 1973): 140, 263-65. In a special section on JFK, Berendt reports that textbooks are diminishing Kennedy the man in stressing his actions and are erecting around JFK a barrier of boring prose.

4211. Boeth, Richard. "JFK: Visions and Revisions." *Newsweek* 73 (November 19, 1973): 76, 90-2. Despite the recent revisionist works, Kennedy remains an authenic hero to most Americans.

4212. Boorstin, Daniel J. "JFK: His Vision, Then and Now." *U.S. News and World Report* 105 (October 24, 1988): 30-1. Boorstin suggests that JFK's untimely death reminds us of how history assesses public figures who die too soon.

4213. Broder, David S. *Changing of the Guard: Power and Leadership in America.* New York: Simon and Schuster, 1980. Contains a chapter on the impact of President Kennedy on the next generation of political figures.

4214. Brown, Thomas. *JFK: History of an Image.* Bloomington: Indiana University

Press, 1988. Astutely addresses the prevalent American images of Kennedy and the reasons for his continued popularity among Americans.

4215. Elfin, Mel. "Beyond the Generations." *U.S. News and World Report* 105 (October 24, 1988): 32-3. Explores reasons for JFK's continued popularity.

4216. Goldman, Peter. "Kennedy Remembered: After Twenty Years, a Man Lost in His Legend." *Newsweek* 102 (November 28, 1983): 61-4. Kennedy has become an authentic folk hero and America's most popular president.

4217. "A Great President? Experts Size Up JFK." *U.S. News and World Report* 95 (November 21, 1983): 51-2, 54. Assessments from scholars such as James MacGregor Burns, Herbert Parmet, Carl Brauer.

4218. Kaiser, David E. "The Politician." *New Republic* 189 (November 21, 1983): 15, 18-19. Kennedy remains a significant historical figure because he was, for better or for worse, the incarnation of an era.

4219. Lasch, Christopher. "The Life of Kennedy's Death." *Harper's Magazine* 267 (October 1983): 32-6, 38. What we now know about Kennedy's life and death suggests that the promise was misconceived from the outset.

4220. Lessard, Suzannah. "A New Look at John Kennedy." *Washington Monthly* 3 (October 1971): 8-18. Lessard recalls President Kennedy's fear at being thought cowardly or sentimental, which Lassard considers a weakness of administration foreign policy and a manifestation of liberal neurosis.

4221. Leuchtenburg, William. "John F. Kennedy, Twenty Years Later." *American Heritage* 35 (December 1983): 50-9. Kennedy's place in history as the romantic hero, cruelly slain in his prime, remains secure.

4222. _____. "Kennedy and the New Generation." In *John F. Kennedy*. Edited by J. Richard Snyder, pp. 11-24. No. **2077**. A mostly personal account of Kennedy's ups and downs with American historians.

4223. Logan, Andy. "JFK: The Stained-Glass Image." *American Heritage* 18 (August 1967): 4-7, 75-8. Analyzes the hero worship of Kennedy found in many of his biographies after his assassination.

4224. Maddox, Robert J. "Kennedy as President: A Ten-Year Perspective." *American History Illustrated* 8 (November 1973): 4-9, 46-50. A balanced account that concludes that any evaluation of Kennedy's presidency must be tentative until a longer perspective develops.

4225. Mazlish, Bruce. "Kennedy: Myth and History." In *John F. Kennedy*. Edited by J. Richard Snyder, pp. 25-34. No. **2077**. The Kennedy myth has faded because it was based only on style and it lacked a larger moral or spiritual quality.

4226. Morrow, Lance. "JFK: After Twenty Years, the Question: How Good a President?" *Time* 122 (November 14, 1983): 58-60, 63-7. Kennedy's assassination much more profoundly affected America than anything he did while he was in the White House.

4227. Parmet, Herbert S. "The Kennedy Myth and American Politics." *History Teacher* 24 (1 1990): 31-9. Kennedy was one of the most popular presidents, but it is difficult to couple him with any particular ideology or substantial accomplishment.

4228. Reston, James. "What Was Killed Was Not Only the President But the Promise." *New York Times Magazine* (November 15, 1964), pp. 24-5, 126-27. The man and the legend one year after the assassination.

4229. Schlesinger, Arthur, Jr. "JFK: What Was He Really Like?" *Ladies Home Journal* 100 (November 1983): 115, 168, 170. Kennedy remains one who was sure of his own identity, confident in his approach to power and responsibility, incisive in his analysis of problems, and optimistic in his search for remedy.

4230. _____. "What the Thousand Days Wrought." *New Republic* 189 (November 21, 1983): 20-2, 25, 28, 30. When the cycle of social concern and progressive reform resumes, Kennedy will again be commonly perceived as a humane and creative political leader.

4231. Sorensen, Theodore C. "Kennedy: Retrospect and Prospect." In *The Kennedy Presidency*. Edited by Kenneth W. Thompson, pp. 285-300. No. **2077**. Argues that Kennedy is not an easy person to summarize.

4232. Toscano, Vincent Lawrence. "Since Dallas: Images of John F. Kennedy in Popular and Scholarly Literature, 1963-1973." Ph.D. diss., State University of New York at Albany, 1975. An examination of how the heroic and positive image of Kennedy persisted ten years after the assassination.

4233. Ulam, Adam B. "Lost Frontier." *New Republic* 189 (November 21, 1983): 10, 12, 14. Compares the consequences of Kennedy's tragic death to Franklin Roosevelt's sudden demise in 1945 in terms of American foreign policy.

4234. "What JFK Meant to Us: Thirty Americans Reflect on the Kennedy Legacy." *Newsweek* 102 (November 28, 1983): 65-6, 71-2, 75-6, 78-80, 83-4, 86, 91. Includes the reflections of Walter Cronkite, Gloria Steinem, Jules Feiffer, Joseph Alsop.

4235. Wicker, Tom. "Kennedy and Our Vanished Dreams." *New York Times Magazine* (November 20, 1983), pp. 73, 124, 148-49. Kennedy's shortened promising presidency has become a personification of our own vanished dreams and defeats.

C. JOHN FITZGERALD KENNEDY LIBRARY

4236. Bergquist, Laura. "The Bright Light of His Days." *McCall's* 101 (November 1973): 81-3, 156-57. Describes Jacqueline Kennedy's ideas about the library and what will be included there.

4237. "Changes in the Kennedy Library." *American Libraries* 5 (October 1974): 465-66. Details the controversy surrounding the plan to build the library near Harvard University.

4238. Fenn, Dan H, Jr. "Launching the John F. Kennedy Library." *American Archivist* 42 (October 1979): 429-42. Written by the first director of the library.

4239. Giglio, James N. "Past Frustrations and New Opportunities: Researching the Kennedy Presidency at the Kennedy Library." *Presidential Studies Quarterly* 22 (June 1992): 371-79. Despite the restrictions still in existence on Kennedy manuscript material, some recent releases have occurred, including the opening of the White House gate logs, which shed light on Kennedy's personal life, and Kennedy's World War II naval medical records.

4240. Hanson, Robert. "Hail to the Chiefs: Our Presidential Libraries." *Wilson Library Bulletin* 55 (April 1981): 576-83. Compares six presidential libraries, including the Kennedy Library.

4241. "JFK's Last Campaign." *Newsweek* 63 (March 9, 1964): 25, 28. Plans are underway for the Kennedy presidential library.

4242. Kay, Jane Holtz. "Architecture." *Nation* 229 (December 15, 1979): 634-35. A critical assessment of the newly dedicated Kennedy Library at Columbia Point, its architecture, contents, and location.

4243. Kinney, Doris G. "JFK Undimned." *Life* 11 (December 1988): 64-9. A ten-year retrospective of the Kennedy Library, with beautiful color photographs.

4244. Marlin, William. "Lighthouse on an Era." *Architectual Record* 167 (February 1980): 81-90. Extensively covers all aspects of the building of the Kennedy Library.

4245. Paterson, Thomas G. "Politics and Perils at the Presidential Libraries." *OAH Newsletter* 21 (May 1993): 5-6. Discusses the deeds-of-gift restrictions at the Kennedy Library.

4246. Schmertz, Mildred. "Getting Ready for the John F. Kennedy Library: Not Everyone Wants to Make It Go Away." *Architectual Record* 156 (December 1974): 98-105. A detailed account of the impact the proposed Kennedy library would have on Cambridge, Massachusetts.

4247. "Unveiling a Glittering Tribute to John F. Kennedy." *U.S. News and World Report* 87 (October 22, 1979): 43-4. A description with pictures of the library dedicated on October 20, 1979.

D. BIBLIOGRAPHIES AND HISTORIOGRAPHICAL ESSAYS

4248. *The American Presidency: A Historical Bibliography*. Santa Barbara, Ca.: ABC-Clio Information Services, 1984. Abstracts of articles, with subject index.

4249. Burns, Richard Dean, and Milton Leitenberg. *The Wars in Vietnam, Cambodia, and Laos, 1945-1982*. Santa Barbara: ABC-Clio Information Services, 1984. A comprehensive bibliography of more than 6,000 items.

4250. Chalmers, David. "The Struggle for Social Change in 1960s America: A Bibliographical Essay." *American Studies International* 30 (April 1992): 41-64. Based on an earlier version in Chalmers's *And the Crooked Places Made Straight*.

4251. Cohen, Norman S. *The American Presidents: Annotated Bibliography*. Pasadena, Ca.: Salem Press, 1989. A very brief bibliography on Kennedy.

4252. Crown, James Tracy. *The Kennedy Literature: A Bibliographical Essay on John F. Kennedy*. New York: New York University Press, 1968. Crown provides useful extensive commentary on the key literature relating to Kennedy and his presidency rather than providing a comprehensive bibliography.

4253. Frewin, Anthony. *The Assassination of John F. Kennedy: An Annotated Film, TV, and Videography, 1963-1992*. Westport, Ct.: Greenwood Press, 1993. An excellent bibliography on Kennedy that covers more than the assassination.

4254. Guth, DeLloyd, and David R. Wrone. *The Assassination of John F. Kennedy: A Comprehensive Historical and Legal Bibliography, 1963-1979*. Westport, Ct.: Greenwood Press, 1980. Accompanied by an excellent introduction that evaluates the major investigations and literature, this bibliography contains virtually everything related to the assassination.

4255. Hess, Gary R. "The Unending Debate: Historians and the Vietnam War." *Diplomatic History* 18 (Spring 1994): 239-64. Focuses on the literature that has appeared in the last dozen years.

4256. Kaufman, Burton I. "John F. Kennedy as World Leader: A Perspective on the

Literature." *Diplomatic History* 17 (Summer 1993): 447-70. There is probably no presidency on which public perceptions and historical evaluations have more remained at odds than that of John Kennedy.

4257. Machin, Maria A. "The Cuban Missile Crisis: An Analysis of a Quarter Century of Historiography." M.A. thesis, Florida Atlantic University, 1990. Recent declassifications of U.S. materials and the availability of Soviet materials have shed new light on the missile crisis.

4258. Martin, Fenton S., and Robert U. Goehlert. *The American Presidency: A Bibliography*. Washington: Congressional Quarterly, 1987. Organized by subjects with chronological breakdown for campaigns and elections.

4259. Menendez, Albert J. *Religion and the U.S. Presidency: A Bibliography*. New York: Garland, 1986. Contains a short chapter on Kennedy.

4260. Newcomb, Joan I. *John F. Kennedy: An Annotated Bibliography*. Metuchen, NJ: Scarecrow Press, 1977. Contains only books.

4261. Ryan, Dorothy, and Louis J. Ryan. *The Kennedy Family in Massachusetts: A Bibliography*. Westport, Ct.: Greenwood Press, 1981. Providing short annotatons, it briefly covers the Kennedy administration as it focuses on the Kennedys and their spouses.

4262. Sable, Martin H. *A Bio-Bibliography of the Kennedy Family*. Metuchen, NJ: Scarecrow Press, 1968. Even though dated, excellent on family members and on works published in other countries.

4263. Stone, Ralph A. *John F. Kennedy, 1917-1963: Chronology-Documents-Bibliographical Aids*. Dobbs Ferry, NY: Oceana, 1971. A short listing of books and articles.

4264. Thompson, William Clifton. *A Bibliography of Literature Relating to the Assassination of John F. Kennedy*. San Antonio: W. C. Thompson, 1968. Unannotated and dated.

4265. VanDeMark, Brian. "Kennedy the Diplomatist: A Historiographical Appraisal." *Society for Historians of American Foreign Relations Newsletter* 15 (December 1984): 21-34. In evaluating Kennedy's foreign policy record, scholars have been hindered by two events: the Vietnam war and his assassination.

4266. Wrone, David R. "The Assassination of John Fitzgerald Kennedy: An Annotated Bibliography." *Wisconsin Magazine of History* 56 (Autumn 1972): 21-36. An excellent early effort by an academic historian who provides a thoughtful introductory essay and evaluative annotations on the key books, articles, and sources.

14

Iconography

A. PUBLISHED WORKS

4267. Barclay, Barbara. *Lamps to Light the Way of Our Presidents: Presidential Portraits by Celeste Swayne-Courtney.* Glendale, Ca.: Bowmar, 1970. Contains a chapter on the "Young Man from Boston."

4268. Blaisdell, Thomas C., Jr., et al. *The American Presidency in Political Cartoons, 1776-1976.* Berkeley, Ca.: University Art Museum, 1976. Contains a small collection of JFK cartoons.

4269. Cross, Robin. *J.F.K.: A Hidden Life.* London: Bloomsbury, 1992. A popular pictorial biography of no use to scholars.

4270. Editors of American Heritage. *The American Heritage Pictorial History of the Presidents of the United States.* 2 vols. New York: American Heritage Publishing Company, 1968, 2: 935-67. Factual information and illustrations.

4271. Fischer, Roger A. *Tippecanoe and Trinkets Too: The Material Culture of American Presidential Campaigns, 1828-1988.* Urbana: University of Illinois Press, 1988. With few exceptions in 1960, Kennedy was poorly served by his material culture.

4272. Harding, Robert T., and A. L. Holmes. *Jacqueline Kennedy: A Woman for the World.* New York: Encyclopedia Enterprises, 1966. A photographic biography with text which focuses on the White House years.

4273. Kunhardt, Philip B. *LIFE in Camelot: The Kennedy Years.* Boston: Little, Brown, 1988. *Life* magazine photographs of President Kennedy and his family.

4274. Lowe, Jacques. *JFK Remembered.* New York: Random House, 1993.

Familiar and unfamiliar photographs of John and Robert Kennedy from 1958 through 1961.

4275. _____. *Kennedy: A Time Remembered*. Quartet Books, 1983. Large format volume of photographs of President Kennedy and his family, many taken by Lowe.

4276. _____. *The Kennedy Legacy: A Generation Later*. New York: Viking Studio Books, 1988. Photographs by Lowe; text by Wilfrid Sheed.

4277. _____. *Portrait: The Emergence of John F. Kennedy*. New York: McGraw Hill, 1961. Text and most photographs by Lowe.

4278. Lowe, Jacques, and Harold Faber. *The Kennedy Years*. New York: Viking Press, 1964. Photographs by Lowe and others covers Kennedy from the late 1930s through his death; Faber provides the text.

4279. MacNeil, Robert, ed. *The Way We Were: The Year Kennedy Was Shot*. New York: Carroll and Graf, 1988. Unusually good selection of illustrations.

4280. Manchester, William. *One Brief Shining Moment: Remembering Kennedy*. Boston: Little, Brown, 1983. Manchester's textual and pictorial tribute to a man he knew and greatly admired.

4281. Meyers, Joan, ed. *John Fitzgerald Kennedy . . . As We Remember Him*. Philadelphia: Courage Books, 1965. A fine pictorial biography of Kennedy along with the reminiscences of those who knew him best--his family, friends, and associates.

4282. *New York Times*. *The Kennedy Years*. New York: Viking, 1964.

4283. Saunders, Doris, ed. *The Kennedy Years and the Negro*. Chicago: Johnson Publishing, 1964. A photographic record of the president's interest in civil rights.

4284. Shaw, Mark. *The John F. Kennedys: A Family Album*. New York: Farrar, Straus, 1964. Informal photographs of the president and his family from the late 1950s on.

4285. Spina, Tony. *This Was the President*. New York: A. S. Barnes, 1964. Mostly photographs from the Los Angeles convention in 1960 through the inauguration.

4286. Stoughton, Cecil, Chester V. Clifton, and Hugh Sidey. *The Memories: JFK, 1961-1963*. New York: W. W. Norton, 1973. A pictorial account by the president's photographer, military aide, and the columnist for *Time* magazine.

4287. Whitney, David C. *The Graphic Side of the American Presidents*. Chicago:

J. G. Ferguson, 1975. pp. 49-69. Dated and favorable, much of it pictorial.

B. UNPUBLISHED MATERIAL

4288. Berinsky, Burton Collection, 1931-91. Audiovisual Archives. Kennedy Library. 30,671 items. Includes photographs of Kennedy's presidential campaign in the Northeast, his inauguration, and trips as president to New York City.

4289. *Boston Globe* Collection, 1910-63. Audiovisual Archives. Kennedy Library. 400 items. Select photographs of John Kennedy, his family and associates taken by staff photographers and others.

4290. *Boston Herald* Collection, 1912-64. Audiovisual Archives. Kennedy Library. 300 items. Copies of photographs from the newspaper's photo library of John Kennedy, his family, and associates particularly prior to 1960.

4291. Democratic National Committee Collection, 1953-64. Audiovisual Archives. Kennedy Library. 1,100 items. File photos taken by the DNC's staff photographer, including the 1960 presidential campaign.

4292. Kennedy Family Collection, 1878-1978. Audiovisual Archives. Kennedy Library. 14,500 items. Permission required. Photographs of the Kennedy and Fitzgerald families taken or collected by Rose Kennedy, Joseph P. Kennedy, and their children.

4293. Library of Congress Prints and Photograph Collection. The varied and extensive collection includes photographs used by the *New York World-Telegram & Sun* and the *U.S. News and World Report*, original political cartoon drawings, posters, and unprocessed material

4294. Look Magazine Collection, 1946-63. Audiovisual Archives. Kennedy Library. 900 items. Photographs taken by staff photographers for use in various *Look* magazine articles about John Kennedy, his family, and associates.

4295. Magnum Collection, 1939-68. Audiovisual Archives. Kennedy Library. 500 items. 35mm contact sheets of the photo agency's complete Kennedy file.

4296. *New Bedford Standard-Times* Collection, 1946-63. Audiovisual Archives. Kennedy Library. 1,000 items. Original file photographs and negatives from the newspaper's photo library on John Kennedy's visits to Cape Cod.

4297. *New Orleans Times-Picayune* Collection, 1960-63. Audiovisual Archives. Kennedy Library. 1,350 items. The complete Kennedy file of the photo library of the newspaper.

4298. *New York Times* Collection, 1960-68. Audiovisual Archives. Kennedy Library. 400 items. Select photographs from the newspaper's photo library of President Kennedy and his associates.

4299. "President's Collection." 1920-63. Audiovisual Archives. Kennedy Library. 1,500 items. Photographs of John Kennedy, his family, and associates, formerly displayed or stored in his congressional and senate offices, and from White House storage.

4300. Press Collection, 1952-60. Audiovisual Archives. Kennedy Library. 900 items. Select photographs of John Kennedy's activities and visits from the photo libraries of major newspapers in all 50 states.

4301. "PX" Photographs Collection, 1894-1984. Audiovisual Archives. Kennedy Library. 8,009 items. Photographs of John Kennedy and members of the Kennedy family taken by private individuals or organizations from many countries.

4302. Steinberg, Gerald Jay Collection, 1963-81. Audiovisual Archives. Kennedy Library. 9,800 items. Researcher and collector of Kennedyana who donated the photographs.

4303. Teti/Miller Collection, 1966-82. Audiovisual Archives. Kennedy Library. 10,700 items. Photographs of John and other Kennedy family members.

4304. U.S. Government Agency Collection, 1934-64. Audiovisual Archives. Kennedy Library. 3,500 items. Photographs from various government agencies, usually showing President Kennedy visiting an agency, installation, or inspecting a program such as Food for Peace.

4305. White House Collection, 1960-63. Audiovisual Archives. Kennedy Library. 42,300 items. Photographs by staff photographers of the president's activities at the White House, on official trips, and vacation.

C. FILM AND VIDEOTAPES

4306. *ABC News Closeup: JFK*. Produced by ABC News, 1983. 120 minutes. Peter Jennings narrates this analytical and balanced documentary, which includes considerable film footage of the era and the assessment of scholars and Kennedy administration members.

4307. *America Remembers JFK*. Produced by Horton Associates, 1983. 2 hours. Documentary narrated and hosted by Hal Holbrook.

4308. *Being with Kennedy*. Produced by Drew Associates, 1983. 2 hours. Uses off-the-record film clips to encapsulate Kennedy's 1960 presidential campaign.

4309. *The Burden and the Glory of JFK.* Produced by CBS, 1964. 90 minutes. Presents a record of Kennedy's quest for peace.

4310. *The Cuban Missile Crisis: Back from the Brink.* Produced by Grenada Television, 1987. 20 minutes. This British documentary is a patchwork of newsreel films connected by some stock film footage.

4311. *From the Bay of Pigs to the Brink.* Produced by VisNews, 1991. 27 minutes. Based largely on American film footage made at the time of the missile crisis, it contains no new knowledge that has come to light in recent years.

4312. *JFK: A Celebration of His Life and Times.* Produced by Reader's Digest and CFL Communications, 1988. 3 hours.

4313. *JFK: In His Own Words.* Produced by Peter W. Kunhardt, HBO, 1988. 60 minutes. With John Kennedy providing the narration, this is a moving romantic rendering of his life with some wonderful film clips of his youth.

4314. *JFK: Reckless Youth.* Produced by Judith A. Polone, ABC Television, 1993. 4 hours. Closely based on Nigel Hamilton's 1992 book, Terry Kinney plays the young John Kennedy.

4315. *JFK Remembered.* Produced by Richard Richter, Judy Crichton, ABC Television, 1988. 54 minutes. Incorporates newsreel footage and interviews with the recollection of Kennedy associates and observers.

4316. *Jacqueline Bouvier Kennedy.* Produced by Louis Rudolph, ABC Circle Film, 1981. 180 minutes. The story of the First Lady from the age of five until immediately after the assassination, with Jaclyn Smith portraying Jacqueline Kennedy.

4317. *John F. Kennedy: The Commemorative Video Album.* Produced by CBS News, 1988. 110 minutes. Covers Kennedy's major foreign policy crises using film clips and excerpts of speeches and press conferences, followed by extensive coverage of the tragic four days in November and ends with Rose Kennedy discussing Kennedy's childhood.

4318. *"Johnny, We Hardly Knew Ye."* Produced by Susskind Associates, 1977. 2 hours. Docu-drama based on the Kenneth O'Donnell and David Powers biography.

4319. *Kennedy.* Produced by Alan Landsburg Productions and shown on NBC Television, 1983. 7 hours. This docu-drama seeks to incorporate the latest scholarship, as Martin Sheen credibly plays JFK even though he sometimes pales in contrast to the real Kennedy.

4320. *Kennedy and Wallace: A Crisis Up Close.* Produced by Robert Drew, Drew

Associates, 1963. 60 minutes. The only time a presidential crisis--the desegregation of the University of Alabama--was filmed from the inside with presidential decisions and the Oval Office dialogue recorded on film.

4321. *The Kennedys.* Produced by Elizabeth Deane and WGBH-TV, Boston, 1992. 240 minutes. Part of PBS's *The American Experience*, it is probably the best documentary on the Kennedys.

4322. *Kennedys Don't Cry.* Produced by Document Associates, 1975. 90 minutes. Excellent documentary that first utilizes Kennedy family film clips.

4323. *The Kennedys of Massachusetts.* Produced by Lynn Raynor, ABC, 1990. 360 minutes. An excellent docu-drama based on Doris Kearns Goodwin's best seller.

4324. "Mr" Films Collection, 1910-64. 253 reels. Audiovisual Archives. Kennedy Library. Films of John Kennedy, his family, and others, produced by and donated to the library by newsreel companies, filmmakers, and individuals.

4325. National Association of Broadcasters Collection, 1953-64. Audiovisual Archives. Kennedy Library. 150 reels. Newsfilm footage of John Kennedy and his associates in various states recorded by local member television stations of the National Association of Broadcasters.

4326. *The Plot to Kill President Kennedy.* Produced by M. G. Hollo, Fox/Lorber Associates and VidAmerica, 1988. 58 minutes. Declassified documents and various inquiries suggest a conspiracy most likely involving organized crime.

4327. *The Pursuit of Happiness.* Produced by Dore Schary, 1956. 30 minutes. Narrated by John Kennedy, it was shown at the Democratic National Convention in 1956.

4328. *Robert Kennedy and His Times.* Produced by Bob Christiansen and Rick Rosenberg, CBS, 1984. Based on Arthur Schlesinger, Jr.'s biography, it covers the period from John Kennedy's congressional race in 1946 to Robert Kennedy's death in June 1968.

4329. *Robert F. Kennedy: The Man and the Memories.* Produced by Sid Feders, NBC, 1993. Narrated by Tom Brokaw, family members and associates warmly remember Bobby in a documentary that includes innumerable film clips.

4330. Television Networks Collection, 1951-83. Audiovisual Archives. Kennedy Library. 877 reels. News film donated to the library by the major American television networks and networks of other countries relating to John Kennedy.

4331. *Thank You, Mr. President.* Produced by World Vision Enterprises, 1983.

Hosted by E. G. Marshall, it includes a narration on and excerpts from President Kennedy's press conferences.

4332. *Twenty Years After the Assassination.* Produced by King Features, 1983. 14 minutes. Pictorial essay of John Kennedy.

4333. U.S. Government Agency Collection, 1961-65. 164 reels. Audiovisual Archives. Kennedy Library. Films of President Kennedy's activities, particularly as they relate to donor agencies such as NASA and the U.S. Information Agency.

4334. *A Woman Named Jackie.* Produced by Lorin Bennett Salob, 1991. 258 minutes. Based on C. David Heymann's biography, Roma Downey superbly captures the Jackie mystique, but Stephen Collins seems more like a young George Bush than JFK.

4335. White House Collection, 1961-63. 87 reels. Audiovisual Archives. Kennedy Library. Film by White House staff cameramen of President Kennedy's official activities, ceremonies at the White House, trips, vacations, and leisure time activities.

4336. *Who Shot President Kennedy?* Produced by Robert Richter and PBS's *Nova*, 1988. 58 minutes. Suggests that we must look further to account for the discrepancies and contradictions in the narrations of the event.

4337. *Years of Lightning, Day of Drums.* Produced by the U.S. Information Agency, 1966. 85 minutes. Narrated by Gregory Peck, this film covers the major events and programs of the Kennedy presidency.

D. SOUND RECORDINGS

4338. Columbia Broadcasting System Collection, 1956, 1960. Audiovisual Archives. Kennedy Library. 71 items. Complete reportage of the 1956 and 1960 Democratic National Conventions as broadcast by CBS Radio News.

4339. Columbia Records Collection, 1964-65. Audiovisual Archives. Kennedy Library. 60 items. Interviews with Kennedy family members and contemporaries, narration, and music used in the disc/book production, *JFK: As We Remember Him* (1965).

4340. Democratic National Committee Collection, 1950-64. Audiovisual Archives. Kennedy Library. 126 items. Recording of political speeches, spot ads, political programs, and other broadcasts produced or recorded by the Democratic National Committee.

4341. "The First Family" featuring Vaughn Meader. Cadence Records, 1962.

Meader was the leading Kennedy impersonator whom even Kennedy appreciated.

4342. "John F. Kennedy and the Negro." A record produced by *Ebony* magazine, Johnson Publishing Co., undated. Includes the Ole Miss desegregation speech and the June 11, 1963 address regarding the desegregation of the University of Alabama.

4343. "John Fitzgerald Kennedy: A Memorial Album." Produced and broadcast by Radio Station WMCA, New York, on Friday November 22, 1963. Includes Kennedy's Inaugural Address and Alliance for Progress and other speeches.

4344. Kennedy Family Collection, 1940-1960. Audiovisual Archives. Kennedy Library. 110 items. Radio transcription discs of speeches relating to public appearances made by various Kennedys, including John.

4345. Library of Congress Sound Collection, 1951-1963. Includes Mutual Broadcasting Network recordings of "Meet the Press" and other Kennedy interviews; the recording of the 1960 Democratic National Convention; Kennedy's presidential press conferences; tapings of presidential meetings, the originals of which are held in the Kennedy Library in Boston; the NBC Radio Collection coverage of the assassination; the "Kennedy" entries in the NBC Radio Collection computerized index; and recordings related to Kennedy.

4346. "Mr" Sound Recordings Collection, 1911-84. Audiovisual Archives. Kennedy Library. 1,830 items. Discs and tapes sent to the White House and to the Kennedy Library from donors, including musical, poetic, and other memorials to President Kennedy.

4347. Oral History Collection, 1964-83. Audiovisual Archives. Kennedy Library. 1,600 items. Tape recorded interviews with appointees associates, friends, and contemporaries of John and Robert Kennedy from which the oral history interview transcripts are produced.

4348. Presidential Assistants Collection, 1965-67. Audiovisual Archives. Kennedy Library. 153 items. Tape recorded interviews made by special assistants to the president David F. Powers, Lawrence F. O'Brien, and Kenneth P. O'Donnell of their activities with John Kennedy.

4349. White House Collection, 1961-63. Audiovisual Archives. Kennedy Library. 245 items. White House Communications Agency recordings of President Kennedy's speeches and other public remarks.

Index to Authors

Numbers in the index refer to entry numbers, not page numbers. Manuscript and oral history material is listed in subject index only.

Art, Robert J., 2551
Artaud, Denise, 3258
Artwohl, Robert R., 3924
Ascoli, Max, 1845, 3091, 3259, 3876
Ashabranner, Brent A., 2937
Ashby, LeRoy, 3678
Asher, George A., 3378
Associated Press, 3925
Attwood, William, 4209
Aubrey, Henry C., 2418
Avedon, Richard, 4179

Baar, James, 2695
Babcock, William A., 2524
Bachrack, Stanley, 3406
Bacon, Donald C., 1724, 3702
Badeau, John S., 3379-80
Bagnall, Joseph, 14
Bahnsen, Uwe, 3298
Bailey, Blake, 1900
Bailey, Stephen K., 2341
Bailey, Thomas A., 4199
Baker, David, 2696
Baker, Dean C., 3926
Baker, Elisabeth, 3272
Baker, Leonard, 2697, 3549
Baker, Robert, 2084, 3548
Baldrige, Letita, 4151
Baldwin, David A. 2874-75
Baldwin, Hanson W., 2552
Baldwin, Louis, 3679
Ball, Desmond, 2553
Ball, George W., 2814, 3381, 3738
Ball, Moya A., 3457-58
Balmer, Donald G., 3878
Balutis, Alan P., 2486
Banks, James G., 3680
Banks, Louis, 2147, 2876
Barbarash, Ernest E., 15, 3382
Barber, James D., 4200
Barber, Richard J., 2148-49
Barber, William J., 2150, 2786
Barclay, Barbara, 4267
Barham, Patte B., 4094
Baritz, Loren, 3459
Barlow, Jeffrey G., 2554

Barnard, John, 2455
Barnds, William J., 3426
Barnes, Catherine A., 2180
Barnet, Richard J., 2555, 2815, 3312
Barnhill, John H., 3804
Barrett, Patricia, 1779
Barrett, Russell H., 2181
Bartlett, Charles, 1588, 3088, 3193
Bartoli, Yvonne M., 3313
Bassett, Lawrence J., 3460
Bassett, Margaret, 1589
Baughman, James L., 3827
Bayard, James, 3030
Bayley, Edwin R., 1700
Beall, Charles, 3880
Beck, Kent M., 1846, 3461
Becker, Robert M., 3767
Beggs, Robert, 3093
Belin, David W., 3927-28
Belkin, Aaron, 3094
Belknap, Michael, 2182
Bell, Coral, 2556
Bell, Daniel, 2044
Bellace, Janice R., 2456
Belli, Melvin M., 3929
Bennett, Meridan, 2943
Berendt, John, 4210
Berger, Caruthers G., 2750
Bergquist, Laura, 1590, 1977, 2751, 3739, 4091, 4180-81, 4236
Berkowitz, Alan D., 2456
Berkowitz, Edward D., 2649
Berman, Larry, 3461a
Berman, William C., 3681
Bernstein, Barton J., 2557, 3061, 3095-3101
Bernstein, Irving, 1591-92, 1901, 2183, 2342, 2650
Berry, Fred, Jr., 3462
Berry, Joseph P., Jr., 2487
Berthold, Carol A., 2787
Beschloss, Michael R., 3102
Best, James J., 2788
Beth, Loren P., 3768

Myers, Hortense, 1665

Nacos, Brigitte L., 2522
Nash, George, 2059
Nash, Jay R., 2403
Nash, Knowlton, 3223
Nash, Philip, 2857, 3165
Nathan, James A., 3166-67
Navasky, Victor, 2258, 2404, 3629
Neal, Steve, 4205
Neustadt, Richard E., 1878, 2024-25,
   3044, 3253
Nevins, Allen, 24-5O
Newcomb, Joan I., 4260
Newell, Homer E., 2717
Newfield, Jack, 1654
Newhouse, John, 3270
Newman, Albert H., 4034
Newman, James R., 2602
Newman, John M., 3506
Newman, Peter C., 3224
New York Times, 4282
Nichols, John, 4143
Nieburg, Harold L., 2728
Nielsen, Waldemar A., 3365
Nitze, Paul, 2858
Nixon, Richard M., 1818, 2026,
   3045
Nobile, Phillip, 4119
Noel, J. V., Jr., 2603
Noer, Thomas, 3366-68
Nolting, Frederick, 3508-09
Norden, Martin F., 1819
North, Mark, 4035
Norton, Hugh S., 2326-28
Nossiter, Bernard D., 2173, 2438
Novak, Robert, 1715, 3551
Nunnerly, David, 3254
Nurse, Ronald J., 1749-50
Nye, Joseph S., Jr., 3107

Oates, Stephen, 2261
Oberdorfer, Don, 2174
O'Brien, Geoffrey, 1946
O'Brien, Lawrence F., 1751
O'Connor, Edwin, 1678

O'Connor, Karen, 2771
O'Donnell, Kenneth, 1752
Oglesby, Carl, 4036
Ohaesbulam, F. Usgboaja, 3369
O'Hara, William T., 30, 2372
Ollestad, Norman, 2406
Olson, Don, 4037
Olson, Gregory A., 3713
Olson, James S., 3509
Ondercin, David G., 2774
O'Neill, Thomas P., 3714
O'Neill, William L., 1947
Opotowsky, Stan, 1948, 3573
Oppenheimer, Martin, 2262
O'Reilly, Kenneth, 2260, 2405
Oren, Karen, 4038
Orfield, Gary, 2105
Orman, John M., 3046
Orwa, D. Katete, 3370
Osborne, John, 1820
Osborne, Leonard L., 2799-2800
Ostman, Ronald E., 2524
Oswald, Robert L., 4039
O'Toole, George, 4040
Oxford, Edward, 4041-42

Pachter, Henry M., 3168
Packenham, Robert A., 2859
Palmer, David R., 3511
Palmer, John D., 2900
Paper, Louis J., 1615, 3169
Park, Bert, 4144
Park, Jong-Chul, 3512
Parker, Edwin B., 3974
Parker, Phyllis, 3012
Parmer, J. Norman, 2957
Parmet, Herbert, 1616-17, 1679,
   1753, 1949, 2074, 4227
Passman, Otto, 2910
Paterson, Thomas, 2860-61a, 3047-
   48, 3170-73, 3904, 4245
Patrick, Richard, 3454
Patterson, James T., 2681
Payne, Darwin, 4043
Payne, Thomas, 1879, 3975
Pearl, Stanley A., 3895

Index to Subjects

Numbers in the index refer to entry numbers, not page numbers.

Bibliographies of the
Presidents of the United States

Series Editors: Carol Bondhus Fitzgerald and Mary Ellen McElligott

1. George Washington
2. John Adams
3. Thomas Jefferson
4. James Madison
5. James Monroe
6. John Quincy Adams
7. Andrew Jackson
8. Martin Van Buren
9. William Henry Harrison
10. John Tyler
11. James Knox Polk
12. Zachary Taylor
13. Millard Fillmore
14. Franklin Pierce
15. James Buchanan
16. Abraham Lincoln
17. Andrew Johnson
18. Ulysses S. Grant
19. Rutherford B. Hayes
20. James A. Garfield
21. Chester A. Arthur
22. Grover Cleveland
23. Benjamin Harrison
24. William McKinley
25. Theodore Roosevelt
26. William Howard Taft
27. Woodrow Wilson
28. Warren G. Harding
29. Calvin Coolidge
30. Herbert C. Hoover
31. Franklin D. Roosevelt
32. Harry S. Truman
33. Dwight D. Eisenhower
34. John F. Kennedy
35. Lyndon B. Johnson
36. Richard M. Nixon
37. Gerald R. Ford
38. Jimmy Carter
39. Ronald Reagan
40. George Bush
41. William Jefferson Clinton

ISBN 0-313-28192-0

9 780313 281921

90000>

EAN

HARDCOVER BAR CODE